PUBLICATIONS OF

THE COLONIAL SOCIETY OF MASSACHUSETTS

VOLUME LXXXV

PORTRAIT OF A PATRIOT

THE MAJOR POLITICAL AND LEGAL PAPERS OF JOSIAH QUINCY JUNIOR

MAGNA CHARTA
CARITAS

PORTRAIT OF A PATRIOT

The Major Political and Legal Papers of Josiah Quincy Junior

EDITORS

DANIEL R. COQUILLETTE

J. Donald Monan, S.J. University Professor, Boston College
Charles Warren Visiting Professor of American Legal History, Harvard Law School

NEIL LONGLEY YORK

Karl G. Maeser Professor of General Education
Chair, History Department, Brigham Young University

VOLUME SIX

Correspondence and Published Political Writings

BOSTON · 2014

The Colonial Society of Massachusetts

Distributed by the University of Virginia Press

ACKNOWLEDGMENTS FOR THE QUINCY PAPERS

This series of volumes represents the tireless and invaluable work of our research and administrative assistants: Brandon Bigelow, Kevin Cox, James Dimas, Jane Downing, Natalia Fekula, Eric Fox, Michael Hayden, Elizabeth Kamali, Michael Morales, Ryan Morrison, Thomas J. Murphy, Christina Nolan, Nicole Scimone, Brian Sheppard, Susannah Tobin, Elisa Underwood, and Mark A. Walsh, with special recognition to the Editorial Assistants to the Boston College Monan Chair, Brendan Farmer, Charles Riordan, and Patricia Tarabelsi, and to Inge Burgess and Thompson Potter at Harvard. Their intelligence and enthusiasm are visible on every page. Of course, we are deeply in debt to John W. Tyler, Editor of Publications of the Colonial Society of Massachusetts, as well as to the Committee of Publications, without whose guidance and support this project would have been impossible. Finally, special thanks are also due to the guardians of the Quincy heritage: the Massachusetts Historical Society with its enormously helpful Librarian, Peter Drummey, and his staff, the Museum of Fine Arts, Boston, and the Quincy family itself.

FRONTISPIECE:

The Frontispiece shows the middle panel of a watercolor triptych painted by Christian Remick in 1768, "A Perspective View of the Blockad of Boston Harbour;" watercolor on laid paper; dimensions: 32.6 cm x 155.5 cm.; courtesy of the Massachusetts Historical Society.

The figure above the center of the banner featuring Magna Charta represents an innocent young woman, trying to cover herself as she urges "CARITAS"—Latin, signifying affection or respect. She is flanked by cherubs, the one on the left holding a spear symbolizing war, the one on the right holding a caduceus, the classical symbol for the herald's staff, or a message from the Gods. Remick's image is a warning that trade would be disrupted and peace shaken with Boston's occupation by British army and naval forces. The left panel, not included here, includes three more British warships. In the right panel, Remick explained in a scroll superimposed over flags, spears, trumpets and drums, that he did the painting as if looking out from town over the long wharf. Paul Revere's more famous engraving of the event—which Remick may have drawn and colored—looks from the harbor toward town, with the troops disembarking.

ISBN 978-0-9852543-3-9

Printed from the income of the Sarah Louise Edes Fund

JOSIAH QUINCY JR.
Political and Legal Works

VOLUME SIX

CORRESPONDENCE AND PUBLISHED POLITICAL WRITINGS

CO-EDITORS:
Daniel R. Coquillette
Neil Longley York

VOLUME EDITOR:
Neil Longley York

"Manus haec inimica tyrannis
Ense petit placidam, sub litertate quietem."
ALGERNON SIDNEY

[This hand, hostile to tyrants
seeks with the sword peace under liberty]

DEDICATION

PAULINE R. MAIER

1938–2013

My co-editor, Neil Longley York, has kindly invited me to write the dedication of this volume, his work. This is the final stage of our six volume, nine year journey together. We both intensely admired Pauline R. Maier. Indeed, without her steadfast and enthusiastic support as Chair of the Committee of Publications of the Colonial Society, this journey might never have begun, and this volume never written.

It was typical of Pauline to appreciate at once the value of Josiah Quincy Jr.'s young life. It was cut off brutally in 1775, at the outset of his great promise as a Founder and a leader of the new American Republic. In the Preface of her magisterial *The Old Revolutionaries*, Pauline wrote that the book was "[A] personal adventure. . . . I wanted to know better what it was to be an American of the late eighteenth century and to live through the American Revolution . . . I was confident that I knew the revolutionaries' politics well, yet I had only a very limited sense of them as people. . . ."[1]

Josiah Quincy Jr., of course, never lived "through the American Revolution." His Atlantic voyage in March and April of 1775, while he was fatally sick with tuberculosis, to deliver important secrets for the patriot cause, put an end to that.[2] But Pauline understood at once that Quincy's papers, a treasure trove of diaries, letters, law commonplace books, and law reports (arguably the earliest law reports in America), presented a unique opportunity to see "all sides" of a brilliant leader—to really get to know Josiah Quincy as a patriot and a person, and to have the invaluable opportunity to see the birth of the American Revolution through his eyes.[3]

Much has been written about the trend in modern historical writing to "prosopography," describing key historical events through the "face" (Greek, "prosopan") of a key individual.[4] Pauline was a master of this genre, not just in her pioneering *The Old Revolutionaries*, but in her great later books, *American Scripture: Making the Declaration of Independence* (New York, 1997), and the award winning *Ratification: The People Debate the Constitution* (New York,

2010). This went hand in hand with Pauline's intense dedication to working with original sources: letters, diaries, newspaper articles, and other direct accounts. That in turn led to her unwavering devotion to the Colonial Society's mission in preserving such sources. In her final days, Pauline was immersed in exactly this type of deeply personal and exacting research, preparing what would have been another one of her great books, this time focusing on the draftsmen of the Bill of Rights.

Much has also been written about another great strength of Pauline's work, its "synchronic" style, i.e., her ability to focus on key historical events and to explain these events from all angles, including ideology, politics, economics, literature, religion, race, and gender.[5] Pauline would have laughed at the scholarly jargon of "prosopographic" and "synchronic" history, but she instinctively appreciated why historical writing should be both deeply personal and unfettered by the old limitations on what the proper "topics" of history should be. Why? Because Pauline was the consummate teacher. Both a great archivist and a great scholar, she still understood perfectly that history must be communicated powerfully to the next generation, or it is a dying enterprise. The magic of modern technology has preserved some of Pauline's finest teaching hours for us, none more powerful than her two hours with the Harvard Extension School students of our distinguished colleague, Robert J. Allison.[6] Pauline made the drama, the hopes and fears, the frustration, and the triumph of the Revolution and the early Republic come alive in the classroom as the struggle of actual men and women. Seeing them as real people, with all their failings and limitations, rather than as mythological Founders, makes their cold courage and stubborn idealism all the more compelling. This was Pauline's great gift.

Thus she naturally and instinctively understood why a major project, restoring to historical life a figure such as Josiah Quincy Jr., was essential to promoting better understanding of the Revolution. Indeed, Quincy's contributions, heretofore largely inaccessible to all but the most dedicated scholars, directly address one of Pauline's fundamental theses: the division of our Revolutionary leaders into distinct "generations." She observed that "[t]he Old Revolutionaries were a generation of American politicians born in the 1720s and 1730s who reached a natural plateau of power and influence four decades later,"[7] exemplified by Samuel Adams (born 1722), Isaac Sears (born 1729), Dr. Thomas Young (born 1731), Richard Henry Lee (born 1732), and Charles Carroll (born 1737), and brought to life by her book, *The Old Revolutionaries*. The next "generation," the "Founding Fathers" who drafted the Constitution of 1789, were, as Stanley Elkins and Eric McKitrick put it, "the young men of the Revolution," illustrated by Pauline by James Wilson (born 1742), John Jay (born 1745), James Madison (born 1750/51), and Alexander Hamilton (born 1757).[8]

But Josiah Quincy's life and works provide uniquely valuable insights into both generational worlds. By birth date, 1744, he was a "young man of the Revolution," in the generation of John Adams, not Samuel Adams, and he would have doubtless taken his place among the Founding Fathers had he lived, as Benjamin Franklin observed to his grieving father, who survived him.[9] His father wrote his epitaph:

> Here rests in humble Hope, his mortal Part,
> Who, when alive, possess'd a patriot Heart.
> A Statesman's Head, with Wisdom's Maxims fraught,
> By which, the Old might learn, the Learn'd be taught.
> Few better skill'd, the Ship of State to steer. . . ."[10]

But, like the older generation, Quincy's life peaked in 1775. Thus his extraordinary collection of writings, journals, law notes, law reports, articles and letters reflects that epoch, caught like a bug in amber at the very outbreak of the Revolution, pure of the intellectual and ideological complicatoins brought on by the War itself and its aftermath. When Pauline focuses in *The Old Revolutionaries* on the importance of "[t]heir experience between 1764 and 1776," she is talking about Quincy's political life, and when she praises "[s]uccessful revolutionary leaders" as "not violent and irresponsible anarchists but political persons of intense discipline for whom the public cause purges mundane consideration of self," she is describing Josiah Quincy himself.[11] Thus *Portrait of a Patriot: The Major Political and Legal Papers of Josiah Quincy Junior*, and particularly this last volume, addresses Pauline's two "generations," the "old Revolutionaries" and the "young men," the "Founding Fathers," on both of which she focused her brilliant work and teaching. So what could be more appropriate than to dedicate this final volume to her?

One final word. How can one express adequately the value of true colleagueship and friendship? Pauline's bright, smiling face at every meeting, her inexhaustible enthusiasm, and her loyal care and concern for all her students and fellow historians were legendary. Pauline's historical subjects, and certainly Josiah Quincy, were concerned with legacy and immortality. They knew that life was short, but that the ripples of a life well and generously lived go on. They go on in family, in institutions, and in colleagueship, forever. How true of Pauline.

DANIEL R. COQUILLETTE

1. Pauline Maier, *The Old Revolutionaries: Political Lives in the Age of Samuel Adams* (New York, 1980), xiii. She certainly did know their "politics well," having written the definitive book on that, Pauline Maier, *From Resistance to Revolution: Colonial Radicals and the Development of American Opposition to Britain, 1765–1776* (New York, 1972).

2. See York, "A Life Cut Short," *Quincy Papers*, vol. 1, 41–43.

3. Quincy, a man way ahead of his time on gender issues, would have appreciated Pauline, who, with Mary Beth Norton, was in the vanguard of women in the historical profession. See Coquillette, "An Odyssey of America on the Brink of Revolution," the *Southern Journal*, *Quincy Papers* vol. 3, 22–28; "First Flower," *The Reports*, *Quincy Papers*, vol. 4, 59–63.

4. See *id.*, vol. 3, 81, for further explanation of jargon.

5. The two great latter volumes, *American Scripture* and *Ratification*, also particularly illustrate one of Pauline's other great talents, spotting what now seem like "obvious" gaps in the massive pre-existing historical studies of the Revolution and the New Republic, and filling those gaps in a uniquely important way. So "obvious" in retrospect, but so brilliant an insight at the time! I owe this to my distinguished colleague and another devoted colleague of Pauline, Mary Sarah Bilder.

6. See http://www.youtube.com/watch?v=ckrFUCTPihg and http://www.youtube.com/watch?v=lqNiOXkXkFk. My special thanks to my distinguished colleague, Robert J. Allison.

7. *The Old Revolutionaries*, *supra*, 270.

8. *Id.*, 280.

9. See York, "A Life Cut Short," *Quincy Papers*, vol. 1, 45–46.

10. *Id.*, 46.

11. *The Old Revolutionaries*, *supra*, 48, 271.

CONTENTS

VOLUME 6

ACKNOWLEDGMENTS

MY GREATEST DEBT is to the late Professor Pauline Maier of MIT; this book exists because she saw the need for it. When Dan Coquillette completed the fifth volume of the Quincy papers, he and I both thought that brought an end to the project. Pauline was convinced we needed a sixth volume, gathering together Quincy's correspondence and published writings. As chair of the publications committee for the Colonial Society of Massachusetts, she joined with editor John Tyler to invite me to take it on and I agreed most eagerly; hence what you have in hand.

Pauline offered her own insights on Quincy and generously worked her connections to help me find any Quincy pieces that had eluded my earlier searches. A few did turn up. Heading the list of those who dug out these gems are Christopher Damiani and David Haugaard at the Historical Society of Pennsylvania, and Maurita Baldock and Tammy Kiter at the New-York Historical Society. Ed Fitzgerald at the Quincy Historical Society, Professor James Cameron of Eastern Nazarene College, Nancy Carlisle and Melinda Huff at Historic New England, Jeanne Solensky at the Winterthur Library, and J. L. Bell, whose blog "Boston 1775" is an Internet treasure trove, also assisted along the way. Even though we came up empty-handed, I am also grateful to Tracey Kry at the American Antiquarian Society, Karen DePauw at the Connecticut Historical Society, and Halley Cella at the South Carolina Historical Society, for their answers to my queries.

My visits to the Massachusetts Historical Society library have gone from annual to semi-annual over the past few years, and I thank Conrad Edick Wright, Peter Drummey, Elaine Grublin, Anne Bentley, and Daniel Hinchen for their patience with me. I could only make those trips because of funding available to me as a Karl G. Maeser Professor of General Education at BYU, and then, after my term in that chair ended, with the resources that came from my being a Mary Lou Fulton Professor within my college at BYU. I was also able to make another trip to London and purchase books, microfilms, and photocopies that otherwise would have been beyond my means.

Thanks too are owed–and offered here–to my department chair, Don Harreld, Julie Radle, who actually runs the department, and to colleague Paul Kerry, who has never doubted that historical editing is important work. And since I can be certain this is the last Quincy volume that I will be producing for the CSM, I once again thank John Tyler, the tireless editor who started it all and has too often put aside his own work on Thomas Hutchinson to help me and others. John teamed me with Dan Coquillette, a constant source of inspiration; it is an honor to once again share a title page with Dan. I was also fortunate that Jane Ward handled the copy-editing as expertly she did on the first volume. Paul Hoffmann provided the exceptionally fine design for this volume and Kate Mertes the index.

And, finally, I must include my wife, Carole, in this list. She has always found Josiah Quincy's dedication to public service inspiring, the relationship between Josiah and Abigail Quincy touching, and the determination of Eliza Susan Quincy impressive. They were remarkable; so is she.

INTRODUCTION

This is the state of man;—to day he puts forth
The tender leaves of hope, to-morrow blossoms,
And bears his blushing honours thick upon him;
The third day comes a frost, a killing frost,
And when 'tis thought —— full surely
His greatness is a ripening, nips his root.

JOSIAH QUINCY JUNIOR BORROWED those lines from Shakespeare's *Henry VIII* to serve as the epigraph for a friend who had just died. That friend, Thomas Leonard, was only twenty-eight. Did Quincy, afflicted with consumption since he was a teen, have some premonitory sense that a similar fate awaited him, that he too would die at a relatively young age—thirty-one—four years later? If so, perhaps he hoped that what he offered in his eulogy might be said of him: that this was a life of much promise, ended tragically early, by "one of the many inexplicable decrees of an unerring Providence."[1] As it turned out, what Quincy said of Leonard would indeed be said of Quincy.

Joseph Warren, Quincy's onetime doctor and longtime ally in Boston politics, lamented that his friend "just lived to come on shore and die in his own Country."[2] James Lovell shared Warren's sorrow. Lovell, like Warren—and

1. Quincy's eulogy for Leonard, which included the epigraph above, appeared on the first page of *The Boston Evening-Post,* 8 July 1771; a handwritten version is in the Quincy, Wendell, Holmes, and Upham Family Papers (hereafter QP), Massachusetts Historical Society (hereafter MHS), at QP 51; also on reel 28 of the microfilm edition of that collection. Quincy added this note for the printer: "The enclosed character was sketched by a very hearty friend to the Deceased. Plain truth has been *aimed* at. Seeing it corrected, or wholly new-drafted, will give *real* satisfaction." The passage Quincy quoted is from Act III, Scene 2, with Cardinal Wolsey, just disgraced by the earls of Suffolk and Surrey at their King's behest, finally realizing that his opposition to Henry's decision to divorce Queen Catherine and marry Anne Boleyn could cost him everything.

2. Warren to Arthur Lee, 27 April 1775, in Peter Force, ed., *American Archives,* 9 vols. (Washington, D.C.: M. St. Clair Clarke and Peter Force, 1837–1853), 4th series, 2:425. Warren erred on the location of Josiah Jr.'s passing. Quincy died aboard ship in Gloucester harbor, not long

unlike others—had honored his promise to keep Quincy abreast of local affairs while he was off in London. "Tis glorious to dye for one's Country," Lovell commiserated with Oliver Wendell, who had also known Josiah Junior well. "Our Friend Quincy died by *thinking* for it, as much as any one has lately died by *fighting* for it."[3] Lovell meant most especially thoughts that Quincy had shared with others, thoughts shaped as arguments in defense of American rights. Those rights, Quincy understood, could only be defended effectively if his fellow colonists had a clear sense of community and identity. He spent much of his short public life trying to build both, first within Boston, then expanded to neighboring Massachusetts communities, and ultimately beyond the Bay Colony to other provinces, and to Britain itself.

Quincy's thoughts about colonial American rights and how to build a sense of American unity, expressed publicly in various newspaper pieces and a pamphlet, as well as privately in numerous letters, are gathered in this volume. They should add to evidence already presented in the previous five volumes that, as my colleague in this enterprise, Dan Coquillette, put it, Josiah Quincy Junior was "a courageous patriot and, by all accounts, a brilliant man."[4] His law commonplace book and reports of cases in the Massachusetts Superior Court, begun while he was an undergraduate at Harvard, are impressive, the former showing his breadth of learning, the latter an attention to detail that would lead, a century later, to their being published and cited as an authoritative source in case law. His journal notes about Charleston society, made in 1773, like his written reactions to London a year later, only add to his reputation for astute observation and incisive commentary. His political commonplace book, compiled between 1770-1774, when he was at the center of the Bay Colony's

after it anchored but before he could be carried ashore. Warren would be slain in the fighting on Breed's Hill on June 17th, prompting John Adams to lament to Josiah Sr. the passing of "two characters as great in proportion to their age, as any I have known in *America*." In ibid., 4th series 2:1751; letter of 29 July 1775. For Adams's initial reaction, and that of his wife, Abigail, as well, see Daniel R. Coquillette and Neil Longley York, eds., *Portrait of a Patriot,* 6 vols. (Boston: Colonial Society of Massachusetts, 2005–2014), 1:43 n. 80.

3. Lovell to Wendell, 5 May 1775, Hugh Upham Clark collection in the MHS, on reel 30 in the MHS film QP collection (see note 1 supra). All three men had been involved in town affairs, joined in opposition to Thomas Hutchinson's attempts to enforce imperial policy. Wendell, like Quincy, had been named to the town's committee of correspondence formed in November 1772.

4. In Coquillette and York, eds., *Portrait of a Patriot,* 2:11.

public affairs, provided the intellectual foundation for speeches that prompted John Adams to remember him as the "Boston Cicero."[5]

Unfortunately, virtually none of the speeches that Quincy made in the Boston town meeting, where he built his reputation as an orator, survive. He quoted from one speech at length in a later letter; bits and pieces of another were jotted down by a listener.[6] The most flattering comments about him came posthumously, when friends who survived him looked back on days that seemed even more glorious over the distance of time. Indeed, a half century would pass before William Eustis, then governor of Massachusetts, told Eliza Susan Quincy that he had never heard a voice equal in clarity and power to that of her grandfather's.[7]

Contemporaneous comments about Quincy the lawyer as opposed to Quincy the politician are even scarcer.[8] Such fragmentary records are a reminder that

5. Adams's "Cicero" allusion is noted in ibid., 1:8. The political commonplace book is reproduced in that volume, along with Quincy's London journal. Quincy's law commonplace book is in volume 2, the Southern journal is in volume 3, and the law reports are in volumes 4 and 5. I edited the first volume, as I did this one; Dan Coquillette and his team of talented research assistants did the other four.

6. Quincy quoted passages from his speech in the Old South meeting house on 16 December 1773, the night of the Boston tea party, in a letter to his wife, Abigail, of 14 December 1774, from London. It is reproduced infra on pp. 335–37. Quincy may have quoted from memory; he may have taken a copy with him, possibly to share with those sympathetic to the American cause. Another of his speeches two days earlier in the town meeting was alluded to and paraphrased in part by an anonymous source that L. F. S. Upton edited for publication as "Proceedings of Ye Body Respecting the Tea" in the "Notes and Documents section of the *William and Mary Quarterly*, 3rd series 22 (1965):286–300 (with the sentiments attributed to Quincy on p. 297). Quincy, who had been involved in debating what to do about the tea for over two weeks, joined others who concluded, as Upton put it, "that the destruction of private property was necessary for the maintenance of public liberty." (Ibid., p. 287.)

7. Eustis, aged twenty at the time of the tea party, had graduated from Harvard the year before and was studying medicine under the tutelage of Joseph Warren. His reminiscence is included as a footnote in Josiah Quincy, *Memoir of the Life of Josiah Quincy, Junior, of Massachusetts: 1744–1775*, 2nd ed, (Boston: John Wilson and Son, 1874), p. 226n. A third edition , virtually identical to this one but published by Little Brown, would appear the next year. Eliza Susan Quincy expanded those volumes from the original, Josiah Quincy, *Memoir of the Life of Josiah Quincy Jun. of Massachusetts* (Boston: Cummings, Hilliard, & Company, 1825). She insisted that her father's name be listed as author, hers as editor, in the later printings, though, from the beginning, the work had been done largely by her. The second edition is the one cited here, as it was in the first volume of this collection.

8. His opening and closing arguments for the soldiers' trial from the Boston "Massacre" do survive, as least as they were recorded in John Hodgson, ed., *The Trial of William Wemms* (Boston, 1770). John Adams famously complained that Hodgson's record is unreliable–see his

the past is forever gone; only vestiges remain. Realistic historians have always known that. They do not have to be "deconstructed" to know that the stories they tell are more constructions than reconstructions, more creations than re-creations.[9] And quite often there is a deeper purpose in studying the past that goes far beyond a simple desire to understand it. "We tell ourselves stories in order to make sense of life," novelist Norman Mailer once commented, and there are times when "life is so absurd" that "nothing makes sense, but stories bring order to the absurdity."[10]

Mailer, perhaps, could not resist playing the curmudgeon, but he hit home when he joined stories to meaning. Josiah Quincy Junior certainly appreciated the value of storytelling when it came to shaping and reshaping identity or promoting one behavior over another. He had a didactic underlying motive in the tales that he wrote as a political essayist, the stands that he took in the Boston town meeting, and the points that he contended in court. But that did not make him disingenuous, his choices determined by convenience rather than conviction. Whether he stood before jurors in court or townsmen in the Old South, he knew that he was engaged in a battle for hearts and minds. Whether he argued a legal case or a political cause, he needed to argue to win. To that extent, John Phillip Reid was right in emphasizing the use of "forensic history"

---

letter to Jedediah Morse of 5 January 1816, in Charles Francis Adams, ed., *The Works of John Adams,* 10 vols. (Boston: Little, Brown, and Co., 1850–1856), 10:201. If Quincy felt the same way, he left no surviving record to indicate it. I did not include Quincy's arguments as reported by Hodgson in this collection, in part because they are so readily available elsewhere, most notably in the printed version noted above, which was in turn included in the final volume of L. Kinvin Wroth and Hiller Zobel, eds., *The Legal Papers of John Adams,* 3 vols. (Cambridge, Mass.: The Belknap Press of the Harvard University Press, 1965), pp. 158–69 and pp. 226–41 for Quincy's opening and closing, resp. But another reason for not including them is that Hodgson went back and forth between purportedly recording what Quincy said verbatim and summarizing in his own words, thus leaving a mixed, incomplete record at best. Nonetheless, it is interesting that Hodgson recorded Quincy as quoting from Portia's "quality of mercy" speech in *The Merchant of Venice* (Act IV, Scene 1), showing that Quincy even took Shakespeare into the courtroom. Hiller Zobel's *The Boston Massacre* (New York: W. W. Norton, 1970) remains the standard study. I offered a few observations that differ from those presented there in "Rival Truths, Political Accommodation, and the Boston 'Massacre'," *Massachusetts Historical Review* 11 (2009):57–95; and *The Boston Massacre* (New York: Routledge, 2010), a documents anthology.

9. Just as I would rather not repeat here what I have already written about Quincy's intellectual world in volume one of this collection, I would rather not rehash what I already wrote about history and memory in *Fiction As Fact* (Kent, Ohio: Kent State University Press, 2001), pp. 127–45.

10. Norman Mailer, *The Spooky Art* (New York: Random House, 2003), pp. 156–57.

in patriot rights talk. As Quincy saw it, his task was to defend *his* position, not that of his opponents. If that meant that he could appear to be one-sided, then so be it. Thus his relentless emphasis on imperial wrongs against colonial rights. "It is astonishing how much the revolutionary controversy was conducted like a common-law litigation," Professor Reid observed, "even though there was no tribunal to which the parties could appeal except to the court of public opinion."[11]

Quincy's pamphlet, the newspaper pieces attributed to him, and his letters all focus on the imperial crisis as Quincy experienced it, mostly in Boston, but then also for a few months in London. Quincy's published writings appeared in Boston before he crossed the Atlantic; he did not write any essays for the London press. Printers Benjamin Edes and John Gill published Quincy's *Observations* and, before that, all but one of his newspaper pieces in their *Boston Gazette*. The lone exception was a piece that appeared in the *Boston Evening-Post*.

Quincy's view of American rights did not change with circumstances. He believed that they came from God as carried through the law of nature, then reinforced by the English constitution and colonial charters, an understanding evident from what he said as a lawyer in court as well as what he wrote as a political essayist.[12] His defense of those rights would not be any more emphatic, any more passionate, in 1775 than in 1767. To those who warned against offending Britain by protesting imperial policy "we boldly answer, that in defence of our civil and religious rights, we dare to oppose the world," he proclaimed in the 1767 essay that Daniel Webster would quote during ceremonies commemorating the fiftieth anniversary of the battle of Bunker Hill.

11. John Phillip Reid, *Constitutional History of the American Revolution,* abridged ed. (Madison, Wisc.: University of Wisconsin Press, 1995), p. 34; and, in more detail, his four-volume magnum opus of the same title, by the same publisher. For what he meant by "forensic history," particularly as it applied to Boston (though with no particular emphasis on Quincy), see his *In a Defiant Stance* (University Park, Pa.: Pennsylvania State University Press, 1977) and *In a Rebellious Spirit* (University Park, Pa.: The Pennsylvania State University Press, 1979). I disagree with Professor Reid, however, on his insistence that American patriots rarely made natural rights arguments before declaring independence. Quincy turned to them from the beginning and in that sense he was typical of his generation.

12. I discuss his ideas, and the sources for them, in detail in Coquillette and York, eds., *Portrait of a Patriot,* 1:47–92. See too Dan Coquillette's observations, in connection with Quincy's trip to the South, in ibid., 3:62–82

"For, under GOD," Quincy proclaimed, "we are determin'd, that whatsoever, whensoever or howsoever we shall be call'd to make our exit, that we shall die free-men."[13] Seven years later Quincy was no less zealous, because no less aggrieved. "They who were the prime movers and instruments" of sending troops to Boston "are stained with a crime, that this people ought *not—they cannot—they will not* forget or forgive."[14] This might seem harsh language indeed for someone who, as a defense counsel, had helped nine British soldiers escape the hangman's noose. But then he expected fellow patriots to differentiate—as he did in court—between the excusable actions of soldiers beset by a mob and the inexcusable imperial policies that put them on the streets of Boston in the first place.[15]

Quincy was a rhetorical populist, a champion of popular sovereignty, arguing that all legitimate political authority was based on how well political leaders, kings as well as governors, served the people. Whether that sovereignty was something the people themselves could exercise or whether it was something more nebulous he never quite worked out—like so many in the Revolutionary generation. Although he preferred discourse to force of arms, he also argued on the soldiers' behalf in their "Massacre" trial—and in various of his newspaper pieces—that self-defense was an undeniable, inalienable right. And yet did that right extend as readily to a society perceiving that it was threatened with a loss of liberty as it did to an individual facing an actual loss of life? To someone looking for an excuse to rise in revolt or foment revolution, the answer was an obvious yes; for Quincy, it was not quite that simple.

Quincy never openly argued that political independence was the only solution to the imperial problem.[16] As Quincy reported to Franklin when they talked just before he left London in March 1775, he preferred to hope that

13. From his "Hyperion" essay of 5 October 1767, reproduced at infra pp. 7–11 (with quotations from pp. 8–9 and 9, resp.).

14. From his "Marchmont Nedham" essay of 10 January 1774, reproduced infra at pp. 152–57 (quotation from pp. 156).

15. See, in this connection, Dan Coquillette's comments in Coquillette and York, eds., *Portrait of a Patriot,* 4:63–75.

16. Nathaniel Appleton reported to Oliver Wendell (as noted in Coquillette and York, ed., *Portrait of a Patriot,* 1:43 n. 80) that Quincy died wondering if a battle had begun that would free his country—a sentiment obtained secondhand, and which could have meant that Quincy hoped that fighting might bring the disputants back to the negotiating table, making independence unnecessary. Appleton's letter is in QP 51 (also on reel 30) MHS.

American rights could be secured within the British empire—this despite all evidence to the contrary and despite all his polemical invective. True enough, thoughtful men on both sides of the Atlantic agreed that nothing lasts forever; the British empire, like empires that had gone before, would eventually decay and fall. "All colonies have their date of independence," advised Isaac Barré, the noted Pittite, in the House of Commons in 1766. "The wisdom or folly of our conduct may make it the sooner or later,"[17] Barré warned. Even eight years later, Samuel Adams, who believed American independence inevitable, still went to the First Continental Congress seeking some sort of reconciliation.[18] He and those who gathered with him at Philadelphia in 1774 wanted to delay, not hasten, the inevitable, which produced a state of mind, and a style of rights talk, that does not put them into neat categories of radical or conservative.[19]

They argued primarily as politicians rather than as political philosophers.[20] They used language carefully, realizing that carrying a point in debate mattered little if the policies they hoped to change remained in place. Quincy could be florid in his writing style and passionate in his denunciations of those who abused the colonists and trespassed upon their liberties. Thomas Hutchinson in particular would suffer from the sharp strokes of his pen.[21] Even so, Quincy wanted to change minds, not simply rouse readers and reinforce existing dispositions. His rhetorical excess was not the result of his having lost personal control and, with it, perspective. He was too experienced a courtroom performer, too practiced a member of the bar, to forget his audience. He knew

17. During debates over repealing the Stamp Act, on 3 February 1766, in R. C. Simmons and P.D. G. Thomas, eds., *Proceedings and Debates of the British Parliaments Respecting North America, 1754–1783,* 6 vols. (Millwood, N.Y.: Kraus International, 1982–1987), 2:144

18. See Adams to Arthur Lee on 4 April 1774 and William Checkley, 1 June 1774, in Harry Alonzo Cushing, ed., *The Writings of Samuel Adams,* 4 vols. (New York: G. P. Putnam's Sons, 1904–1908), 3:100–1 and 3:128, resp. Pauline Maier explains how Adams predicted independence long before he advocated it in *The Old Revolutionaries* (New York: Alfred A. Knopf, 1980), 3–50.

19. On this subject see my "The First Continental Congress and the Problem of American Rights," *Pennsylvania Magazine of History and Biography* 122 (1998):353–83.

20. Which is not to say that no political philosopher ever holds back, unconcerned with the socially acceptable; thus the debates over "esotericism" and the "noble lie," discussed, notably, in Catherine and Michael Zuckert, *The Truth about Leo Strauss* (Chicago: University of Chicago Press, 2006), pp. 42–46, 120–36.

21. See most especially his "Marchmont Nedham" pieces between December 1773-February 1774, at infra, pp. 143–72.

that successful arguments, spoken as well as written, relied on a mastery of performance arts; all criticism, he understood, runs the risk of offending. But, if done skillfully enough, it might have the desired effect, no doubt offending some but quite possibly changing the minds of others. He had to believe that political debate could affect political decisions. Otherwise he would not have risked his fragile health in a transatlantic voyage to meet with those whose views differed from his. In that sense he was almost naively optimistic.

As Hannah Arendt once observed, most revolutions begin as a quest for restoration or renovation.[22] Rather than thinking of Quincy simply as a revolutionary in the making—which he may well have become, had his life not been cut short—we should place him in an eighteenth-century Whig tradition that emphasized securing rights within the existing political system, not creating new forms of government, much less an entirely new nation state.[23] He may have given up on the idea of an Anglo-American empire of liberty, as did so many of his colleagues in the Boston town meeting, but we cannot say for sure. Not all of the colonists who engaged in protest or supported revolt went on to embrace revolution, or, if they embraced it, they did so reluctantly, like Quincy's friend and correspondent, John Dickinson. Whatever changes would result from colonial agitation, Quincy was determined to be part of the process. In his mind he put public need over private preference, with virtuous service being the measure of his success.

He fits nicely into a frame of mind that the historian Douglass Adair described for the Revolutionary generation as a whole. Adair did not profess to know what truly drove the men of Quincy's generation—motivation being ever elusive, our power to explain it frustratingly limited—but we can examine the ideals they professed to revere and "fame" stood high among them. This was more than a quest for honor or glory. As Adair explained it:

> To be famous or renowned means to be widely spoken of by a man's contemporaries and also to act in such a way that posterity also remembers his name and

22. Hannah Arendt, *On Revolution* (New York: Viking Press, 1965; orig. ed., 1963), p. 30. Also see Gordon S. Wood, *The Creation of the American Republic, 1776–1787* (Chapel Hill, N.C.: University of North Carolina Press, 1969), for how this tendency played out for American Revolutionaries (but with no mention of Quincy in particular).

23. An attitude that became more difficult to sustain after both the American and French revolutions. For this changed setting see Bernard Crick, *In Defense of Politics*, 2nd ed. (New York: Penguin, 1982).

> actions. His desire for fame is thus a dynamic element in the historical process; it rejects the static complacent urge in the human heart to merely *be* and invites a strenuous effort to *become*—to become a person and force in history larger than the ordinary. The love of fame encourages a man to make history, to leave the mark of his deeds and his ideals on the world; it incites a man to refuse to be the victim of events and to become an "event-making" personality—a being never to be forgotten by those later generations that will be born into a world his actions helped to shape.[24]

Adair did not mention Quincy. I do not think he would mind my adding Quincy's name to a list that included Washington and Franklin, Adams and Jefferson. After all, the writers that Adair turned to for the source of that Revolutionary Era thinking—Plutarch and Francis Bacon standing foremost—were among Quincy's favorites.[25] They had shaped his way of thinking, even his view of himself, and he wanted their influence to continue on into future generations. His contingency plan to set aside part of his estate to endow a chair in his name for moral philosophy, law, and oratory at Harvard should be understood with that purpose in mind.[26]

Quincy wrote his will many months before he set sail for England, mortality never being far from his consciousness. Although he may not have consid-

24. Adair's 1967 essay can be found most conveniently in the eponymous *Fame and the Founding Fathers,* edited by Trevor Colbourn (New York: W. W. Norton, 1974), pp. 3–26 (quotation from p. 11). Adair steered clear of the distinction between "becoming" and "being" made by Oswald Spengler in his *The Decline of the West,* 2 vols. (New York: Alfred A. Knopf, 1929; orig German ed., 1918), as part of Spengler's argument that a "spiritual life force" is lost as a dynamic culture inevitably devolves into a more materialistic civilization. Even though I am avoiding repeating in this volume what I already stated in the first, Pauline Maier's caution offered in *From Resistance to Revolution* (New York: Alfred A. Knopf, 1972), p. xx, cited there, is worth quoting here as well: "Motivation remains the most elusive of historical problems, and efforts to attribute it to any one cause, or to identify conceptual structures as causes in themselves, seem to me inadequate."

25. For the inclusion of books by Bacon, Locke and Sidney in Quincy's posthumous portrait, painted by Gilbert Stuart, see Coquillette and York, eds., *Portrait of a Patriot,* 1:xxix–xxxvi, 88.

26. Should his son die young, which of course he did not. My collaborator, Dan Coquillette, has pointed out that, had the Quincy bequest in fact carried through, Josiah Quincy Jr. rather than the slaveholding Loyalist Isaac Royall could have become the initial benefactor of what would become Harvard Law School. (In Coquillette and Bruce A. Kimball, *On the Battlefield of Merit: Harvard Law School, The First Century,* forthcoming.) See Quincy's will of 28 February 1774, with a codicil added on September 9th, after his daughter, Abigail, had been born. Joseph Warren acted as a witness in both instances. In QP 51 (also reel 29), MHS, and reproduced infra, pp. 173–79 (with £2000 for the endowed chair at p. 176).

According to Eliza Susan Quincy, her father had a copy of this political cartoon hanging on the wall of his room in Massachusetts Hall when he was a student at Harvard. It was quite likely among the items that his father brought back with him from England. It ended up in the mansion built by the future mayor's grandfather, Josiah "the Colonel," in Quincy, where Eliza Susan included it in an 1879 description of the house's furnishings. She misidentified the rider being thrown as Lord North in a scene from 1770. The mezzotint, done by John Dixon of London, actually dated from September 1774. The horse could be taken to be the colonies in general or Massachusetts in particular, and the rider an Englishman or perhaps General Thomas Gage, who had been sent over by George III to restore peace in a province churning with unrest since passage of the so-called "Coercive" Acts. Interestingly enough, in 1776 Lord North would indeed be thrown by his horse while he was riding in Bushy Park, near Hampton Court, and the fall apparently took a toll on his physical health just as the American war was beginning to drain him emotionally. Dixon image, Courtesy of the British Library.

ered himself a disciple of Plato's Socrates, he nonetheless had the same concern about how a young man should be prepared to lead as an adult that Plato ascribed to Socrates in *The Republic.* When his son—only two at the time that he made his will—reached sixteen, he wanted him to be given certain books from his personal library, books that very likely he had filled with marginalia: the works of Algernon Sidney, Francis Bacon and John Locke, Thomas Gordon's translations of Tacitus and Sallust, *Cato's Letters* that Gordon had joined with John Trenchard to write, and Catharine Macaulay's history of England. "May the Spirit of Liberty rest upon him," Quincy admonished after listing the titles—a charge to those who in the event of his death would care for his son, and a charge to young Josiah himself, which he accepted as he grew to manhood.[27] Both his widowed mother and heartbroken grandfather saw to it. The mourning ring that Josiah Junior had had made for his father in London,[28] his father in turn passed on to his grandson. Inscribed was this motto: "Oh, save my country, were his last." His grandfather bequeathed it, "wishing the Motto" his father "caused to be engraved upon it may never be forgot nor Neglected by his Son." According to Josiah the Mayor's daughter, Eliza Susan Quincy, he wore the ring throughout his adult life.[29]

Josiah Junior had secured his reputation as an orator when speaking at the

27. From Quincy's will, cited supra n. 26, and the passage just quoted at infra, p. 174.

28. Which he described in the letter that he dictated to a sailor on board *The Boston Packet,* 21 April 1775, anticipating that he would not survive the crossing. In QP 51 (and reel 30) MHS. He also described the ring that he had made for his wife, Abigail, to wear in memory of him. For context (without any mention of Quincy's rings) see Sarah Nehama, *In Death Lamented* (Boston: Massachusetts Historical Society, 2012), a companion volume to a Fall 2012 exhibition at the MHS on "The Tradition of Anglo-American Mourning Jewelry."

29. Quincy, *Memoir,* pp. 425–26, from Eliza Susan Quincy's editorial notes to the volume. The wording of the inscription is taken from Josiah Sr.'s will, dated 23 March 1781, with a codicil added 17 February 1784, not long before he died. It is in QP 72 (also reel 32) MHS. The motto itself came from Alexander Pope's epistle to Lord Viscount Cobham, with "Popes Works" listed as no. 312 in the "Catalogue of Books," in Coquillette and York, eds., *Portrait of a Patriot,* 5:901. Drawing from the classical past as well as English history, to work in Caesar as well as Cromwell and the complicated nature of human motives, Pope ended: "And You! BRAVE COBHAM, to the latest breath Shall feel your *ruling Passion* strong in Death: Such in those Moments, as in All the past, 'Oh, save my Country, Heav'n!' shall be your last." Pope also included this cautionary note earlier in his poem, which all biographers should take to heart: "And yet the fate of all Extremes is such, Men may be read, as well as Books, too much." Josiah Sr. would quote another passage from this same poem in a letter to his daughter-in-law Abigail, after Josiah Jr.'s death. See infra, p. 398. Also see his letter to his grandson, written not long before he died, at infra, pp. 403. It is, fittingly, the last letter in this volume.

Old South meeting house on the evening of the Boston Tea Party. His son marked his own rise as a public figure by a July 4th speech at Faneuil Hall a quarter of a century later. The younger Quincy called on the audience to remember their forefathers, those who had settled the colony and those who later founded the nation. In a style reminiscent of his father he lectured listeners that "the ark of liberty is, among the virtuous, union invincible," while warning them away from democratic enthusiasms leading to the anarchy of Revolutionary France, whose "new temple of liberty,' he thundered, "has NO GOD."[30] The speech may have helped launch a political career that eventually took him to Washington, D.C. as a Federalist for four terms in the House of Representatives. He would return to Boston, be elected mayor, then serve as Harvard's president for well over a decade. Dying in 1864 at the age of ninety-two, he lived nearly three times as long as his father.[31]

It was while mayor that he put the finishing touches to the biography of his father begun by his daughter, Eliza Susan. They had received mixed signals about the effort, one friend advising that there would be readers for it, another cautioning that something broader would be required—that the story of Josiah Junior alone would not be intriguing enough to sell copies.[32] The book did well, at least locally, but it would be another half century before a new edition, with expanded editorial comments by Eliza Susan Quincy, was published. Another followed soon after, though Eliza Susan admitted that she

30. Josiah Quincy, *An Oration Pronounced, on July 4, 1798, at the Request of the Inhabitants of the Town of Boston, in Commemoration of the Anniversary of American Independence* (Boston: John Russell, 1798). Quotations from pp. 31 and 24, resp. In calling for his audience to remember and emulate great patriots, he alluded to John Adams, James Otis, even Jonathan Mayhew, but not explicitly his father—though he did use a variation of a phrase his father had once used as well: "This is history. May we now say, it is also prophecy?" (p. 17). See infra, p. 216. He also used as the epigraph for the printed copy an extract from his father's 1774 *Observations,* p. 78.

31. His second son became his first biographer: Edmund Quincy, *Life of Josiah Quincy* (Boston: Ticknor and Fields, 1867).

32. See the notes that Eliza Susan Quincy wrote in 1876 and 1892 that she tipped into her "Memoir of Josiah Quincy jun.r" QP 46 (also reel 6) MHS. Directly under the title she wrote the epigraph: "The history of his Life, his Children shall venerate." It is the second volume in her two-volume memoir, the first taking the family history up to Josiah's Jr's life. That first volume is QP 45 (also on reel 6) MHS. Therefore the "Memoir" for Josiah Jr. will be cited as volume 2, and not as a freestanding manuscript. As Eliza Susan recalled, "Mr. Ticknor"—probably Professor George Ticknor of Harvard—had advised against publication of what became the 1825 first edition of the published *Memoir* (see supra p. xxi, n. 7), whereas Joseph Savage had urged them to proceed. Her father decided that "Savage's opinion is enough for me."

pushed for both, using still powerful family connections to offset the lack of reader demand.[33]

She held her post as keeper of the family flame to the end of her life, gathering Josiah Junior's papers, arranging them, donating them in stages to the Massachusetts Historical Society. It was Eliza Susan who had commissioned Gilbert Stuart to do the portrait of her father and deceased grandfather. She restricted the use of both likenesses, only allowing those whose judgment and motives she trusted to reproduce them.[34] She even tried to arrange for the perpetual care of her grandfather's grave in the Hancock Cemetery. He had been re-interred there after his initial burial in Gloucester. His wife Abigail's body was placed alongside his when she died in 1798. His father, who died in 1784, was placed, as he requested, in a separate crypt at the foot of their burial mound.[35] Eliza Susan offered to give the town of Quincy $100 to invest, the interest from which could be tapped periodically to repaint the wrought iron rail fence around the monument at the top of the mound. "It may reasonably be expected that this duty will be performed for the next ten to twenty years, by some member of our family" but, with fading memory and flagging interest, she feared that the grave site—prominently situated in the cemetery though it was—might thereafter fall into disrepair.[36]

Hancock Cemetery, despite being in the heart of downtown Quincy, can be charmingly peaceful, acting as the refuge for meditation and contemplation that Eliza Susan Quincy had hoped it would be. Time may work against its staying that way much longer. Even the best maintained cemeteries give only the illusion of permanence. The mound built over Josiah Junior's crypt is practically barren, the foundation for the stone shaft at its summit is cracked, the inscriptions on the shaft itself are nearly worn away, and the old iron fence

33. See the note in Coquillette and York, eds., *Portrait of a Patriot,* 1:11.

34. "As I was the entire cause of Stuart's painting both portraits," she explained in a letter to historian Justin Winsor of 23 May 1881, "I have a right to object if copies prove unsatisfactory." QP 47 (reel 64) MHS.

35. More details about Josiah and Abigail's burials are in Coquillette and York, eds., *Portrait of a Patriot,* 1:44–46.

36. See her letters to George Gill, Quincy town clerk, beginning on 12 September 1881 (the one quoted in the text above) in QP 48 (reel 64) MHS. She hoped that the fund would also cover the maintenance of family graves in nearby Mt. Wollaston Cemetery, where her remains now lie in quiet hillside repose. Her father had been interred in Mount Auburn Cemetery in Cambridge, not far from the Harvard campus that had defined so much of his later career.

surrounding it could use a fresh coat of paint. And yet there lingers the sense of caring that a family and community put into preserving the memory of one of their own.[37] Only later generations can decide if what he did, and what he stood for, are worth honoring still. But it would be a shame indeed if memory of Josiah Quincy Junior were allowed to fade away. He personified what it meant, in his age, to be an American patriot.

Josiah Quincy Junior's burial mound, in a watercolor painted by Eliza Susan Quincy, ca. 1822; pen and ink wash; dimensions: full page: 18 cm x 22.1 cm; image only: 15.3 cm x 20.1 cm; Quincy Family Papers; courtesy of the Massachusetts Historical Society.

The mound itself now is essentially as it was then, although the general setting—other grave stones and a tree nearby within the cemetery, and buildings just outside it—have altered the overall appearance. Eliza Susan included this painting, one in a series of nine that she did of landmarks in Quincy, in her manuscript "Memoir" honoring her grandfather. Her painting of the Quincy "mansion" is reproduced in volume one of this series, as is a photograph of Josiah Junior's grave, taken just over a decade ago.

37. As Dan Coquillette witnessed firsthand when he participated in events honoring Josiah Jr. in the spring of 2011.

A NOTE ON EDITING

INCLUDED BELOW, in chronological order, are Josiah Quincy Junior's surviving letters, those he received as well as those he wrote, the first dating from December 1764, the last from March 1775; newspaper pieces printed between 1768 and 1774 that have been attributed to him, either in his lifetime or later by his granddaughter, Eliza Susan Quincy; his one published pamphlet, the 1774 *Observations;* and a handful of letters written by others about him that are useful in painting his portrait. Nearly all of the letters are housed in the Massachusetts Historical Society library, as part of the Quincy, Wendell, Holmes and Upham Family Papers, in a box marked QP 51. The vast majority of them were later reproduced on microfilm (on reels 28–30 of the 67 reel collection, under P-347 at the MHS). Those that were not are indicated below; likewise those that are in other collections. It appears that the bulk of Josiah Junior's writings ended up with the MHS because of Eliza Susan Quincy, who, in 1884, the year she died, donated many of the manuscripts relating to her grandfather that she gathered over a lifetime. She had placed her two volume "Memoir" of the Quincy family—QP 45 and 46 in the collection noted above (reel 6 in the film version)—with the MHS for safekeeping fourteen years before. She stipulated in her bequest that the "Memoir" never be loaned to anyone outside the MHS library. There it remains with the other materials she donated, after having been bound on the eve of World War I. Volume 1 eventually came apart; volume 2 is still intact.

Reading through the letters, it will become obvious how few pieces from a once extensive correspondence have been passed down to the present.[1] Indeed, some items that Eliza Susan Quincy used in writing the "Memoir" between

1. For example, Quincy listed at the beginning of his Southern journal the date and addresses of sixteen letters that he wrote on his trip. Ten of those were to his wife Abigail (who would again be his primary correspondent when he traveled to London the next year). Of the sixteen total, only two appear to have survived, both of which are reproduced below (to Abigail on March 1st and his father on April 15th, infra at pp. 126–27 and 135–37, resp.). He forgot to include in his list a letter that he wrote to his brother Samuel on April 6th (see infra, pp. 128–30). Did he forget others as well? The list is in Coquillette and York, eds., *Portrait of a Patriot,* 3:86.

1822 and 1824 did not make it to the MHS and their whereabouts are now unknown—to me, at least, and various archivists and librarians I have pestered over the years in my quest to find them. Eliza Susan pasted a few letters into her handwritten "Memoir" but others that she transcribed have since disappeared. Those transcriptions fill many of the pages of the biography that her father had published under his name in 1825—under his name, because she demurred in using her own—as the *Memoir of the Life of Josiah Quincy, Junior, of Massachusetts: 1744–1775*. As in Volume 1 of this series, I cited the second edition released in 1874, which was much expanded from the original text. Apparently Eliza Susan had the drafts of all the newspaper essays that she attributed to Josiah Junior, some of which she quoted at length in both her handwritten "Memoir" and in the printed *Memoir*. None—not a single one—is now to be found.

Eliza Susan Quincy edited some of the letters that she transcribed for her "Memoir," which were later printed in the *Memoir*, quite heavily. I too have done some editing, with a lighter touch but for the same purpose. Eliza Susan did not want readers to think that Josiah Junior's language was sloppy or that he was in any sense unlearned in its use. She therefore sometimes changed noun/verb relations so that they conformed to the then-current usage; she likewise altered the spelling and substituted different words for those whose connotation had changed over time. Occasionally she excised entire paragraphs and, yes, in a few instances she bowdlerized the text for one reason or another. Only she could say precisely why, and she did not.

I followed the same editorial guidelines as I did in the first volume. To repeat here what I explained there, when Quincy used as a shorthand the runic thorns "ye" for the and "yt" for that, I substituted the fuller forms; likewise with "yr" for your and "shoud" for should, as well as other shortened words. Quincy's contemporaries would not have stumbled over the informal shorthand; modern readers might and thereby lose the import of what Quincy said, as well as the style in which he said it. Quincy often underlined words in his letters that he wanted to emphasize. Here those underlines have been turned into italics. I also substituted "and" where he (and his correspondents) had written "&." Words that he habitually misspelled (writing "beleive" rather than "believe" is one notable example) or misconstructed (writing the contraction "it's" where he should have used the possessive pronoun "its") I corrected silently. His punctuation often differed from current standards, particularly in the use of colons and semi-colons, and even commas and periods. He and his correspondents used dashes as substitutes for all of them. I edited punctuation that could prove too jarring to modern readers. Therefore I kept a few of those dashes, but only where they seemed to be intended for a particular emphasis. Words that Quincy and his correspondents left out inadvertently, I inserted in brackets. Quincy and his correspondents varied how they dated their letters and quite often signed them with abbreviated names. I moved dates that came at the end to the beginning, but did not otherwise alter them, or the signatures at the end.

As in the previous volume, I did not aim for a perfect consistency, making all that Quincy wrote conform to modern standards. In some places he wrote "public" and in others "publick"; I let those differences stand. He capitalized as he saw fit, as was the convention of his age. I let that stand too, except in instances where he put the first letter of a word in lower case at the beginning of a sentence.

What I have explained to this point applies to manuscript letters. I did not change the grammar, punctuation or spelling of Quincy's pamphlet and newspaper pieces. I also kept the emphasis where Quincy placed it on certain words or phrases, but I could not duplicate precisely, in either the size or type of font, the form that the emphasis took. Without the manuscript originals before me I could not tell how or even if printers Benjamin Edes and John Gill altered the prose in Quincy's newspaper essays. The manuscript original to Quincy's pamphlet does survive and shows an author's careful attention to detail—one word larger than another or capitalized for emphasis, and full passages underlined to stand apart. Edes and Gill followed the author's directions for the pamphlet; presumably they did for the newspaper pieces as well. From here, Josiah Quincy Junior can speak for himself.

MAG
NA
N.º 19
N.º 22
N.º 20
N.º 10
N.º 3

LETTERS, ESSAYS, AND PAMPHLET

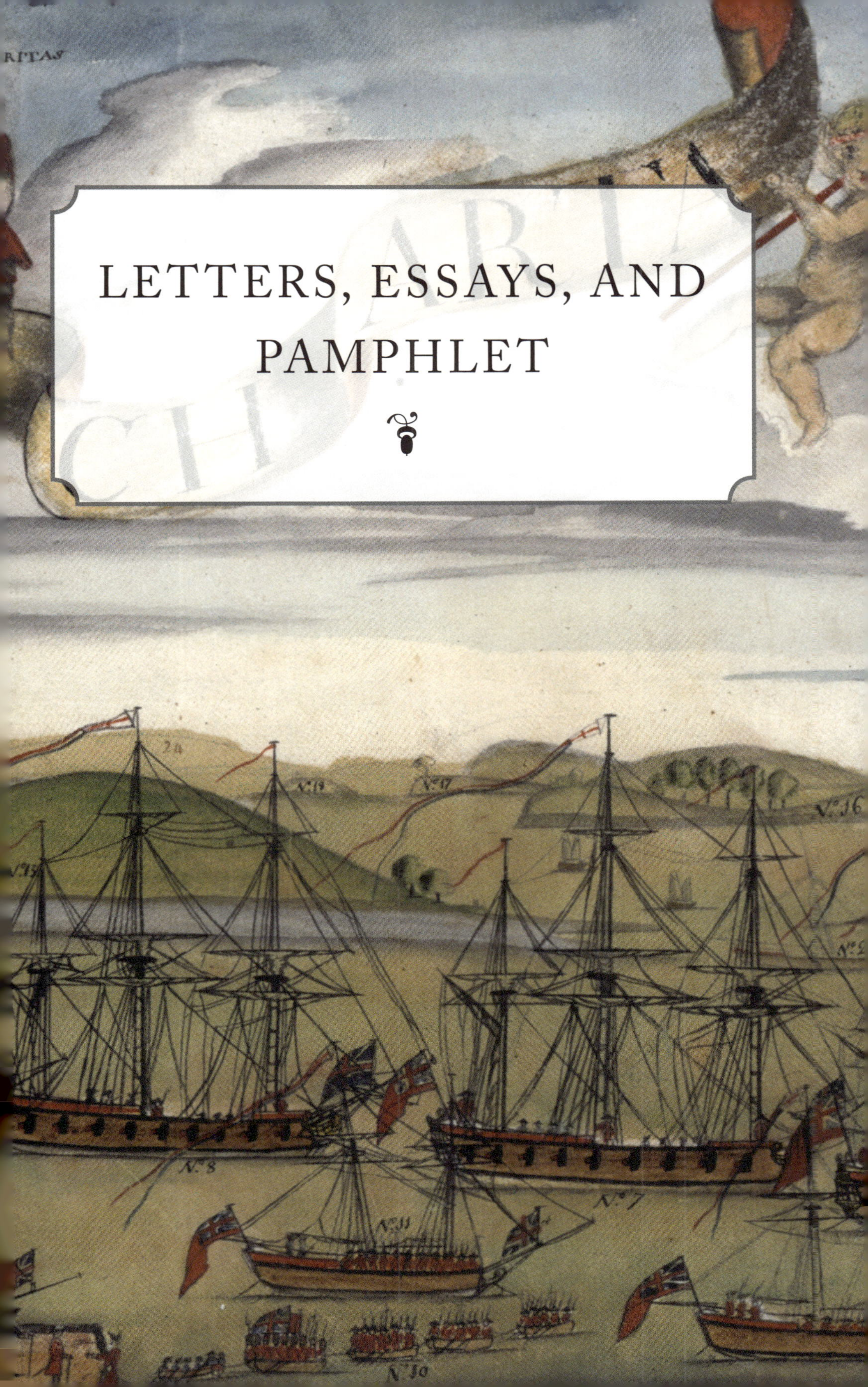

JQ TO BELA LINCOLN

25 December 1764[1]

Dear Sir Boston December 25th 1764

This I hope will find you in London, happier if possible, than even your warmest wishes ever desired. Yet indeed, this is little better than mere selfishness, for being so nearly connected with you by family alliance, and more especially by that hearty and I believe sincere friendship, which has ever since our relation, strictly subsisted between us, I must, at least, greatly participate, if not equally share with you, every smile of fortune. In your present situation, the letters of your friends can do little more than bear their love and regards, surrounded with so many new and striking objects, some of them, I am sure, very disagreeable, not to say detestable, to one of your turn of mind, and others perplexing, as well as entertaining. In such a situation it must necessarily be the greatest mark of regard, not to perplex you still more, with long and unimportant letters; but as I know you will willingly spare a minute in hearing the welfare and well being of your friends, on this side the water, I have taken the present opportunity to inform you of the health of your father, and brother, and my sister, all of whom I lately saw, and who heartily joined, with other friends, in wishing you the greatest success, together with dear Sir,

your affectionate friend and brother,

J. Quincy jun.

I must again renew the request I made before you sailed, if the time can be spared from the hurry of business, that you would give me your sentiments of London, &c., and of men and things in general; and let me know whether you do not find human nature every where the same, though perhaps in different garbs, in London, and at Sherborn. Your sentiments will be such (you must be conscious) as may strictly be depended upon by every one. At least you know they will be highly relied on by me, both for veracity and judgment. For Caelum non Animum mutant, qui trans mare currunt;[2] and if this is true, I think you will comply with my request. I have lately seen an account in the Monthly Review for January last of a book entitled: "The Life of the Honourable Sir John Holt, Knight, Lord Chief Justice of the Court of Kings Bench, containing several arguments touching the rights and liberties of the people, delivered by his Lordship with great reason and remarkable courage, upon most important occasions, during the reigns of their Majesties King William 3d and Queen Anne, taken from the Reports of Lord Chief Justice Raymond &c&c&c., never before published. By a gentleman of the Inner Temple".[3] This book with the above pompous title is highly recommended by the aforesaid Reviewers, as curious and useful, to all Gentlemen of the Law especially. If this book should deserve the character here given, and you will purchase and send the same to me, I will account with you, as you shall direct, and return if in my power, the favor with gratitude.

1. Bela Lincoln, an informally trained (as was typical of the age) physician in Sherborn, had gone to Britain to improve his expertise. After completing his studies in Aberdeen he moved to his hometown of Hingham to practice. He was married to Josiah Jr.'s older sister Hannah. He died in July 1774; they had no children. Eliza Susan Quincy had the original letter in hand and used it for her "Memoir," 2:2–4, QP 46 (reel 6) MHS (cited as volume 2, which is explained at supra, p. xxx, n. 32) and presumably the printed *Memoir,* p. 7n, although she only carried a portion of the letter below Quincy's signature into the *Memoir,* and none of the rest. The letter does not appear to be among the papers that she later donated to the MHS. See the brief entry for Lincoln in John Langden Sibley, *Biographical Sketches of Graduates of Harvard University,* 18 vols. (Boston: Massachusetts Historical Society, 1873–), 13:455–57. Conrad Edick Wright, who took up the work begun by Sibley, also wrote an interesting study of "Harvard Men and the Consequences of Independence" in *Revolutionary Generation* (Boston: University of Massachusetts Press, 2005).

2. Meaning, essentially, a person can change the scene—in this case, cross the ocean—but that does not necessarily mean he or she is changed by it. From Horace's epistle 11, to Bullatius, which Quincy could have taken from any number of collected works then in print and published in London. His "Catalogue of Books," no. 119 in Coquillette and York, eds., *Portrait of a Patriot,* 5:895, simply says "Horace."

3. A Gentlemen of the Inner-Temple, *The Life of the Right Honourable Sir John Holt, Knight, Lord Chief Justice of the Court of King's-Bench* (London: J. Worrall, 1764). Lincoln may have purchased the copy for his brother-in-law that is no. 113 in the "Catalogue of Books" in Coquillette and York, eds., *Portrait of a Patriot,* 5:894. Quincy drew upon Holt from the bench for both his law cases (ibid., 4:45 n. 28, 198n , 201, 216 n. 2, 298n and 300n) and his political commonplace book (ibid., 1:139, 201–2).

"HYPERION"

28 September 1767[1]

"Still be this Truth, this saving Truth confess'd,
Britain is great, because with Freedom blest;
Her Prince is great, because her People free,
And Power here springs from public Liberty.
Hail mighty Monarch of the free and great!
Firm on the Basis of a prosp'rous State.
The Wealth, the Strength of happy Millions thine,
United rise, united shall decline.
For Time will come, sad Period of the brave,
When Britain's Humble Prince shall rule the Slave;
When Traffic vile shall stain the guilty Throne,
And King's shall buy our Ruin and their own."[2]

Tis a political maxim, that all government tends to despotism, and like the human frame brings at it's birth the latent seed which finally shall destroy the constitution. This is a melancholy truth—but such is the lot of humanity. The art of an ingenious physician may, indeed, for a time illude the desperate poison, the skill of an able patriot may prolong, awhile, the political existence of a state; but the constitution still hastens with increasing velocity to inevitable death. This truth is founded in nature: Experience has, in every age, verefied this maxim of politics, and the approaching fate of our Mother Country shall but confirm the observation.

An insatiable appetite, an enormous thirst of despotic sway is a threatening symptom and sure presage of the fatal catastrophe of the constitutional system. A desire of absolute government prompts to the extension of legal authority, and states, like men, are precipitated headlong, by a boundless ambition, from the giddy precipice of power into the gulph of ruin & destruction.—Oh Britain! hold thy cruel hand, suspend the bloody sword an instant, and while, with an out-stretched arm, thou art forcing from thy injured Colonies one Right after another, while even now thou art making the desperate pass, which stabs the very vitals of thy children, reflect one single moment upon the unnatural, the brutal action; but if the dismal scene of woe, thy sons and daughters weltering in their infant blood, touch not thy adamantine heart, look back to distant ages, and see the rise and fall of ancient kingdoms!—Behold their fate and learn thine own!—Such a retrospective view of grandeur and declension in former states will show the genuine origin of a nation's glory and magnificence, and mark the putrid source of it's decline and final dissolution. Remember, Britain! human nature is every where the same, and similar effects will always flow from the same cause.[3]—An extensive commerce will produce opulence; riches create power; these united soon beget insatiable luxury; luxury, opulence and power soon gender fell oppression and a hideous offspring; the next immediate consequences, though various, according to the manners of the age and temper of the people, yet work certain death; political economy is quick destroyed, and sudden desolation shall swallow up the kingdom.

The powers of the human mind were never made for an unlimited jurisdiction over the extensive realm of science, neither was the sceptre of civil society form'd for arbitrary and universal empire. The political, like the animal body is in the best health, while the original constitution is kept pure and undebauch'd. But despotism has been the alluring syren, the inticing sorceress of the most flourishing nations, whose histories are inroll'd in the annals of fame. The boundless power of Rome was her mortal disease. Rome trod the path that leads up to the high and lofty tower of dominion: She tumbled head-long from the giddy elevation.—Britain now totters on the same dreadful precipice!—The British flag and Roman standard flourish'd in the days of *public virtue*. The *one* was disgrac'd and trampled under foot, when vice and tyranny rear'd their execrable heads, the *other* shall surely kiss the dust with like infamy.—But, methinks, I hear my injur'd countrymen exclaim—What comfort doth this voice of prophecy afford? To know the destin'd wrath of an avenging GOD shall blast the head of Britain; to see our mother's honours kiss the dust, her children too become the slaves of miscreant lordlings, to bear the galling yoke and cumberous load of merciless oppressors, doth rather add a tenfold pang to the keen anguish of our heart's distress. We! the sons of glorious Sires who nobly bled for civil and religious liberty in fame's immortal field, who dauntless fought with many a crimson wound the cause of freedom, and with many a blushing honor, godlike, won the victory of the day. We and our children must become the ignominious slaves of haughty, cruel and oppressive masters!—And that Britain, at some future period, shall receive the full reward of all her crimes, her aggravated guilt and her abhorred oppressions is now the only word of peace and consolation!—Think not, my countrymen! I meant to sooth you into peace, or lull your fears of tyranny asleep: too well I know the loss of Liberty, the spectre of departed freedom, the terrors of approaching bondage will haunt you day & night, & harrow up your souls.—No consolation can I whisper to my fellow-slaves and countrymen: No lamp of hope and pleasing expectation can I hold up to light our feet in this dark night of deep distress and woe.—Our fathers sacrificed their blood—they died freemen—they purchas'd Liberty with death—they left the legacy of freedom to their offspring.—We their sons, shall leave the *royal* gift of bondage to our sons and daughters.—Think you not, my brother-slaves, *our children will arise and call us blessed?*—The valor and the blood of our fore-fathers purchas'd their freedom.—The purple current of our noble ancestors still swells our veins—but oh the *British Virtue's* fled!—the *ethereal spark* which fir'd our father's blood is quite extinct!—the flames of patriotism blaze no more!—Hence then all consolation!—away!—

"—Let no man speak of comfort;
Let's talk of graves, of worms and epitaphs,
Make dust our paper and with rainy eyes
Write sorrow on the bosom of the earth!
Let's chuse executors, and talk of wills!
And yet not so—for what can we bequeath,
Save our deposed bodies to the ground?
Our lands, our lives, and all are *Britain's*
And nothing can we call our own, but Death;
And that small model of the barren earth,
Which serves as paste & cover to our bones!"[4]

HYPERION.

1. *The Boston-Gazette and Country Journal* [hereafter *Boston Gazette]*, 28 September 1767. This piece took up over half of the first page of that (typical) four page issue. In Greek mythology Hyperion was one of the twelve Titans, linked with the power of the Sun. He was imprisoned–in some renditions of the tale unfairly—by Zeus when Zeus overthrew Kronos. He is alluded to in *Hamlet* (Act I, Scene 2), Quincy's favorite play by his favorite playwright, in a positive light, with Hamlet's assassinated father a "Hyperion to a satyr"–the satyr being the elder Hamlet's own brother Claudius, a murderous usurper.

2. From "An Epistle to the Right Honourable the Lord Cornbury," quite likely taken from

Robert Dodsley, ed, *A Collection of Poems in Four Volumes,* 4th ed. (London: J. Hughs, R. and J. Dodsley, 1744), 2:172. This title is not in the "Catalogue of Books," but there are two listings that say simply "Poems." See Coquillette and York, eds., *Portrait of a Patriot*, 5:900 (nos. 287 and 291).

3. A theme that Quincy returned to, again and again, a theme repeated in much that he wrote, just as it was repeated in much that he read. See Coquillette and York, eds., *Portrait of a Patriot,* 1:47–76.

4. From Shakespeare's *Richard II*, Act III, Scene 2, Richard himself speaking, realizing that his kingdom was slipping away and that he might never regain the throne.

"HYPERION"

5 October 1767[1]

"—, *Are we unpregnant of our Cause?*
Can we do nothing: no, not for our Country,
Upon whose Property and most dear Life
A vile defeat is made? Are we all Cowards?
————————————. *It cannot be,*
But we are Pigeon-liver'd and lack Gall
To make Oppression *bitter, or e're this*
We should have fatted all the Region-Kites
With the Offal of these Slaves. Bloody Villains!
Remorseless, treacherous, kindless Villains!
Oh Vengeance! ————————
O, all you host of Heaven! O Earth! What else?
And shall I couple Hell? O fy! hold, hold my Heart,
And you, my Sinews, grow not instant old,
But bear me stifly up. Can I forget Thee?
Oh, my poor Country, while Memory holds a Seat
In this distracted Globe; I will remember Thee!
Yea, from the Table of my Memory,
I'll wipe away all trivial fond Records,
All sawes of Books, all Formes, all Pressures past,
That Youth and Observation copied there;
And thy Commandments all alone shall live
Within the Book and Volume of my Brain,
Unmix'd with baser Matter:—Yes by Heaven!"[2]

When I reflect upon the exalted character of the ancient Britons, when I call to mind the fortitude of our illustrious Predecessors, when my memory retraces the noble struggles of the late memorable period; when from these reflections, a very natural transition is made, and I contemplate the gloomy aspect of the present day, my feeling heart is alternately torn with doubt and hope, despondency and terror.—Can the true, generous magnanimity of British heroes be entirely lost in their degenerate progeny? Is the GENIUS of *Liberty,* whose breath, but a few days since, inflamed our bosom with a celestial ardor, fled forever? Is the spirit of the prophets departed from among us, that our enemies should become triumphant, and those who seek our destruction shortly rejoice? Or does the Lion of the wood but sleep, that when he is rous'd from his slumbers, the roaring of his mouth, and the flame of his nostrils may be the more terrible? Oh ye ravenous blood-hounds! who eager stand, with wide-expanded jaws, to seize your prey, to you I call, *but with no friendly voice*. Have you not seen the young Lion of the forest enrag'd—have you not heard the thunder of his voice—have you not beheld the lightnings of his eyes?—Come not too near his sacred retreat—disturb not his peaceful repose—tempt not his wrath, lest he gnash his teeth with indignation, lest he tear you in pieces in the frenzy of his passion, and give thy flesh to the birds of the air, & thy bones to the wild beasts of the field.[3]

An attentive observer of the deportment of some particular persons, in this Metropolis, would be apt to imagine that the grand point was gain'd; the people intirely broken to the yoke,—all America subjugated to bondage.—Does the baleful blasts of calamity blow upon our land?—see these accursed betrayers of their *native* soil snuff with joy the tainted gale. Does the herald of report sound forth the doom of a Sister Colony?—see these *vipers of our bosom* swell with triumph; see them even now devouring in imagination, the vitals of their country, and anticipate the riotous feast they expect shortly to make upon the blood and treasure of their fellow-citizens; and as if, already, they had fatten'd and grown wanton upon the spoils of the land, see them toss the head of insolence, put on the haughty air of contemptuous disdain, and insultingly display their lordships and dominions, their potentates and powers; nay, they dare to tell us, our only hope is to crouch and cowl under the iron rod, and kiss the scepter of oppression. Precious sample of the meek and lowly temper of those who are destin'd to be our imperious lords and masters!

Be not deceived, my countrymen, by these venal hirelings, these mercenary tools of power. Let them not cajole you by their subtleties into submission, or frighten you by their vapourings into compliance.—Should some wretched minion, who would palm himself "*a true Patriot*", endeavour to flatter you into "*moderation and prudence*"—tell him, that calmness and deliberation are to guide the judgment; courage and intrepidity are to command in action.[4]

Should he tell us "*to perceive our inability to oppose the Mother Country*"—we boldly answer, that in defence of our civil and religious rights, we dare to *oppose* the world; that with the GOD of ARMIES on our side, even the GOD who fought our Father's battles, we fear not the hour of trial; tho' the host of our enemies should cover the field like locusts, and set their Armies in dreadful array against us, yet the sword of the Lord and of Gideon shall prevail.—But "*away with political enthusiasm*"! If this, thou blasphemer! is enthusiasm, then will we live and die enthusiasts.

"IF YOU ARE AGGRIEVED, *says the true Patriot, strive by all prudent means to obtain redress.*"

—Go, thou dastard! Get the[e] home! A rank adulterer riots in thy incestuous bed, a brutal ravisher deflowers thy only daughter, a barbarous villain now lifts the murtherous hand and stabs thy tender infant to the heart—see the sapphire current trickling from the wound, & the dear Boy, now as he gasps his last, cries out the Ruffian's mercy—Go! Thou wretch! be calm and sooth the frenzy of thy soul into tame *moderation*:—Go! *Doubt the injuries you feel* Go! *question with the assassin of thy wrongs*;—and when insultingly he brandishes the fatal dagger, reeling with thy infant's gore, nay, holds the crimson-tinged point to thine own bosom, and bids defiance to thy utmost rage, then in the very instant of tumultuous fury,—Go! Let e'en thy coward soul boast, if it can, of "*prudence, calmness and deliberation.*"

Out thou abandon'd caitiff! Desist thy vile, but impotent, attempts to lure my fellow-countrymen to the hidden snare. Thy blandishments will not fascinate our eyes, neither do thy threats of an "halter" intimidate us. For, under GOD, we are determin'd, that wheresoever, whensoever or howsoever we shall be call'd to make our exit, that we will die free-men.[5] And well do we know, that all the regalia of death cannot dignify a villain's past life, nor diminish from the ignominy with which a slave shall quit his existence; neither can it taint the unblemish'd honour of a son of freedom, tho' he should make his departure on the already-prepared gibbet, or be dragg'd to the new-erected scaffold for execution: With the plaudit of his conscience he will go off the stage, the crown of joy and immortality shall be his reward; the history of his life, his children shall venerate; the virtues of their Sire shall excite their emulation.

Hear me, thou *Patriot*-Traytor and all ye despicable tribe of great and petty villains! Display not too soon thy "*halter, fire and faggot,*" quaff not our blood *before your time,* lest your eagerness to anticipate forestall the delights of fruition.

My much-respected countrymen! Be not terrify'd by the threats and vaunting of your sworn foes: For even in our times, we have seen the finger of the Lord: And we have heard with our ears, and our fathers have told us the great things, which GOD did for them in their day; how he deliver'd them, in the howling wilderness, out of the paw of the Lion, and out of the paw of the Bear; how, with an out-stretched hand, he led them thro' the dreary desert, giving them the manna of Heaven for food, and the water out of the rock for drink; how he miraculously preserved his chosen people from tempest, fire, sword and famine, and put all their lurking and insiduous enemies to flight: Surely his ear is not heavy, that he cannot hear, nor his arm shorten'd, that he cannot save.—Did he not plant us with his own hand? Hath he not nourish'd and brought us up as children? Surely he will not now altogether cast us off! If we seek him, he will be found of us; while we serve him, he will never forsake us.—And if our GOD be for us—who shall stand against us?[6] Tho' our enemies should be as the vermin of the field, or as the insects of the air, yet will I not be dismay'd; for the breath of his mouth shall scatter them abroad, the power of his strength shall confound and overwhelm them with mighty destruction.[7]

HYPERION.

1. Printed on the first page of the *Boston Gazette,* for that date, filling two of the three columns there.

2. These are lines from *Hamlet*, the first eleven (through "Vengeance") from Act II, Scene 2; the remainder are from Act I, Scene 5. Quincy was a great admirer of Shakespeare in general and *Hamlet* in particular. According to Eliza Susan Quincy in her "Memoir," 2:7, QP 46 (reel 6) MHS, "the mighty genius of Shakespeare appears to have captivated his youthful imagination. Extracts from that author forming a manuscript of seventy closely written pages still remain among his papers." Also see Quincy, *Memoir,* p. 6. Insofar as I can determine, Eliza Susan did not pass that item along to the MHS. For context see my "Hamlet as American Revolutionary," *Hamlet Studies* 15 (1993):40–53, though I say nothing there about Quincy; and, more generally, Alden T. Vaughan and Virginia Mason Vaughan, *Shakespeare in America* (Oxford: Oxford University Press, 2012). Quincy turned to *Hamlet* as well on his Southern journey and, not surprisingly, to *The Tempest;* see Coquillette and York, eds., *Portrait of a Patriot,* 3:123 (*Hamlet*) 102 and 117 (*Tempest*).

3. Quincy assembled an Old Testament literary pastiche, from the Psalms to Amos to even Esdras in the Apocrypha before closing with a slight reworking of 1 Samuel 17:44 KJV ("give thy flesh . . ."), as the mighty Philistine Goliath hurls his challenge at the stripling David of Israel.

4. The *Boston Evening-Post,* 21 September 1767, printed a piece by "A true Patriot" that warned the people of Massachusetts against being drawn by local agitators into a dispute with Great

Britain, a dispute they could not win and was unnecessary anyway. Much that follows is aimed at the author of that essay.

5. Beginning with "blandishments' and ending with "free-men," Daniel Webster quoted this piece in his speech at the dedication of the Bunker Hill Monument on 17 June 1825. Josiah Jr.'s son and namesake, then mayor of Boston, was there, as was Josiah the Mayor's daughter, Eliza Susan. See Coquillette and York, eds, *Portrait of a Patriot,* 1:7–8. After the event Eliza Susan wrote: "How little did Josiah Quincy Junr anticipate when he wrote this sentence, fifty-eight years ago, at the age of twenty-three, that his children would hear it sounded over Bunker Hill, on such a day, and amid such a scene as this." In 1775, she marveled, the firing of cannon meant "death and destruction" for the Americans fighting on that battlefield; in 1825, cannons "proclaimed the triumphs of American Liberty and Independence." From the "Journal of E. S. Quincy of Lafayette's Visit, 1824–1825" QP 44 (also reproduced on reel 7, no. 1) MHS.

6. Quincy resumed his Biblical allusions, with Hebrews 13:5 (never forsake) and Romans 8:31 (God be for us) KJV.

7. More of the same, ranging from Psalms 33:6 (breath) to Micah 7:16 (confound) KJV.

"PRO LEGE"

4 January 1768[1]

Messieurs EDES & GILL,

Please to insert the following.

"*IF to differ ever hereafter with an upstart Minister, is to be construed as a* Crimen laesae Majestatis;[2] *if the Giant* Prerogative *is to be let loose, and stalk about, to create* unusual *Terror, and inflict* unpractised *Punishment; if the fiercest thunderbolts of Jupiter are to be launched by a low Miscreant against the slightest Offence, and even against Innocence itself; if the favourite Motto of the* North, *the* Nemo me impune lacessit,[3] *is to be adopted as the future Rule of Government in our once happier Land, we may then boast as much as we please of our invaluable Liberties, purchased with the Blood of our heroic Ancestors;—but let us watch narrowly, lest, before we are aware, they should depende upon too slight a Thread.*"

READER! Make thine own Comment ___ Permit me also to make my own Application. If the preceeding Quotation excite Sentiments in thy Mind, different from those Sensations which affect my Breast, I will not pluck out thine Eyes, or tear out thy Heart. My Creed will not condemn thee, neither will thy Faith obtain my Salvation. Theoretic Opinions are of but little Consequence to Mankind: It is the practical Deportment which is of Importance to the Community. For let a Man's Thoughts in Religion and Politicks, be what they may, they are of inconsiderable Moment to his Fellowmen: but when once the Principles of a Man prompt him to prostitute his Office, or neglect the sacred Duties of his Station, the State has an undoubted Right to demand the Infliction of due Punishment; and it is incumbent upon every Individual of Society to forward a rigourous Execution of Justice. And when it happens, that any one Man has obtained, *by a general Amassment of Power*, such an unlimited Sway, in the State, as to be able with Impunity, *to condemn the Innocent as a Judge, and destroy the Constitution as a Statesman,* deplorable indeed is the fate of that Nation. But there is Hope, that the Case is not desperate, unless this rapacious Grasper of Sovereignty, elated with a Plenitude of Power, has had the Effrontery to make an open Avowal of his Designs, and Hardiness sufficient to proclaim his Resolution to fulfill their Accomplishment. When such is the Object, such the Determination, such the Boldness of only one single Tyrant, irremediable indeed, in all human Probability, is the Malady of the Commonwealth. For when despotic Views of this Complection are form'd and executed, tis Demonstration, that the Minds of the People are sunk in Submission; and should some dauntless Champion of the Cause of Freedom, providentially arise for their Defence, they would fly, like a timid Herd, and leave the virtuous Hero to be sacrific'd as a Victim. Never indeed was there a Wolf of the State, who did not think the People were but Sheep:—Strange Infatuation of Mankind! They bow the Knee to the Image they themselves have form'd, and tremble before the Bug-bear of their own Creation.—Strip yon gorgeous Monarch of his Regalia, take from that despised Tyrant, the Powers with which a despotic Rabble have invested him;—the *one* sinks, a weak, pusillanimous Mortal, the *other* hides, a wretched, contemptible and execrated Monster.

It is almost incredible, that one, who had enjoy'd the Felicity of living under a British Government, should be endued with so insatiable a "*Lust for Power*" as to wish the Subversion of it's Constitution.—It is equally incredible, that any Man, who knew the characteristic Bravery of freemen, should dare make the Attempt.—*Quid non mortalia Peclora cogis Imperii sacra Fames*?[4] An exorbitant Thirst of Dominion, united with a desperate Mind, will do Wonders. Restless Ambition will be unwearied in the Race for the Prize of Power; an intrepid Spirit will, at all Hazards, win the Palm. With a Wish to Command, and Ability to Execute, Conquest is inevitable.—The Thirst of Rule renders the Plan of Empire obvious to the Aspirer; a Determination to accomplish, facilitates the Progress of Attainment.—Happy for Americans, their wise and venerable Ancestors, conscious of the predominant Vices of Mankind, have been eminently careful in guarding every Avenue, where it was probable, the ambitious and intrepid Enemy would labour to enter, by Stratagem and Force, in order to destroy that noble Fabrick, the complicated Work of Heroes, Saints and Ages, the *British Constitution*.

A short Attention to the following Extracts will abundantly convince every intelligent Mind, that, while the first Principles of our Constitution, the Fundamentals of all our Liberties, are adher'd to, no Subject, however great and powerful, is beyond the Reach of a strict Examination into his Conduct, or out of Danger of a Scourge for his Crimes.

A Peer of the Realm may be impeached *in Parliament* by Articles exhibited at the Suit of the King, by the Attorney General, as against the Earl of Bristol. Rush. 249.[5]

By Articles exhibited by another Peer. Rush. 254.

So the *Commons* may *by Parol*, charge a Peer before the King & Lords. Seld. Jud. Parl. 24.[6] (3 Vol. 2 p. 1596. 1598, 9)

Or a Commoner. Vide Seld. 3 Vol. 2 p. 1598, 9.

So before the Lords at a Conference. Seld. Jud. Parl. 30, 31, 32, (3 Vol. 2 p. 1598, 1599)

The Right of Impeachment by the Commons was allowed by the Lords, 20 June 1701.

In the Proceedings upon an Impeachment by the Commons, a Member stands with others at the Bar of the Lords, there, in the name of all the Commons of England, impeaches such an one, and acquaints the House, that the Commons in due Time will exhibit Articles against him, and maintain them. Lord Journ. 1. 15. Ap. 1751. 1701.

Though the Commons impeach only for a particular Grievance, they may afterwards exhibit other Articles against him. Seld. Jud. Parl. 21. (3 Vol. 2. p. 1595.)

And the Delivery of such Articles is not necessary till the Party appears. Seld. Jud. Parl. 23. (3 Vol. 2. p. 1596)

If Articles are not exhibited against against the Lords impeached, the Lords, by Message remind the Commons of it. Lords Journ. 5 May 1701. 15 May 1701. 4 June 1701.

But the Commons are Judges of the proper Time for exhibiting them. 31 May 1701. Yet the Lords *claimed* a Power to limit the Time. 4 June 1701.

Articles of Impeachment need not pursue the strict Forms of Law. Seld. Jud. Parl. 22, 27 (3 Vol. 2 p. 1595, 7)

Where an Impeachment is for a capital Offence, he shall be committed to Custody. Seld. Jud. Parl. 97. (3 Vols. 2 p. 1624.)

Yet the Commitment will sometimes be omitted, at the Discretion of the Lords, Raym. 382.[7]

And when an Impeachment is for High Treason, generally, without special Matter, it is usually omitted. It was omitted in the Case of Ld. Clarendon, though the Commons complained of it. Life of Clar. 251. & 302.[8]

After Answer by a Lord impeached, a Copy is made, and sent to the Commons. Lords Journ. 14.24.

After Answer, the Commons join Issue by Replication. 23 May 1701.

And may consider whether they will reply or not. Seld. Jud. Parl. 199. (3 Vol. 2. p. 1628.)

CAUSES FOR IMPEACHMENT

The Duke of Norfolk was impeached for high Treason. 28. H. 6. Art. 1,2,3. Seld. Jud. Parl. 27 3 Vol. 2. p. 1597.

For high Treason in subverting the fundamental Laws, and introducing arbitrary Power. Lord Finch, Sir Robert Berkley. Lord Strafford. 2 Rush. 606. 3 Rush. 1365. (Vid. Rush. Pt. 3. Vol. 1. 136.)

Michael de la Pool was impeached, 10 R. 2. That he excited the King to act against the Advice of Parliament. Seld. Jud. Parl. 25. (3 Vol. 2 p. 1596.)

The Spencers, *that they gave bad Counsel to the King.* 4 Inst. 54.[9]

Michael de la Pool was Impeached, that he, being Chancellor, acted contrary to his Duty. Seld. Jud. Parl. 26. (3 Vol. 2. p. 1596.)

The Duke of Buckingham was Impeached for a Plurality of Offices. 2 Car. Rush. 306.

The Earl of Oxford for exercising incompatible Offices. 8 May 1701.

So Lord Halifax. 9 June 1701.

The Spencers, Father and Son, were Impeached, for that they prevented the great Men of the Realm from giving their Counsel to the King, except in their Presence. 4 Inst. 53.

That they put good Magistrates out of Office, and advanced bad, 4 Inst. 53.

Lord Finch was Impeached for threatning the other Judges to subscribe to his Opinion. Art. 4, 5, 6. Vide Rush. Part 3 Vol. 1. 137.

For delivering Opinions which he knew to be contrary to Law. Art. 7. Vid. Rush. Pt. 3. Vol. 1. 137.

Is the Sword of Justice become pointless, that the Wicked go unpunish'd? Why is the Sabre of the Law sheathed, when the exhorbitant Crimes of the *peerless Man* demand the Arm of the Executioner?—Woe unto the Land, when the Greatness of the Criminal shall dismay his Accusers, and his Authority shall make *the righteous Man* to tremble; when the enormous Power of Guilt shall exalt itself above the Judgment-Seat, and bid Defiance to the Tribunal of Justice!

PRO LEGE.

1. From the *Boston Gazette* for that date, all but filling the first two of three print columns, Quincy writing "for law" (pro lege).

2. High treason.

3. Often translated as "no one attacks me with impunity," a familiar phrase to Quincy's generation, as the motto of the Scottish Order of the Thistle, and a couple of British army regiments. Marchmont Nedham—which would be Quincy's most frequent nom be plume–also employed it in his writings.

4. Quincy owned various editions of Virgil, as listed in the "Catalogue of Books," nos. 118, 265, and 337, and only the last is identified—an edition done by Joseph Trapp, in 1718, with Trapp providing his own English translation, but not the Latin. See Coquillette and York, eds., *Portrait of a Patriot*, 5:895, 599, 902. Quincy may have owned and turned to Christopher Pitt, *The Works of Virgil, In Latin and English*, 4 vols. (London: R. Dodsley, 1763), 2:192 (for the Latin) and 2:195 (for Pitt's translation into English) from the *Aeneid*, Book III. Pitt translated the line as "Cursed gold! how high will mortals rise" (the next line being "In ev'ry guilt to reach the glittering prize?"). Note that Quincy added "Imperii" to the passage—which he could have expected at least some of his readers to realize, as he attempted to make the reference more specific to the problems of the British empire at that moment. Remember that Quincy was proficient enough in Latin to consider doing his own translation of Virgil's *Eclogues*–see his comment about doing so on his voyage south in February 1773, in Coquillette and York, eds., *Portrait of a Patriot*, 3:91, and his quotations from the *Eclogues* in ibid., at 3:89 and 92. For the Latin passage from the *Aeneid* cited above, repeated on that voyage, see ibid., 3:193. For Quincy's transcription of the Earl of Chatham's famous speech on American reconciliation in the House of Lords on 20 January 1775, where Chatham alluded to Virgil's *Aeneid*—as did Quincy in commenting on Chatham's delivery—see ibid., 1:252–54.

5. John Rushworth, ed., *Historical Collections*, 7 vols. (London: Richard Chiswell and Thomas Cockerill, 1659–1701), which Quincy used for his political commonplace book as well. See Coquillette and York, eds., *Portrait of a Patriot*, 5:892 (no. 35) and 1:181–82, resp.

6. John Selden, *Of the Judicature in Parliaments* (London: Joseph Lawson, 1681). A three volume collection of Selden's works was published in London in 1726. Quincy turned to Selden's translation of Sir John Fortescue's *De Laudibus Legum Angliae* for his political commonplace book, but he did not refer to this particular work, nor did a copy (if he owned one) appear in his posthumous "Catalogue of Books."

7. Robert, Lord Raymond's *Report of Cases Adjudged in the Court of King's Bench and Common Pleas*, 2 vols. (London: Henry Lintot, 1743), or perhaps the three-volume 1765 edition. Listed in the "Catalogue of Books" in Coquillette and York, eds., *Portrait of a Patriot*, 5:892 (no. 39; author misidentified as Sir Thomas Raymond).

8. Edward Hyde, Earl of Clarendon, *The Life of Lord Clarendon* (Oxford: Clarendon Press, 1759).

9. Sir Edward Coke, *The Fourth Part of the Institutes of the Laws of England*, with no less than five editions being printed in London between 1644 and 1681, but none in Quincy's lifetime. Coke, in some form, can be found in the "Catalogue of Books" in Coquillette and York, eds., *Portrait of a Patriot*, 5:892 (no. 34) and 893 (no. 81), the former listed as "A Comment: upon Littleton" and the latter as "Cokes D."

JQ TO JONATHAN BLISS

5 September 1768[1]

Sir September 5, 1768

The inclosed Letter I left, about a month since, with Mr. Brackett, to be conveyed to Sheriff Brown. To my surprise, he returned it to me this morning, no Opportunity of conveyance having presented. I am told, that through your hand, the Letter will probably arrive safe to Mr. Brown, and have, therefore, taken the freedom to put it under cover to you. As the time of service will be out the first Tuesday of October, you will be pleased to send it forward, as soon as you can with convenience. An opportunity of returning a similar favour will be, with pleasure, embraced by your very humble servant,

Josiah Quincy junr.

1. Bliss was a lawyer in Springfield; Quincy was anticipating riding the circuit there in the fall. Letter in the Simon Gratz Autograph Collection, #250B, Case 8, Box 16, Historical Society of Pennsylvania mss.

JQ TO REV. JOHN EAGLESON

15 September 1768[1]

Respected Sir, Boston September 15th 1768

Your friendly letter came to hand a few days since, and a leisure moment now presenting, I with pleasure seize the opportunity of hitting off something that may please the fancy "of a partial friend, tho' probably it will afford but little satisfaction" to his benevolent "mind."

The *rights* and *liberrties* of Americans become every day more and more the serious object of attention. As political disputation increases, a settlement of the point in question removes further and further from the design of both parties. Private pique, envy, and personal resentment soon preclude a fair and candid discussion, an infernal group of intemperate passions will forever prevent any equitable decision. But, thank God! whatever may be the execrable schemes of ministerial parasites, or popular incendiaries, the *Rights* of *Man* stand upon a foundation which (with reverence I affirm) *Omnipotence* cannot shake. This I hold may be easily demonstrated; if I am indeed mistaken, you, who know my fervent zeal in the cause of an oppressed people, will pardon a too strong expression: the recording Angel, who knows my sincerity, will, it is trusted, "drop a tear and blot it out forever."[2]

The present aspect of the day is gloomy indeed, yet we are far from despair. Though the clouds, full charged, rise thick and fast, the thunders roll, and lightnings play, nay it is said, are just within striking distance, there are not wanting those among us, who believe that proper conductors will safely carry off all the political fluid, the clouds disperse, and the sky soon become calm and serene. Visionaries, you know, are credulous, enthusiasts are bold and enterprizing. Many such, Mr. Eagleson is sensible, inhabit these northern regions.

We, Americans, have a righteous cause. We know it. The power of Great Britain may oppress, nay, for a time, apparently subdue us. But, before all the *free born sons* of the North will yield a general and "united submission," to any tyrannic power on earth, fire and sword, famine and slaughter, desolation and ruin, will ravage the land. When thus I venture, without any pretence to the spirit of prophecy, at a hasty prediction, you will probably smile at my reverie; but, you know political dreamers are the most obstinate and incorrigible of sinners. You will see, by our public prints, the late transactions of this town, and the situation that we are in at present. Daily in expectation of troops, some say three regiments, and seven ships of the line. Opinions differ respecting what *might*, and what *will* be, the deportment of this people. On the one hand, a swarm of court dependants, and a standing army in the bowels of a state; in all ages and nations, thought, and found to be the bane of civil freedom. On the other, an open rupture with Great Britain (I had like to have said *mother* state) is a dreadful alternative.

But our all is at stake!

The pulse of the people beats high, and it may well be imagined that in our present state, all ranks among us are much agitated. This therefore may apologize for my not being in a facetious and proper frame of mind to answer some parts of your entertaining letter. To see the daily blunders which are committed, and the deep tragedy which is now acting on the political theatre, and not to be moved, is to be an unfeeling wretch indeed. If the contempt and indignation of every sensible and humane man in Christendom, was sufficient to explode a political system, there would be some hopes of seeing "Venice preserved and the plot discovered."[3]

But waving politicks, we rejoice with all the heartiness of honest friends, at your promising settlement. May friend Eagleson always be provided with something to moisten the clay, and support the tabernacle, in the laundry and cellar—"till superstition, bigotry and oppression shall be banished the world and all mankind on the genuine principles of *universal benevolence* write heart, and hand, hailing the halcyon days of peace and concord, and singing with the shepherd"

"Ultima Cumaei venit iam carminis aetas,
Magnus ab integro saeclorum nascitur ordo.
Iam redit et virgo, redeunt Saturnia regna:
Iam nova progenies Ca[e]lo dimittur alto!"[4]

Josiah Quincy junr.

1. Eliza Susan Quincy transcribed this letter for her "Memoir," 2:8–11, QP 46 (reel 6) MHS, which she carried over, but only in part, into the printed *Memoir*, pp. 12–13. The original has apparently since been lost. Eagleson's letter, which prompted this response, is also missing. With the differences between the two versions of the text, it would seem that Eliza Susan went back to the original when producing the printed edition. Unlikely as it sounds, this may have been

the Reverend John Eagleson, who worked as an Anglican minister near Fort Cumberland, in what had been, until the last of the wars for empire, Acadia. Once a Presbyterian, by the time of Quincy's letter he had converted to mainstream Anglicanism and represented the Society for Propagating the Gospel in that region. A confirmed loyalist, during the war he would be taken prisoner to Boston. He eventually made his way home. The basics of his story are told in Ernest Clarke, *The Siege of Fort Cumberland, 1776* (Montreal: McGill-Queen's University Press, 1995). There is an entry for him in the *Dictionary of Canadian Biography Online* as well as in the print version of that collection.

2. It is quite likely that Quincy borrowed, one way or another, from Laurence Sterne's *Tristram Shandy* (Book 6, Chapter 8), which circulated in various editions at the time, the relevant passage reading: "the RECORDING ANGEL as he wrote it down, dropp'd a tear upon the word and blotted it out forever."

3. Thomas Otway's play *Venice Preserved: Or. A Plot Discover'd* was first staged in London in 1682 and was continuing to be performed, with the text being reprinted, in Quincy's lifetime. Scholars dispute the extent to which Otway intended it as an allegorical commentary on English history—possibly the 1605 "gunpowder plot" against James I or the 1678 "popish plot" against Charles II.

4. These lines are from Virgil's *Eclogues*, Book IV: "Now comes the last age of the Cumaean song; the great order of the ages rises anew. Now the Virgin returns, and Saturn's reign returns; now a new generation is sent down from heaven." Cumae was a Greek colony in Italy. Virgil would celebrate it in The *Aeneid* as the home of Sibyl, a priestess and prophetess. Eliza Susan Quincy combined the first and second paragraphs above to make one, with everything after "decision" in that paragraph deleted in the printed version. She cut the final paragraph and passage from Virgil as well.

"HYPERION"

26 September 1768[1]

Messieurs EDES & GILL,

Please to give this a conspicuous Place in your next, and you shall have another Piece for the Monday after.

H.

"*Free government alone preserves the free*
And righteous rule is gen'ral liberty;
Their guiding law is freedom's native voice,
The publick good defin'd by publick choice;
And justly should the bold offenders fall
Who dare invade the sovereign rights of All."[2]

IT is now about a twelve-month since I addressed my countrymen, in terms, which were dictated by a heart pregnant with grief and indignation. Those, who had whispered the blackest falshoods against the whole continent, at that time, thought proper publickly to threaten every one, who dared to assert the rights of America, with "halters, fire and faggot." With these menaces, they, then, vapored away, and they now exult, with a temper truly diabolical, at the prospect of carrying those threats into execution.

To bruit abroad, that, as soon as the troops shall be quartered upon us, some were to be pilloried, some whipped, some to lose their ears, and others their heads, has been, lately, the delightful task of those, who lie in wait for innocent blood. "An ill-timed oppugnation of the Commissioners' authority",[3] a manly boldness in delivering patriotic sentiments to the world, and an open daring to discuss the rights of mankind, the liberty of the press, and the freedom of speech, are those unpardonable crimes, for which the scaffold alone can work an expiation.—Thus placemen and pensioners, and all those, who live by reaping where they have not sown, become the most maliciously inveterate persecutors of every friend to his country.—What a prospect here presents itself to the imaginations! A virtuous people on the very borders of absolute slavery; a wise and understanding people, capable of discerning, was there any friendly hand to point out their salvation; a people, hardy and brave, capable of extricating themselves from the toils of bondage, was there any voice to inform them of the danger; Dragoons and executioners to awe and terrify, with fire and sword, every man, who should dare give his countrymen one timely caution. What wonder that a nation, in such dreadful circumstances, should remain uninformed, spiritless and inactive; till their hands were fast-manacled, and the whole herd of great and little tyrants rush violently on, seeking whom they may devour? A people, in this state, it is likely, would never be roused from their lethargy, till the soldier was ravaging their fields, invading their most sacred property, and tearing the dearest pledges of nature from their bosoms; till the executioner was at the door, the scaffold erected, and the fire kindled:—What heaven-inspired paragon of virtue, at such a gloomy crisis, would rise to save the sinking land, and, nobly resquing all for GOD and his country, would dare—

"—— *Unfold a tale, whose lightest word*
Would harrow up the soul, freeze the young blood,
Make the two eyes, like stars, start from their spheres,
The knotted and combined locks to part,
And each particular hair to stand on end
Like quills upon the fretful porcupine?
O, horrible! O, horrible! most horrible!
If thou hast nature in thee, bear it not."[4]

HYPERION

1. *Boston Gazette*, in the supplement for that date, running about a half-column in length. Quincy was adding his voice to the chorus of complaints against the posting of troops to Boston, with the first regiments arriving within days of this piece, and another two just over a month later. It is not clear if Quincy had been involved with the extralegal gathering of town delegates that had assembled, starting the week before this essay appeared, to protest. Despite passing resolutions to resist the troops' landing—as the Boston town meeting had already done—the delegates went home and no militia was mustered or sent forth from any town. There were those in London who thought the locals thereby proved they were cowardly, full of bluff and bluster and little more; politically, choosing not to resist proved wise in the long run. Hiller Zobel's *The Boston Massacre* remains unmatched for overall context; John Phillip Reid's *In a Defiant Stance* and *In a Rebellious Spirit* are indispensable for examining the uneven contest between theoretical imperial authority and real local power.

2. Lines from Earl Nugent, *An Ode to Mankind* (London: R. Dodsley, 1741), p. 4. Quincy would draw from this same poem as "Hyperion" for 3 October 1768—see infra, pp. 24–28.

3. Governor Francis Bernard's dismissive characterization of the convention.

4. *Hamlet*, Act I, Scene 5. Lines spoken by the ghost of Hamlet's father to a stunned Hamlet that Quincy pasted together to create his own sense of treachery and betrayal.

JQ TO MR. ELIOT

28 September 1768[1]

Sir Boston September 28 1768

To compassionate and relieve the distressed, is the highest gratification to a benevolent heart; therefore, with sorrow, I inform you that it is utterly inconsistent, with my present plan of business, to take a Clerk into my office. As my reasons are many, and most of them of a private nature, you will chearfully excuse my giving you any enumeration.

But permit, a stranger, to inform you, from experience, that *the law* is an arduous science indeed. He, who enters into the study, ought to have an ambition to reach the summit of his profession; and resolution enough to cleanse an augean stable, to attain the object of his wishes. Antient and modern learning in general, great mathematical knowledge, and a sound, logical head, joined with an *undissipated* mind, are but some of the pre-requisites for our student. To almost every pleasure, except what results from science, he must bid a long adieu.

Dear Sir! I feel for you indeed. Think cooly, reflect maturely, before you engage; once engaged, persevere to the end.

With the most tender sympathy in the sorrows of a worthy family, for your past imprudent conduct, and the most fervent prayers for your future felicity, I am, Dear Sir,

Your hearty and very
Sincere well wisher.
Josiah Quincy junr

1. This is a draft copy, which Quincy composed as he went, apparently, based on the number of words that he crossed out, then re-inserted. It is in QP 72 at the MHS; it was not microfilmed. The Identity of "Mr. Eliot" remains elusive. There is no Eliot among the list of lawyers practicing in Massachusetts in 1775 compiled by Charles R. McKirdy and attached as an appendix to his "Massachusetts Lawyers on the Eve of the American Revolution: The State of the Profession" in Daniel R. Coquillette, ed., *Law in Colonial Massachusetts, 1630–1800* (Boston: The Colonial Society of Massachusetts, 1984), pp. 313–58.

"HYPERION"

3 October 1768[1]

Messieurs EDES & GILL,

Please to insert the following.

"Warm in my country's rights and nature's laws,
I call forth all our hope *in freedom's cause;*
Assert an empire to ALL belongs,
And vindicate a world's long suffer'd wrongs;—
In strains no slave dare sing, nor tyrant hear."

"*THE aggregated judgment of the common people,* says an eminent writer, *discerns most truly the errors of government, for as much as they are the first to be sure that smart under them.* In this only they come to be short sighted; that tho' they know the diseases, they understand not the remedies; and tho' good patients, they are ill physicians."[2] What are the present sentiments of the Inhabitants of North America? *Discern* they not *most truly,* and *smart* they not most severely *under the errors of government?* The disease is known and felt—but where is the remedy, where is the physician? For the people to ask council is deemed treasonable; to assemble themselves to consult is denominated rebellion. Thus would some potentates terrify mankind with a few founding, technical expressions. It has been found, in all ages, very difficult to perswade men, by the most refined court-chicane, out of their reason, and tyrants have ever found it impossible to argue, sooth or frighten the common people out of their feelings. And it is truly strange to hear the arguments and see the parade of some, at this day: One would, from their conduct, be induced to imagine, they thought it the most likely way of dispiriting the *people,* to render *their* case irremediable. Certainly such politicians have little studied the volume of nature. A nation, not as yet intirely enervated by luxury, not wholly depressed by slavery, when reduced to despair, are invincible to a proverb.

After what has been said and wrote, on both sides of the atlantic, upon colony-affairs; after the most perspicuous demonstration of the illegality and ill policy of the measures pursued, against this continent; it would be an affront to the understanding, to attempt setting the matter in a clearer point of view: The meanest capacity must perceive, the remotest peasant, in the wilds of America, must feel the consequences.

British taxations, suspension of legislatures, and standing armies are but some of the clouds which over-shadow the northern world.—Heaven grant, that a grand constellation of virtues may shine forth with redoubled lustre and enlighten this gloomy hemisphere! If ever there was a time, this is the hour, for Americans to rouze themselves, and exert every ability.—Their all is at hazard, and the die of fate spins doubtful!—In vain, do we talk of magnanimity and heroism, in vain, do we trace a descent from the worthies of the earth, if we inherit not the spirit of our ancestors. Who is he, who boasteth of his patriotism? Has he vanquished luxury and subdued the worldly pride of his heart? Is he not yet drinking the poisonous draught, and rolling the sweet morsel under his tongue?[3] He, who cannot conquer the little vanity of his heart, and deny the delicacy of a debauch'd palate, let him lay his hand upon his mouth, and his mouth in the dust. Now is the time for this people to summon every aid human and divine, to exhibit every moral virtue, and call forth every christian grace. The wisdom of the serpent, the innocence of the dove, and the bold, inflexible intrepidity of the lion, with the blessing of GOD, will yet save us from the jaws of destruction.

Where is the boasted Liberty of Englishmen, if property may be disposed, charters suspended, assemblies dissolved, and every valued right annihilated, at the uncontroulable will of an external power? Does not every man, who feels one etherial spark yet glowing in his bosom, find his indignation kindle, at the bare imagination of these wrongs? What would be our sentiments, were this imagination realized? Did the blood of the ancient Britons swell our veins, did the spirit of our fore-fathers inhabit our breasts, should we hesitate a moment, in preferring death to a miserable existence in bondage? Did we reflect on their toils, their dangers, their fiery trials, the thought would inspire unconquerable courage, unless we are indeed bastards and not sons. Who has the front to ask, wherefore do you complain? Who dares assert every thing, worth living for, is not lost, when a nation is inslaved?—Are not pensioners, stipendiaries, and salary-men (unknown before) hourly multiplying on us, to riot in the spoils of miserable America? Does not every eastern gale waft us some new insect, even of that devouring kind, which eat up every green thing? Is not the bread taken out of the childrens mouths and given unto the Dogs? Are not our estates given to corrupt sycophants, without a design, or even a pretence, of solliciting our assent, and our lives put into the hands of those, whose tender mercies are cruelties? Has not an authority, in a distant land, in the most public manner, proclaimed a right of disposing *the all* of Americans? In short, what have we to lose, what have we to fear? Are not our distresses more than we can bear; and to finish all, are not our cities, in a time of profound peace, filled with standing armies, to preclude us even from that last solace of the wretched;—to open their mouths in complaint and send forth their cries in bitterness of heart?

But is there no ray of hope? Is not G. B. inhabited by the children of those renowned barons, who waded thro' seas of crimson gore to establish their liberty? And will they not allow us their fellow-men to enjoy that freedom, which we claim from nature, which is confirmed by our constitution, and which they pretend so highly to value? Was a tyrant to conquer us, the chains of slavery when opposition would be less useless, might be supportable; but to be shackled by Englishmen, by our equals, is not to be borne!—By the sweat of our brow, we earn the little we possess; from nature, we derive the common rights of man, and by charter we claim the liberties of Britons:—Shall we, dare we, pusillanimously, surrender our birthrights? Can the debt of nature be cancelled,—is the obligation to our fathers discharged,—is the debt we owe posterity paid? Answer me, thou coward! who hidest thyself in the hour of trial.—If there is no reward in this life, no prize of glory in the next, capable of animating thy dastard soul; think and tremble, thou miscreant! at the whips and stripes thy master shall lash thee with on earth, and the flames and scorpions thy second master shall torment thee with, in hell!

Oh my countrymen! what will our children say, when they read the history of these times, should they find we tamely gave away the most invaluable earthly blessings? As they drag the galling chain, will they not execrate us? If we have any respect for things sacred, any regard to the dearest treasure on earth, if we have one tender sentiment for posterity, if we would not be despised by the whole world, let us in the most open, solemn manner, and with the determined fortitude of a Corsican, sware, *We will die, if we cannot live Freemen.*[4] Be not lulled, my countrymen, with vain imaginations, and idle fancies. To hope for the protection of heaven, without doing our duty, and exerting ourselves as become men, is to mock the Deity: Wherefore had man his reason, if it was not to direct him; wherefore his strength, if it be not his protection?

To banish folly and luxury, correct vice and immorality, and stand immoveable in the freedom, in which we are free indeed, is eminently the duty of each individual, at this day. When this is done, we may *rationally* hope for an answer to our prayers; for the whole council of GOD, and the invincible armour of the Almighty. However righteous our cause, we cannot, in this period of the world, expect a miraculous salvation. Heaven will undoubtedly assist us, if we act like men; but to expect protection from above, while we are enervated by luxury, and slothful in the exertion of those abilities with which we are indued, is an expectation vain and foolish. With the smiles of heaven, virtue, unanimity and firmness, will insure success; while we have equity, justice, and GOD on our side, tyranny, spiritual or temporal, shall never ride triumphant in a land inhabited by ENGLISHMEN.

"Avert it heaven! you love the brave,
You hate the treach'rous, willing slave,
The self-devoted head.
Nor shall an hireling's voice convey
That sacred prize to lawless sway,
For which a nation bled.
Vain prayer, the coward's weak resource!
Directing reason, active force,
Propitious heaven bestows.
But ne'er shall flame the thund'ring sky,
To aid the trembling herd that fly
Before the weaker foes.
In names there dwell no magick charms,
The British virtues, British arms
Unloos'd our father's bands:
Say, Greece and Rome! *If these should fail,*
What names, what ancestors avail,
To save a sinking land?"[5]

HYPERION.

1. *Boston Gazette,* 3 October 1768, p. 3, filling nearly the first two of the three columns.

2. Quincy was both quoting and paraphrasing from Andrew Marvell's *The Rehearsal Transpros'd: The Second Part* (London: Nathaniel Ponder, 1673), p. 193, which he would later include in his political commonplace book; it is also in his posthumous "Catalogue of Books." See Coquillette and York, eds., *Portrait of a Patriot,* 1:103 and 5:900 (no. 295), resp.

3. Here is a fine example of the difficulty of pinning down every source that Quincy paraphrased, quoted directly, or quoted from memory. He may have borrowed the phrase "rolling the sweet morsel under his tongue" from Matthew Henry's *An Exposition of all the Books of the Old and New Testaments,* 6 vols., 3rd ed. (London: J. Clark and R. Hett, et al., 1721–1735), Henry's exposition on Job 20:12 (at 3:206) or variations on that phrase in Henry's discussion of Psalms 34 and 73 (at 3:206 and 295, resp.), or from another edition of Henry's *Exposition,* or from yet another writer, in New England as well as Old, who borrowed from Henry. The same could be said of finding the source of other borrowed phrases that precede and follow this particular one, whether from a Biblical source or not.

4. Pascal Paoli, fighting to keep republican Corsica free from French rule, had become a famous figure, in some sense the darling of his age in certain social circles, especially in London, where he would soon be living in exile. Perhaps he came to mind to Quincy just then because he had bought a copy of James Boswell's recently published *An Account of Corsica* (London: Edward and Charles Dilly, 1768), with Boswell singing the praises of Paoli as a freedom fighter. Quincy quoted from Boswell in his political commonplace book and a copy is listed in the "Catalogue of Books" as well. See Coquillette and York, eds., *Portrait of a Patriot,* 1:165–66 and 5:898 (no. 240), resp.

5. Quincy borrowed again from Nugent's *Ode to Mankind,* pp. 12–13 (see p. 22, n. 2 supra for an earlier excerpt).

JQ TO JOSIAH QUINCY SR.

December 1768[1]

An independency, in the strict sense of the word, I know is not the lot of man; but to restrain, to a certain degree, the instability of fortune, is much in our power. So far, then, an independence is attainable. Let those who will laugh at the paltry certainty which is to be gained. Surely, it would be some alleviation, under the pressure of misfortune, to think that our own folly and rashness contributed in no part to the heavy burden. Alas, how few of the sons of men have this happy consolation! Hence, most of those idle and vague declamations, which we so often hear, upon the fickleness and inconstancy of fortune. When thoroughly examined, the grand source is found in the hasty presumption of a foolish vanity, or the weak irresolution of a vicious heart. To apply for assistance, where my own foresight might have prevented the necessity, would be to me worse than death. Early in life I was fixed, experience has confirmed me, to suffer every stroke of adversity, let it be as severe as even imagination can paint, ere I would implore any earthly relief from distress, against which my own prudence might have armed me. To ask assistance, where, if it were declined, your redoubled efforts would supply your exigence, is the daily course of human affairs: but to seek relief, where a denial reduces you to despair, would be torment beyond expression.

Through your watchful care of my education and your kind munificence, I am out of a temptation to the meaner vices, and in that state which, to one of my temper, is the happiest human nature can boast, an independency, save on God and myself, for a decent support through life, and the hope of quitting the stage with that best human standard of true worth, the general approbation of my countrymen. How deeply my heart is affected, by those invaluable favours, is not for profession to convince you, but will be, I trust, best manifested by the uniform tenor of my life, who wishes ever to be esteemed, as, *he thinks,* he really is.

Your affectionate son,
Josiah Quincy junr

The interruptions, which perplexed the composition and transcribing of this Letter plead some excuse for Errors.

1. Quincy, *Memoir,* pp. 19–20. Eliza Susan Quincy noted this is just an "extract" from a full letter. She did not transcribe it for the manuscript "Memoir" but she did paste in a portion of the original there, between pp. 16–17, beginning at the second paragraph, which includes the closing to his father missing from the printed *Memoir.* The top portion may have been lost since that time. Quincy Sr.'s response follows.

JOSIAH QUINCY SR. TO JQ

21 February 1769[1]

I can therefore only add, that I am so far from wondering, at your Care and Solicitude to preserve, the Felicity you now enjoy, I wish, from my Soul, every Branch of my Family, had an equal Share of it, and I esteem it my Honor, as well as Happiness, that you attribute any Part of your Felicity, to my Care and Indulgence, in the Course of your Education.

That our universal Parent may, of his abundant Goodness, continue Me in; and by granting Success to our honest Endeavours, in his own due Time, raise you up to, that *Independancy* you so feelingly express, and having exerted, the Faculties with which We are indued, to improve our Selves, and all around Us, in virtuous Habits and usefull Knowledge, that, We may finally make, a decent *Exit* from this mortal Stage, and then find our Selves encompassed, with his Love and Favour in a better State, is the ardent, and unalterable Wish and Prayer, of him, who always esteemed You his dutifull Son, and who is unreservedly

Your affectionate Father
Jos. Quincy

1. Pasted into the "Memoir," 2:16, QP 46 (reel 6) MHS; and, like Josiah Jr.'s of December 1768 (see previous entry), this is only a portion of a longer letter.

"PRO ARIS ET FOCIS"

11 September 1769[1]

Messieurs EDES & GILL,

Please to insert the following.

______"*O vain surmise!*
To deem the grandeur of a crown
Consists in lawless pow'r! to deem them wise
Who change security and fair renown,
For detestation, shame, distrust, and fear!"[2]

IT is the indispensible duty of every good citizen, when he thinks his country in jeopardy of bondage, to offer his sentiments on the state of publick affairs, with that zeal and resolution, which the exigency of the times demands. Wherever the right of delivering opinions and arguments, touching political transactions, is restrained by any thing, but the *common good* of the whole, the natural, the just claim of freemen is so far *unnecessarily* infringed: And in the same degree, as this infringement is extended, by the legislative or executive body of any state, so far is the grand, the sole end of all government defeated: — Hence the *body of the community,* whose safety and protection is the only rational standard of obedience, have an indefesible right to assert and establish this *prerogative* of the people: And as the multitude, when united, ever have the power, so unless debauched by vice, they will ever, without any procrastination, repell such daring invaders. For let the executioners of oppression, who are cloathed with the regalia of power, in proportion to their own infamy and the corruption of age;—I say, let these execrable tools trumpet forth the *mysteries* of government, with as much unintelligible jargon, pomp, and diabolical hypocrisy, as they may; they will always meet, from an intelligent people, just indignation and vengeance.—What must be the emotions of any honest man, who, in his day, should have seen the herald of Slavery enrobed in the sacred scarlet of the judgment-seat;—one fitted by nature, for fraud and deception, confirmed, by habit, in the despicable arts of low cant and cunning; *pensioned,* by monies drawn from the bowels of an impoverished people, to instill, and peerless enough to inculcate, in a land of light, the abhorred doctrines of passive obedience:—and, finally, the villain, who contrived, hardy enough to accomplish the accursed project of prostituting the sacred tribunal of justice—

to promote the little designs of private policy, and establish the broad plan of a determined, imperial tyranny! But a delineation of the thoughts, which naturally arise on this head, would exceed the limits of this Paper:—Perhaps the subject will be handled with more copiousness and fidelity, by some future historian, who need not dread the *"summary procedure"* of a star-chamber tyranny, or imprisonment and torture from the fangs of power.—But a rising generation of freemen will scarcely believe, that doctrines were ever advanced, and avowedly practised upon, which would have better graced the court of a Spanish inquisition, than a land famed for its free constitution.

When we look on the historic page of old time, or survey, with attention, the present face of the globe—When shall we find, where shall we see a nation, who, with justice, can boast a freedom, confirmed by the laws of state, worthy to be placed in competition with that liberty, which is derived from the grand charter of nature:—a liberty which the people have an indefesible right to enjoy, *unimpaired,* except so far as is necessary for the *general felicity;*—a liberty, which no nation, that the Sun ever saw, enjoyed in that plenitude and perfection, which it ought to expect—and *demand.*

Have not the British nation vaunted their patronage of freedom?—Yet traverse the globe—and where do you find the flame of liberty blaze with the greatest lustre?—Poor America! Distressed Corsica!—How does my Heart bleed?—Oh Britain do you not blush? Ye, worthy few, of a degenerate nation—do you not weep tears of Blood?—France and England have to a proverb, been denominated natural and sworn enemies.—But in what instance will posterity find them combining into a close Union? Great Britain is oppressing the American!—France plundering the Corsican!—And are they not unnaturally united totally to extinguish the few remaining sparks of patriotism, which yet enliven and vigorate two little spots of this subjugated World?—A melancholy and alarming reflection!

What, my honest countrymen—you I mean who are willing, like your venerable forefathers, (if such be the decree of heaven,) to eat your bread, with sweat of brow and sorrow of heart;—nay, if your GOD and country require, are willing to wade thro' blood and carnage to extirpate that bondage, with which the *Egyptians* seek to enthrall us;—what, I say, my fellowmen, are your feelings at beholding the infernal miscreants, who are even in your own bosoms, and are seconding the blood-thirsty designs of those who would devour your very vitals?—Declare, my countrymen, freely declare your sentiments—avow your determinations—and execute your righteous resolutions,—

Our merchants have done worthily; but it is the body of the people, who must, under GOD, finally save us. For while there are debauched consumers of foreign luxuries, there always will be, in this depraved state, mercenary creatures enough to import the *bane of their country.* And it is no derogation from the disinterested conduct of our merchants to imagine, that their efforts will prove ineffectual, if not established by the virtue of the people.—Nay, my fellowmen, the servile emissaries and wicked minions of your inveterate foes have insultingly prophesied and blazed it abroad, with a rancorous malice, characteristic of themselves, that the mercantile endeavours would prove utterly abortive;—that no dependance was to be had upon the virtuous stability of the generality among us;—that the common people, or, as they disdainfully term it, the herd, were sunk in luxury, intemperance and every degrading vice;—and that hence, any *commercial plan* of political salvation would prove, only, an amusing dream—a transitory phantom.

There are a black tribe of ignoble and abandoned wretches, in almost every community, who would entail poverty and servitude on all mankind, if they might be allowed the temporary gratification of revelling in the unbounded wantoness of power and plunder. Such wretches cannot fail, when fully known, of meeting from their injured fellow-men, that righteous judgment, sentence, and prosecution, which will effectually mortify their pride, subdue their insolence, and frustrate their damnable designs.

For if once a servile clan of infamous prostitutes, with impunity, lay and carry on their detestable schemes—All is upon the brink of destruction:—but, if a daring band of rebels to their GOD, and traitors to their Country, plot with the malice of Hell, labour and persevere with the obstinacy of Devils, for the ruin and rapine of a happy land, *unchecked* and *uncontrouled,* by the vigilance, the union, the vigour and firmness of the *people*—All is lost!—

"*Superior virtue, wisdom, might,*
Create and mark the ruler's right,
So reason must conclude:
Then thine it is, to whom belong
The wise, the virtuous, and the strong,
Thrice sacred Multitude!

Thy will's thy rule, thy good it's end;
You punish only to defend
What parent nature gave:
And he who dare her gifts invade
By nature's oldest law is made
Thy victim or thy slave."[3]

PRO ARIS ET FOCIS.

1. *Boston Gazette,* 11 September 1769, filling two columns, spilling over to the third. "Pro Aris et Focis," the motto of a number of organizations that have sprung up since Quincy's day, the phrase is often translated idiomatically as "For God and Country," a variation from Cicero's "for altar and hearth" (or "home"). See the comment on possible sources in Coquillette and York, eds., *Portrait of a Patriot,* 1:67 n. 47. In the "Catalogue of Books," in ibid., 5:899 (no. 256) "Cicero's Thoughts" are listed–which well could be the 1750 London edition noted at 5:926, with English-French-Latin included, but this particular phrase is not there. It is in M. T. Ciceronis [Marcus Tullius Cicero], *De Natura Deorum* (Glasgow, 1748), at p. 244, but that seems an unlikely source for Quincy to have used. Fourteen years before William Bollan, then agent in London for the Massachusetts General Court, reported that Sir Thomas Robinson, then secretary of state for the southern department, used the phrase for Bollan to pass along to the colonists, to encourage them to prepare for the coming war with France. See Bollan's letter to the Mass. house speaker of 4 September 1755 in the William Bollan Papers, Box 1, folder 6, New England Historic Genealogical Society mss.

2. Quincy could have taken these lines directly from *The Institution of the Order of the Garter. A Dramatick Poem* (London: R. Dodsley, 1742), p. 63, or a number of anthologies published since then that included it.

3. Quincy returned to Nugent's *Ode to Mankind,* p. 6, for these lines. See his "Hyperion" pieces of 26 September and 3 October 1768 for earlier instances (supra pp. 21 and 27, resp.).

"AN INDEPENDANT"

12 February 1770[1]

Messi'rs EDES & GILL,

IT has been the general apprehension of all parties, among us, that the publications in Messirs. Mein and Fleeming's paper, have tended much, to promote that very cause, they were designed to defeat. "The great encouragement those persons received,"—and "gratitude for that encouragement," they so *publickly professed,* gave some grounds to imagine, that they would have pursued a scheme, widely different, from the one, it seems, they have adopted. The "plan of their weekly paper," when proposed, was to "be of no party"—to "publish & propagate with the greatest industry whatever might promote THE GENERAL GOOD": How plain a deviation from this eligible plan! How did those specious pretenses gull the good people of this province?

Messieurs Mein and Fleeming have so thoro'ly discovered themselves, and their weekly efforts have, thence, been thought so feeble, as that a dangerous disregard of their publications seems to have taken place. But I conceive, that when any thing is said, tho' by the worst of men, which is plausible, and may deceive the unwary, that some strictures should be made to prevent any bad consequences. Hence, I have been influenced to offer a few remarks, upon the BOSTONIAN, of Monday last.[2] But before I enter upon that task, I would desire Messirs. Mein and Fleeming to peruse the following passage, in the plan of their paper, which was presented to the Public.—"Be independent;—your *interest* is intimately connected with this noble virtue;—if you depart from this, *you must sink from the esteem of the public,* to the *partial praise of a party, who, when their purpose is served or defeated, may, perhaps, desert you;* and then, HOW CAN YOU EXPECT THAT THOSE, WHOM YOU HAVE REVILED, WILL SUPPORT YOU."

The BOSTONIAN, in common with most of the writers, who have appeared in the Chronicle, is guilty of very illiberal reflections, wicked misrepresentations, and unjustifiable *personal* abuse. However, it is not my design to enter upon a defence of gentlemen whose characters are unblemished, and thereby to divert the public attention from matters of general moment, to the, comparatively, trifling concern of private individuals. If particular men are knaves, or fools, the public will soon find them out—but it is too late, to play the old game:—Philanthrop and many others, of lesser note, have had their time of deception:—but what is the interest of America, who espouse it, and who seek it's destruction, we want, at this day, but little information

A writer who sets out, with telling us, that "our attention has long been engrossed *with wild chimeras*", carries "a title page that speaks the nature of his volume." The objects, that have attracted our eyes, as well as the hearts of all N. America, need no further elucidation to shew their value and importance.—If there is any "charm" that is like to ensnare us;—any "fascination" that should be dispelled, it is the "fascinating charm" of imitating the inticing luxuries of those who riot on the toil of others:—A great danger, a danger, that is alarming, in proportion as it is not generally perceived;—a great danger of the present day is, that we should be allured by the affluence and splendor of the creatures, among us, who are insinuating their poison, by increasing their connections, and corrupting the minds of the young and unwary, with flattering expectations of eating idle bread. Here is a source of danger, my countrymen are not normally apprized of, and of a much more fatal nature, than we, in general, imagine.

The BOSTONIAN tells us, what we well knew before, namely, that "our cause is good": This is a concession quite unexpected; and as it seems a generous one, we wish he had been more explicit in telling us what he imagined that "*cause*" to be. For this indeterminate mode of expression, may give an opening, for future evasion, and some may conjecture, that this ambiguity was designed for that purpose.

If the words "good cause", mean the present plan of non-importation, the gentleman's argument is apparently futile; nay absurd: But if an intire exemption, from any British tax on America, is the idea affixed to those words, it may be worth while to enquire, how this concession squares with the purport of this BOSTONIAN performance. One of these things, it seems, was intended, by that "granted good cause," which "my countrymen" had embraced. Now if this latter construction is a fair and just one, my fellowmen will be at no loss by what standard to examine and measure their past and future conduct.

The enquiry, then, will be reduced to a very few heads;—whether any individual is a free man, whose property and person is subject to a power, over whom he has no influence? Whether a state can, in any sense, be free, who are under a foreign, legislative, controul? These are questions, which a *New-England* yeoman, with his domestic companions, his BIBLE and *Law-book,* can answer, without the *pensioned* assistance of a corrupt judge, "whose education was behind the counter," and "whose hands are yet dirty; with sweeping a shop."—Whether tamely to submit to a merciless oppression, an insatiable tyranny; to drag out a miserable life of ignominious vassalage, and bequeath the chains, he can wear no longer, to the offspring of his loins;—or nobly to hazard all that is dear, in the defence of the household of his fathers and the *household of his faith,* would cause little deliberation, in the *breast* of an AMERICAN husbandman, with his mattock and hayfork, as it would, in the mind of a wretched miscreant, whether to *turn from his way, and live,* or sacrifice his country, his soul and his GOD, for *the mammon of unrighteousness, the wages of his iniquities?*

If these things are true, and, if they are not, let them be confuted; I say, if these remarks are just, we call on the BOSTONIAN and his abettors to convince us, we are in no danger, or point out the way of relief.

To be free, we are resolved. To obtain a great good, or defend from a destroying evil, without some danger, and some difficulties, is the vain expectation of the ignorant or the dastard. For the greatest blessings all good men will make the greatest sacrifice. This alone is a sufficient answer to all the fallacious cries of the hirelings, who have been pretendedly lamenting the distresses of non-importation.

"If I ask, says the BOSTONIAN, an advocate for the non importation agreement, what end it is to answer, I am told it is to bring about a REPEAL of the revenue laws." But, by the gentleman's leave, I, who am an advocate for the same agreement, would make a very different answer. I believe, if those laws are never repealed, it will be happy for my country; and therefore, as a good citizen I wish their continuance. My reasons for this creed are founded on many circumstances, and arise from various considerations; and when I think it expedient, I shall enlarge on this subject: But, as I know there are multitudes who think, with me, I wave, for the present, extensive observations on this head. Yet, as the BOSTONIAN, may, possibly chuse to hear what answer, some others would make to his question; I give him the following reply.

From a conviction, in my own mind, that America is now the slave of Britain; from a sense, that we are every day, more and more, in danger of an increase of our burdens, and a fastment of our shackles, I wish to see my countrymen break off—OFF FOREVER!—all social intercourse, with those, whose commerce contaminates, whose luxuries poison, whose avarice is insatiable, & whose unnatural oppressions are not to be borne. That Americans well know their rights, that they will resume, assert and defend them are matters of which I harbour no doubt. Whether the arts of POLICY, or the arts of *war* will decide the contest, are problems we will solve, at a more convenient season. He, whose heart is enamoured, with the refinements of political artifice and finesse, will seek one mode of relief; he, whose heart is free, honest and intrepid, will pursue another, a bolder, and more noble mode of redress.—This reply is so intelligible, that it needs no comment, for explanation.

When the BOSTONIAN "observes, that a *town (a single one* is only mentioned) within this province would not very readily meet with a redress of grievances by such conduct*", he seems to be either guilty of palpable sophistry, or to have produced a case, no way applicable or pertinent to the times.

"That all is not gold that glitters", we are convinced of, by the *friendly* information of the BOSTONIAN, "that we have hurt our own cause, so as to lose our *best friends,* and that we are in danger of frustrating the *intentions of Administrations* IN OUR FAVOUR"! *Risum teneatis amici?*[3]

"The cause of the repeal of the stamp-act" we are not solicitous to inquire; for we knew, at the time, and we have been confirmed since, that the repeal was not made on *right-principles.*

Of "the riches of the East and the West"; of the "greatness, traffic & rivalship" of our neighbours, we are not envious: The genuine cause of their riches, greatness and traffic, we can well ascribe to that industry, frugality and oeconomy which is more and more prevalent: And we would be far from easily believing those are knaves and villains, whose interest is inseperably interwoven with our own, more especially, as the intelligence comes from such a suspicious quarter.

AN INDEPENDANT.

*Non-importation conduct is meant.

1. *Boston Gazette,* 12 February 1770, taking up most of the first page, from the second half of the first column through nearly the bottom of the third.

2. *The Boston Chronicle,* 5 February 1770, nearly filling the first page and spilling over onto the second. "A Bostonian" derided the advocates of non-importation as self-interested, duping the working men in the Boston town meeting who were foolish enough to support their self-

interested efforts. The author of "A Bostonian" responded to "An Independant" in the *Boston Chronicle* for March 5th. John Mein and John Fleeming had started the newspaper near the end of 1767. It tended to favor imperial authority as extended through the governor, and law and order in general. John and Thomas Fleets' *Boston Evening-Post* attempted to steer a more middle course. Richard Draper's *Massachusetts Gazette* was, unofficially, as much the administration's newspaper as, unofficially, Benjamin Edes and John Gill's *Boston Gazette* was for the opposition. For Edes and Gill see Robert E. Burkholder's entry in Benjamin Franklin V, ed., *Boston Printers, Publishers, and Booksellers: 1640–1800* (Boston: G. K. Hall, 1980), pp. 117–35. Also see *The History of Printing in America* (Worcester, Mass.: Isaiah Thomas, 1810) by Isaiah Thomas, who founded the anti-administration *Massachusetts Spy* in July 1770; and Mary Ann Yodelis, "Boston's Second Major Paper War: Economics, Politics, and the Theory and Practice of Political Expression in the Press, 1763–1775" (Ph.D. dissertation, University of Wisconsin 1971). The print duel that pitted "An Independant" against "A Bostonian" was but one of many. For another example see my"Tag-Team Polemics: The Centinel and His Allies in the *Massachusetts Spy*," *Proceedings of the Massachusetts Historical Society* (1995):85–114. There I suggest (on p. 107 n. 68) that Quincy may have been the "Centinel," but I do not push the point. Eliza Susan Quincy did not mention this particular pen name as being one of Quincy's.

3. Essentially an ironic response, a rhetorical question: "Can you help laughing, friends?" It is a line from one of Horace's epistles that Quincy could have found in various editions of Horace's works or even in a number of anthologies. The "Catalogue of Books," no. 119, says "Horace" and no more. In Coquillette and York, eds., *Portrait of a Patriot,* 5:895.

"AN INDEPENDANT"

26 February 1770[1]

Messi'rs EDES & GILL,

"This is the master-piece of a *modern politician,* how to qualify and mould the sufferance and subjection of the people to the length of that foot, that is to tread on their necks; how rapine may serve itself with fair and honourable pretences of public good; how the puny law, may be brought under the wardship, and controul of *lust,* and will, in which attempt if he fall short, then must a superficial colour of reputation, by all means, be gotten to wash over the unsightly bruise of honour. To make men governable in this manner, precepts are inculcated, that mainly tend to *break* a national spirit and courage by countenancing open riot, luxury, and ignorance, till having thus disfigured and *made men beneath men,* as *Juno* in the fable of Io, the *poor* transformed *heifer* of the common-wealth is delivered up to be stung and vext with the breeze and goad of oppression."[2]

HAVING observed, that the publications, in the Chronicle, were passed over, with general neglect, I took occasion, in the Gazette of the 12th instant, to express some concern, at this disregard:—the *cause* and the *consequence* of this neglect were also mentioned;—and the truth of what was remarked, on those publications, it was thought, wou'd serve as an apology, for the notice paid to a writer, in the Boston Chronicle.

The Bostonian, at his first appearance, was unjust, in his insinuations, abusive to individuals, and flagrantly false in his account of facts;—of this all ranks among us, were so well convinced, it would have been time mispent to enter upon a long confutation of what gained no belief.[3] Accordingly, I openly declared, that I would not "divert the public attention from matters of general concern:" And after collecting the most plausible part of the Bostonian, I endeavoured to show the absurdity and sophistry of his reasoning. How far this endeavour was attained, the candid will judge, without being much influenced by the indiscreet vapour of the BOSTONIAN, on "the imbecility of my performance."

When an author informs his readers, that he is about to "wave his plan to answer what has been advanced by another gentleman, who signs himself AN INDEPENDANT", one would not naturally be led to conjecture, that this

Independant, "instead of contending any, gave up several of the points started by the answerer": I say one would not readily think, that a writer of the Bostonian's *"kidney"* would lay down his important plan, to encounter sentiments, that, it should seem, no way interfered with his own: And now we are upon this head, I wish the BOSTONIAN for his own credit, would give us a minute delineation of his plan and his *schemes,* in order that we may judge of his consistency. For some sagacious minds are but too jealous, that his indeterminate expressions, and his inaccurate reasonings forebode no laudable design.

Since the BOSTONIAN has assured us, that "it would be unreasonable in him to expect that his assertions should be received as facts," many would be pleased to find his conduct, more conformable to his professions. It is, in general, a just observation, that matters of fact may be so fully proved, that mankind will be well satisfied of the truth; but should we make the gaining credit, the standard, by which to determine the merits of the present dispute; the BOSTONIAN and his party, when tried by this scale, would certainly be found wanting. After such an apparently generous declaration, it is *reasonable for me to expect,* that the BOSTONIAN will prove his *plump assertion*, that The INDEPENDANT "gave up several of the points started by him."

As there appears a diffidence, in the "defence of the Printers," and the matter is not very momentous, severe animadversion is declined, and we come to that part of our opponent's "answer," where he, with singular assurance affirms, that "the INDEPENDANT does not deign to take notice of the misery brought upon the town by the *eligible* scheme of non-importation; not a word does he administer to sooth the needy, but to aggravate their distress, he tells us of such as indulge themselves in luxuries."—I am at loss to determine, whether the author, here, intended to be pathetic or to insult.

Something, however, was offered, by the *Independant,* which, he imagined, was "a sufficient answer to all the salacious cries of the hirelings, who were pretendedly lamenting the distresses of non-importation:"—And this surely was, at lest, "a deigning to take that notice," which the Bostonian roundly declares to have been omitted.

Will any thing *"sooth"* a good mind so much, as to be sure and certain, that the inconveniencies that are felt, result from a noble struggle, in the most noble cause, that can inspire the human breast? Little minds are pleased with *soothings:* the hope of Americans is in greatness of soul: We determine to repel the stroke of adversity: we are animated in the trial, by the example of our persecuted, suffering and triumphant ancestors. Fired by their virtues, we will fight the good fight of faith, and protected by that ARM, which wrought their salvation, we, yet, hope to do valiantly for this goodly heritage of our fathers.

It is recommended to the BOSTONIAN, that while he is weeping over the calamities of the poor, that he would make some effectual discovery of their true source. For notwithstanding all that has yet been offered, the very *poor* themselves believe, that the enormous clogs and burdens of trade contribute much to deprive them of their daily bread. They have heard, that the very breath of tyranny blasts the luscious fruits of industry; and they are foolish enough to believe, that the misfortunes, they now bewail, are but the natural consequences of a fatal bondage;—they view present distress only as ominous of future woe, and the first fruits of oppression, however artfully gilded, are unpleasing to the eye, and ungrateful to the taste. And, at this day, even the studied productions, and harrangues of *the sweet-speech maker,* will gain no proselytes:—the man is known:—the charm is dissolved:—*"Hic niger est, hunc tu Romane cavete."*[4]

And tho', like *fallen* BELIAL,[5] "he seems
For dignity compos'd and high exploit;—
Yet all is *false* and *hollow*: *tho' his tongue*
Drop manna, and he make the worse appear
The better reason, to perplex and dash
Maturest counsels; yet *his thoughts are low:*
To vice industrious, but *to nobler deeds*
Timorous and *slothful.*"[6]

That *Cincinnatus* was called from the "*plough*" to conduct in the *field* of Mars, the histories of Rome mention; but that any of the Fabian name were husbandmen, I do not recollect to have heard. But in the days of Roman freedom, "*Pensioners*" of the great were not intrusted with the *chief command,* either in the camp or senate.[7]—

In the purity of the *Roman* state, the great Fabius would have been *more* than "*taxed* with the meanness of his occupation, and the dirtiness of his hands," had he displayed the contracted notions of a warehouse education—the little pique of private resentment;—the wicked byass of a party-policy;—and the indefatigable *lust* of restless ambition;—when, in solemn judgment, upon the property, life, and liberty of the citizen—in senatorial debate upon the privileges and rights of the comon-wealth;—and in awful decision upon points, which intimately affected the fate of empires!

The same Johnson, who supplied the "definition of a pension"—affords the following account of a PENSIONER:—"One, who is *supported* by an allowance *paid at the will of another;* a dependant; a *slave of state hired by a stipend to obey his master*"[8]—Good GOD! What must be the distress, the sentiments, and feelings of a people, legislated, condemned and governed, by a creature so mercenary, so dependant, and so ——— But I forbear: my anguish is too exquisite—my heart is too full!

We will resume then, our enquiry, whether the BOSTONIAN was not a little precipitate in his unwary intimation, that the INDEPENDANT had not "*contended any* of the points he had started."

Were the observations I made on the Bostonian's "*good cause*" pertinent and unanswerable? Is not that gentleman caught between the horns of a fatal dilemma? Must not the gentlemen either frankly own his concession to be "futile and absurd," or endeavour to answer the purport of what was offered, on the only rational constructions of his words? On this head, I will not, here, press the gentleman further.

The "impertinence," or "the palpable sophistry" of the Bostonian's reasonings, was so sufficiently evidenced, that, *to save appearances,* it would have been more politic and decent for the gentleman to have given a better reply, than barely to suggest, that *no points he had started were contended.*

Lest I should give further occasion to PACIFICUS, and other such *courtly* writers, to descant on a *very fertile* and *interesting* subject:—and animate "my countrymen to *confide* in the *experienced* justice and generosity of G.B." I close, with the sentiments of a man, whose genious, learning, fortitude and piety, rendered him the scourge of tyrants, and a glory to the world.[9]

"What stirs the *Englishmen* sooner to *rebellion,* than violent and heavy hands upon their properties and persons? yet there are those, who (in spight of our charter, and the souls of our progenitors, that wrested their liberties out of the *Norman* gripe, with their dearest blood and highest prowess) have not ceased to set at naught and trample under foot all the most sacred, life blood laws, statutes and acts of parliament, that are the holy covenant of union and marriage, between the king and his realm, by proscribing and confiscating, from us, all the right we have to our bodies, goods and liberties. *What is this, but to blow a trumpet and proclaim a fire-cross to an hereditary ad perpetual* CIVIL WAR?"[10]

AN INDEPENDANT.

1. *Boston Gazette,* 26 February 1770, p. 2, starting at the bottom of the first column and filling the remaining two.

2. Quincy took this paragraph from the second book of John Milton's "Of Reformation in England," possibly as found in *The Works of John Milton,* 2 vols. (London: A. Millar, 1753), 1:15. Quincy ended his quotation mid-sentence. He owned several sets of Milton's writings. See Coquillette and York, eds., *Portrait of a Patriot,* 5:901 (no. 323). He turned to Milton for his political commonplace book (though not this passage) and for his "Marchmont Nedham" essays as well. See ibid., 1:177 for the commonplace book entry. The fable of Juno and Io, to which Quincy alludes, is the Roman version of the Greek tale of the goddess Hera and princess Io. Hera suspected that Zeus lusted after the beautiful Io; Zeus, sensing Hera's approach, turned Io into a heifer. Hera, knowing what he had done, demanded that the heifer be given to her. Io suffers greatly, from one indignity after another, until eventually Zeus restores her to her human form and she bears him a son.

3. Quincy first addressed "A Bostonian" two weeks before as "An Independant" in the *Boston Gazette,* 12 February 1770 (supra, pp. 36–40); "A Bostonian" first appeared in the *Boston Chronicle,* 5 February 1770.

4. Quoting from Horace's "Satires," Book I, the warning being that "that man is dark; Romans beware." For the particular printed source, see p. 40, n. 3 supra.

5. A fallen angel, one who rebels against God; to some, even Satan himself. (As in 2 Corinthians 6:15 KJV, "And what concord hath Christ with Belial? Or what part hath he that believeth with an infidel?")

6. Quincy returned to Milton, this time Book II, lines 108–17 of "Paradise Lost," with some slight changes, perhaps as taken from *The Poetical Works of Milton,* 2 vols. (Edinburgh: A. Donaldson and J. Reid, 1762), which, again perhaps, is the source listed the Catalogue of Books" in Coquillette and York eds., *Portrait of a Patriot,* 5:892 (no. 28).

7. (Lucius Quinctius) Cincinnatus, famous for having saved republican Rome in the 5th century BCE, giving up his dictatorial authority once the republic was secure; and Fabius (Maximus), for his tactics against the Carthaginians under Hannibal, after they had overrun much of Italy during the second Punic War in the 3rd century BCE. George Washington would eventually be celebrated as both, first as Fabius, for his decisive strikes at Trenton and Princeton, and later as Cincinnatus when he resigned his commission as commander-in-chief. Quincy could have read much about Fabius in his copy of John and William Langhorne, *Plutarch's Lives,* 6 vols. (London: Edward and Charles Dilly, 1770), 2:56–95. Livy may have been his basic source for Cincinnatus, though Livy, unlike Plutarch, was neither cited in Quincy's political commonplace book nor listed in the posthumous "Catalogue of Books," and was much rarer, available only in Latin. Still, there were many commentaries on Caesar in print and a fair number of them at least alluded to Cincinnatus in an unfavorable (to Caesar) comparison of the two.

8. Samuel Johnson, *A Dictionary of the English Language,* 2 vols. (London: W. Strahan, 1755–1756), volume I [unpaginated].

9. Essays by PACIFICUS had appeared in the London *Gazetteer* some years before, with some reprinted in the colonies (see the *Boston Post-Boy and Daily Advertiser,* 3 March 1766).

10. Once again, a quotation from Milton's "Of Reformation in England," in 1:23 of the source at p. 45 n. 2 supra.

"AN INDEPENDANT"

12 March 1770[1]

Like a scurvy politician seem,
To see the things thou dost not.
SHAKESPEARE.[2]

A Writer, in the Boston Chronicle, has not only been charged, in direct terms, but *proved,* by irresistable demonstration, guilty of *impertinence, absurdity, sophistry & falsehood.* That, all this has been done, with fair argument and good manners, the BOSTONIAN ought, with blushes, to concede. But should that gentleman think such a concession too great a sacrifice to truth and justice, it is then hoped, that his future publications, *tho' unanswer'd,* will meet little attention, and less credit. For, surely, when a writer, after such *charges* and such *proofs,* continues to *vapour* and *froth,* in futile strains and indeterminate expressions, devoid of reason or excuse, he cannot rationally hope even the countenance of *a party.*[3]

Such a *profound ignorance* of the laws and constitution of our government is displayed in the last production, signed A BOSTONIAN, that it is very difficult to refrain, from expressions of contempt; such trifling evasion and despicable argument are below serious confutation.

"To acknowledge *allegiance* to the *King,* and deny obedience to the *laws* of *Great-Britain,* the BOSTONIAN says would be preposterous." As well might he assert, that an acknowledgment of DUTY to a *natural* parent was incompatible with an absolute denial of obedience to his *unnatural* demands. But the weakness of what is, here, called "preposterous", must be peculiarly evident to those, who are acquainted with the spirit of our laws: And if same says true, our BOSTONIAN ought to be *much ashamed* of his defects, in handling this subject.

I would chuse to treat every publick writer with politeness, but when palpable lies are asserted, for truth, in the face of all mankind, it is difficult to abstain from an appearance of incivility.—The BOSTONIAN is called upon to offer the *least* shadow of evidence, that—"the Independant would convert *every* province or island, *however insignificant* some of them may be, into *separate* and *distinct* states:"—

It would require little less than a spirit of divination to find out, what reason or propriety there was in the stated supposition, about "the people of Main". The BOSTONIAN surely exposes himself to very just ridicule! Matters of greater importance, than viewing the defects and deformities of the BOSTONIAN, demand our instant attention. I therefore, close with the very applicable sentiments of an author, whose strength and life were spent in the service of his GOD and his country.

"Few words, well considered; few and easy things, now seasonably done; will save us. But if the people be so affected, as to prostitute religion and liberty, to the vain and groundless apprehension, that nothing, but a lucrative trade can make them happy; and if trade be grown so craving and importunate thro' the profusion of men, that nothing can support it, but the luxurious expences of the community upon trifles or superfluities, so as if the people should generally betake themselves to frugality, it might prove a dangerous matter, lest tradesmen should mutiny, for want of trading; and that, therefore, we must forego and set to sale, religion, liberty, honour, safety, all concernment divine or human, to keep up trading; if, lastly, after all this light among us, the same reason shall pass for current to fix our necks under illegal impositions, as was made use of, by the Jews, to return back to Egypt, because they foolishly imagined, that they would then live in more plenty and prosperity;[4] our condition is not sound but rotten, both in religion and all civil prudence; and we shall soon be brought to those calamities, which attend always and unavoidably on luxury, that is to say, all national judgments under foreign and domestic slavery.

Thus, with hazard, I have ventured what I thought my duty, to speak in season, and to forewarn my country in time. Many circumstances and particulars I could have added; but a few *main matters,* now put speedily into execution, will suffice to recover us from bondage, and set all right.—What I have said, is the language of the GOOD OLD CAUSE: If it seem strange to any, it will not seem more strange I hope, than convincing to backsliders. Thus much I should perhaps have said, tho' sure I should have spoken, only, to trees and stones, and had none to cry to, but with the prophet; *O earth, earth, earth!* But, I trust, I shall have spoken persuasion to abundance of sensible and ingenuous men: to some, perhaps, whom GOD may raise of these stones, to become children of liberty; and may enable and unite in noble resolution to give a full stay to the ruinous proceedings of tyranny and rapine."[5]

AN INDEPENDANT.

1. *Boston Gazette,* 12 March 1770, filling the first column and carrying over to a small portion of the second.

2. *King Lear,* Act IV Scene 6, Lear ranting to Gloucester in despair, his life a tatters–Gloucester's too, surrounded and undone by lies, their own as well as those of others.

3. In this, his third essay under this pen name, Quincy again attacks "A Bostonian." See supra, pp. 36–40 and 41–46, "An Independant," for February 12th and 26th, resp.

4. In their complaints against Moses less than two months after they had escaped Egypt through a parted Red Sea, as recorded in Exodus 16.

5. These two paragraphs are excerpted from John Milton's "The Ready and Easy Way To establish a Free Commonwealth," perhaps from Milton's *Works,* 2:652 at p. 45, n. 2 supra.

JOSIAH QUINCY SR. TO JQ

22 March 1770[1]

My dear son Braintree March 22d 1770

I am under great affliction at hearing the bitterest reproaches uttered against you, for having become an advocate for those criminals who are charged with the murder of their fellow citizens.—Good God! Is it possible?—I will not believe it.

Just before I returned home from Boston, I knew indeed, that on the day those criminals were committed to prison a sergeant had inquired for you at your brother's house, but I had no apprehensions that it was possible an application would be made to you to undertake their defence. Since then, I have been told that you have actually engaged for Captain Preston, and I have heard the discreet reflections made upon the occasion, by men who had just before manifested the highest esteem for you as one destined to be a Saviour of your country.

I must own to you, it has filled the bosom of your aged and infirm parent with anxiety, and distress, lest it should not only prove true, but destructive of your reputation and interest, and I repeat, I will not believe it unless it be confirmed by your own mouth or under your own hand.

Your anxious and distressed parent
Josiah Quincy

1. Transcribed in the "Memoir," 2:19–20, QP 46 (reel 6) MHS; also in the printed *Memoir,* pp. 26–27, with slight variations. Which of the two is closest to the original? For now it is impossible to say; the original appears to be missing. For Quincy and the "massacre" trials see Zobel, *Boston Massacre,* passim; and my comments in Coquillette and York, eds., *Portrait of a Patriot,* 1:21–27. Quincy's closing argument during the soldiers' trial can be found in John Hodgson, *The Trial of William Wemms* (Boston, 1770), pp. 139-48. John Adams complained that Hodgson did not record his arguments accurately. See his letter to Jedediah Morse of 5 January 1816 in Charles Francis Adams, ed., *The Works of John Adams,* 10 vols. (Boston: Little, Brown & Co., 1850–1856), 10:201. If Quincy had similar complaints, they do not appear in his surviving writings.

JQ TO JOSIAH QUINCY SR.

26 March 1770[1]

Honoured Sir Boston March 26th 1770

I have little leisure and less inclination, either to know or to take notice of those ignorant slanderers, who have dared to utter their "bitter reproaches" in your hearing against me, for having become an advocate for criminals charged with murder. But the sting of reproach, when envenomed only by envy and falsehood will never prove mortal.—Before pouring their reproaches into the ear of the aged and infirm, if they had been friends, they would have surely spared a little reflection, on the nature of an attorney's oath, and duty.—Some trifling scrutiny into the business and discharge of his office and some small portion of patience in viewing my past and future conduct.

Let such be told, Sir, that these criminals charged with murder, are not *yet legally proved guilty:* and therefore however criminal, are entitled by the laws of God, and man, to all counsel and legal aid.—That my duty as a man obliged me to undertake, that my duty as a lawyer strengthened the obligation. That from abundant caution, I, at first declined being engaged, but that after the best advice and most mature deliberation had determined my judgment, I waited on Captain Preston and told him that I would afford him my assistance, but prior to this, in presence of two of his friends, I made the most explicit declaration to him of my real opinion, on the contests (as I expressed it to him) of the times, and that my heart and hand, were indissolubly attached to the cause of my country; and finally, that I refused all engagement, until advised and urged to undertake it by an Adams, a Hancock, a Molineux, a Cushing, a Henshaw, a Pemberton, a Warren, a Cooper and a Phillips.[2]

This, and much more might be told with great truth, and I dare affirm that you, and this whole people will one day *rejoice* that I became an advocate for the aforesaid "criminals," *charged* with the murder of their fellow citizens.

I never harboured the expectation, nor any great desire, that all men should speak well of me. To enquire my duty, and do it, is my aim. Being mortal, I am subject to error, and conscious of this I wish to be diffident. Being a rational creature, I judge for myself according to the light afforded me—When a plan of conduct is formed with an honest deliberation, neither murmuring, slander or reproaches move—For my single self, I consider—judge—and with reason, hope to be immutable.

There are honest men in all sects. I wish their approbation. There are wicked bigots in all parties. I abhor them.

I am truly, and affectionately
your son
Josiah Quincy junr.

1. The original letter, like the one that prompted it, is now missing, although Eliza Susan Quincy had it in hand at the time she wrote the "Memoir," 2:20–21, QP 46 (reel 6) MHS) that became the basis of the *Memoir* (see pp. 27–28). The version printed here follows that transcribed for the "Memoir," although I capitalized the first word in each new sentence, which Eliza Susan Quincy did not—presumably because Josiah Junior did not either.

2. Samuel Adams, John Hancock, William Molineux, Thomas Cushing, Joshua Henshaw, Samuel Pemberton, Dr. Joseph Warren, the Reverend Samuel Cooper, and William Phillips (Quincy's father-in-law), town leaders all.

BOSTON TOWN MEETING INSTRUCTIONS TO ITS REPRESENTATIVES IN THE GENERAL COURT

15 May 1770[1]

Gentlemen—

The Town of Boston, by their late choice of you to Represent them in the ensuing General Court, have given strong proof of their confidence in your abilities and integrity. For no period since the perilous times of our venerable Fathers has worn a more gloomy and melancholy aspect. Unwarrantable and arbitrary exactions made upon the people—trade expiring, grievances, murmurs, discontents convulsing every part of the British Empire, forbode a day of tryal, in which under God nothing but strict virtue and inflexible fortitude can save us, from a rapacious and miserable distruction. A series of occurrances, many recent events, and especially the late Journals Of the House of Lords afford great reason to believe, that a Deep laid & desperate plan of Imperial despotism has been laid, and partly executed, for the extinction of all civil liberty; —— and from a gradual sapping the grand foundation from a subtle undermining the main pillars, breaking the strong bulwarks destroying the principal ramparts and battlements, the august and once revered, fortress of english freedom—the admirable work of ages,—the BRITISH CONSTITUTION seems fast tottering into a fatal & inevitable ruin. The dreadful catastrophe threatens universal havock, and presents an awful warning to hazard all if, peradventure, we in these distant confines of the Earth, may prevent being totally overwhelm'd and buried under the ruins of our most established rights. For many Years past we have with sorrow beheld the approaching conflict; various have been the causes, which pressed on this decisive period, and everything now conspires to prompt a full exertion of our utmost vigilance wisdom and firmness;—and as ye[2] exigencies of the times require, not only the refined abilities of true policy; but the more martial virtues; conduct valor and intrepidity; So, Gentlemen, in giving you our suffrages, at this Election, we have devolved upon you a most important trust; to discharge which we doubt not you will summon up the whole united faculties of mind and body.

We decline, Gentlemen, a minute detail of many momentous concernments, relative to which it is believed no Instructions need be given; but we shall express our thoughts on such matters as we suppose you will choose to have our explicit sentiments.

A Grievance which will early present itself in the ensuing Sessions (and to redress which you are to take all proper and spirited methods) is that of holding the General Court at Harvard College, not only against antient usage and established law, but also against the wellfare of that Seminary of learning, the happy advancement of which, this Province ever had and still have so much at heart.[3]

We would have you Gentlemen particularly Scrutinize into the wise and cautious transactions of our worthy Fathers of 1721. They, it should be known, in that year tho not directly called to weigh the high importance of the question, yet, on this very matter, behaved with a political foresight, and segacious circumspection, truly admirable and worthy imitation. The small pox then almost as pestilential as the plague, rendred the Meeting of the General Court in Boston morally impossible; yet so convinced was the Governor of the Province of his own defect of authority to remove the General Assembly out of Town, than when all the Members daring to attend the Court in that infectious season, were assembled in the Council Chamber, unable to make a quorum of the lower House, they were expressly assured by his Excellency that the proposed adjourning into the Country shown not be drawn into President. Accordingly a reliance doubtless being had on such solemn assurance, no objections appear entred on record against the Adjournment, when thro' a providential calamity, a transaction of business in the proper place was become really impracticable. No Proverb is more familiar, than that necessity knows no law; and the Court no doubt on this natural consideration was immediately adjourned out of this Town. Yet so universally sensible were the people of that duty, and especially the three branches of Legislature, that an act of the whole Court, even when such a fatal emergency had forced the Adjournment, absolutely requisite to legalize and capasitate for their proceedure to publick business:—and accordingly a vote passed the honourable House to that purpose, the same was concurred by his Majestys Council, and approved & formally assented to, by the Commander in Chief:—all which appears on the publick records of the Province. Now we should be glad to be informed, how these proceedings in essence sense and spirit, differ from a full ample and final denunciation of the law establishing the seat of Government.

We are not ignorant that in 1728/9 a controversy was forced on relative to this point. This dispute had its rise, like many of more modern date, in consequence of ministerial Instructions, which to borrow a phrase of the then House "are not pleasant to mention." We are not unacquainted that his Majestys Attorney and Solicitor General were at this time consulted relative to our legal seat of Government. We also know that the then Governor (Burnet), treating upon the same subject, informed the House of Representatives, that the *King Determined* the point," according to the Attorney General and "Solicitors opinion, that the SOLE *power* of dissolving, proroguing and adjourning *the* General Court or Assembly as to time or place is IN HIS MAJESTYS GOVERNOR, and that the reasons against it from the tenth of King William had no real foundation; *there being no clause in that Act laying any such restraint upon the Governor.*"

Here it should be well observed is not barely a tacit but an express declaration that the sole power of dissolving is "devolved entirely" *upon*, and exclusively vested "*in the Governor*" From hence in our opinion, this consequence unavoidably follows, that no Instructions orders or mandates whatever ought to direct and control *such power solely in the Governor.* For it is not merely absurd in theory, and most mischievous in practise, that an authority incapasitated by distance to Judge of local and other critical circumstances, should have a power to fix such an imporant movement, but moreover it is palpably contrarient to the plain words of the preceeding determination. We freely own it would have given us more satisfaction to have seen this opinion under the hand of those Lawyers. But we would here Gentlemen direct you carefully to notice and remember, that as we always expect to defend our own rights & libertys so we are unalterably fixed to Judge *for ourselves* of their real existence, agreable to law. Yet as we believe this same opinion is far from being well grounded, so we now offer a few comments thereon; for your future consideration. But let it be recorded that we enter upon this task, protesting against the pretended right or power of any Crown Lawyer, or any exterior authority upon Earth to determine, limit or ascertain all or any of our constitutional or charteral, natural or civil, political or sacred Rights, liberties and privileges or immunities. These words there being no clause in the "Act of 10th. of William laying any such *constraints* upon the Governor" contained in the afore cited opinion are, we conclude, intended to convey that as the Kings *prerogative* to remove the General Court at pleasure is not by express words taken away, so such a power remains inherent in the Crown. We do allow indeed that the Kings Prerogative was once thought "a topic too delicate and sacred to be profaned by the pen of a Subject, that it was ranked among the *areana imperrii* [state secrets], and like the misteries of the *bona dea* [good Roman goddess, connected with fertility] was not suffered to be pried into by any but such as were initiated into its Service: because perhaps the exertion of the one, like the solemnities of the other, would not bear the inspection of a rational & sober enquiry." We also have heard that there hath been a British Potentate who "dared to direct an English Parliament to abstain from discoursing of matters of state; that even that august assembly ought not to deal to Judge or to meddle with *Majestys Prerogative Royal*"—and James the first with his high notions of the Divinity of regal sway, more than once laid it down in his speeches, that "as it was athesm and blashemy in a Creature to dispute what the Deity might do so it is presumption and sedition in a subject to dispute what a King might do in the height of his powers; Good Christians, he adds, will be content with Gods will revealed in his word, and good Subjects will rest in the Kings will, revealed in HIS Law." Surely when such mistical Jargon, such absurd and infamous rant was thus openly denounced in a Realm famed for understanding, freedom and true magnanimitie, nothing except an ineffable contempt of the reigning Monarch diverted that indignant vengeance, which would otherwise have made his illustrious throne to tremble and hurl'd the Royal diadem from his forfeit head.

The Kings prerogative in its largest extent includes only certain rights and privileges which *by law* the King hath as a third power of the Commonwealth, intrusted with the execution of *laws already in being.* This prerogative our law pronounces to be *solely governed by the laws of the land*; those being the measure as well of the Kings power as the Subjects obedience. For as the laws assert & bound the Just rights of the King; so they likewise declare & maintain the Rights and liberties of the people; hence it is adjudged law, that all prerogatives must be for the advantage and good of the people, otherwise such pretended prerogatives are to be allowed by law. Even our Crown Lawyers will inform us "that one of the principal bulwarks of civil liberty, or in other words of the British constitution, is the limitation of the Kings prerogative by bounds so certain and notorious, that it is impossible he should ever exceed them, without the consent of the people on the one hand, or without on the other a violation of that original contract, which in all states implicidly and in ours most expressly subsists between the Prince and the Subject—And for a consideration of the extent and the restrictions of the Kings prerogative, this conclusion will evidently follow that the powers which are vested in the Crown by the Laws of England; are necessary for the support of society; and do not retrench any further on our *natural* rights then is expedient for the maintenance of our civil. Sir Henry Finch under Charles the first, tho' he lays down the law of prerogative in very strong and emphatical terms, yet qualifies it with a general restriction in regard to the liberties of the people.[4] The King (says he) hath a prerogative in all things that are not injurious to the Subject, *in them all* it must be remembered, that the *Kings prerogative stretcheth* not to the doing of any wrong. And finally the best definition of the *prerogative,* which our law books afford, is "that discretionary power of acting for the *public good* where the positive laws are silent" and if this discretionary power is abused to the publick detriment, such *prerogative* is exerted in an unconstitutional manner.[5]

We, Gentlemen, have been thus particular in our instructions on this head, because we apprehend that this point of prerogative thro' great inattention hath been much mistaken; and also because every *other* matter, set forth in the aforesaid opinion of Mr. Attorney and Solicitor General, has been irrefragably confuted by diverse Judicious replys of succeeding houses of Assembly.[6] Now the clear law laid down (to the spirit of which we do order you punctually to adhere) proves beyond a cavil, that if the late removal of our General Court was not against plain provincial law, yet that such removal is not only unwarrantable by the principles of Crown Law, but is directly repugnant to the fundamental institutions even of prerogative law—For will any one be so weak or wicked nay, will even a Crown lawyer for his stipend or pension have the front publicly to maintain, that the late alteration of the seat of our General Assembly is "for the advantage and good of the people," or "for the necessary support of society," or that this assumed "prerogative stretcheth not to any wrong." Now if all this, and much more, is not maintained, then waving our provincial law relative to the seat of government, we with good authority say, that the holding the General Court, from its antient and proper station, is unwarrantable, unconstitutional, illegal and oppressive. We have given you Gentlemen our full sentiments touching this important concern, because you ought not to be at any loss how to conduct your self herein conformable to the Judgment of your Constituents.—But had we not here spoken so largely, nay, had the express letter of the law been less favorable, & were it possible to romack up[7] any absurd, obsolete notion, which might have seemed calculated to propagate slavish doctrines, we should by no more means have been influenced to forego our birth rights. For the prime and only reason which originated all laws, but more particularly and expressly the prerogative, was the general emolument of the state, and therefore when any pretended prerogatives do not advance this grand purpose, they have no legal obligation; and when any strictly Just prerogatives are exerted to promote any different design, they also cease to be binding. Indeed was a Solicitor General of Majesty in an express treatise "of the Kings prerogative will teach us" that mankind will not be reasoned out of the feelings of humanity nor will sacrifice their liberty by a scrupulous adherence to those political maxims, which were originally established to preserve it.

The despicable situation of our provincial militia you will make the object of your peculiar attention; and as it is apparent From what putred source, this decline of military emulation hath flow'd, we press, that such animated steps may be taken as shall speedily remove this Just reproach from the land.—When every method is obstinately pursued to enervate with foreign luxuries, every artifice practised to corrupt, in order to inslave, when we are denyed a free constitutional exercise of our rights as Men and Citizens; when high handed invasions are made on our property, and audacious attempts to intimidate not only from resistance but complaint; surely the constitutional watchmen and centinels of our liberties are asleep upon their stations, or traitors to the main body, if they not rouse and risque from this insiduous plot.

As a laudable and voluntary renunciation of a baneful Commerce has naturally occasioned a general stagnation of trade; and as the true riches of a people are numbers and industry, we warmly recommend to you such measures as will tend to increase population, incourage industry and promote our own manufactures; and as this is a very pacifick political devise for the defeat of our malicious foes, we presume it may be less obnoxious to the virulent slander of ministerial dependants—but these salutary methods of genuine policy ought never to exclude or supersede the more open, manly, bold and pertenacious exertions for our freedom.

One of the most weighty matters, which attracts our affection, and lies deep in the heart of every honest, sensible American, is the firm and lasting union of the Colonies; There is no one point which ought more to engage our affectionate zeal. Our enemies well knowing the consequence of this great acquisition, have bent their whole force to render it abortive. Without the least foundation, Jealousies have been assiduously infused, diabolical falsehood forged, idle tales propogated, little discords fomented; and every engine that fraud could invent, and hardy villains manage, has been set to work in order to retard if not utterly overthrow this desirable atainment, but all has not done it. The Eyes of our worthy Brethren thro' the Continent are open. Yet as we know the plotting mallice, inveteracy & indefatigueable labour of the desperately wicked, we strongly inculcate that you be zealous to keep up a cordial intercourse, with our Sister Colonies; and as our interests are so apparently inseparable, nothing but an intimate Communion is requisite to cement our political and natural attachment.

We have for a long time beheld with grief and astonishment the unwarrantable practise of ministerial instructions to the Commanders in Chief of this Province; it is high time, Gentlemen, for this matter to be searched into and remidied.

Such an enormous stretch of power, if much longer unchecked, will eventually annihilate the essentials of all civil liberty. It is repugnant to the very first principle of true government (which was alone instituted for the good of the governed) that a remote power not only much disconnected but often different in interests should undertake at pleasure to controul any command in affairs of the last moment for the benefit and relief of the people—a power 3000 transmarine miles distant, not only ignorant of our true wellfare, but if perchance discovered, interested to oppose it; not only attempting to oppress, but actually oppressing—that such a power should be allowed, wontonly to proscribe patricians & plebeins, at will to fix the residence of our parliament; to order that parliament when and how to proceed, and where to retire; at one time to forbid the best improvement of our own produce, at another time effectually to force us to purchase forreign merchandize; and again, as it were, sword in hand, to demand our property; and anon to forbid our own disposal of a certain part of it.[8] These are doctrines & political solicisms which may take root and spring up, under the meridian of modern Rome; but we trust in God will not flourish in the soil and climate of British America. We therefore strictly charge you not to grant any supplys to the instruments of government, if through their defect or misapplication the grand end for which we support and pay our Rulers are not accomplished. We also recommend to you carefully to enquire into the state of criminal Prosecution in our executive courts; and endeavor to revive the antient method of appointing the Attorney General, agreable to charter; for we believe that such a step will be attended with very salutary consequences, in the advancement of public Justice, the punishment of offenders and the general good order of the Province.

Our choice of you Gentlemen to represent us at this hazardous Juncture is a sufficient evidence of our great dependence on your wise, honest and steady conduct. We therefore leave all other matters to your best discretion and Judgment; till we shall see fit to give further instructions. We greatly confide that you will bear in strong remembrance, the hardships and sufferings of our pious fathers, to find out and purchase this remote asslym from ecclesiastical persecution and civil tyranny; that inspired by their glorious example, you will vigorously repel even unto the uttermost the insults and violences of internal and external enemies to our peace. We remind you that the further Nations recede and give way to the gigantick strides of any powerful Despot, the more rapidly will the Fiend advance to spread wide desolation; and then should an attempt be made to stay his ravaging progress—the dogs of war let loose and hot for blood rush on to waste and havock![9] *Obsta principiis* is the maxim now held in view.[10] It is now no time to halt between two opinions: the demands of fraud, violence and usurpation are insatiable. It is therefore no season to stand listning to subtle alurements, deceitful cajolings, or formidable threatenings. We therefore enjoin you at all hazards to deport (as we rely your own hearts will stimulate) like the faithful Representatives of a freeborn, awakened and determined people—who being impregnated with the spirit of liberty in conception, and nurtured in principles of freedom from their infancy are resolved to breathe the same celestial ether, till summoned to resign the heavenly flame by that omnipotent God who gave it.

1. Record Commissioners of the City of Boston, *Boston Town Records, 1770–1777* (Boston: Rockwell and Churchill, 1887), pp. 23-32. I added commas and even a few periods to ease the reader's way through. The other committee members were Richard Dana, Joseph Warren, Joshua

Henshaw and Benjamin Kent. The newly-elected representatives were James Bowdoin, Thomas Cushing, Samuel Adams, and John Hancock. A handwritten copy is in QP 51 (also on reel 28 MHS), with various differences in spelling, capitalization, and punctuation. Unfortunately, various errors crept into the printed version, making Quincy's handwritten copy the better rendition. That that copy appears to be in Quincy's hand, and is in his papers, is of course not proof, in and of itself, that he was the primary author of the final draft of these instructions. Eliza Susan Quincy added a note to the folder holding the manuscript copy, commenting that Hutchinson, in the third volume of his history, had noted that this particular set of instructions "not only afforded a strong presage of the measures of the House, but, in words more open and express than those that had been before ventured on, indicated to government in England the design of a general revolt, and excited the first measures taken with an apparent design to guard against it." See Thomas Hutchinson, *The History of the Province of Massachusetts-Bay,* 3 vols. (Cambridge, Mass.: The Belknap Press of Harvard University Press, 1936), 3:209, and the text itself in Appendix R, pp. 370–77, with the expected changes to capitalization found in a later printing; edited by Lawrence Mayo. Eliza Susan left out part of Hutchinson's sentence in her note.

2. Quincy, who often used "ye" instead of "the," in this case actually wrote the latter.

3. Donald C. Lord and Robert M. Calhoon discuss this dispute in "The Removal of the Massachusetts General Court from Boston, 1769–1772," *Journal of American History* 55 (1969):735–55.

4. Sir Henry Finch, *A Description of the Common Laws of England* (London: A. Millar, 1759), p. 57, from the Second Book, Chapter 1, "Of the Common Law, Customs, Prerogative, and Estates." Finch, who died in 1625, the first year of Charles's reign, was a barrister affiliated with Gray's Inn.

5. As taken from Blackstone's *Commentaries,* Book I, Chapter 7, 1:244, "Of the King's Prerogative."

6. The House challenged Hutchinson, as it had Francis Bernard before him, to provide the basis for his authority to move the General Court from Boston to Cambridge. Hutchinson responded that the attorney general and solicitor general supported him—in effect, giving him legal backing. To which the House replied on 31 July 1770: "The opinion of the Attorney and Solicitor General has very little weight with this House in any case, any further, than the reasons which they expressly give, are convincing. This province has suffered so much by unjust, groundless, and illegal opinions of those officers of the Crown, that our veneration, or reverence for their opinions, is much abated." In other words, the House would determine for itself what was legal and what was not, thereby drawing a line in the political sand. *Journals of the House of Representatives of Massachusetts,* 55 vols. (Boston: Massachusetts Historical Society, 1919–1990), 47:64.

7. Bring to light by rummaging about.

8. Quincy wrote in his copy this comment in the margin: "See some extraordinary proceedings at the late sessions of the General Court relative to the manufactory house."

9. Marc Antony, having done nothing to stop the conspirators from assassinating Caesar in the Senate, returns to the scene of the crime and, with the lines that inspired this phrase, announces his plot against the plotters, his intention to wreak bloody vengeance, in Shakespeare's *Julius Caesar,* Act III, Scene 1.

10. Quincy wrote "Obsta Principiis" twice in the margins of his political commonplace book. See Coquillette and York, eds., *Portrait of a Patriot,* 1:125, abbreviated to "Obsta Prin." in another entry at p. 12. Also see ibid., p. 96, n. 3, for John Adams's use of the phrase in one of his "Novanglus" essays in early 1775. The admonition had probably become familiar to both men as they learned legal Latin, which means to resist or withstand from the beginning in order to nip the undesirable in the bud.

"AN OLD MAN"

6 August 1770[1]

The fittest Time to corrupt a Man's Wife,
is when she's fallen out with her Husband.
SHAKESPEAR.[2]

WHAT this great master of the human heart pronounces concerning the dearest connections in life, is equally true, when applied to every other social union. And those great villains, who have degraded the human species by their infernal practices, have even tread upon that grand principle of corruption. No tyrant could plunder and slaughter, if union in resistance opposed his ravage. One would think, that at this period of the world, mankind could need no instructions on this head. The greatest ornaments of the world have foretold the mischiefs of discord, and the annals of all countries confirm those interesting truths; yet the ingenuous and unwary are still frequently off their guard. The wiles of iniquity are so many and various; the snare is so deep laid and artfully covered; that fraud will insure success in those schemes, which power could never effect. Hence we find, that tyranny & oppression in their first approach always come disguised, in some friendly appearance, and the emissaries of power and rapine ransack earth and hell for plausible pretexts of their first advances: And the progress from the admission of unlawful controul to the full sway of despotic usurpation, is so insidious and rapid, that mankind are trampled upon and butchered, before they have time to meditate their deliverance. Good GOD! How is it possible for a sensible people to think of relaxing their vigilance a moment, when they all hear the clank of their shackles, and see the fiend entering the door! Are not the monitions of your best, your *disinterested* friends, enough to alarm you? Does not the miseries of a parent country awaken? Has the historic page no instruction? Did not the nobility and people of England at first oppose those encroachments and burdens, under the pressure of which, they now tremblingly despond?—But their weakness—their wickedness—their infamy remains—they became corrupt, they were sold and bought—they are—Oh my heart! a dagger for the bowels of every traitor!—and GOD knows hundreds could be *honestly* bestowed!

I need not inform my countrymen who inhabit near this metropolis, of the malevolence and obstinate perseverance of the enemies of our Israel. Their conduct has been uniformly treacherous and abandoned. Yet I will offer a few thoughts to the public, on some late artful efforts to tempt us to precipitate into ruin. A belief of their success does not so much move me, as a certain knowledge of the baseness and infamy of the agents: for surely, we have been wanting in observation indeed, if we have not frequently noticed, who among us are of the tribe of Issachar.[3] Notwithstanding the pretended variation of their attacks, the views, motives and actions of the tribe, have been pretty generally seen through. Even that arch fiend of the North, whose baleful influence did heretofore frequently reign, has at last discovered his cloven foot; his duplicity is detected, his nakedness is seen, and his odious form driven from all good men, seems in the course of nature, but a little way from that bottomless pit, where the *father of lies* must be bound his thousand years.[4]

It is a great truth, that in an age like this, more self-denying virtue is necessary, to entirely cease the importation of British manufactures, than to wade thro' crimson gore, in hot pursuit of our worst enemies. Every wound we received in such a conflict, would revive our indignation, and every drop of vital blood from such foes would inspire and invigorate our heart. Such is human nature! The glorious spirit of extirminating from the earth, it's reproach and scourge, would inspire enthusiasm, and a noble death would happily deliver us from slavery, and be an acceptable sacrifice to our dear country.

It is the great unhappiness of man, that the fruition of a small good, when present, is often preferred to the highest acquisitions when remote. Hence every day, we find a momentary gratification is hazarded at the risque of the future; tho' eternal, vengeance. Sensible of this, and in order to take advantage of a weakness too predominant in the human mind, the ministerial faction, in America, are perpetually declaiming on the stagnation of trade, and the poverty arising from a decline of British commerce. As, if that commercial intercourse was our *summum bonum*, & foreign manufactures the grand *desiderata* of Americans. When no truth is more apparent, or oftener conceded, than this, that the stoppage of importation is to the great general emolument of the colonies, however detrimental to a few individuals. Now allowing the plea of commercial poverty its full extent, surely the sacrifice of the *few* is far more eligible than that of the *many*. And a community convinced of its true, nay, its only interest will never hesitate, whether to forego the public welfare and become compleat bond-men, rather than occasion the rise or fall of stock; or an alteration in the balance of exchange.

A wise people will inquire thoro'ly into every scheme proposed for their adoption, and when its baneful or salutary effect is discerned, will be inflexible in their resolutions. A nation would be mad indeed should they see, as in the meridian sun, a design to enslave them, and after a feeble opposition be cajoled or bullied into timid acquiescence. But their disgrace would be singularly infamous and deplorable should they tamely surrender their birthrights to pimpls, parasites and harpies, when their solemn protestations of resistance, to their hearts-blood, had been registered in the records of eternity. Dead also must they be to every moral sentiment should they be actuated to commit the most atrocious crime by a fondness and a precipatude to imitate the perfidy of others. Surely it is to good men and christians a strange doctrine, that the villainy of one part of society is a sanction for the wickedness of the residue. Men, who have a genuine attachment to their most important concernments will examine, what is their duty, and what the Lord their God requireth of them; and then will walk as a well informed conscience shall dictate. On such men alone, under GOD, do we depend: On those, who despising the disingenuity of fraudulent subterfuge, will persevere with untainted probity to the end.

There is no one argument, founded on *right* principles, which heretofore was urged in favour of our disuse of British commodities, but what now subsists in its primary force. Hence every defection, whether of individuals or communities, from former pretences of supporting our common liberties, is an open disclosure of consummate ignorance, deep hypocrisy or deliberate and exquisite malice.

We have been verging an unexpected length of time to that trying period, which is to delineate and mark forever our true characters. If we are blind, we shall surely be deluded;—if discerning, we shall escape the snare. If we are pusillanimous wretches, we may easily be frightened; if brave our courage, vigour and stability will accumulate strength by opposition. And let those who fear the wants arising from loss of trade, remember the toils and labours of their forefathers, and blush, when they repine at fancied miseries. If it did not move our derision, it would excite the sharpest anger to hear the difficulties, we now sustain, mentioned with a complaining regret. Good God! Consider my fellowmen, what you are strugling for—consider what you oppose and what you seek!—In defending your fair inheritance, it is impossible for you to suffer half the pains and sorrows, your pious ancestors bore, in the arduous acquisition.

In short, my friends, you have nothing to fear, but the deceitfulness of your own heart and the variegated and unremitting malevolence of your enemies. Struggle with half the spirit and obstinacy to save yourselves, that they seek to destroy you, and victory will crown you with success.—You have often been enlightened, and often been warned. It is your own fault, if you do not discern, if you do not avoid destruction.

Shall then the wretch, whose dastard heart
Shrinks at a Tyrant's nobler part,
  And only dares betray;
With reptile wiles, alas! prevail,
Where force, and rage, and priest-craft fail
To pilfer power away?[5]

AN OLD MAN.

1. *Boston Gazette,* 6 August 1770, taking the first column and a half on p. 1.

2. *Coriolanus,* Act IV, Scene 3, Nicanor, the Roman, to Adrian, a Volscian, as he comments on the unrest in Rome and Coriolanus's banishment. Coriolanus (Caius Martius), once Rome's great battlefield hero, has been betrayed by rivals in Rome. He allied himself with former enemies in Volsci for revenge, ultimately relents, and is slain by those former enemies, now supposed allies, who felt in their turn betrayed.

3. Issachar was one of the twelve tribes of Israel (because one of Jacob's twelve sons), being used here for a sarcastic aside, a jab at would-be scholars or those who thought they knew best.

4. Apparently a poke at the Earl of Bute, long out of power but still a symbol of the corruption of court politics at Whitehall because of his supposed influence on an impressionable George III. If Bute was the intended target—Hutchinson, in this instance, seems unlikely, given the "North" (Scotland) reference—Quincy was simply following the lead of opposition members of Parliament. For Bute and Hutchinson as scapegoats see Peter Shaw, *American Patriots and the Rituals of Revolution* (Cambridge, Mass.: Harvard University press, 1981), an intriguing attempt at psychohistorical explanation that nevertheless goes too far in asserting that "Quincy's politics began and ended with Thomas Hutchinson." (p. 153) Michael Wynn Jones, *The Cartoon History of the American Revolution* (London: London Editions Limited, 1975) reproduces various broadsides where an image of Bute—identifiable by Scottish garb (tam, kilt, broadsword, or the like)—was used to criticize policies coming out of Whitehall and Westminster, despite the fact that he had had little to do with them.

5. Nugent, *Ode to Mankind*, p. 12.

"MENTOR"

11 February 1771[1]

To the Publishers of the BOSTON EVENING-POST.

No despotic government can ever *subsist* without that support of the *instrument* of tyranny and oppression, a STANDING ARMY. For all *illegal* power must be supported by the *SAME MEANS* by which it was *at first* acquired.

MONTAGU.[2]

AS the month of March is so nigh at hand, I have wondered to hear so little discourse, relative to a decent, manly and instructive commemoration of the melancholy tragedy of the last year.

I think it will be agreed on *all sides,* that the fatal effects of *standing armies and quartering troops in populous cities,* are apparent from the various transactions, which took place, while the soldiery were stationed in this town; and more especially from the mournful catastrophe of last March. However we may differ in opinion concerning the real *state of facts,* as they existed between the *agents* on the unhappy evening, yet surely none will deny, that such consequences were easily deducible, for such effects naturally flowed, from such causes.

A strict research into remote antiquity will teach the ends of making *the military* a *distinct* body in the state; and even a cursory retrospection on the conduct of our ancestors will show their wisdom, jealousy, fore-cast, nay *spirit of prophecy,* touching this important manoeuvre of state-*cunning.**—Equally instructive also will be an attention to the state of former nations, on the establishment and use of disciplined armies:—nor of less import is it to recollect and remember British history, as to this formidable engine of tyranny.

How happily might these, and other similar ideas be awakened at the approaching anniversary of the fifth of March. To call to mind the deeds of our fathers, and at stated periods to review the complicated machinery of government, is certainly a very profitable and interesting duty. It serves, among other valuable purposes, to call forth our notice of matters, which would otherwise escape our observation; to imprint on the mind of the rising youth (the hopes of their country) those truths which serve as governing directories of future life; it gives a check to that incroaching and aspiring lust of domination, which, more or less, actuates the great and powerful in every community.—If these were all the good ends such an annual commemoration would answer, it ought not to be omitted; but the one half has not been told: those who are acquainted with the affections and movements of the human heart will supply the residue.

I therefore propose it to the understanding and discreet, as well as the zealous, friends of liberty and mankind, that a regular plan be formed for an annual & solemn remembrance of the 5th of March.

I would speak my own mind on this occasion with freedom, tho' with becoming diffidence. And I own, that in my present view of the matter, it seems to be expedient to *exclude,* the reverend and worthy gentlemen of the Clergy from being concerned in any part of the exercises of the day. This proposed *exclusion* does not arise from any aversion to that useful order of men, or from any doubt of their learning, integrity or fortitude. But I conceive that this celebration ought to be considered and conducted solely with a reference to *civil* society and domestick policy. And it is in general, perhaps, of little advantage to true religion, or good government, that the clergy should interfere in matters purely temporal, and wholly affecting social compacts and political oeconomy.

It may therefore be proper to chuse two persons to deliver (one in the forenoon and the other in the afternoon) a dissertation on—THE POLICY OF STANDING ARMIES; AND THE NATURAL TENDENCY OF QUARTERING REGULAR TROOPS IN POPULOUS CITIES IN TIME OF PEACE.—This choice should be at such a convenient time as to give the speaker opportunity to mature his thoughts, digest his arguments and form his diction. By this means, it is likely the performance will be devoid of crude sentiments and inelegant language; and if the audience are not instructed with a sensible, judicious and useful disquisition on so important subjects, yet their time will not be wholly misemployed in giving countenance to those efforts of genius, which may throw some new ray of light upon those sciences, the knowledge of which can never be too generally diffused, or too universally inculcated.—But might we indulge the pleasing hopes, that on these occasions some rising worthy, some genius yet unborn, will pervade the mazy system and perplexed labyrinth of fraud and usurpation;—that will rescue one right from the jaws of power, and restore one liberty to oppressed mankind;—how would the flattering thought inspire our hearts—how would grateful millions bless the institution!

Many benefits resulting from this plan, I decline pointing out; of some plausible objections I am aware, but do not think myself obliged, at present, to obviate them. I have offered my sentiments in a manner becoming a good citizen:—they claim, I trust, some small attention. What is proposed with decency is intitled to candid treatment; but ill-placed ridicule, illiberal and censorious dogmatism, never promoted the cause of GOD or man.

MENTOR.

*Cunning, says Lord Bacon, is a sort of *left-handed* wisdom.

1. *Boston-Evening Post,* 11 February 1771, filling the first column of three, carrying over to part of the second.

2. This passage from E[dward] W[ortley] Montagu, *Reflections on the Rise and Fall of the Antient Republicks* (London: A. Millar, 1759), p. 153, is in the political commonplace book, and the title is listed in the "Catalogue of Books." See Coquillette and York, eds., *Portrait of a Patriot,* 1:102 and 5:898 (no. 233), resp.

"INTELLIGENTIBUS"

20 May 1771[1]

INTELLIGENTIBUS

At last August Term, continued by Adjournment to December 1770, the honorable Justices of the Superiour Court, passed the following Order.

"ORDERED, That it be recommended to the Court of General Sessions of the Peace to make the Jurors, that were impannelled and sworn for the Trials of Capt. Thomas Preston, Esq; and the Soldiers, as also the Officers who kept them, a reasonable Allowance for said Service: said Preston's Trial holding six Days, and said Soldiers nine Days; said Juries being kept together every Night by two or more Officers."

In consequence of this order, the jurors above named petitioned the Court of Sessions, for the above allowance; and the court having a doubt of their power touching the grant of the prayer thereof, ordered the petition to stand over for argument at the sessions in April:—and on last Wednesday THE POWER OF THE COURT to grant the prayer of the petition was argued by four gentlemen of the bar (pro and con) by desire of the honorable justices of the sessions.

It seemed agreed by bench and bar, that the only power of the sessions to *grant monies* must be derived from *provincial* law; that such a power could be derived from no where else.—And the QUESTION was, whether the act of 4 of W. & M. C. 12. gave the Court a power to grant monies for the allowance before mentioned?

The act is intitled "an act for the settlement of the bounds, and defraying the PUBLICK and NECESSARY CHARGES *arising within each respective county* in this province."

"And for the due and equal *raising of monies* for *defraying of the charges arising within each respective county* for the necessary repairs and amendments of bridges, prisons, the maintainance of poor prisoners, and ALL OTHER PROPER COUNTY CHARGES: It is enacted, that when and so often as there shall be NEED OF RAISING MONEY FOR THE ENDS AFORESAID in any county, the justices in quarter sessions for such county, receiving information thereof from the county-treasurer, shall agree and determine the whole sum to be raised, &c. and issue their orders, &c. to assess the same upon the inhabitants," &c.

The debates, at the bar, took up the day. And the justices, after this solemn hearing, (Mr. Justice Dunbar only doubting), were unanimously of opinion, that the prayer of the petition of the jurors should not be granted; and the petition was accordingly dismissed.

It gives a most sensible pleasure, *in these times,* to find a court of justice, deciding a *point of law,* against an extension of *their power: especially as* that power would affect *the purse of the subject.*—This decision is of no small moment: It's importance will appear, more conspicuous upon a close examen and reflection. However, it is yet a matter of deep concern with some, that the Superiour Court seem to entertain a different opinion on the point in question. They *ordered a recommendation of this allowance to be made:* They are presumed to know the law; and we are willing to suppose they would not *influence,* and *much less recommend* to a subordinate court, the exertion of an *illegal power;* a power derogatory to the natural and primary right of the subject over his property; and of the highest consequence to the community, considered in a seperate or collective view.

The EXISTENCE and EXERTION of such a power in the sessions are of very extensive concernment: We, therefore, imagine all due consideration was had at passing the above *order of recommendation:*—and, if so, does not a becoming deference to the Supreme Court lead us to conjecture, that they were of opinion, that the court of sessions was *by law* vested *with power to take money out of the pockets of the people* to make that *allowance,* which it was thought expedient thus *formally to recommend?*[2]

1. *Boston Gazette,* 20 May 1771, p. 2, filling just over half of the third column. Quincy uses this particular pen name to enlist readers in his cause, translated as, "to those who know" or "those who understand." My thanks to Professor Paul Rahe for suggesting this reading of the word, in the dative case.

2. This case resulted from the October 1770 trial of Captain Thomas Preston, and, following him nearly a month later, that of eight enlisted men also accused of murder in the Boston "Massacre" of 5 March 1770. Quincy was of course deeply involved in both trials as a counsel for the defense. His summary of the subsequent May 1771 case involving a petition from the jurors for payment, which he essentially repeated for newspaper readers in the piece above, is in Coquillette and York, eds., *Portrait of a Patriot,* 5:798–807, 847–48 (with the text of "Intelligentibus" being reproduced from the *Boston Gazette* on p. 807).

"TERTIUS IN NUBIBUS"

20 May 1771[1]

Messieurs EDES & GILL,

YESTERDAY, *immediately*, after public worship, Charles Paxton, Esq.; a commissioner of the customs, waited on his Excellency at the Province House. The good people of the town suppose something of great importance *to the people* under his excellency's administration, must have given rise to this *friendly* interview, at a season especially set apart, for the service of GOD. It is of great consequence for the subject to know, when publick affairs are so urgent as to require a portion of holy time for their dispatch; and therefore we wish that when the officers of the crown are to advise, consult, &c. upon the Sabbath, that they would appear in the face of day, and not sneak thro' *the covered way* or a by-alley. It had a bad look. People are *jealous* at these times. No wonder:—These are times of court-addresses—not to say adorations: and *panting lovers* are always *jealous* of their *mistresses*.

However no good and liege-man will dare suspect his Excellency of a wanton breach of the Lord's-Day—"Who contrived, framed, and got passed into a law the W rd-n A-t?"[2]—Who in a populous assembly asserted in support of the same act, that the Sabbath was *no where* so remissly kept as in this town; an assertion as remarkable for it's truth, as for the unhypocritical gravity with which it was delivered?—May the just reward of such unfeigned *regard for religion,* without one interested view to that popularity or HONOUR, *which his Excellency has experienced in this life,* prepare him for the smiles of that master, who abhors hypocrisy, slavery and tyranny.

May 13th 1771

TERTIUS IN NUBIBUS.

1. Latin for "third in the clouds," from the *Boston Gazette,* 20 May 1771, p. 3, the same issue as the preceding piece by "Intelligentibus." It is Quincy's shortest newspaper essay ever to be printed in the *Boston Gazette* (if, again, Eliza Susan Quincy's attributions are taken as the source). Could it be that Quincy mocked Hutchinson so subtly that Hutchinson himself might have wondered what he meant—that he was accusing the Governor of thinking he was on the same level as the Father and the Son, when it came to deciding how the Sabbath ought to be observed?

2. The "Warden Act" alluded to a 1761 law stipulating that towns appoint wardens to make sure people observed "the Lord's Day" each week.

"HYPERION"

25 November 1771[1]

Messieurs EDES & GILL,

Please to insert the following,

To the Man whom Conscience forbids to stile my Governor.

SIR,

A Patriot Prince on his death bed left this sage admonition to his heir; "Beware my son of *doing wrong* to any one *yourself;* or of suffering any one (particularly *your servant)* to do wrong to others: For one wrong *done* or *connived* at by you, will produce a million by its example; and each of these will multiply others, in their justification or defence."

How happy had it been for you, Sir, had you made this sentiment your own at setting out in life! The moderate share of genius you possess, if *warmed* with a *love* of *Right,* and animated with that *benevolence* for your *fellow creatures,* which *exalts* the human mind above its *little self,* would have rendered you beloved, if not considerably admired.

Give me leave, Sir, to imagine your undebauched heart then glowing towards your countrymen with the feelings of a christian, and judgment of a man. What rapture would have returned upon your mind from considering yourself in league with the Deity, an instrument in his hand to diffuse his blessings impartially among his people? A virtuous habit, would have preserved a humane sympathy with every sensitive being within your knowledge.

This you may say would have given you trouble and some degree of pain, but surely the pleasures arising from that *peace* which passeth all understanding, would have been to you an exceeding great reward.

Are riches the desire of your eyes? In the right hand of wisdom and virtue are riches, yea, durable riches, and pleasures for evermore—Does power inflame your ambition? Consider you can be but a subordinate ruler, you must please a master, or be at lest '*dismissed* and *punished*', let the denunciation seem as grating to you as it will; and who so great, so powerful or honorable a master as the King of Kings, who requires you on pain of his highest displeasure, to govern this great people as one that must give an account? The meanest peasant is as much the darling of heaven as the finest courtier—Is honor (*a good name)* better to you than silver? You cannot certainly expect much of this, from ensuring to yourself the reputation of having the principal hand in subverting the constitution of your country—Is a good conscience a most cordial companion through life, and a comforting stay to the soul, when, sublunary things receeding, the DIVINITY *enlarges* upon the mind? This is only to be maintained in *doing unto others*, as by change of circumstance you would *wish them to do unto you.* A timely check to the *rabies dominandi* which early infected your mind, would have secured you all these. But alas such a conquest as this was too hard for a stripling, who early confessed he had sucked *prerogative milk,* and observed *it would never be good times till the landed interest was got into few hands*—Who with the celebrated Claudia felt always a sovereign contempt for the *scoundrel mob*, meaning by these the bulk of the citizens.

Were you ignorant of the numberless and inconceivable calamities, usurpation, tyranny and oppression, inevitably bring upon a brave & free people, I should pity your head, & in some measure excuse your heart. But I presume you would as readily ruin me for discovering a doubt of your capacity as integrity, or may I add, humanity? Indeed while I am upon that head, I know not how I can expect to escape destruction from you in one shape or other, if you proceed in the manner you are now said to be going on. If you can of your own motion, without the pretence of one iota of authority for it, erect yourself and as many as you please of your council into a court of judicature, and barely on suspicion, hale a gentleman before you to answer for an affront pretended to be offered yourself: Nay some go so far as to say, that even during this process *pendente lite*[2] before you, the same atrocious crime (no doubt as *dangerous* to the very *being of government,* as was the modest address to governor Bernard, which made so much noise a day or two) is to be bro't *by information* before another tribunal. It also seems the matter is to be remarkably *hurried* along, and threats we hear are given out, that if any attorney dares to vindicate the publication, he shall be thrown over the bar. Here Sir, my text most remarkably applies itself. How *terrible* a thing is it for a little tyrant to begin a deviation from the beaten path of his duty! One would think that a people who in seven years had been declared *controulable* in every action, taxable i. e. *deprivable* of every farthing, liable to the imposition of an indefinite number of revenue officers, invested with such powers as destroy utterly the notion of a man's house being his castle, and this too augmented by the virtue of those baleful death warrants to the constitution, called writs of assistance, to all the wanton exertions of a pretended prerogative in the hands of a ministerial creature, to a fleet and standing army to carry these dreadful measures into execution; to a seizure of the principal fortress in the dominion, and garrisoning it with troops utterly independent of the legislature of the province; to the virtual, absolute incapacitation of that legislative to act with any efficacy, for the protection of the rights of their constituents; one I say would have thought that such a people allowed to be sensible enough, in all the foregoing trials of temper, would hardly be irritated anew, with an entire invasion of every remaining security that ever a Caracalla or a Dionisius of Sicily could wish to deprive them of at once.[3] If perhaps one oppression will make a *wise man mad,* what must be the outrage and despair of a people over whom the coercive power is absolute, and by them uncontroulable; where grievances may be multiplied by millions, and even the most fundamental of them cannot be so much as enquired into without exposing a worthy citizen to the unconstitutional hardship of suffering a persecution in the *Star-Chamber* mode of prosecuting by information, and even then deprived of counsel for his defence: If menaces of loss of living, can deter men of conscience and spirit from stemming the torrent which aims to sweep off the last resource of the wretched, the opportunity of complaint; surely, Sir, these steps are alarming; these strides are very rapid.

What hope, Sir, have we left, if our representatives are reduced to cyphers, with whom it seems you have very little business, however universal and earnest be the complaints of the people of a long neglect of most interesting matters to them: If our courts of Justice be filled with expectants, of whose behavior no Printer is by me requested to advertise the world, having already thoroughly established its own reputation, without the pains. If denied of that inestimable and indefeasible birthright of an Englishman, which secures to him his liberty and fame, 'till a majority of twenty-four of the grand inquest of his county find him guilty of a crime, if put to the difficulty of sending to another government for lawyers to defend us, and after that harassed with prosecutions in such distant countries as are supposed to have pliant jurors?

You know, Sir, that to prevent such cruel treatment of man to man as this, government itself was instituted; and I cannot realise it yet, that you could bear to contemplate the horror and confusion, perhaps carnage and desolation, that might follow such a train of most glaring injustice and intolerable stretch of power!

Your party gives out that you have not a fair chance if a bill is presented to a grand jury, having found the aversion of these sort of people to the star chamber law of libels, which holds the *truest* representation of the villainy of any ruler to be the most *false*, scandalous and seditious libel upon government itself. Had you compared small things with great, you might have been ashamed to have attacked the press for telling you in a pretty indeterminate hypothetical way, what all the world believes true to a tittle. The very notice you take of it confirms it to every one! Call me a *seditious incendiary*, a fellow of *no property* who aims at nothing but a *revolution* in the *state* that he may enrich himself with the substance of others, I laugh at the pointless invective: And how dirt can stick to such excellent hands, as some say you possess, rather than mine, may be accounted for by your vindicators, if any of them please to undertake it. Your master has been treated with ten times the freedom you have been, and of late has declared his aversion to meddle with the press any further.

The King of Prussia ordered the paper which reproach'd him bitterly to be stuck up again; but well does Montesquieu observe that petty sovereigns are much more irritable than great one's; the reason is plain. But considering the advantage you have over him in one shape, and the uneasy terms on which you hold this odious, this formidable tenure, 'tis no wonder you endeavor to rid your side of such a pricking thorn. Were I in your place, I would tremble at being tho't a *usurper*, and knowing that I was incapable of denying that I held more power than was possibly reconcileable with any idea of freedom in the people I governed. The case between Mucius and you is as short and plain as an honest man could wish.[4] Should it be determined by a *grand* and *petty jury* of this county, that you are a governor *nominated* and *appointed*, only, by the King, and such a one, as holds no powers inconsistent with the liberty and security of men entitled to all the privileges of natural born subjects of Great-Britain, they will undoubtedly find him guilty of writing and publishing a *false*, scandalous and seditious libel against you. But on the contrary, should they in conscience believe you are in possession of an independency unknown even to your master; and that independency assumed in downright opposition to the will of the people you govern, and exactly reversive of their and your conditions; i. e. that whereas your constitutional condition is that of a servant, your assumed one, is that of an uncontroulable despot, they will be hard set to find the *falshood:* And if you cannot bear to be told of such attrocious crimes as conspiring the destruction of so great a people, for the gratification of a humour becoming only the Devil himself, to vex and torment; and directed in a like manner more especially at the most noble, disinterested and virtuous members of the community, do not further deserve it.

All men of sense must be convinced of the badness of your cause when you discover a reluctance to leave it to the legal determination of an impartial grand jury. If you deny they are impartial, the implication is strong against you, that you are driving measures alarming to the whole community; and such as writers ought to be rewarded rather than punished for exposing to every one. They know that a free Press can never hurt an honest man; and I presume the secretion of the crimes of a traitor or usurper from the knowledge of the public, will not yet become a public engagement.

Could yourself or any one for you, deny a tittle laid to your charge, or set your behaviour in any thing of a better light than we receive it from those authors your tools affect to call the *faction,* it would certainly be attended to; but the complement of our freedom of complaint, is too important, to be made to any man, much less a man to whom this province feels so little obligation. It would be infernal injustice to hinder your puppey to yelp in proportion to the pain you gave him by trampling on him; and if Englishmen will bear a treatment too base for a puppey, they may yelp to eternity under your tramplings, without the pity or further regard of their much neglected monitor.

HYPERION.

P.S. A certain writer addressing a great man in a situation similar to your's says, "You have voluntarily abdicated the *love* of this people, & have rendered yourself too ridiculous to move their *fears.*" If your privy council persuade you otherwise, pursue your malicious prosecution in your *own way,* and it will at least ensure the sale of another edition of Zenger's trial with additions, &c.[5]

1. *Boston Gazette,* 25 November 1771, on p. 2, filling most of the second column and all of the third. Boston shopkeeper Harbottle Dorr, Jr., Quincy's contemporary and a Son of Liberty, marked his copy "By Dr. Young"—Thomas Young. Dorr did not mark the earlier "Hyperion" pieces in his collection that way; he did identify Quincy as the author behind "Marchmont Nedham (on 8 June 1772, and later issues). See the *Harbottle Dorr Collection of Annotated Massachusetts Newspapers, 1765–1776,* 4 reels microfilm (Boston: Massachusetts Historical Society, 1966); and Bernard Bailyn, "The Index and Commentaries of Harbottle Dorr," *Proceedings of the*

Massachusetts Historical Society 85 (1973):21–35. Was Dorr right and Eliza Susan Quincy wrong? We may never know.

2. More legal Latin: a pending action or litigation, which Hutchinson, serving until recently as chief justice, would have understood.

3. Caracalla (a nickname; more formally, Marcus Aurelius Severus Antoninus Augustus), a Roman emperor whose reign in the early third century CE was noted for barbarity and cruelty, he having murdered his own younger brother to become sole ruler after their father (Septimius Severus) died. He eventually would be assassinated as well. Dionysius, onetime student of Plato in Athens, fell far short of ruling Syracuse as Plato's idealized philosopher king in the 4th century BCE. Deposed, he died in exile, a victim of his own violent and greedy ways, a petty tyrant—like his father before him.

4. Hutchinson wanted to silence "Mucius Scaevola," whose essays began appearing in the *Massachusetts Spy* on 30 May 1771. In Hutchinson's view press freedom extended only to forbidding prior restraint; anything appearing in the press critical of government policy he believed could be prosecuted for seditious libel. A grand jury refused to indict Isaiah Thomas, the *Spy*'s printer, and Hutchinson decided not to attempt a prosecution of the paper by pressuring the attorney general to proceed on the basis of an "information" (accusation). "Mucius Scaevola" continued to appear in the *Spy*. For details see York, "Tag-Team Polemics," pp. 93–105.

5. I have not been able to locate the source that Quincy quoted at the beginning of this postscript. Accounts of the famous 1735 libel case prosecuted against John Peter Zenger in New York had appeared in pamphlet form in at least three different editions since that time; hence Quincy's reference. The best modern version is Stanley Nider Katz, ed., *A Brief Narrative of the Case and Trial of John Peter Zenger* (Cambridge, Mass.: Belknap Press of the Harvard University Press, 1972); and it figures in Leonard Levy's discussion of *The Emergence of a Free Press* (New York: Oxford University Press, 1985). There Levy revises some of the arguments that he had made in an earlier book on the subject. Also see Jeffrey A. Smith, *Printers and Press Freedom* (New York: Oxford University Press, 1988). The Zenger case helped strengthen the idea that truth can be a defense for printers, but the burden of truth was still on defendants and the Zenger case did not serve as a formal precedent for press freedom cases in other colonies or in England either.

"CALLLISTHENES"

10 February 1772[1]

Messieurs EDES & GILL,

WE have heard much in our public prints of the *exemplary* treatment of one EBENEZER RICHARDSON, who many months ago, was in due course of law found guilty of wilful murder. It has never been pretended that the jury of trial were infamous or corrupted. We have frequently had broad hints, that political motives influenced to a delay of judgment and execution of this criminal: This matter ought to be seriously considered by the whole community.[2] If political views should ever actuate the Judges of the land, who have the lives, liberty and property of us all in their power, society is worse than a state of nature: because the members of it have a greater opportunity, more abilities to do mischief, less danger of detection, and a more flattering prospect of impunity. These are incitements to villainy, which human nature in it's present state cannot withstand.—To consider the dangers to which citizens are exposed, when justice is retarded, and the course of the laws diverted by the power and influence of the great and guilty, is the duty of all good men.

Do, my countrymen, use the faculties, which GOD has given you—think—weigh—and *consider.*

Punishment loses it's efficacy, when it does not immediately overtake the criminal. A delay in punishing, begets either a doubt of the heinousness of the crime, the truth of the fact, or the integrity of administration. It is a bad omen, when this takes place.

A subject should never have reason to believe that those who are set over him, are deserving of the halter and gibbet. This he will be prone to do, when he can account for the manoeuvres of the magistrate upon no principle of reason, law, good conscience or policy.

A goal was never intended for punishment; but only to hold the *debtor,* till he fulfilled his voluntary contracts; *the Suspected*, till his offence could be conveniently ascertained; and *the convicted,* till speedy justice could be executed.

Being a citizen of the world, I cite no mouldy authors to confirm my observations:—the book of nature and volume of society are my authorities. The well-tempered substance contained in *these,* are too elastic to suffer by the wrestings and twistings of a black gown or a scarlet robe: I have often smiled, to see grave and learned lawyers, cite and recite, as if they thought all wisdom existed a century ago, and no improvements were every day making in the circle of the arts and sciences.

I am, Messi'rs Printers, one of your *better sort of people:* zealous for the dignity of government; strenuous to support administration (as the phrase is.) It gives me much pain, when I find governmental matters indefencible. I too like other great men have my travels. But as I make a conscience of not saying what I disbelieve, I am often non-plused with the home-spun reasonings of my plain-spoken countrymen.

The vulgar in substance argue thus, Mess. Printers, and YOUR BETTERS (gentlemen) ought to know it.

This Richardson is either guilty or innocent.—If guilty, why not punished; if innocent, why not released. TWENTY TWO months imprisonment for a capital crime—in a tormenting suspense between life and death—is what no man undeserving of death ought to bear. Either the laws want mending, or the ministers of justice want *something else.*

To say his cause is difficult, is to say nothing of weight. All men are innocent, till they are *proved guilty.* There ought in every well regulated state to be some order of men whose business it should be *to try this matter,* and whose decision should be *conclusive.* Surely within this two years past, affairs of much less importance than the life or imprisonment of a citizen have been heard and ended in our courts. Therefore they who have the face to pretend that there has not been time enough to determine touching this prisoner, I trust would not blush to make a much worse pretext.

Is Richardson kept in goal in order to recommend him to mercy? The *honour* of magistracy ought openly to avow it:—the wisdom of the recommenders ought to justify it. A *secret cunning-like* conduct in persons of *judicial* characters is base, odious and execrable! It is base, because little: odious, because wicked: execrable, because destructive of social security and happiness.

The pretence that Richardson has been a profligate and abandoned wretch, is no good argument for his present treatment. At most, it should operate only to deter an application for extraordinary efforts of royal grace. Public justice can take no cognizance of facts not in issue; it can punish nothing but what is legally established. A dangerous doctrine this, that imprisonment can be justifiy'd upon a principle, that is too absurd and wicked to be openly avowed.

In short, Mess. Printers, the serious part of the people are conscientiously uneasy:—the sagacious and penetrating think that those consequences may flow from this precedent which destroy individuals and ruin communities. And those who are acquainted with the human heart, know, that a precedent which will warrant oppression, is soon consumed by usage.

PUBLIC JUSTICE should never be *suspected.* I have heard arguments brought to justify all manner of political and judicial movements. But I have seen "no tolerable colouring" given *this affair.* All are enquiring, but none can answer. There was a story propagated—I hope it is not true—that a certain—publickly said, "when the people have done calling upon us, something may be done—but, for my part, at present I am for doing nothing about it."

For GOD's sake, Have the people no right to ask questions about the progress of justice thro' the land—the progress of *criminal* justice too? When a breach of criminal law is made, it is *the publick* who *are injured* by the infraction:—this gave rise to the crown law—this alone (to speak as a citizen) warrants it's progress.—Shall *the injured* not *call for redress?*

Say you imprisonment is punishment enough. If he is convicted of any crime, it deserves DEATH. If of no crime, the punishment is undeserved. If he is held in order to give an opportunity to enquire into the *truth* of the offence; time hath already been given—every day puts it more and more out of the power of man to ascertain *the truth of the case. The accused is injured then. Public justice is impeach'd.* He who is thrown into a prison will complain, unheard; he will languish, unpitied. Let not the infamy of the man give origin to an acquiesence in unjustifiable confinement; all imprisonment is oppression, that is not necessary for the advancement of justice. Patience to hear, is the honour of a judge: but celerity of execution is a first principle of justice. For *the safety* of the people, prisons were erected: They, for whose sake the prisoner is confined, are bound by *the laws of GOD* to see that *the rights of the prisoner* are not forgotten: for prisoners, have *their rights* as well as all other men. Remember my friends & countrymen, remember PUBLIC JUSTICE is in question—THE PEOPLE are interested—*they are injured.* COMPLAINT IS THE PREROGATIVE OF THE INJURED. No order of men are too high to be *called upon*—too honest to *exclude suspicion*—too good to be *drawn aside of their own hearts*—too pure to be tempted—or too powerful to be amesned[3] to the tribunal of the public, and punished by—THE PEOPLE.—Remember this important truth—What is law for a *Richardson,* is law for a SIDNEY. If oppression is warranted by law, the PATRIOT is much more likely to fall a victim than the pimp and pander. HAMPDENS will stain the scaffold with blood, while a robber or murderer finds a city of refuge.[4]

No tyranny so secure, none so intollerable, none so dangerous, none so remediless, as that of EXECUTIVE COURTS!

CALLISTHENES.

1. *Boston Gazette,* 10 February 1772, p. 2, all of the first column, carrying over to about a quarter of the second. Callisthenes was a Greek writer and orator who initially promoted Alexander the Great, then became his critic. Accused of treason, he was thrown into prison and apparently died there, after being tortured. His writings only survive in excerpts quoted later by others. Quincy could have come across Callisthenes in the Langhornes' *Plutarch's Lives,* in the chapter on Alexander (at 4:295–99).

2. In February 1770, Richardson, a minor customs official, shot and killed a young boy, Christopher Seider, who had been part of a crowd that gathered outside Richardson's house. Richardson was tried for murder in April and the jury found him guilty, to the obvious displeasure of the judges presiding at the trial—the same four who would preside at Preston's and the soldiers' trials. Quincy had acted as defense counsel in the trial. The judges did not pronounce sentence and, awaiting a royal pardon, held Richardson in jail until they could slip him out of the province. The best discussion of Richardson's case in the context of Quincy's complaints as "Callisthenes" is Zobel, *Boston Massacre,* pp. 164-79; which builds on the earlier work Zobel did with L. Kinvin Wroth as editors of *The Legal Papers of John Adams,* 2:396–430. Zobel notes that Quincy wrote as "Callisthenes" (citing the *Memoir*). Wondering if Quincy wrote to "provoke" Richardson's execution, Zobel also noted (*Boston Massacre,* p. 410) that such a position "would seem to contrast sharply not only with his duty as an attorney to his erstwhile client, but also with his stand in the Massacre trials." But, if Quincy had also written as "Mentor" (see supra, pp. 66–68 from the *Boston Evening-Post,* 11 February 1771) in the aftermath of the "Massacre trials," as Eliza Susan Quincy claimed, that would serve as an earlier example of the same phenomenon—which could simply be the result of Quincy taking off his lawyer's hat and putting on that of the political activist. Besides, neither position—as "Callisthenes" or as "Mentor"—was literally inconsistent with the position that he argued in court, or his notions of how the law should be used to achieve justice.

3. Should be "amensed." In this context, it meant to compensate or offer restitution.

4. Sidney was executed in 1683. John Hampden, the bane of Charles I, died in 1643 from wounds suffered in battle, fighting on the side of Parliament and therefore, to Parliament's supporters, a martyr in the cause of liberty.

"HYPERION"

4 May 1772[1]

Messieurs EDES & GILL,

SUPPOSING it admitted that the Governor's Speech is artful, nay suppose further, what I would freely allow, that he has manifested as much ability as assiduity in his vindication of the force of ministerial Instructions, considered as legally binding on any branch of the Provincial Legislature, I cannot be of opinion, it can have any tendency to enlarge his influence in the Country. His jesuitical return of thanks and acknowledgment of great harmony, are as readily seen thro' by them as by us: And shallow indeed must be the capacity which cannot perceive the labor and struggle he is forced upon to give even a coloring *to his pretensions.*

To support his opinion, he engages to lay before the house "what appears to be the true spirit of the Charter." And to go to the bottom of the affair, they are informed that by the first Charter the Crown had constituted a Corporation in England, impowered to appoint under its *direction and* instructions *Governors and other Officers in the Colony. By the second Charter the Crown reserves to itself the power of* appointing *and* commissionating *a Governor and Lieutenant or Deputy Governor. But what more says the Charter to the point in question? Nothing surely, that the Governor has been kind enough to produce! The very artful induction of their* Commissions, *and the clause of* Instructions *mentioned in them, though indeed the sole support of the doctrine, is so far from imagining, in these instructions a power to controul the laws, legislators or any branch of them, that even in their Commissions (no part either of the letter or spirit of the Charter) they are to be considered in subordination to, or pursuance of their determinations. Indeed the Governor himself after saying a great deal about it, and at last confesses that the reserve in the Governor's Commission is not made to deprive the People of any Privilege, but to restrain the Governor from using to their oppression or hurt, or to the dimunition of the just Prerogative of the crown, that power and authority with which he is intrusted. If this be true, why are the People deprived of their privileges, and oppressed, hurt, and affronted by means and pretence of authority from these rascally instructions?*

I would beg leave to ask the Governor whether any unprejudiced person can be informed of the general tenor of instructions, since we were favoured with that famous one for rescinding the circular letter on pain of dissolution of the legislature, and of all the abuses, indignities, and affronts heaped upon the people themselves or their representatives from that time to this, and conclude that instructions have had no other aim than to restrain oppressive powers in Governors? But taking it for granted he has represented the matter fairly, I hope we shall have no more complaints of want of power to indulge the just demands of the people, by pretending any further inhibitions from Lord Hillsborough.

It seems strangely inconsistent with a desire to have his conduct appear in a favorable light with the people, for the Governor to take the blame of so wretched a Scene of administration entirely upon himself; but the path of deceit is dark and full of windings.[2]

HYPERION.

1. *Boston Gazette,* p. 3, filling roughly half of the first column.

2. Quincy demonstrates here, as well as anywhere, his ability to wield sarcasm and irony as rhetorical weapons. The resolutions sent in the circular letter to which he referred passed the Massachusetts House of Representatives on 11 February 1768, asserting the basic rights to which the Bay Colony was entitled while at the same time swearing loyalty to crown and empire. The Earl of Hillsborough, first to hold the new post of secretary of state for American affairs, instructed Governor Bernard to in turn instruct the House to repeal the resolutions or face prorogation (immediate end of the session) or dissolution (no new session until an election was held). The same held true for those legislatures in royal colonies that had endorsed them. Hillsborough's instructions went to all of the royal governors. His letter to Bernard of 21 April 1768 is in the Public Record Office, Colonial Office 5/757, in the National Archives, Kew; for his instructions to the other governors, see, as an example, his letter to Governor Henry Moore of New York in E. B. O'Callaghan, ed., *Documents Relative to the Colonial History of New York,* 15 vols. (Albany, N.Y.: Weed, Parsons and Company, 1853-1857), 8:58–59. The Massachusetts House refused to rescind its resolutions and endorsed them by an even larger margin. They are printed in *Journals of the House of Representatives of Massachusetts,* 55 vols. (Boston: Massachusetts Historical Society, 1919-1990), 44:20–23 (Appendix). A proud Massachusetts celebrated the stand taken by those who refused to rescind (and included various documents connected with the controversy) in *The Glorious Ninety-Two* (Boston: The Massachusetts General Court, 1949).

"MARCHMONT NEDHAM"

8 June 1772[1]

"*The Serpent, subtlest* Beast of all the Field."[2]

I SCARCE ever inspected the face of Mr. H. or considered his conduct in public and private life, but some passage of my beloved Milton came to my mind. And however "*doubtful or equivocal*" his behavior may appear to the *gullable* and gaping,* he is easily 'kenned and seen thro' by the sagacious and penetrating. Worldly policy and serpentine insinuation have in general been his characteristicks: these have so often served his turn, and a dolt must become so considerable an adept by practice, that when he obviously stumbles out of his common track, I suspect he is ridden by a *superannuated* driver, or urged on by one, who has been *a blunderer* from the beginning.

It was Mr. H's business on his meeting the general assembly at Cambridge on *Election*-Day, to sooth and conciliate: Accordingly this gentleman sets out with a formal protestation, that—"*in* EVERY *measure, as far as shall consist with my duty to the King and with the welfare and prosperity of the province, I will chearfully concur with you.*" From this we may fairly conclude, that no desire of the Council and House, compatible with these pretended objects of concern, would be non concurred by his Excellency: Undoubtedly he was, and intended to be, so understood: The Council indeed thought proper to *thank* his excellency for the *readiness* he *expressed* to this purpose. Whether it was necessary, politick, prudent, polite, or christian-like to *thank a ruler for doing his duty,* I am too unskilled in parliamentary forms to say: However the phraseology in the reply is shrewdly indicative of a suspicion not over-favorable to his Excellency's sincerity.

The Council with much delicacy and caution proceed explicitly to declare to his Excellency, that "*the sitting of the General Court out of Boston is in* MANY *respects* VERY INCONVENIENT":—And—"therefore *pray* his Excellency to remove it to the Court House in that Town"—And solemnly deliver it as their opinion, that—"*it will* be more for his Majesty's service and the true interest of the Province the Court should be there held."

The whole, (and not a favorite, picked and—junto) of the Council are here *deliberately giving their Judgment,* and are *supplicating* the chair to advance that service and interest which Mr. H. is pledging his honour and faith that he has at heart.

A matter of state, in "*many* respects *very inconvenient,*" and incompatible with the *highest interest of king and people*, must be "very grievous" to their honest representatives. In this sentiment the House concur with the second branch of government, and accordingly make their reply;—and as his Excellency had not acted correspondent to the same impressions, they are CONSTRAINED *earnestly to request a removal to Boston as a matter of the greatest public advantage.*

No reasonable person could expect or desire that the Council and House should be more cautious, civil and polite. His Excellency, had he been the man he pretends himself to be, would have here closed, droped the controversy, and instantly prorogued the assembly to Boston. But with an ostentatious solemnity, he formally takes "the matter into consideration", and declares with seeming sincerity, that "if it shall not appear to him *necessary for his Majesty's service and the good of the province* to continue the court in some other place than the town of Boston, *he will remove it there.*"

Let us consider this conduct: One who fills the seat of Governor surely ought not to answer a message he does not fully understand, or pass his word without intending to perform it. The *necessity* of his Majesty's service and the good of the province is the standard to determine the Court's continuance out of Boston. If there is no *such necessity,* Mr. H. promises to gratify the House and remove the assembly to Boston. Now we presume that it is incumbent upon his Excellency to *show forth this necessity*, or fulfill his declaration. A failure in either of these points will leave casuists to decide between an egregious blunder or a worse falsehood.

Three days consideration are had upon the afore-mentioned necessity; this necessity, we therefore conclude, was discovered, if it existed. If it was discovered, his Excellency had nothing to do, but to show it, and the matter would of course end: there is no pretence of any such discovery; we have therefore a right from this alone to suppose there is no such necessity, and further from our own knowledge, we affirm there is none in nature or sound policy. His Excellency, his dependants and expectants, are therefore now to clear his truth from suspicion. *Prove this necessity—or give up his veracity.*

His Excellency raises a doubt, for what end others must conjecture; but for my own part I tho't *this necessity* was the criterion; and if so, what need of solving a question of words:—I say, a doubt is raised, whether the House intended the convening of the assembly at Cambridge when Mr. H. *first removed it there,* or the convening this year. Now I will venture to affirm no man of common sense could have any doubt about the matter; and whether his Excellency had any in his own mind, people will believe with discretion. The House thought and declare, with the approbation of nine hundred and ninety-nine out of a thousand of their constituents, that "all expressions in their message are sufficiently clear and plain, and that it is needless to make any explanation of them."

But I have some other reasons, besides that of believing Mr. H. a man of good common sense, which make me a little uncharitable in this instance: I will mention one.

His Excellency "*the first time he removed the assembly from Boston, did not* in the PARLIAMENTARY sense of the word CONVENE *the assembly at Cambridge.*"

Every statesman knows, that this word *convene* as used in parliament, *is a technical* expression; and no doubt was thus used by the house in it's peculiar and appropriate sense, which must preclude all honest pretence of doubt upon the subject. However, would it cleanse Mr. H.s' reputation to admit that there might be made a doubt on this head? I think not.

In the first place, the rules of construction in law, reason, and charity are to take words in their *best* sense; had Mr. H. been what *his station* denotes him, *the father of this people,* he would have so done. Further, it is past the art of man to make any just inference from that message, injurious to the service of the King or his prerogative—those darlings, to which all that is truly desireable must be sacrificed. All pretext is therefore taken away; all that quibbling is able to except to, turns our to be a bare *non-appearance:*—"It does *not appear* to us, that there was any necessity" say the house—For heaven's sake! Is the declared *non-appearance of a matter of necessity* to be a foundation for the denial of the united request and prayer of the LORDS and COMMONS of this land?—A declaration made too by those, who are the constitutional guardians of the people, the legal advisers and councellors of the first magistrate! Into what times are we fallen? NO BRITISH MONARCH EVER DARED THE LIKE EXPERIMENT.—INDEPENDANCE—*insult,—oppression—and madness* from the beginning were inseperable!

MARCHMONT NEDHAM.

**He who does not like the Word may substitute another.*

1. *Boston Gazette,* 8 June 1772, p. 2, filling half of the first column, all of the second and a dozen lines onto the third; more commonly "Marchamont" Nedham. Quincy would use this nom de plume more than any other, a total of eleven times, all for this newspaper, and in two distinct groupings, the first beginning now and running over five consecutive issues into the next month; the final six beginning in December 1773, carrying through consecutive issues to the beginning of February 1774. I discussed Nedham's shifting political loyalties ever so briefly in Coquillette and York, eds., *Portrait of a Patriot,* 1:85–86. Since then, Blair Worden has written an interesting essay on Nedham for his edition of *The Excellencies of a Free-State; Or, The Right Constitution of a Commonwealth* (Indianapolis, Ind.: Liberty Fund, 2011), pp. xv–cv. As Professor Worden noted there, Nedham "is a figure troubling to readers who expect political thinkers to pursue a disinterested search for truth. He is the serial turncoat of the civil wars." (pp. xx–xxi)

2. Quincy was quoting lines from Book IX in Milton's "Paradise Lost."

"MARCHMONT NEDHAM"

15 June 1772[1]

"Fain would a LELIUS[2] for *a favorite* plead,
Fain would he form some *reconciling plan,*
To spare the person ———
"Allied alas! for ever to the crime,
No kind exemption can *the person* claim;
But blackens downwards on the lapse of Time,
The equal object of eternal shame."[3]

HOWEVER "posterity may be careless of enquiry concerning the fautors[4] of a junto," it is not probable that they will be less affected with the subject-matter of the political treatises of the present day, than their ancestors:—and, if I am not mistaken, the Lelii, the Philanthropes,[5] and the Hutchinsons of futurity will find the next generation as refractory as their fires. There is a degree of imposition beyond which man will not suffer; hypocritical solemnity, and base duplicity may deceive for a season; but an awakening people are not easily appeased; and when thoroughly roused, *inward* murmurings and execrations will not satisfy their feelings.

Whether Lelius or myself are "worthy to be ranked among the *sagacious* and *penetrating*", is not matter of sufficient moment to divert the public attention; and this artifice so successfully played off in times past, on similar occasions, shall not prevent my considering those subjects which are infinitely more important to my countrymen and posterity. However, tho' my inclination does not prompt me to expatiate on literary trifles, yet it may, in some cases, be profitable to gratify a word-catcher.

Lelius suggests that I have "mistaken myself" in saying "it was his Excellency's *business* on *Election*-day, to *sooth and conciliate*:"—"For if it was his *business,* (says this acute logician) *it must* have been his *duty,* and if his *duty,* doubtless *justifiable.*"—As if a governor might not, with sinister designs and odious machinations, be *as busy,* as the *Prince of the air,* without once doing, or even thinking of, his *duty.* Should an Historian of the next age, in recording the present aera, inform our countrymen, that Mr. ——— though his whole life sacrificed understanding, conscience and peice of mind, to gratify a "lust of power" and avarice of wealth; and that from the moment he was elevated in authority, he made it his whole BUSINESS to prostitute the sanctity of office to the same execrable purposes; would even Lelius plainly say, this "*business must* have been *his duty?*"—and "doubtless justifiable."—That a man's *business* is not always his *duty,* but frequently his *engagement,* EMPLOYMENT and *delight,* and that this is a current sense of that word, as used by the best authors in the English language, would not be exemplified in any instance, did not Addison afford one, of which Lelius, and such critics may make a very happy application.

"*I never knew one,* who made it his *business* to lash the faults of other writers, *that was not guilty of greater himself.*" Addison.[6]

It was never thought "unpardonable in Mr. H. to ask any question in order to determine his judgment." But when a governor on an *Election*-day, makes high *professions of his affection for the welfare of his country,* and as soon as the *Election is over,* takes measures, which must incense and exasperate; we want no other index of his heart:—We have a right to presume and say, 'till he gives good evidence to the contrary, that he designed "to sooth and conciliate," "to *invite and charm*" those, who unawares of "*the serpent*" in the grass, were tho'tlesly gazing at "*the subtle beast.*"

But Lelius asks, "Did his Excellency in his speech promise to comply with the requests of the Council and House at all events?" Was this query put for information or deception? Let us consider.

In answer to the message of the House, in which they make an "earnest request" for removal, Mr. H. *as governor,* declares, "I will take *the* subject-matter of your message into consideration, and IF IT SHALL NOT APPEAR NECESSARY to me for *his Majesty's service and the good of the province* to continue the Court in some other place than the town of Boston, I WILL COMPLY WITH YOUR DESIRE, AND REMOVE IT THERE."[7]—Now, I say, that here is an EXPRESS "PROMISE, *at all* events to comply with the requests of the Council and House," unless the JOINT *necessity* of the *service of his Majesty* AND *the good of the province prevented.* This I affirm his Excellency declares shall govern his conduct: and if no such necessity, in the estimation of "*his Majesty's Council,*" the House, or the people of the province is existing, we have good reason to say, it does not exist at all; because if these are not proper judges of what *Mr. H. means* by "his Majesty's service," yet

I say they are fit judges of "the good of the province." And Mr. H. (in the *zeal* of HIS PROFESSION) has made a necessity *unitedly* affecting *both "King and Province"* the standard of his conduct, and *such necessity alone is now to be the criterion of his veracity.* Now I again call upon Mr. H. the cabal, and the "fautors of the junto," either to prove, that this "PROMISE" had no meaning, or that he who made it, did not know what he said, *or what he designed;* if neither of these can be satisfactorily done, then let those gentlemen exhibit some *specious* evidence of the existence of such a necessity as we have been considering, or I am afraid, that if at present there is no formal "presentment" (or IMPEACHMENT) "accusing his Excellency of *insincerity, prevarication,* and *falshood,*" yet a day of *search and trial,* of arraignment and condemnation is approaching, in which neither the sophistry of *an Advocate,* the eminence of the Criminal, or *the number of his Accomplices,* will be able to blind, warp or elude the justice and vengeance of an ALMIGHTY JUDGE.

Had Mr. H. however found that the fervor of *his profession* had carried him too far, that his heart or his instructions forbid a compliance with "the good of the province," and then like a bold, a hardy and INDEPENDANT VETERAN had plumply declared his sentiments and determination, we might perhaps have let such open frankness mitigate the warmth of our resentment; but when the little wiles of timidity and the arts of subterfuge and evasion unite with a malevolence of intention, our scorn and abhorrence alternately predominate.

Lelius may think, that it is his best answer to talk of "vermicular convolutions," and the "taking up too much of Draper's paper";—but this will do only with gulls and gudgeons. Sensible and honest men see, and sufficiently despise such little *gubernatorial* tricks. This game will not do now.—Therefore, Sir, show that the answer of the house was of enigmatical or doubtful meaning;—show us that the word "convene" is ever used in parliament or in our charter in the sense Mr. H. pretends;—show that his excellency did not understand a message he had *three days to consider,* and *as a governor* was undertaking to answer;—give us a rule of construction, that admits a private individual or a judge; a *governor and a prince, when treating with his commons,* to take doubtful words in an unfavorable sense; give us a specimen from *English* history of that monarch, who dared to disregard *"the prayer"* of his LORDS and COUNCELLORS, and *"the earnest request"* of his COMMONS.—This is the work, this is the labor.

Till this is done, Lelius will serve his reputation more by his silence, than by such false affirmations as these:—that "the very respectable body of the Council are saluted (by Me) with a broadside, as being HIGHLY CRIMINAL in thanking his excellency." This charge is not true. I never did salute *the Council* as being *highly criminal,* in what they did. I did think and intimate my own sentiments of thanking *a ruler* for doing his duty, tho' it went no further than an "*expression of* readiness" to perform it. That such kinds of gratitude and such modes of thanks *to rulers* never did any good, and have done much mischief, we need not spend time to prove. The design and tendency of such political manoeuvres are equally obvious to the statesman, the patriot and the discerning citizen. And if they had the sanction of "*Faneuil-Hall* in a unanimous plaudit, to one *for his moderation*", it would by no means prove or convince me, that it was *therefore* "politick, prudent or christian-like." All understanding and honest men will view with a like watchfulness, perhaps not with equal indignation, the *Tribunitian* declaimer, and the *Patrician* prostitute, *the pirate* of northern seas, and the plunderers of American revenue; the venal and corrupt judge, and the rapacious and dutiful governor.

MARCHMONT NEDHAM.

1. *Boston Gazette,* 15 June 1772, p. 2, the entire first column and most of the second.

2. The pen name of an essayist who first took on "Marchmont Nedham" in the *Massachusetts Gazette,* 11 June 1772, and for several subsequent issues thereafter. This newspaper, printed by Richard Draper, produced as many pieces supportive of Hutchinson's actions as Edes and Gill's *Boston Gazette* printed squibs critical of them. "Lelius," who may have been Hutchinson himself—Quincy seems to have thought as much, but then could not be absolutely sure—also aimed barbs at "Mucius Scaevola," yet another writer whose essays criticized the Governor and his policies. "Mucius Scaevola" and "Marchnont Nedham" were joined by still others engaged in rhetorical battle with Hutchinson and his supporters. See my "Tag-Team Polemics" for details. The historical (Caius) Lelius had been the right-hand man to Scipio Africanus in the second Punic War, in Spain as well as Africa, and perhaps most notably as cavalry commander in the Roman victory over the Carthaginians at the battle of Zama.

3. These verses are from *An Elegy on the Late Rt. Hon. W...... P..., Esq.* (London: G. Kearsly, 1766), p. 3, condemning the "great commoner" for abandoning political principle and the people by accepting a peerage and taking a seat in the House of Lords. Quincy appears to have been more forgiving; he continued to admire Pitt, even when he had become the Earl of Chatham.

4. Abettors.

5. In reference to pieces by "Philanthrop," whose essays first began appearing five years before, in defense of Governor Francis Bernard, Hutchinson's predecessor.

6. Joseph Addison, *The Whig-Examiner* for 14 September 1710, which Quincy could have found in a number of sources, including various editions of Addison's collected works. Quincy quoted from Addison's *The Free-holder* in his political commonplace book, which was also listed in his "Catalogue of Books. See Coquillette and York, eds., *Portrait of a Patriot,* 1:176 and 5:899 (no. 259), resp.

7. Taken from Hutchinson's message to the House of 30 May 1772, printed in the *Mass. House Journals,* 49:15. Many House members were still smarting from the assertion that Hutchinson made about his prerogatives as governor on 5 July 1771, printed in ibid., 48:115–17. His messages were usually printed in the Boston press soon after he delivered them.

"MARCHMONT NEDHAM"

15 June 1772[1]

Messieurs EDES & GILL,

SINCE I sent you my last, Mr. H. has adjourned the General Court to Boston; and all are busy with their Animadversions. His Dependants and Expectants are extolling his pretended Condescension; his Enemies and heated Observers are ridiculing, or smiling at, the Conduct and Situation of our Adventurer:—While the cool and judicious are inquiring into his Motives of Action, and deriving Knowledge for their future Guidance.

It is a Matter of Speculation, what new Occurrence has altered the Operations of the first Magistrate: Whether there has been a Change in any Way affecting the real Service and Welfare of the Province (since the 3d of this Month) many doubt; but more believe that some *Illumination* has so purified his Excellency's Capacity, or his Conscience, that the one is better calculated for *the Solution of Problems,* or the other for *the Service of the Man.*—However if any one can reconcile the Governor's late Windings and Revolutions, with a real Concern for the Welfare of his *native Country,* with the Probity of an honest Mind, or even with the Circumspection and Wisdom of the Statesman, he will do a greater Work, and deserve a greater Reward, than Philanthrop did for his notable Feats in endeavouring to cleanse the *Augean* Stable of Governor Bernard.[2]

"Verily they have their Reward."[3]

MARCHMONT NEDHAM.

1. From the same issue of the *Boston Gazette,* 15 June 1772 immediately preceding, the following being a brief note near the bottom of the first column on p. 3, taking just under thirty lines.

2. Cleaning the Augean stables in a single day, which housed thousands of cattle and had not been attended to in years, was the fifth of twelve tasks assigned to Hercules to humble himself before the Gods (most especially his father, Zeus). He performed them all successfully, despite their seeming to be impossible. In the case of the stables he diverted two rivers to flow through them, which flushed them quickly.

3. "And when thou prayest, thou shalt not be as the hypocrites are: for they love to pray standing in the synagogues and in the corners of the streets, that they may be seen of men. Verily I say unto you, They have their reward." Matthew 6:5 (KJV), from Christ's sermon on the mount.

"MARCHMONT NEDHAM"

22 June 1772[1]

"When one in Viciousness grows hard,
On Misery on't! the wise GOD seals his eyes;
——— makes him
Adore his Errors, —— *while he struts,*
To his Confusion." SHAKESPEARE.[2]

IN political, as well as other matters, there is nothing like research and examination to determine our judgment: It is not every man who bawls—LIBERTY! is a patriot; neither are all they who croak—GOVERNMENT! friends to peace and good order. It becomes therefore a wise people to attend to their own interests; remembering that *there are powers, in every state, perpetually operating on the most important concerns of the community.* Believe no man for his professions; but consider whether he is in the service of those, who dispose *the loaves* and *the fishes.* Trust with discretion. The people have in general nothing to bestow, but their plaudit—and Heaven knows!—that is sufficiently precarious. No wise man will enter into conflicts for the people, for such a poor reward, unless a sense of his duty impells him to action. It has ever been the bane of man, that he has generally neglected, or not sufficiently supported and revered, those who have sacrificed health and fortune, in the service of the common cause. Neither does the history of the world afford us reason to hope, that the enemies of public felicity, the partizans of public oppression, and the advocates of tyranny (under the sacred name of government) will receive from their injured fellowmen—justice—justice!——Hence encouraged by impunity, the most atrocious criminals have their abettors, and every day affords us an instance that shameless man is capable of espousing the most shameless measures.

Let any one review the history of this country for the last seven years; let him consider what has been done and said, and *by whom;* let him advert to the transactions of this day, and trace their operation to what will probably be the consequences; I say let this be done, and my remarks will receive confirmation.—But I must hasten to attend upon Mr. Hutchinson and his defenders,—LELIUS and THE COBLER:[3]—the renowned triumvirate who gave rise to my observations.

Lelius may think it *uncourtly* to have the truth publickly told of him, when such a declaration bespeaks his falsehood. As well might a thief or robber complain of the incivility of the post and gallows, as many whom I could name, who are eternally lamenting the just rewards of their crimes and infamy.

Lelius after a public conviction of one falsehood, if he had any respect for the understanding and virtue of his countrymen, any modesty or feeling, would not have hoped any success from the same little artifice. He tells us, in the front of his last publication, that "Marchmont Nedham, to the charge against his Excellency of inconsistence, prevarication, insincerity and falshood, has added, hypocritical solemnity, base duplicity, and malevolence of intention! Language (adds Lelius) better becoming the porter, than *the instructor of youth* and *the guardian of the people*."—What a scurvy trick have some men got of lying? What sentiments concerning the design and use of language?

Lelius knows that either of these charges was never made by me against his Excellency in my *first* publication. I stated facts, and reasoned upon them. What those facts and that reasoning supported and proved, and no more, the Governor or his friends might answer as they were able. Mankind were to judge between the ruler and the people. Lelius or others who penetrated into matters, and properly considered them, would decide for themselves, and denominate the transactions by such names as seemed best expressive of their sentiments. But for myself, whatever I tho't, or believed, I *charged his Excellency with nothing but his own public conduct;* and if this eventually convicted him of "inconsistence, prevarication, insincerity and falshood," his advocates will not better his cause by pursuing the same practices in the Governor's vindication. ——My *last* contained this great truth, that "hypocritical solemnity, and base duplicity, may deceive for a season." And tho' a naked position by itself, unapplied to any individual, and (as connected with the rest of my observations) equally relative to Lelius, Philanthrop and Mr. Hutchinson, yet Lelius tells us, this is *an additional charge* against the governor. Was it thought, that the truth of this position was so strikingly exemplified, as that all, who read or heard, must make the application? Or did Lelius wish to be considered, or did he know himself, so intimately *incorporated* with the three notable adventurers, as that a truth which affected any one of them, must equally touch his Excellency?

A curious figure this writer makes with his "language of a porter," when his remark had no sanction from truth of fact or brilliancy of thought. For he ought to know, that *propriety of language* must be determined by a joint consideration of the sentiment to be conveyed, the person addressed, and him who is spoken of. Now, when the sentiment of the heart is justly abhorrent of the turpitude of the culprit, the language of the lips ought to be expressive of the feelings. Hence it is becoming the man, who acts from principle, to treat all villains with words and actions correspondent to their crimes. This alone ought to silence one half of the clamour made about civility and politeness to dignified knaves and robbers. FACT is a test of just sentiment: TRUTH is an eternal standard of propriety in language.

The celebrated author, who tells us, that "he who goes about to persuade a multitude they are not *so well governed as they ought to be,* will not fail of finding *attentive* and *favourable* hearers," delivered a truth:—but as it would have been as fair and as profitable to mankind, had he told us the reason, which he has chose to conceal, let me do it for him. He who goes about to persuade a multitude of this EVERLASTING TRUTH, will always find abundant matter for his discourse; matter *deeply interesting* to *the many, greatly galling* to *the few:* matter that deserves the attention and favor of *all* good men, and will *therefore ever have it from some;*—while he who attempts thus to persuade, properly feels for his fellows:—has understanding to know their wrongs, ability to display them, and spirit to redress them. Heaven knows that a want of more of these "PERSWADERS," a deficiency in the number of THE "ATTENTIVE AND FAVOURABLE," has been the bane of human happiness—an encouragement of those, who have been the scourges of GOD, and the plagues of mankind.

We are informed by Lelius, that he will "*endeavor* to shew forth several matters," for "reconciling the conduct of the governor, with *truth, wisdom* and *integrity*". This is said with reference to my last, which I hope will be read by all those who are inclined to think Lelius has performed what he has undertaken. However Lelius takes care not to proceed in his *reconciling plan* "*in the way* Marchmont has pleased to point out." Proceed in any honest way in your labours, and I am content:—Take *the stone Sisiphus,* as a device for your standard, and "the thirst of Tantalus" for your motto.[4] Philanthrop held forth in 1767, a "fixed resolution, to examine *in his own way* every charge bro't against G — r B — d, and, if it could be fairly done, to set his (BERNARD's) CHARACTER FOR INTEGRITY, AND TRUE FRIENDSHIP

TO THE PROVINCE *in a just point of light.*" Philanthrop and Lelius on a comparison of their "fixed resolution" and "endeavour" '*in their own way*' to "examine" and "reconcile" seem as likely to be the same "*single soul,*" as Mucius and Marchmont; and I have no doubt but the hero of 1767 and 1772 will be alike deserving, if not alike rewarded. However, going your "*own way*" will not succeed so well now as formerly.—But we will attend Lelius in "*his way*".

"In last week's papers every thing bad was said of the governor *because* he would NOT remove the court to Boston": Not barely for this only; but for his not doing it conformable to the *words and spirit of his promise,* and agreeable to his ostentatious *professions and pretences.* "In the next paper (continues our advocate) he is abused for doing it." It is not true Lelius, and you know it. This is plain truth and *good manners, among men,* whatever you may say about *porters and politeness.* Mr. H. has not been *abused* by me, or any one else that I know, *for removing the Court to Boston.* He has been sifted rather more thoroughly than common touching this point: he has been weighed and found greatly wanting. He acted a part that no honest man will attempt to palliate, much less justify: a part, which, with them *who know the man, his aims* and *measures,* precludes all charity, till he shows, true contrition and reformation

He apparently designed to bring the House into his plot; and if once ensnared, we are not ignorant who would make it a merit, and who have *pensions* at disposal. It is not every day, that *such a subtle ruler, as our present* is exhibited in true colours. There are a thousand ways to act the villain in a mask: and an equal number of ways for the great and guilty to elude conviction or defeat justice. He, who with so odious, so poor, so mean a motive, *openly practice* such devices, is capable of ——— all that a free people dread and abhor. Such conduct ought to be fixed up as a land-mark, to the present and future generations, and as a genuine standard by which to judge *the ruler* and *the man.*

Who "told" Lelius that "the governor would not even now have regarded the earnest request and prayer of his councellors and commons, *had he not been afraid* to do otherwise; and his remanding the Court to Boston was an act of *compulsion* or design, not of will"? Lelius after having affirmed this tale, which I am well satisfied he never saw in print, knight errant-like sets about "determining the truth of it with precision." But "his review" has not shown any thing to prove even this tale, (which *he pretends to have been "told"*) was untrue in fact; tho' it should seem a mighty easy matter to knock down *a man of straw of our own formation.* One ground of complaint against Mr. H. was directly the reverse of all this. It was his dependence upon a minister,[5] and his *monstrous* independance of this people, which we supposed made him *so little afraid of doing what he did.* It is no easy thing to compel a man to forfeit the approbation of one who *feeds* and *pays* him; especially when *this man* has a herd of *monsters* in his train, an army at his heels, and a fleet at his command. Hence Lelius was called upon to shew THE VERY REVERSE of what *he pretends to be told:*—"Give us a specimen from *English* history of that monarch, who *dared* to disregard *"the prayer"* of his LORDS and COUNCELLORS, and "the *earnest request" of his COMMONS."* Plainly pointing out, that Mr. H. *so far from "being afraid,"* had actually *dared to do* what NO KING OF ENGLAND, from the *Norman* tyrant to the present occupier of the throne *defacto, had ventured to attempt.*—Lelius surely must know, that *to serve a turn,* the most hardy and daring oppressor[6] may resort to "the little wiles of timidity", and practice, *for a time,* "the arts of subterfuge and evasion."

Lelius tells the world, that the GOVERNOR WAS UNDER A NECESSITY *of continuing the Court out of Boston, while the king's authority to appoint the place for holding it was disputed."* THIS I UTTERLY DENY: And I call upon Lelius to prove it. I have good reason to believe that Mr. Hutchinson HAD NOT EVEN AN INSTRUCTION *from the king* to this purpose. I have been well informed, that when he lately asked the advice of council he read a letter from Lord Hillsborough, the purport of which was no more than simply this: – that so long as the house continued such dispute, "*his excellency would* BE JUSTIFIED *in holding the Court out of Boston."* These I say, I am told are the words of that letter, which one would suppose, as the advice of Council was asked on it, was recorded: However it is said, this was forbid: If I am wrong, let me be set right. Now if this letter contains "the necessity" talked of; if this letter is the only *instruction* which has influenced his conduct, let people consider how his behaviour is aggravated.—What a farce to seek advice under such circumstances and on such an occasion? What a poor incentive to actuate Mr H. in his explanatory Message? A resort *to Council* will not serve the purpose.

Lelius informs us, that the "Governor sends the House a second message, *civilly* desiring them to resolve a doubt, which upon *consideration* had arisen in his mind respecting the intent of one expression in their answer." But before this can serve as any excuse, let it be owned, that he had *not considered it to be in the three days* precedent to his first message; and what is still more important, give us some shadow of plausible pretext for the doubt he pretends to raise upon FURTHER *consideration.* Shameless as men are in these days, from the highest to the lowest, no one attempts this. Therefore this FURTHER *consideration* which gave rise to a *declaration* of this doubt, serves only to evidence a deeper plot at the bottom, and, of course, gives a ten-fold blackness to the despicable project. And publickly, *as a governor,* to affirm "that as plain as the words were *to the House, to him* they were *doubtful* and *equivocal,*" adds a new shade to the exhibition. Neither does it at all better the matter to say (let who will say it) that the words of the House "*might be construed* in such a manner, as if the Governor complied with the desire of the House" he would depart from the KING's *instruction*"; unless some evidence besides a bare *ipse dixit*[7] is given to support *the fact*, and then some rule of language, of common sense or of parliament, *which will warrant "such a construction."* The application to the Council is seen thro' by all wise men, and will never be tho't anything more, than a new specimen of his Excellency's dexterity in methods *to save appearances,* unless as many suppose, that there was a further view of getting the Board unwarily and suddenly to go into a measure, which "*might be construed,*" as the phrase goes, a tacit or implied allowance of a *right* to give the *modern* kind of instructions to continental governors. If this was, also, the design, the keeness of my resentment surpasses the expression of my pen.

I shall now leave my intelligent countrymen to determine, whether Lelius has succeeded in an "endeavor" precisely in my way, or any other, to show these "several matters":—"That the answer of the House was of enigmatical or doubtful meaning; that the word "convene", is ever used in parliament or in our charter in the sense Mr. H. pretends; that his Excellency did not understand a message he had *three days to consider,* and, *as a governor* was undertaking to answer; that rule of construction, that admits a private individual or a judge; *a governor and a prince, when treating with his commons,* to take doubtful words in an unfavourable sense; and that specimen from English history", which we have heretofore mentioned. "This work, this labor" must be performed, before Lelius or any other, will accomplish the arduous task "of reconciling the conduct of the Governor, with truth, wisdom, or integrity."

I would just inform *"the Cobler"* that agreeable to his "prayer",[8] I have taken a new, I wish it may be "a full draught" of Milton: And let me recommend to his serious meditation and improvement, this one passage from that sublime author, that wise, great & good man.

"They undoubtedly, that by their *labors, counsels* and *prayers,* have been *earnest* for the *common good of religion* and *their country*, shall receive above the inferior *orders* of *the blessed,* the *regal* addition of *principalities, legions,* and *thrones,* into their glorious titles, and in super-eminence of beatific vision, progressing the dateless and irrevocable circle of *eternity,* shall clasp inseperable hands with *joy* and *bliss*, in over-measure forever.

"But they on the contrary, that by the impairing and diminution of *the true faith,* THE DISTRESSES AND SERVITUDE OF THEIR COUNTRY, ASPIRE TO HIGH DIGNITY, RULE AND PROMOTION HERE, after a shameful end in this life (which GOD grant them) *shall be thrown down eternally into the darkest and deepest gulph of hell, where under the despightful controul, the trample and spurne of all the other damned, shall remain in that plight forever;*—THE BASEST, THE LOWER-MOST, THE MOST-DEJECTED, MOST UNDER-FOOT AND DOWN-TRODDEN VASSALS OF PERDITION."[9]

MARCHMONT NEDHAM.

1. *Boston Gazette,* 22 June 1772, a long piece taking up the first two columns and half of the third on p. 2.

2. From Act III, Scene 13 in *Antony and Cleopatra,* altered somewhat by Quincy to suit his purposes. In this scene Marc Antony lashes out verbally in frustration, fearing that he and Cleopatra were doomed and that his lover might try to save herself by accepting Caesar's offer of mercy, leaving him to suffer his fate alone. To make it clear that Hutchinson was his target, Quincy changed "our confusion" to "his Confusion."

3. "C ---- The Cobler" went after "Marchmont Nedham" in the pages of the *Massachusetts Gazette,* joining "Lelius" in the 18 June 1772 issue.

4. Quincy turned again to Greek mythology, the stone of Sisyphus referring to King Sisyphus, who, having betrayed Zeus, was obliged to try to push a huge rock to the top of a steep hill in Hades. He could never complete the task; the rock would roll back down, even over him, before he could get it to the summit. (The moral of the tale would later be reworked by the

existentialist Albert Camus.) Tantalus, a more unsavory character, fell afoul of Zeus as well and was forced to stand in water that would recede every time he tried to drink, beneath a tree whose branches would rise out of his reach when he tried to grab its fruit (thus to "tantalize").

5. That is to say, Wills Hill, the Earl of Hillsborough, secretary of state for American affairs. Like others who protested the policies coming out of Whitehall and Westminster, Quincy objected to any extension of prerogative power–whether it be Hutchinson as governor putting the instructions of an imperial administrator like Hillsborough over the wishes of the Massachusetts House and Council, or his deciding to move the location of the General Court from Boston to Cambridge, or his willingness to accept his salary as part of a civil list rather than from the people through the General Court. To Quincy these issues were every bit as important as the question of Parliament's authority to regulate commerce or raise revenue through the navigation system. Hillsborough has come down to us as an ideologue, the personification of the imperial hardliner, determined to impress the colonists with Britain's power. Actually, he was far more pragmatic in his approach to managing the empire, as was Lord North, who has been stuck with the same misleading label.

6. A relatively soft criticism of George III, compared with what would soon follow, but a reminder that colonial protest did not run in some simple sequence, with the king being criticized only after Parliament had been condemned and utterly rejected.

7. Legal Latin: he himself said it, trying to make that bare assertion stand as proof, without further evidence. (In effect, asking that a claim be accepted as true at face value.)

8. Which "C — the Cobler" returns to mockingly in the *Massachusetts Gazette,* 25 June 1772, at p. 2, column 1, hinting that he knew Quincy masqueraded as Marchmont Nedham: "Pray *drink again,* my dying Creature, And thus shew *Life* in ev'ry Feature, For even *Mucius* must allow, Th' Symptoms of *Death* are on you now."

9. From Milton's "Of Reformation in England," in the *Works,* 1:31. Quincy, with Edes and Gill's help, highlighted as he saw fit with italics and capitalization.

"MARCHMONT NEDHAM"

29 June 1772[1]

The Day of Grace,
They who neglect and scorn, shall ——
—— *hard be harden'd, blind be blinded more;*
That they may stumble on, and deeper fall.
MILTON.[2]

THERE is a degree of depravity, to which individuals and communities sometimes arrive, that seems to extinguish not only every moral but every intelligent principle: Men lose all affection and attachment to things which are laudable, and yet wear a mask which screens from *common* observation and resentment; this, comparatively, is not surprizing; but when we behold a traitor to his species, with the genius and obstinacy of a devil, fulfilling his part; regardless of the *universal* observation, the curses and vengeance of his injured brethren; dead to those *rational* sentiments and general feelings, so usual and prevalent in man; we can account for the prodigy in no way better, than by supposing that in wrath GOD hath sealed the eyes and hardened the heart, for the purpose of his own wisdom and glory.

When I first perused the last production of Lelius, I was inclined to think his designs were too apparent to be undiscovered, and his efforts were too feeble to do mischief. For when a man is so shameless as to make his cause appear with resplendent badges of ignorance, fraud and falshood, he becomes less capable of deception and injury; and more the object of scorn and derision, than of fear or solicitude. Being quite unambitious of the last word with Lelius, the Cobler, or Mr. H, and entertaining better sentiments of my countrymen, than to imagine them influenced by the despicable arts of the lowest cunning, I was much disposed to leave the three adventurers to share the emoluments of their labors, amid the enmity of the wise, the imprecations of the honest, and the scorn even of their companions in guilt: but recollecting that in this world, there are all degrees of intelligence, morality and vice, and therefore perhaps some may be deluded and carried away, even by such leaders, I am prompted to say a few things more,—peradventure for the benefit of my country!—tho' not hopeful of making any good impression on those who are candidates for the reproach of a world, the infamy of ages, and the torments of an eternity.

Lelius tells us, that "IF the GOOD PEOPLE over whom governor H. presides, have no greater reason to complain of his administration, than that about which Marchmont has seen fit to exercise his talents, few will be willing to join in the clamour, and fewer still who would ever wish his removal." Does Lelius really believe that the GOOD *people* will not cry out against that administration, which is so irreconcileable with TRUTH, *wisdom* and INTEGRITY, that even a Lelius, hardy and shameless as he is, shrinks from *his labor?* Is it with Lelius or the GOOD PEOPLE of this land, a trivial matter for a governor triply bound by his duty, as a man and a ruler, and by the oath of GOD, to act for the welfare of those over whom he is ordained? is it a matter of small consideration for *such* a magistrate, professing himself a christian in a christian land, to pretend a zeal for public happiness, in order to *serve a turn* on an *Election-day—to promise* to do what he intends to evade, as sinister purposes and *appearances* may require;—to persist in the being of a *necessity,* while he (with his veracity as a man, his faith as a ruler, at stake) is unable, tho' publickly called upon, to give the lightest proof of its existence;—to hold forth the substance of *an instruction from the King,* when all that is produced is a *ministerial epistle;* shamelessly, "in the face of broad-eyed, watchful day," to avow *this epistle*, as a sanction for that *serpentine* conduct, to justify which, it has not the remotest tendency;—to labor and toil *for hire* to entrap the guardians of public liberty in the snares of ignominious vassallage and thraldom?—I say, are these matters, which *good subjects* and GOOD *people* are to view with unconcern, or observe without a murmur?

But let Lelius be mindful, and let him consider it upon his pillow—There is yet "GREATER reason of complaint," and that his hypothetical IF gave no grace of truth or modesty to his observation. Lelius has already been told, that "it is not *every day,* SUCH A SUBTLE RULER, *as our present,* is exhibited in true colours": An elevated oppressor may make a trade for life of his oppression, and there may be none found to detect, or of ability to punish: he may by betraying the interests of a single town, make his way to a station more fitted for the destruction of a province: the fall of a province may give a rise sufficient for accomplishing the sacrifice of a new world: the reign of a tyrant—(shame to the morals & virtue of man!)—is seldom thought a time for complaint, conviction or punishment. Thousands become interested to obey, thousands to serve, thousands to protect: the few discern, the many gaze, and the lowest tremble:

the deceivers and deceived, the oppressors and the oppressed, make so great a part of the community, that the wise and good, the noble and brave are often crushed and overwhelmed in the general calamity.

Every sensible man knows, that this is not a time to review or display in a true light Mr. H's *whole* public conduct. Our business is to take such parts of his administration, as we may treat of with freedom and safety; to form a proper estimate of the man from his *more open* operations, and draw that *useful* knowledge which may serve to counteract or defeat his *most secret, but not less dangerous and desperate* machinations.

I have known this gentleman a Selectman of the Town, a Representative and a Counsellor: I have seen him sit in judgment, heard his speeches and his charges, and have now lived to see him in the chair of government. I have attended and marked him, & think *I know him.* As *an individual,* having never received any *private* injury from him, I bear him no enmity. As far as he is an adversary of *my native country,* I am his foe. Disappointed ambition (of which we have sometimes heard) has not moved me; for I never had an ambition, which Mr. H. had *an opportunity* to gratify; and at my present time of life and health, I ought to feel no higher ambition than that of fulfilling the more important duties. Being advanced in age & infirmity, I wish to see my country free and happy; that my children may partake as fair an inheritance as I received. These and similar motives actuate me in my present works, and I hope will lead me to those pursuits and labors, which may render the small residue of my days profitable to my species, to whom I bear much affection.

Believe me, my countrymen, that a love to the human race is a moral and religious duty. It is a great, and too successful, art, which is often practised, to deseminate an aversion of man to man. More of this seed is sown, & more evils spring from it, than is generally apprehended. Disunion inevitably succeeds this aversion, till the divided *many* fall an easy prey to the compacted *few.* For this infernal purpose, the execrable WALPOLE propagated his accursed maxim—"EVERY MAN HAS HIS PRICE." For similar purposes the servile imitators of that odious prostitute have continued to inculcate like principles and doctrines: and whether *carolled* at a noisy riot, or *retailed* in Draper's paper, the same object is still ultimately in view.—To destroy all faith and confidence among men, that the subtle and rapacious may sooner subjugate the poor and innocent. This is the true LEVELING PLAN of the rich and powerful;—a plan that levels virtue with vice, benevolence with selfishness, and all that is good and great with all which is vile and despicable.—To oppose a project so pregnant of every moral and political evil, is a common duty. He who sneers at all public virtue, denies or ridicules the supposed existence of an affection for mankind, betrays that turpitude of heart, which characterised Satan in the garden of Eden:—he ought to be avoided as a pestilence.—Cultivate an affection for each other, and for the world; and let this love be fervent, and it will do mighty works. Oppose with bitterness all who go about to disunite the members of that great body—THE MULTITUDE. I bless GOD, that in early youth, I considered all men, as my brethren; and now, in the decline of life, if I have one predominant desire, next to the plaudit of MY CREATOR and my conscience, it is, that of having THE MANY *to arise and call me blessed.*

MARCHMONT NEDHAM.

1. *Boston Gazette,* 29 June 1772, p. 2, full first column and over half of the second.

2. Milton's "Paradise Lost," Book III, lines 198-201, quite possibly from *The Poetical Works of John Milton*, 2 vols. (London, 1731), 1:59–60, which, again, Quincy edited to suit his purposes. There was also a three volume edition of Milton's poetic works published more recently, in London in 1761. "Milton's Po Works" is no. 28 in the "Catalogue of Books" in Coquillette and York, eds., *Portrait of a Patriot,* 5:892.

"MARCHMONT NEDHAM"

6 July 1772[1]

"*In every Breast inspire a virtuous Flame*
And teach them to revere their Country's Fame."[2]

TO the benevolent and feeling, it is painful to review the stale artifices of those whose folly and weakness are not sufficiently despicable to exempt their malice and turpitude from detestation and resentment: The bulk of mankind, being engaged in eager pursuit after temporary gratifications, are supine and careless about their future well-being, and afford but little for the weightier matters of consideration and thought; the few whom subtility of nature, servile assiduity, and lust of controul have buoyed into place, are so greedy of gain, so devoid of reflection, and destitute of conscience, that, in general, they may be justly dreaded as the deceivers and destroyers of their species: Hence amid the carelessness of some, and the ambition of others, the COMMON INTEREST OF ALL is forgotten and trampled on. Inattention is the bane of man.—It becomes therefore eminently the duty of the wise, the good and the great, to appear in behalf of their deluded brethren. Of *one blood* did GOD make all nations of the earth—an eternal memento of the great obligation we owe to the innocent MULTITUDE.—And when we find, that the *wages of an hireling,* the temptations of riches and grandeur, or *the deceitful sweets of spoil and riot,* prompt a few venal prostitutes—the disgrace and curse of the human race—to be active, sedulous and enterprising in their odious service, the TRUE FATHER OF HIS COUNTRY, the friend of mankind will arise with his strong armour:—Reason, the helmet of his head; integrity, the shield of his heart;—assuming the fortitude of virtue, he gives a new keeness to his shaft, and a more than youthful vigour to his bow.

"O mihi praeteritos referat si Jupiter Annos!
Qualis eram."———[3]

I thank the great giver of every good gift, that I am addressing a people, probably, of as much natural capacity and acquired knowledge, as any in recorded time: As vicious, and as corrupt, as they are, yet the most virtuous and pure of any now upon the stage of action. This encourages me in the labours of my age. I trust, I have spoken conviction to many worthies; and intend to devote many of these my latter hours in the detection, and exposure of those, who hug themselves in their fancied security of wealth and splendor:—Not doubting, but I shall share the prayers of the pious, and the benisons of my countrymen.

To them, if I speak the words of truth and soberness, it will be very immaterial whether I am *the master of a grammar-school, the instructor of youth, the physician or the lawyer;* or, peradventure, a minister of the word of GOD: So long as *the word in season* is spoken, so long as it is heard and *done,* it pertains little to *universal* happiness whether the speaker is called Lelius or Marchmont. But let me tell Lelius, that were it a matter of sufficient moment to point out *the fine gentleman,* and COURT-*subaltern,* I might touch, perhaps, with a *more lasting* tint than "*the limner,*" and *cut* with a *deeper chizzel* than the statuary.— And as a warning I insert, with *as much propriety* and *good grammar,* the *Nemo me impune lacessit*[4] of Scotland, as Lelius the "*esto perpetua!*"[5] of father Paul.

Lelius has thought fit to *indict* "*Master* Nedham" as a "*madman*", or *something of this sort.*" But so long as *the peers* or the *betters* of Lelius are circumscribed by the laws of the land, they may proceed with governor Bernard to "*the end of the tether.*" However, *mad* as I am, I have yet *reason* sufficient to expose the *Lelii,* as they exhale in the sunshine of a despot, from the foeces of corruption. It is a ridiculous vanity to treat one whom we are too impotent to refute, as a "presumptuous dogmatist and vain babler." Confute the *dogma,* and expose the *babbling.* The sting of satire is the truth of observation: the poignancy of sarcasm consists in justness of remark. Lelius, I scorn to recriminate—in words without ideas. I challenge you to point out the position which is not founded in truth, reason or experience. I bid you defiance in an attempt to refute a *single fact* I have advanced; or show the futility of an argument I have used. Surely Lelius, you have sense eno' to know, that you have been detected: If you want information of your egregious errors, your gross and unpaliated falshoods, I will give you a new edition; though a review of my former publications will save the trouble. Had you any feeling, you would blush even in a mask. To betray the rights of your species, to aim at the bondage of *those who have given you bread,* is a sufficient load of guilt;——but to defend to the meanness of falshood, in the odious service of oppression, adds new infamy to baseness. But what shall we say? Most of your countrymen can read and consider; you must know, that even those whom you serve will despise the creature they employ, when it's prostitution is exposed. Remember, Lelius, that you *are now certainly known by some,* and will probably in time be known to many more:—What will you say—what torments will sting you, when *promotion* shall mark the degenerate offspring of an ancestor who expired with the first honors, and in the best service—*of his country!*

To insinuate that this continent, and its worthies, who have nobly conducted the public affairs for seven years past, are all "*inebriated;*" that "restless temper," and "unbounded ambition," actuate those whose arguments force conviction, and whose deportment is characteristic of the noblest affections, will serve to deceive but a very few. We have not yet forgot the measures of the Bernard-administration:—we know who prated of his love for this province: we know that even Bernard held forth a zealous *profession of good-will*—while he was stabbing *in secret* the vitals of this people:—we know his friend and his adviser, his justifier and successor. But Lelius thinks it "turbulence" to use our faculties, and hopes no doubt to suppress our emotions. He would make us believe, that "*civil dissention*" is the greatest calamity of society; whereas but a common knowledge of the history of man teaches a very opposite truth. The sloth, the indolence, the submission and tameness of *the many,* has ever given rise to the enormous power, domination, rapine and ravage of *the few.* To what does man owe his safety? To his using the faculties, and exerting the powers of his nature. A nation in security are slaves, or soon will be. But this country must do something more than either reason or write, or they will soon be the most miserable and ignominious of the Earth.—For the richness of the spoil invites the Vultures of plunder—And the sun is darkned with these unclean birds of prey.—Indeed Lelius, I believe we are, and shall continue to be, what you call "turbulent:" would to GOD you may see, what you, with misapplied derision, would call—ENTHUSIASTS *for freedom.*

Whatever you may *pretend to think,* Lelius, I will venture to say, & doubt not *all my readers* will join with me, that *you did not believe yourself* when talking about the *truth* and *integrity* of Gov. H. Hast thou not learned, that "the weapon of invective" will *not* "*avoid* the confusion of a defeat;"—that he who sees an Adversary's weakness and wickedness, having prov'd and displayed it, has *a right to inveigh;* that in the cause of public liberty and right, he who *properly feels* for his country is *inexorable* towards it's enemies; while his heart, his pen and his tongue, glows in the glorious contest:—This will point *the invective;*—this will speed the shaft, & pierce it to the marrow of a traitor.

——A Demosthenes *inveighed* against a Philip of Macedon, a Tully[6] against a Catiline and Verres, a Pitt against a Bute and a Holland:—and the wise and honest will re-echo the *bitter* "*invective,*" while the spark of genius and the beam of divinity illuminate and inspire the world of mankind.

Marchmont has stated facts, reasoned upon them, and leaves every man to judge for himself relative to Gov. H's late conduct. He proposes, if his life is spared, in some future period, further to consider Mr. H. as a man, a citizen, legislator, judge and governor. There are striking lines in his character, which have marked him from the beginning: And I could name as venerable a worthy as ever honored this land, who while a co-temporary member with Mr. H. in the house of assembly, many years ago, was frequently heard to say—"Mark that man! he will be the ruin of this country." How far this prophecy is, or will be, history, others are left to consider. The deepest dissimulation is early seen thro' by the penetrating: 'tis a much longer space, sometimes an age, before a compleat hypocrite is thoro'ly detected and abhorred.—Lelius, if he wants information, may be pointed the way, for as depraved a person as ever breathed, to gain a temporary reputation in the office he refers to. But if Lelius will go to *orphans,* instead of WIDOWS, his enquiry may save part of my trouble.

We are told, that "the contest is NOT now *a common* cause." This implies that there was one *once:* Pray how is the cause changed? Show us some difference between our injuries & complaints now and formerly. Unless you can suppose an INDEPENDENT *ruler,* a MONSTER *in a free state,* interested *by his price,* to rivet the chains of slavery, makes a *favourable* distinction. Tis in vain Lelius, to ring *or puff* the changes of "*personal* revenge, liberty the *pretence, interest* the pursuit; and disappointed ambition." Where is the *personal* revenge? Is the making pretences to *liberty,* the way to promote *interest?*—Or rather is not servility and prostitution to the basest purposes the road of preferment? Indeed Lelius, a common capacity is sufficient to expose thee.

Does Lelius believe, dares he avow in the face of day, that "EVERY MAN HAS HIS PRICE"? Shameless miscreant! Can you expect ever again to place faith *even in thyself,* or hope any will trust you? Will your fellow citizens attend to one who declares, that *his idol,* like to Judas, or a Devil, he may be *bought for his price?* At what price have you rated?—for it seems you have made the computation;—At what price do you *hawk* in the market of venality?—integrity, conscience, honour, peace of mind and a good name? It is a deplorable time, when a principle is *openly* advanced, (without *universal* resentment) which saps the foundation of moral virtue and mutual confidence among men: If this infernal maxim be true, where and what is the essential distinction between the benevolent patriot and the meanest miser—the man of piety and the slave of Satan? Many curses, and much infamy would the GREAT VILLAINS of the world *escape,* if they could find a refuge in this abominable doctrine: No wonder the marrow of it is preserved and retailed with such abundant industry.—Did I believe myself in a city or a country, where *all men* adopted and practised upon this odious principle, I would fly from the society of man to the wilderness of nature. For wherefore should I live in that country, ALL whose Inhabitants are of that LELIAN race, who for *their price,* would plunge a dagger to the heart, for plunder of the purse—or, Judas-like, crucify the LORD OF LIGHT, and SAVIOR *of* MANKIND, for a few pieces of silver.

MARCHMONT NEDHAM.

1. *Boston Gazette,* 6 July 1772, p. 2, all of the first two columns and roughly a third of the last.

2. Near the closing lines of Gilbert West, *The Institution of the Order of the Garter* (London: R. Dodsley, 1742), p. 64. It was also reprinted in various poetic anthologies. It is not clear which particular source Quincy used.

3. From Virgil's *Aeneid,* Book VIII, lines 560–61: "If Jupiter would only restore the bygone years."

4. "No one attacks me with impunity;" from the Order of the Thistle.

5. "Let it be perpetual."

6. Nickname for Cicero (Marcus Tullius Cicero).

"CALLISTHENES"

28 September 1772[1]

Messieurs EDES & GILL,

IN your Gazette of the 10th of February last, I took occasion to deliver my sentiments on the imprisonment of Ebenezer Richardson. A truth I then delivered, give me leave to repeat—"NO TYRANNY so *secure,* none so INTOLLERABLE, none so DANGEROUS, none so REMEDILESS, as that of EXECUTIVE COURTS."

———— This is a truth all nations bear witness to, all history confirms. And so sensible are all tyrants of the importance of *such courts* to advance and establish their system of oppression, they never rest 'till they have compleatly corrupted or BOUGHT THE JUDGES OF THE LAND. I could easily show that the most deep-laid and daring attacks upon the rights of a people might in some measure be defeated or evaded by upright judicatories:—that bad laws with good judges make little progress. "Let me make the judges," said the Pedant King James, "I care not who makes the laws"; and this was very far from being the worst speech of that vain-glorious monarch.—How would the silly tyrant have hugged himself in fancied bliss, if he had been gratified with making laws, judges, lawyers, sheriffs, &c. and then to have PAID and *displaced* them ALL AT PLEASURE? Cou'd a Nero wish more? The people then would have no more real life, than might be extinguished with one single stroke.—

My countrymen, Great-Britain with legislative solemnity has told you, she can bind you and yours by her laws, when the parliament please:—the parliament have so bound, and are still so binding you:—Who appoints—who displaces our judges, we all know; but *who pays them?* THE LAST VESSELS from England tell us, THE JUDGES AND THE SUBALTERNS HAVE GOT SALARIES FROM—GREAT-BRITAIN![2] Is it possible this last movement should not rouse us—and *drive us*—not to desperation—but to OUR DUTY!

Let us consider what has been done in the *Green*-tree—We may form some judgment what will be done in the *dry.* Richardson's Case we all know.—Capt. Preston is called to his trial; TALES MEN *are wanted.* Stephen Greenleaf, Esq; is to return them. *Accidentally* suitable Persons are at hand. They are returned.

Mankind know them, their sentiments, their political conduct, their engagements in extensive trade—their usual attention to it, and *to scarce any thing else.* However, they urge no objection—they set, and Preston is acquitted.[3]

Pierpont and Davis are to be tried.—A TALESMAN is wanted.—Chandler returns two *from Hardwick.* The Judges sum up the case. Pierpont is ordered to pay £15 and Costs—.[4]

These and a multitude of other like facts, which all the world ought properly to resent, need no comment: the blind may see—the callous must feel:—*the spirited will act.*

Surely we may think as freely, as the Reviewers write, who are under the Nose of Lord Mansfield.[5]—Leaving wise and good men to comment and apply their words, I close with their Expressions in the review of December last. "It is not be accounted surprising in an age, when virtue is, in some measure, a reproach, and men of high Quality are only noted for debauchery, THAT JUDGES should dispossess themselves of *every appearance of integrity, and assume the boldest and most unpardonable latitude in the interpretation of the Laws.*"[6]

CALLISTHENES.

N. B.[7] The judges of England have salaries *independent of Crown* and people, with commissions during good Behaviour: *If the reverse of this was true,* according to the account of the reviewers, it is very certain, they would soon be—incarnate.—Awake my countrymen! Arise—*consider*—AND ACT LIKE MEN! C.

1. *Boston Gazette,* 28 September 1772, p. 3, a briefer piece filling half of the first column.

2. The crown had already begun paying the salaries of royally-appointed governors, which also stirred protest. Charles Townshend is most famous—infamous in patriot circles—for wanting to create a civil list with part of the revenues raised by the new navigation act that he shepherded through Parliament in June 1767. He did not originate the idea, even if he pressed it harder than most and was more successful in having it carried through. For Quincy, it was one of many inter-related issues, pitting American rights against British authority, issues that expressed themselves politically but were at heart constitutional.

3. See Zobel, *Boston Massacre,* pp. 245–46 and 270–71 for the selection of jurors in Preston's trial and that of the soldiers that followed.

4. This refers to a case first tried in Worcester in April 1771 and continued to the next term in September, where Quincy and John Adams represented the defendants, Caleb Davis and Robert Pierpont (Pierpont would be one of the coroners involved in the "Massacre" post-mortems),

in a suit filed by Ebenezer Cutler against them. Cutler accused them of being involved (with many others) in seizing goods he was taking out of Boston that he had imported in violation of the non-importation agreements that numerous merchants had signed. Davis was acquitted; Pierpont was fined the amount noted by Quincy. There were comments on the case in the *Boston Gazette,* 23 September 1771 and 22 September 1772. See too L. H. Butterfield, ed., *The Diary and Autobiography of John Adams,* 4 vols. (Cambridge, Mass.: Belknap Press of the Harvard University Press, 1961), 2:8–9.

5. William Murray, Earl of Mansfield and lord chief justice of the Court of King's Bench, was also active in the House of Lords. He made a point of skewering what he dismissed as colonial political pretensions. Often, what men like Quincy considered rights, he considered privileges. On the bench he was notorious as an opponent to expanding the notion of press freedom beyond the elimination of prior restraint.

6. Quincy was quoting from a brief notice on *Free Thoughts on Seduction, Adultery, and Divorce,* By a Civilian (London: J. Bell, 1771) that appeared in the *Monthly Review* 45 (December 1771):497. That same issue carried a full review of Sir Robert Talbot, *Letters on the French Nation,* a title first published in French that had recently been translated into English, and that Quincy drew from for his political commonplace book—see Coquillette and York, eds., *Portrait of a Patriot,* 1:213–14. Even if Quincy already owned a copy of Talbot before he turned to that issue of the *Monthly Review,* it is interesting to think that he, like many modern academicians, went to book reviews when looking for titles to add to his personal library.

7. Abbreviation for nota bene: to note well.

"EDWARD SEXBY"

12 October 1772[1]

The following came to Hand last Saturday se-nnight, but too late to be inserted in our last Week's Gazette.

—*"He who* dares *my rights invade*
By NATURE'S *oldest* LAW *is made*
My VICTIM *or my Slave.*[2]

DRAPER's last Thursday's Paper tells us, that "the extravagant licentiousness of the Press is arrived to such a pitch *of late,* that unless it be in some measure curbed, bids fair to be the destruction of all government in this province."[3] It is curious to observe the variant accounts we have, from the same quarter, of *the licentiousness of the Press;*—that hackneyed theme of knaves who *feel* and *fear* the lash of truth.—At one time they aim to amuse by pretending *this licentiousness* to be so *enormous* as to be *contemptible;* at another so *extravagant* as to become *formidable* to *all government.* And I have observed these changes to be rung, according as they *who bear rule* imagine *the body of the people* FEAR or HATE their power and oppression. If timidity and supineness are thought to predominate among the populace—*the licentiousness of the Press must be in some measure curbed;*—if rage and revenge inflame the injured multitude;—*the liberty of the Press is too contemptible for notice.* However no writer has ever yet shown us a government destroyed by licentious Printers; and what is more, such a phenomenon never did or will appear in the political world: Though I could easily name states, nations, colonies and provinces for whom it would be HAPPY, *if any licentiousness* could be found sufficient to dissolve ALL that, *among them,* is called GOVERNMENT. Now if this be true, and moreover that it is the duty of *every* man to aim at *this happiness* of such a community, I need not spend time to prove, that ONE AND ALL ought to arise and *overturn, overturn, and continue to overturn,* till they "leave not a wreck (of their bondage) behind."

Let us suppose, for a moment, a nation, sunk in vice, and prostitute to a herd of plundering villains, assuming & exerting *a supreme power* over many millions of people in a distant land; let us realize this people as having a charter from GOD and Nature to be free from *all manner of foreign controul without their consent;* let us also consider that the *whole administration* of what is called government, in this *assuming nation,* to be wicked and corrupt to a degree unparalleled in history; and that *all officers* over these subjugated millions do and must, upon the present plan, hold their offices by the tenure of slaves and vassals to the worst of men; let us suppose these things and many more impositions and thraldoms needless here to enumerate;—and I ask whether such a government as is over *this distant land* is worth preserving; yea rather I ask,—whether the cry ought not to be as in the days of Sampson, *know you not that the Philistines are rulers over you?* Whether firebrands, or the jaw-bone, the first weapon just rage can lay hold on, may not be *lawfully* employed against *the oppressors?*[4] For the word of GOD in the example of an Ehud has pointed the remedy against tyranny, and the mode of relief from *Moabitish* oppression. Prayers and tears *with the help of a dagger,*—crying to the Lord and *the hand of an Ehud.* DEVOTION and ACTION united: Tyrants are of that race of Devils that they are not cast out by fasting and prayer *alone.* The light of nature has not left us in the dark relative to the way of exterminating robbers and destroyers: We have natural light sufficient to show us how an enslaved people are to obtain deliverance. But the LORD OF LIGHT has given us *the fit message to send to a tyrant:*—A DAGGER OF A CUBIT IN HIS BELLY:—and every worthy man who desires to be an Ehud, *the deliverer of his country,* will strive to be the messenger.[5]

From hence, I infer, that bad men and bad measures, are not exempted from "opprobrious epithets"—nay; not from death and extinction itself, by being shrouded under great names and dignified appellations. "Ministers" of state, foreign "jurisdictions" and "immediate executors of laws," in certain cases, are to be pursued—not with "epithets and abuse"—but with execrations and death. *Desert,—desert,* I say, is the standard of such pursuit and punishment:—this is the touchstone by which we are to determine the justice of those who *thus pursue,* and the lawfulness of the punishment they inflict on *the overtaken.*

It seems the writer in Draper's paper thinks that "*Americans* DO and ought to contend for the trial by Jury with a becoming assurance." We should be glad to know;—Whether Americans *have* and DO thus contend, while they submit with tameness, cowardice and eternal infamy, to the extended and extending jurisdictions of Admiralty Courts on this Continent? Whether so gross impositions, rapine and barbarity were ever practised upon any other people, under colour of law, as those Courts decree, execute and record?—Whether it is not the policy of the times from Mansfield to the lowest subaltern in office to eradicate, render useless, *or worse than useless,* the trial by Jury?

As to the Account of the Trial of Pierpont and Davis, which it seems provoked *Draper's* COMMON SENSE to issue forth; whether true or no I am unable to say: I own that part of the publications which have been by some thought to relate to that cause would have pleased me better, had they been otherwise worded and more clearly expressed.[6] And I have good reason to believe that *if the whole of the matter* was before the world, it would much serve that Cause, which Draper's employers seek to destroy. For I have taken great pains to enquire and know the truth relative to every hearing of Cutler's case, and find the uniform account from almost every one who inhabits the county of Worcester, serving to confirm the sentiment, I ever entertained concerning the Judges and lawyers who bore a part in that trial. I am verily perswaded that the eyes of that county have been much opened and their opinions of certain men and things much changed in the course of this cause:—A knowledge of this, I have no doubt contributed to certain steps and manoeuvres, which otherwise COMMON SENSE, prudence and policy would have forbidden.

Till last Thursday's paper, I never heard it suggested that "Pierpont's *management* at the trial was *extraordinary*" in any degree; and if it was so much so as "to more than counterbalance the extraordinary management of others," the Public ought to know it. And as there can be no manner of *danger* in telling *the whole truth with regard to Pierpont,* we have a right to expect this writer will give it to us; and I am well informed that others would do the like with respect TO ALL CONCERNED, if FINES and IMPRISONMENTS, STOCKS & PILLORIES were not in the administration of some, who will not permit *the one half to be told.* But the breath of man is in his nostrils, he dieth—and *his deeds are recorded.*

We all know that "the *whole* Jury bring in the verdict": but it is as well known, that some men have much more art, address, powers, and influence with their fellows, than others: now I cannot say, how far McClanathan and Wheeler were fitted for the purpose of perswasion or influence, but this I firmly believe that *every* man sees a reason why McClanathan was permitted to set, tho' objected against, and why *two* Hardwick men should *successively* strike the pupil of Sheriff Chandler's eye in preference to any others of a large multitude who were about him. And as I have over and over again heard, that the Council for Pierpont and Davis made repeated offers to draw a Jury by lot, or strike a Jury, as 'tis said they do in England, none of which were accepted, it serves to confirm me and many others, that *all was not right.* I presume our sentiments of this affair is no evidence, that we are unfriendly to trials by Jury in general, any more than an opinion, that *some one beguiled Jury* were insidiously drawn to give an unrighteous verdict, could be fairly construed as "villifying" that excellent institution for the purposes of distributive justice.

A jury *acquitted* a Preston and a Killroy; A jury *convicted* a SIDNEY of high-treason: This is the difference between the reigns of a Brunswick and a Stuart![7]—But still juries are admirable inventions. Laud with his religion was a curse, Caesar with his Senate was a curse, Charles the second with his Parliament was a curse, and JEFFRIES[8] with his JURY was a curse; but religion, senates, parliaments and juries have and will be blessings to mankind for ages past and to come.—"A fair trial, in GOD's name" said a Jeffries, and prostituted his office, his conscience, and stained his robes with blood—the blood of a SIDNEY!—Execrable villain! Historians have told his speeches, his windings, his arts and his—! at the trial of this first of men!—History also can and *will* tell *more modern stories.*—We execrate Jeffries, while to this day we almost adore a Sidney:—and generations unborn will do the same. These different fates are not peculiar to the judges and convicts of the last century.—But THE WHOLE TRUTH is never told of THE GREAT AND GUILTY, while they live and *bear rule.* 'Tis succeeding ages relate the frauds, the ravages, and butcheries of enormous villains.

"Hear this—& tremble! ye who 'scape the laws."[9]

What the C—J—said or did in Cutler's cause, I am unable to relate; but if the concurrent testimony of 50 people who were present may be relied on, he did deliver it as his opinion, that "the non-importation agreement was against the laws of GOD and Man." And if so, how it can be considered as "demonstrating a gross want of regard and respect" to inform the world of it, I leave others to say: For though I have heard lawyers often talk of *their reports,* I never before heard it intimated that *reporting* was exclusively confined to the Long-robe. Thus much is certain, if this doctrine concerning the non-importation agreement is law, we should be glad to know it: And it may have this valuable tendency;—to make the next efforts for freedom favour more of that virtue and valour for which Englishmen in former ages have been justly renowned;

and may turn this GREAT PEOPLE to call on the name of the LORD, and to seek a redress of their grievances, with the spear and the lance, at that GLORIOUS SEAT OF JUSTICE,—where Moses brought the Egyptian; and Sampson the Phillistines.

EDWARD SEXBY.

1. *Boston Gazette,* 12 October 1772, filling almost the entire first page—except for a portion of the third column devoted to a "letter" from the same author to Joseph Hawley (see the following piece). Quincy may have encountered Sexby in his reading of Catharine Macaulay's history. Sexby was in his own way as much of a political opportunist as Marchmont Nedham, though Quincy probably did not realize it. See my brief comments in Coquillette and York, eds., *Portrait of a Patriot,* 1:85-86; and ibid., 1:58–60, 109–12, 209–10, for Macaulay's history and his use of it in the political commonplace book.

2. Once again Quincy quoted from Nugent's *Ode to Mankind,* and, once again, altered the text (from p. 8) to achieve the desired effect (the original reading "And he who dares her Gift invade, By Nature's oldest Law is made, Thy Victim or Thy Slave.")

3. This is the opening sentence to a piece by "Common Sense" for the *Massachusetts Gazette,* 1 October 1772, supplement.

4. Samson's tale is told in the Old Testament book of Judges 13–16.

5. The essay was indented for a half dozen lines to squeeze into the margin, as a source for the reference to Ehud, Judges 3. Although angered by the behavior of Israelites who had strayed off into evil ways, God forgave them and allowed Ehud to lead them out of captivity by the Moabites.

6. See supra p. 112, n. 4.

7. Quincy referred here to Algernon Sidney, one of his favorite writers in what historian Caroline Robbins called the "commonwealth" tradition. By Quincy's era he had become revered as a champion of republicanism, a martyr to the cause of English freedom when he was convicted of treason and executed in 1683 for participating in the so-called Rye House Plot against Charles II. He had supported the dethroning of Charles I but ended up as appalled by the actions of Cromwell and the army in forming the Protectorate as he had been by those of the king they displaced. For Sidney and the American Revolutionary generation see Caroline Robbins, *The Eighteenth-Century Commonwealthman* (Cambridge, Mass.: Harvard University Press, 1959); Peter Karsten, *Patriot-Heroes in England and America (* Madison, Wis.: University of Wisconsin Press, 1978); and Alan Craig Houston, *Algernon Sidney and the Republican Heritage in England and America* (Princeton, N. J.: Princeton University Press, 1991). Quincy owned a compilation of Sidney's writings that included an account of his trial: see Coquillette and York, eds., *Portrait of a Patriot*, 5:893 (no. 61 in the "Catalogue of Books").

8. As the newly-appointed chief justice of the Court of King's Bench, Judge George Jeffreys presided at Sidney's trial, the villain to Sidney's hero in Quincy's pantheon of important figures from the past.

9. Taken from Alexander Pope's *The First Satire on the Second Book of Horace* (London: L. G., 1733), p. 17, though Quincy could have turned to any number of editions printed during this period or to a later compilation of Pope's works; it is not clear which he actually used.

"EDWARD SEXBY"

12 October 1772[1]

To the honorable JOSEPH HAWLEY, *Esq;*

SIR,

THE great respect I have for your understanding, and the deep veneration I entertain of your integrity, prompt me thus publickly to give you information of a report which has been industriously propagated from one end of the province to the other;—by whom I need not inform you.—The report I mean is the same with that which makes it's appearance in Draper's last week's paper, under the head of "Extract of a Letter from London, August 3, 1772." In which pretended extract by the "Gentleman of distinguished character" is meant yourself.—That you declared yourself in the General Assembly at the Spring-Sessions for making an addition to the Judges salaries I have very little doubt; because if their commissions were *during good behaviour,* I presume every friend to his Country, would second the motion:—but that you then declared "that if the Assembly refused to make any addition to the small salaries of the Judges, you thought NO EXCEPTION could be taken to Parliament's providing for their salaries", is what I will not believe, unless you give your own testimony to this report, or by silence give your consent to it.—The interposition of the Parliament of G. B. in this matter and at this time, being in my humble opinion the most fatal and daring measure in the whole deep-laid and compacted system of American bondage:—A measure which if suffered to take effect, will in future render our lives and *personal* Liberties as precarious and insignificant, as our rights and properties are at present worthless and transitory in the hands of British Legislators and American Judges of Admiralty.

With unfeigned regard,

I am your friend and fellow countryman,

EDWARD SEXBY.

1. This brief piece appeared on the bottom right of the same page as the previous essay. Joseph Hawley practiced law in Northampton and sat in the Massachusetts House. He would become one of the leading patriots from the western part of the colony, an ally of Samuel Adams when it came to protesting imperial policy. He figures prominently as one of Hampshire County's "river gods" in Robert J. Taylor, *Western Massachusetts in the American Revolution* (Providence, R. I.: Brown University Press, 1954).

JQ TO JOSIAH QUINCY SR.

Late 1772[1]

Honored Sir, Thursday, 2 o'clock

I thank you very sincerely for your solicitude and good wishes; being convinced of their sincerity. The expression of them gives me a proportionate satisfaction. My fever the last two days and nights seems almost wholly to have left me. My slumbers are sound and undisturbed, and the light of the morning finds me refreshed. The Dr. (Warren) thinks (at least very solemnly says) that my symptoms are very favorable, and my prospect of health (humanly speaking) certain. Be this as it may, my appetite and my relish for food extends beyond the limits of my prescription.

Thus much to gratify you Sir with particulars, and to do it has been as much my pleasure as my duty—A little now to gratify myself.

The decease of giving advice is one of the most difficult of any. Yet both the male and female would think themselves adept in it. But of the few who are any way skilled in this nice art, how few know their mode of application and the time to administer.—But of the empyrics in this mystery with which the world swarms, how few are truly solicitous about the real welfare of the pretended object. How many are actuated by the felicity they feel, from gratifying the pride of their own hearts? This may not be any justification of an obstinate mule, but they may serve as some palliation for the conduct of those who feel, and those who can see. There are those who have the gift of prophecy, and many who have the gift of tongues, but also how few have the gift of persuasion.

Don't be concerned that I worry myself with this letter. Tis' rather sport than labour.—And it gives me some pleasure to see you puzzled to find out its meaning.

For how to apply
(says Hudibras) Has vexed me more
Than all the fellow said before[2]

Give my hearty and sincere love to my mother, and tell her, I will be very compliant with her advice if she will give it to me as *in times past* for I do not recollect she ever pleaded with me in vain.—Give my warm affections to sister Lincoln, and tell her that our friend Governor Hutchinson is always telling us "*we shall never all think alike* in this world".—With my best wishes for the family, and a grateful remembrance of your attachment, and goodness to me.

I am your very affectionate son
J. Quincy jun.

1. Eliza Susan Quincy transcribed this letter for her "Memoir," 2:38a, 39a, QP 46 (reel 6) MHS, and included most of it in the printed *Memoir*, pp. 54-55 as well. The original is not among the Quincy Papers at the MHS.

2. Inspired by, but not taken directly from, Samuel Butler's *Hudibras?* These lines (along with some others) are among those from Quincy's letter not included in the printed biography.

PETERSHAM TOWN RESOLUTIONS

4 January 1773[1]

At a meeting of the freeholders and other inhabitants of the town of Petersham, *in the county of Worcester, duly assembled according to law, held by adjournment on the 4th of* January, 1773, *the committee chosen the 30th ult. made the following report, viz.*

"THE town having received a circular letter from the town of Boston,[2] respecting the present grievances and abominable oppression under which this country groans, have thereupon taken into their most serious consideration, the present policy of the British government and administration, with regard to Great-Britain and these colonies, have carefully reviewed the mode of election and the quality of the electors of the commons of that island, and have also attentively reflected upon the enormous and growing influence of the crown, and that bane of all free states a standing army, in the time of peace, and in consequence therefore are fully confirmed in opinion, that the antient rights of the nation are capitally invaded, and the greatest of the most precious and established liberties of Englishmen utterly destroyed: ——— And whereas, the Parliament of Great-Britain by various statutes and acts, have unrighteously destroyed our trade, denied and precluded us from the setting up and carrying on manufactures highly beneficial to the inhabitants of these territories, restricted and prevented our lawful intercourse and commerce with other states and kingdoms, have also made laws and institutions touching life and limb, in disherison of the ancient common law of the land; and moreover, have, in these latter times, robbed and plundered the honest and laborious inhabitants of this extensive continent, of their property by mere force and power, and are now draining this people of the fruits of their toil, by thus raising a revenue from them against the natural rights of man, and in open violation of the laws of God: This town in union with the worthy inhabitants of Boston, now think it their indispensible duty to consider of the premises and the present aspect of the times, and to take such steps as upon mature deliberation are judged right and expedient, and hereupon this town

"*Resolved,* That, with a Governor appointed from Great-Britain (especially at this day) during pleasure, with a large stipend, dependant upon the will of the crown, and controled by instructions from a British Minister of State;

with a council subject to the negative of such a governor, and with all officers civil and military subject to his appointment or consent; with a castle in the hands of a standing army, stationed in the very bowels of the land,[3] that amazing number of place-men and dependants, with which every maritime town already swarms, no people can ever be truly virtuous, free or brave.

"*Resolved,* That the parliament of Great-Britain, usurping and exercising a legislative authority over, and extorting an unrighteous revenue from these colonies, is against all divine and human laws. The late appointment of salaries to be paid to our Superior Court Judges, whose creation, pay and commission depend on mere will and pleasure, complete a system of bondage equal to any ever before fabricated by the combined efforts of the ingenuity, malice, fraud, and wickedness of man.

"*Resolved,* That it is the opinion of this town, that a despotic, arbitrary government is the kingdom of this world, as set forth in the New-Testament, and is diametrically opposite to the establishment of christianity, in a society, and has a direct tendency to sink a people into a profound state of ignorance and irreligion; and that if we have an eye to our own and posterity's happiness (not only in this world but the world to come) it is our duty to oppose such a government.

"*And further Resolved,* That the depriving the colonies of their constitutional rights, may be fitly compared to the dismembering the natural body, which will soon affect the heart; and it would be nothing unexpected for us to hear, that those very persons who have been so active in robbing the colonies of their constitutional rights, that they have delivered up the constitution of our mother country into the hands of our King.

"*Therefore, Resolved,* That it is the first and highest social duty of this people, to consider of, and seek ways and means for a speedy redress of these mighty grievances and intolerable wrongs; and that for the obtainment of this end, this people are warranted, by the laws of God and nature, in the use of every rightful art, and energy of policy, stratagem and force.

"And while we are thus under these awful frowns of divine providence, and involved, as this people are, in heavy calamities which daily increase in number and severity, it is highly becoming towns and individuals to humble themselves before almighty GOD, seriously to commune with their own hearts , and seek carefully with tears, for the causes of the prevailing distresses of the land: And while it is apparent that pristine piety and purity of morals have given place to infidelity, dissipation, luxury and gross corruption of mind and morals, there is a loud call for public humility, lamentings and reformation; and it is at this time eminently incumbent upon one and all, to seek at the throne of the Great GOD, for those special and remarkable interpositions of divine providence, grace and mercy, which have so often saved New-England from both public and private distress and misery: And as there is great reason to believe that in past times we have too much depended upon the exertions of worldly wisdom and political devices, it becomes us in our present melancholy situation to rely no longer on an arm of flesh, but on the arms of that all-powerful GOD, who is able to unite the numerous inhabitants of this extensive territory, as a band of brothers in one common cause; who can easily give that true religion which shall make us his people indeed, that spirit which shall fit us to endure temporary hardships for the procurement of future happiness; that spirit of valour and irresistable courage which shall occasion our aged and our youth to jeopard their lives with joy in the high places of the field, for his name and service sake, for the preservation also of this goodly heritage of our fathers, for the sake of the living children of our loins, and the unborn millions of posterity.

"We believe that there are very many, who in these days have kept their integrity and garments unspotted; and hope that God will deliver them, and our nation for their sake. GOD will not suffer this land, where the gospel hath flourished, to become a slave of the world; he will stir up witnesses of the truth, and in his own time spirit his people to stand up for his cause and deliver them. In a similar belief, that Patriot of Patriots, the great ALGERNON SIDNEY, lived and died, and dying breathed a like sentiment and prophecy, touching his own and the then approaching times;[*4] a prophecy however not accomplished until a glorious revolution.

1. These resolutions, plus the town's instructions to Ephraim Doolittle, its representative in the General Court, were printed in the *Boston Evening-Post* and the *Boston Gazette,* in the 18 January 1773 issue for both papers. The transcription here is from the *BEP* version. Edmund B. Wilson, *Address Delivered in Petersham, Massachusetts, July 4, 1854* (Boston: Crosby, Nichols and Co., 1855), p. 99, noted that town leader Sylvanus How had readily acknowledged Quincy's assis-

tance with the resolutions and that Quincy's son—Josiah the Mayor—had a handwritten copy in his possession. Solicitor General Alexander Wedderburn, in his 29 January 1774 excoriation of Benjamin Franklin before the privy council, quoted in part from the Petersham resolutions as an example of the wrong thinking encouraged in Franklin's "school of Politics." See Leonard Labaree, et al., eds., *The Papers of Benjamin Franklin*, 38 vols. (New Haven, Conn.: Yale University Press, 1959 —) 21:63–64.

2. Quincy had been a member of the twenty-one-man Boston committee of correspondence, formed after a motion made by Samuel Adams, that drafted those resolutions. They were approved by the full town meeting on 20 November 1772, and then sent out "to the several Towns in this Province and the World." See Record Commissioners, *Boston Town Records*, pp.95–106 for the "Rights" and "Infringements," those rights being grounded in the law of nature. For context see Richard D. Brown, *Revolutionary Politics in Massachusetts* (Cambridge, Mass.: Harvard University Press, 1970).

3. Of the four British regiments sent to Boston in 1768, two (the 64th and 65th) had been re-assigned in less than a year. The remaining two (the 14th and 29th) had been removed from the town proper to barracks on Castle William within two weeks of the March 1770 "massacre," with the 29th being transferred to New Jersey the following June. The 14th had been transferred to the West Indies in August 1772 and the 64th came down from Halifax to replace it. Hutchinson had effectively turned Castle William over to the army and he had begun to accept his salary from the crown rather than from the General Court; so had superior court judges. Whether Castle William should be garrisoned by militia or regulars, whether munitions stockpiled at public expense (an issue that would be brought to the fore during the "powder alarm" of September 1774), or whether the king's troops had right of access on a road through town (such as would be seen at Salem and the near-confrontation there in February 1775)—all raised complicated questions of local versus imperial authority.

4. The asterisk was placed after the town's instructions to Ephraim Doolittle, which advised: "*See* SIDNEY's *Apology in the Day of his Death.*" Sidney's "Apology" had been printed in various editions of his writings—one of which Quincy, a great admirer of Sidney, owned. See the posthumous "Catalogue of Books" in Coquillette and York, eds., *Portrait of a Patriot*, 5:893 (no. 61). The last paragraph was essentially taken from the Apology, most likely the version that appeared as an appendix to the *Discourses Concerning Government* (London: A. Millar, 1763), Appendix, pp. 197–98: "But I believe that there are many who haue kept their garments unspotted; and hope that God will deliuer them and the nation for their sakes. God will not suffer this land, where the gospell hath of late flourished more than in any other part of the world, to become a slave of the world; he will not suffer it to be made a land of grauen images: he will stirre up witnesses of the truth. And, in his owne time, spirit his people to stand up for his cause, and deliure them. I liued in this belief, and am now about to dye in it. I knowe my Redeemer liues; and, as he hath in a great mesure upheld me in the day of my calamity, hope that he will still uphold me by his spirite in this last moment, and giuing me grace to glorify him in my death, receaue me into the glory prepared for thoes that feare him, when my body shall be dissolued. Amen."

JQ TO ABIGAIL QUINCY

1 March 1773[1]

Charleston, South Carolina March 1st 1773

The first emotion of my heart is,—gratitude to Heaven,—the second—love to my friend nearer than a brother.—How much, my dear wife, we owe to God, can only be known by reflection on the felicities we have enjoyed, those we hope:—the pleasures of our union, the dread of our seperation,—and the iminent dangers from which I have been delivered. A voyage more disagreable, dangerous, and terrible perhaps was never passed than that which landed me on this distant shore.[2]

I omit lesser hardships, disappointments and affliction. I cannot say that I was ever well at sea, although I was not always very ill. My dear partner, what cause have we of thankfulness. I had not the least expectation of ever seeing you or my dear boy again. I was fully convinced that we must perish. Heaven has gratified me with satisfying a frequent wish of my heart, that I might once see Death before my eyes, as striking his dart—that I might know if possible the stability of what I lean on.—Whether the pillared firmament or rottenness.

How often did I wish that my first and best friends knew my hazards that they might share my calamities. How often did I rejoice that ignorance freed them from pain on my account and that long expectation of hearing from me would lessen the weight of what length of time would convince them of. How often did I imprint the loss of seperation, and look forward[3] to that 'bourn' from whence 'no traveller returns'![4] How frequently clasp my dear boy, and view him in a wide, corrupt world, destitute of the instruction, vigilance, care, and protection of a father!

You will doubtless wish to know what real damage our vessel sustained: and when I tell you but a very trifle to her rigging, you may be surprised. But the wonder may cease when I inform you that our ship was remarkably well found, new sails, rigging and in very fine order, active, and good seamen, and a most incomparable commander. Such precaution before danger, such vigilance, activity and firmness in it were truly astonishing. We passengers almost idolized him. But before the storm was over, all were nearly beat out–master and mariners:—as good as ever steped between stem and stern of a ship. But

I must have done. The last eve[5] at dusk I landed here, in better health than could be expected, especially when you are told that the wet of the Cabin, and dampness of my bed, were so great, as that the one was flowing, and the other might have been wrung. This town makes a most beautiful appearance as you come up to it, and in many respects a magnificent one. I have not been here twenty hours, although I have traversed the most populous parts of it, I can only say in general, that in grandeur, splendor of buildings, decorations, equipages, numbers, commerce, shipping, and indeed in almost everything it far surpasses all I ever saw or ever expect to see in America. Of their manners, literature, understanding, spirit of true liberty, policy and government, I can as yet form no adequate judgment. But some omen forbade ill touching the truly great, and able. All seems at present to be trade, riches, magnificence, and great affectation of state is every thing: much gaiety and dissipation. . .

There are such a multitude of ghosts and shadows here that I make not so bad a figure on comparison. I shall give you an account of my health when I can with certainty; every thing looks favourable at present that way.[6] At sea, sometimes it was extreme hot, but here the weather has been uncommonly cold. Snow and hail in plenty this last week. Want of paper compels me to put an end to converse with her, with whom I could commune with pleasure all the day long. I do not want room to say

I am the same Josiah Quincy junr.

1. Letter from Quincy to his wife Abigail, 1 March 1773, which Eliza Susan Quincy transcribed for her handwritten "Memoir," 2:54–56, QP 46 (reel 6) MHS, and then included in the printed *Memoir,* pp. 71–73, with various small changes to punctuation and small additions to the latter version. The original is not in the MHS collections. A transcription of Quincy's journal of this trip (by Michael H. Hayden, with copious notes) is in Coquillette and York, eds., *Portrait of a Patriot,* 3:85–350. See too Dan Coquillette's introduction for that volume on pp. 11–82.

2. Eliza Susan Quincy may have deleted some material that followed between this point and the next paragraph. Without the original for comparison, it is impossible to know how much.

3. The words from this point to the end of the paragraph are not in the handwritten "Memoir"—perhaps just a simple error in transcription.

4. *Hamlet,* Act III, Scene 1, from Hamlet's most famous soliloquy.

5. "Last evening" in the printed *Memoir*, p. 72.

6. The remaining sentences and closing are not included in the *Memoir.*

JQ TO SAMUEL QUINCY

6 April 1773[1]

Dear and respected Brother, No. Carolina Apr. 6th 1773 Edenton

Engagements and considerations not worth enumerating have prevented a transmission of that knowledge of my wellfare and adventures which would please the Brother and amuse the friend. An account of my passage has reached Boston, and, previous to your reception of this, Mrs. Q will be able to relate how far my excursion has already proved salutary and promises future success. Indeed, if an entire ease and hilarity of mind, together with a delightfull temperature of air and moderate exercise can give me health, I shall obtain that mighty boon. If I had not experienced the effect, I should scarce have believed it possible, for one of my turn and past life so speedily to become that man of carelessness and pleasure. Horace has said *caelum non animum mutant qui trans currunt*[2] and therefore you may perhaps be obliged to exercise your faith in order to credit me: but I am incapable of self-sensation and discernment, if the fact is not thus. Not however that I am altogether the Idler, or the man of dissipation and intemperance: we may enjoy true ease and chearfullness, and be neither one or the other. It is natural to a man of sense and enquiry to desire some information of the laws, constitution and police of countries he can not visit in person, with some account of the variances which are observable in the customs, manners and improvements of the Inhabitants. As far as my power extends I would gladly gratify your expectations from me. But to say all on this subject that I would chuse (if I say any thing) will exceed the limits of a Letter, if not those of your patience. Having, however, near finished my tour through the Carolinas, I may hazard a general, and in some measure a comparative view of North and South province, to one who will consider the necessary defects of a brief sketch and will in brotherly love be lenient towards deficiencies of a more capital nature.

The genius of the South Carolinian seems much confined; whether by nature, education or some other cause may be doubtfull: but I believe Dame Nature is not only a bounteous, but a pretty even handed dispenser. Their taste is more delighted with salt and spices, with the goblet and the Cup, with magnificence and splendor, with equipages and the turff, than with enquiries, disquisition, and improvements of the severe, liberal, and enlarged kind:—nay according to my observations, than even with engagements and pursuits of the softer and more enlivening sort. In short, Bacchus, nay a Bucephalus, is in this climate a more influential being, than a Venus or Apollo. But though the glass circles in quick revolutions I saw little of that exuberanic hilarity and roar which are so incident to a Northern festival and entertainment: indeed in point of genuine vivacity and fire the Northern Bells and Sparks surpass those of the South whose point and blaze seem exhausted or extinguished by a warmer sun. Should you tell me that my *ruling planet* at the North so extended its *polar influence;* that I was but a poor or blind observer of the meteors and luminaries of the South, I will readily accede to an imputation that pays a complement to my virtue, though at the expense of my judgment.

It is not be wondered at then, that politicks becomes an uninteresting theme, that discourses on law, government and civil society give place to a conversation of Rice, indigo, Negroes and horses:—the bottle oftener revolves round the table than a sentimental story or burst of wit and humour: Gallantry and the delights of Venus are more the employment of Baccanalian loquacity, than of Carolinean pursuit and vigour: neither is this incompatible with a former remark, for the voluptuary who talks much of intrigue and women does not always follow an amour with the most perseverance or push an address with the greatest activity.

Little more than an imaginary, mathematical line parts the two Carolinas, but one would be induced to think from the different appearance of men and things , that—"Eden roll'd between, and mountains interven'd."[3]

The face of most here is quite changed—comparatively little splendor or show—more solidity and real improvement. The political pulse beats high, and men of taste and sense came to redouble in number and strength. Small talk and the lighter Conversation is supplanted by nobler and more worthy engagements. Industry is risen and labor is at work in the woods and fields. Agriculture is carried to higher perfection, flocks and herds increase, and greater equality and social happiness is diffused abroad. The natural concomitants of all this is easily conjectured: freedom of thought, inquisitive dispositions, a more general flourishing in arts and sciences. I need not now say, which country pleased my fancy, and had the preference in my heart.

But I must wave a subject which will lead me into thorny and dangerous paths; and should certainly suppress the effusions already written, if I did not remember, that an only Brother has a claim to a considerable share in my pleasures and confidence, and will make no use of my remarks injurious to me or prejudicial to the good fame of a country where I experienced much civility and politeness.

I need not say, that general observations like general rules must be allowed their exceptions, neither would I be understood as speaking decisively upon matters of which is probably I am no competent judge: but as giving to a friend those impressions and sentiments which in a reversal of circumstances I should wish to receive from him.

Present me in the bonds of love and esteem to your worthy Consort, and tell your little ones that I remember them with the feelings of affection:—and accept my wishes for them and you, as those of a real friend and Brother,

J Quincy junr.

PS. Tell Sister Q I have as yet seen no table surpass her's in true elegance and taste:—several in richness of glass and china, and magnificence of plate:—and but one in point of gratification to the palate.—Mrs. Hill who happened to be a guest promised to send a small edition of recipes.

1. From the original in QP 51 (also reel 29) MHS. Eliza Susan Quincy did not transcribe it for either memoir. Samuel Quincy was Josiah Junior's older brother by a decade. He had joined the Massachusetts Bar in 1758, four years after completing his studies at Harvard. A good lawyer, even Whiggish in his politics (and acting as prosecutor in two of the three "Massacre" trials" in opposition to his brother as a defense counsel), he eventually chose law and order over protest, and sided with the those defending the empire against men like his younger brother who kept pressing their opposition to policies coming out of London, and the actions of Thomas Hutchinson in their support. He left for London after fighting erupted at Lexington and Concord, then made his way to Antigua, and eventually secured an appointment as the governor of St. Croix. In the meantime, he had been proscribed in Massachusetts and his remaining property there was sold at public auction. He perished while voyaging to England in 1789. He, his younger brother, and their father had done their best to try to keep political differences from breaking family ties. There is a nice sketch of him in Sibley's *Harvard Graduates,* 13:478–88.

2. Quincy went to Horace, as he did in his December 1764 letter to Bela Lincoln (see supra, pp. 1-2); his underlining there was converted to italics here, as in other instances.

3. It is not clear who Quincy quoted here. It may be a reference to the valley of the river Eden above Solway Firth, separating England and Scotland.

JOSIAH QUINCY SR. TO JQ
9 April 1773[1]

My dear Son, Braintree April 9th 1773

The Contents of your first Letter gave your Friends both Pleasure and Pain: Pain to hear you were called to endure so much upon your Passage but greatly overballanced by the good News of your safe Arrival at the Port you were bound to, and that notwithstanding the Fatigue and Anxiety you underwent you thought your Self better than when you left Us. If my Wishes and Prayers are heard and granted, we shall ere' long meet and rejoice together, with Hearts filled with Gratitude to our divine Benefactor, for every Instance of his unmerited Goodness to us, whilst absent from each other.

As to what has occurred in private and publick Life since you left us, the publick Prints and Letters from your Friends in Boston will inform you much better than I can. I forget whether it was just before, or soon after you sailed, that the good old Lady Madam Marsh, began sensibly to decline, by losing her Appetite and other Symtoms of her approaching Dissolution. She has been confined to her Chamber above these six Weeks past, and is now scarce able to get from her Bed to the Fire. She is free from Pain, and sleeps the greatest Part of her Time. Her understanding is remarkably clear and Vivacity of Spirits that almost excites Envy. She often asks if any more of your Letters are come to hand.[2] Your two Sisters have had the Measles and almost got well again as also Tower and Nat. Your poor Mother has had a most fateguing Time of it; has never been to Boston since she took Leave of you. We depend upon your Wife and my dear little grandson's coming, the last Week in this Month or the first week in May, to tarry with us till she goes home to prepare for your Reception. This is the Favour we expect, but whether it will be granted, remains in Contemplation. I had the Pleasure a Day or two since of seeing this dear little Babe run alone. I am perswaded the Country Air and Exercise would contribute greatly to His Health and Strength. Your Sister Lincoln paid us a Visit this Week, but almost worn out with her constant Attendance upon a gloomy fretfull and sick Husband [missing portion] seems to be more and more a Burthen to himself and of Course to all about [more missing] is truly pitiable, and the more as it seems to be without Remedy.[3]

A Revolution in our Braintree Politicks began at our election in March.

Major or rather Colonel Thayer had not Interest enough to carry his Election, for Select Man and our Country Wits say, they have cut down the Tree in March, and intend to bark it in May, from whence it's generally concluded your Cozn N. Quincy will supply his Place in the next general Assembly unless the Colonel Rum should prove strong enough to defeat the Designs of his Enemies.[4] We have had a very favourable Winter upon the Whole; and this fortnight past some of the pleasantest Weather I ever knew at this Time of year; which makes me fear, least where you are, it may be [portion missing] tender Constitution.

I am under some Concern least you should think the Contents [portion missing] not worth the Charge of Postage; which I will prevent by a private Conveyance if [portion missing] however, if the inclosed Letters to two of the principal Gentlemen in Philadelphia should procure you the same Civility and Politeness as was shown to me, I assure my Self you will have no Reason to regret, this otherwise impertinent Scribble of—

Your affectionate Father
Jos. Quincy

P.S. All the Family send their Love and best Wishes for your safe Return

1. Transcribed from the original in QP 51 (also filmed, on reel 29) MHS; Eliza Susan Quincy copied most of it into her "Memoir," 2:93a, QP 46 (reel 6) MHS, but it was not included in the printed *Memoir.* Portions near a torn right margin are missing, as noted above.

2. The widow of the Reverend Joseph Marsh of Braintree, whose son, also named Joseph, had acted as a tutor to prepare Josiah Junior for Harvard, as he had John Adams before him, and other boys in the town. Josiah Senior had married as his third wife Ann Marsh–sister of the younger Marsh, daughter of the elder Marsh, a good example of the kinship ties formed in this small farming community to the south of Boston that so many Quincys and Adamses would call home.

3. Her husband Bela was Josiah Junior's first correspondent in this collection (see supra, pp. 1–2).

4. Norton Quincy, who had retired to Braintree to escape the hubbub of Boston, was sympathetic to the patriot cause but would have preferred to be left alone and live the life of a country gentleman. He was actually defeated in the election, then appointed to the governor's council by the House, but General Thomas Gage, Hutchinson's successor as governor, refused to approve the appointment. See the brief sketch in Sibley's *Harvard Graduates,* 10:75–78.

SAMUEL QUINCY TO JQ
13 April 1773[1]

Dear Brother Boston April 13th 1773.

Wherever or However this may meet you, accept the tenderest Salutations of a Brother.

I have been waiting some time for an Opportunity to Lodge a Letter for You with my Friend Mr. Thomas Smith of Philadelphia, and having this minute heard of a Vessel that sails this Evening, am set down first to tell you that I am well with my Family, and Connections; my Father and his Family, save an accident which happened to Mother by a Fall down Stairs, by which her leg and ancle are much bruised. I had in my Arms a few minutes ago your fine Little Boy; and the pleasure of seeing Sister Quincy, your Father Phillips &c. at their house, where I went upon a Visit, and upon hearing of this Conveyance, left them almost as soon as I had Spoke to them, to write you a line.

I hope by this time we may congratulate You on the Recovery of your health to the utmost of your Expectations. We have accidentally heard of your being about a Fortnight ago at Cape-Fear; but What of your health, or What of the prosecution of your intended Journey, we are wholly at a loss.

Things public and private remain much as they were when you left Us. The Spring Ships arrived Yesterday and the day before, but not a Word of News respecting America.

The Business of the Courts and your Office, I suppose You will be punctually informed of by Mr. Moreton.[2] I know of Nothing that has taken place other than you could have wished.

Mr. Smith you will find a humane, courteous Gentleman; and I hope receive a Civility from him that will do honour to my Recommendation, and prove a Satisfaction to you equal to most of the Letters you have been favored with.

It would give me pleasure had I time to enlarge but the Vessell is ready to put to Sea, and I must have done.—I depend upon hearing from you soon, and intend to write you, if I have an Opportunity in New York.—May the Almighty Sovereign of the Universe bless You, continue and confirm your

Health and Prosperity, and return you soon to the Society of your Family and Friends and among the Rest, to

Your Affectionate Friend and Brother,

Josiah Quincy Junior Esq Saml. Quincy

1. In QP 51 (and reel 29) MHS; also in the "Memoir," 2:94a, QP 46 (reel 6) MHS.

2. Perez Morton, who had completed his studies at Harvard two years before and worked in Quincy's law office as he prepared to become a member of the Massachusetts bar, the next year. He would become one of the town's leading patriots and delivered the eulogy for Joseph Warren (Quincy's doctor) in April 1776, nearly a year after Warren had been slain at the Battle of Bunker Hill, doing so when Warren's body was re-interred in Boston after the British evacuation just weeks before. In later years he would serve as the state's attorney general. There is an entry for him in Sibley's *Harvard Graduates,* 17:555–561. Also see p. 370, n. 1 infra.

JQ TO JOSIAH QUINCY SR.

15 April 1773[1]

Virginia, Port Royal April 15th 1773.

Honored and dear Sir

The occurrences of every day (however vexatious some of them are for the present) give me new reason to consider my present undertaking, as a salutary and happy adventure.—I know I fled from fortune and fame—but

"What's fame? a fancied life in other's breath
A thing beyond us, e'en before our death
It begins and ends
In the small circle of our foes and friends."[2]

Shall I in conformity to the model of the Ancients boast of more valuable acquisitions —— an acquaintance with mankind, a knowledge of the world, a contempt of my own country &c. ("The fame of Tully"—says my Lord Bacon somewhere—"had scarce lasted a day, or at least not as fresh and fair if it had not been joined with *vanity* and *boasting*, for boasting seems to be like varnish that not only makes wood shine but last.")[3] But alas! to what will even this acquisition amount? A new series of evidence; to show forth the source of the great, the fruits of the little, the insolence of the rich, the knavery of the poor, and the depravity of all, this will make up the sum . . . I think that it is Seneca who says, that "he who would enjoy many friends and live happy in the world, should be deaf, dumb, and blind to its follies and vices."[4] Whoever said this, said truly, and yet he who acts upon this principle through life, will scarce be a good citizen or great character.

Should I tell you Sir that, the more I see of mankind the greater is my desire of retirement—that the more I mix with the world, the less I am pleased with it; that the oftener I blend in public companies the more I long for solitude. I should only re-echo the trite tale of many who have advanced on the other side of the hill of life, and are verging swift down the declivity; but thus to moralize is seldom the part of one in the hey day of his youth surrounded with pleasures and amusements.

It is a happiness to be able to inform my friends that I am in better health than I remember ever to have experienced before. It gives me a yet more sensible pleasure when I communicate this information to those who will share the joy of my acquisition. You may wonder, perhaps, that while my blood flows with an unusual current, when my spirits vibrate with uncommon velocity, I should seem so sick of the world, its engagements, pursuits, and pleasures. But who that hath felt the languor of study, the perplexities of his ways, the lassitude of application and the despondence of sinking nature and dread not the miserable sensation? Who that has exchanged such feelings for those of ease, air, and exercise, and health, would hazard all for wealth and honors? You may tell me I am now remote from temptation; that necessity will drive me to study and toil, that moderation and mediocrity are repugnant to my nature, that *video meliora proboque deteriora sequor*[5]—You perhaps judge right, and say truly, but it does not therefore follow that I now think and reason wrong. The moralist, the philosopher, the Bra[h]min, and the Mystic have their essays, maxims, doctrines, and dogmas; but their words and doctrines are at perpetual variance. It is not strange then, that the *dicta* and practice of a poor, simple, uninspired, common lawyer should be at variance and opposition. But it is a little mysterious, however, that consistency, and stability seem the honour of a man while contradiction and change form his characteristic. Having an idle moment, I have employed it in giving you my thoughts as they rose and fluctuated, having neither leisure [n]or inclination to review and correct them, you will consider this latter a tribute of my heart rather than my head.

With much love and gratitude,
yours J. Quincy junr.

1. Transcribed by Eliza Susan into her "Memoir," 88a–90a, QP 46 (reel 6) MHS, with the original now missing.

2. Drawn from Alexander Pope's "An Essay on Man," Epistle IV, lines 237–38, 241–42; probably from "Popes Works" as listed in the "Catalogue of Books" (no. 312) in Coquillette and York, eds., *Portrait of a Patriot,* 5:901. There are too many possibilities to list here–and he may have gone to a copy of the "Essay" that had been printed separately, which only adds to the number of potential sources. He turned to Pope's piece a number of times in his journal while on this Southern trip—see ibid., 3:88, 120, 122.

3. Quincy worked from memory, and was just a bit off. He was correct that it was Bacon—in this case, his essay "Of Vain-Glory," the relevant passage of which is: "For the Fame of *Cicero, Seneca, Plinius Secundus,* had scarce lasted to this Day, or at least not so fresh, if it have not been joined with some Vanity and Boasting in themselves. For Boasting seems to be like Varnish, that makes Wood not only Shine, but Last." The "Catalogue of Books" (no. 42) lists "Lord

Bacons Works 4," which, if it was a complete set, could have been the edition published in 1740 in London by A. Millar. Even so, Quincy did not have that edition in mind when recalling this particular passage. Instead, he was drawing on what he had read in an earlier edition of Bacon's *Essays* rather than the complete *Works* (the phraseology from the translated Latin being notably different). For those other possibilities see my comments in Coquillette and York, eds., *Portrait of a Patriot,* 1:202.

4. He may have thought it was Seneca, perhaps one of his epistles, but the more likely source is Adam Fitz-Adam [Edward Moore], *The World,* 4 vols. (London: R. And J. Dodsley, 1753–1756), 1:2.

5. A passage from Ovid's *Metamorphoses,* Book VIII, lines 20–21—"I see and approve the better course, though I follow the worse"—that has passed into legal Latin. Quincy owned a copy of *Metamorphoses*: see the "Catalogue of Books" at Coquillette and York, eds., *Portrait of a Patriot,* 5:899 (no. 257), which could have been a translated edition or one in the original Latin. He turned to it for his journal too at this same time: at ibid., 3:275.

JONATHAN SMITH TO JQ

12 May 1773[1]

Sir Philadelphia May 12 1773

Agreeable to my promise I now inclose you a copy of one of the first American charters. It is made out from an impression of (1600 Anno Domini), Hackluit's voyages which is now out of print, and perhaps the copy from which it is taken is the only one in America.[2] Had your Governor. Hutchinson a copy within his reach it might have furnished him with perhaps not the least curious, and, it may be, important paper in his Collection.[3] How far this and the other papers of those early times may discover the intentions of the adventurers to America, and of Government, with respect to the unlimited authority of Great Britain over the Colonies to be planted, is a question that may admit of a quick decision; especially if the approving act of Parliament sometime after passed be attended to. As for the inclosed, I think you may depend on it as exact and correct, only that in some instances I have used the common abbreviations in spelling.

I hope this may meet you happy in the injoyment of your family and friends, and in a confirmed state of health.

I am, Sir, very respectfully, your very humble servant[4]

Jon. B Smith

1. QP 51 (and reel 29) MHS; also in the "Memoir," 2:107b, QP 46 (reel 6) MHS; and the *Memoir*, pp. 117–18. Smith, the son of a wealthy merchant involved in trade himself and just a couple of years older than Quincy, was one of the rising leaders among Philadelphia radicals.

2. He probably referred here to Richard Hakluyt's *The Principal Navigations, Voyages, and Traffiques of the English Nation,* the first three volumes of which appeared in London between 1599 and 1600. There were no eighteenth-century editions printed in either Britain or the American colonies.

3. [Thomas Hutchinson] *A Collection of Original Papers Relative to the History of Massachusetts-Bay* (Boston: Thomas and John Fleet, 1769). Quincy quoted from the *Collection* twice in his political commonplace book. See Coquillette and York, eds., *Portrait of Patriot,* 1:103, 173–74.

4. Which Smith abbreviated as simply "v. h. s."

THOMAS BEE TO JQ

15 June 1773[1]

Sir Chas. Town, South Carolina 15 June 1773

I hope this will find you safe returned to your Friends & your Health quite established after your long Journey—You have herewith inclosed a Copy of the several Letters &c., you marked off in the Committee's Book of Correspondence with our Agent. It was sometime before I could procure a Clerk to copy them, and at last was Obliged to pay 14 Dollars to the Person employed, which I thought too much but could not otherwise have got them done in time to be sent by Mr. Lynch, the Bearer hereof, who with his family intend passing a few Months your way this Summer. He will inform you of any Matters passing in these Southern Regions much better than I can communicate them on paper. I shall be glad to be favoured with your Correspondence, whenever convenient. And am Sir

Your very humble Servant
Tho. Bee

1. QP 51 (also reel 29) MHS; and in the *Memoir,* p. 115. Bee would become one the leaders of the Revolutionary movement in South Carolina, and he sat in the Continental Congress during the latter part of the war. Bee studied at Oxford and had been a member of the South Carolina bar for well over a decade before Quincy's arrival in Charleston. There are various references to Bee in Quincy's Southern journal; see Coquillette and York, eds., *Portrait of a Patriot,* vol. 3 passim.

GEORGE CLYMER TO JQ

29 July 1773[1]

Dear Sir Phila. July 29, 1773

I returned home a few Weeks ago considerably the better for my Eastern Journey, and have already let too long Time slip without acknowledging the Obligations your many Civilities have laid me under.

I have Thanks to return many Gentlemen at Boston on that Score, and could wish my own Countrymen were not justly accused of falling so far short of yours in the great Virtue of Hospitality.

But Hospitality was not the only Virtue I had reason to admire there. Your Patriotism is the great Support of the common Cause, and I trust will in Time diffuse itself so universally as to make all Attempts against American Liberty as vain as they are wicked. At present indeed it seems to have taken but shallow Root in some places, particularly at New York, where all political Principles are truly as unfixed as the Wind. One Year sees the NewYorkers, Champions for Liberty, and the next hugging their Chains.

Our Pennsylvanians I take to be in the mean betwixt both, I cannot call it the golden Mean, for surely it is not alone sufficient where our Liberties are so greatly threatened, to think justly of the Danger, or to have the Principles of Freemen, these Principles should direct the Conduct of every Individual and of the publick.

I beg you will make my particular Compliments to Mr. Hancock and Mr. S. Adams. There are no Men more worthy of general Esteem. The latter I cannot sufficiently respect for his Integrity and Abilities. All good Americans should erect a Statue to him in their Hearts.

Our Acquaintance has yet been but short, but believe me, it will leave an Impression on me of longer Date, and a strong Desire with it of cultivating your Friendship. I sincerely wish you and Mrs. Quincy every possible Happiness and am

Dear Sir
Your most obedient Servant,
Geo. Clymer

1. QP 51 (and reel 29) MHS; the "Memoir," 2:108b–109, QP 46 (reel 6) MHS; and *Memoir,* pp. 118–19. Clymer was a wealthy merchant, deeply involved in patriot politics. He would serve in

the Continental Congress during the war and as a delegate to the constitutional convention in 1787. Gaspare Saladino's sketch in John A. Garraty and Mark C. Carnes, eds., *American National Biography,* 24 vols. (New York: Oxford University Press, 1999), 5:90–92 is the best introduction to Clymer.

JQ TO GEORGE CLYMER

August 1773[1]

Dear Sir, Boston. August. 1773.

It gives me great pleasure to hear of your safe return to your family. The reflection of having contributed to Mr. Clymer's happiness, while in this town, gives his friends a real satisfaction. I hope your confidence in the universal diffusion of public virtue will not be frustrated; but the die spins doubtful. Force is not all we have to fear. Fraud is a more concealed, and therefore a more dangerous enemy. Political artifice is used to divide, while ministerial manoeuvres destroy us. Instability is not peculiar to the New-Yorkers: it is the characteristic of men in all ages and nations. Let us forgive each other's follies, and unite while we may.

"To *think justly* (is certainly) not sufficient;"[2] but we must think *alike,* before we shall form a union: that truly formed, we are invincible. They who have the principles of freemen, feel them. The sensation once felt, it directs "the band of the undivided and free." A spark of fire inflames a compact building. A spark of spirit will as soon enkindle a UNITED PEOPLE.

Our hemisphere is calm, but the diviners of our political sky see a cloud at the horizon, though not bigger than a hand. They who have reason to fear the storm will seek a shelter. The impression of our short acquaintance was most certainly mutual, and a cultivation of future friendship, as cordially embraced as it is offered. A mutual exchange of sentiments will give us, as men, a knowledge of each other; that knowledge naturally creates esteem, and that esteem will, in the end, cement us as colonists. As men, and as brethren then, in one common cause, let us think, converse, and act. When the guilty combine, let the virtuous unite; else individuals and communities will fall a sacrifice, one by one, in an inglorious, despicable struggle. Present me, in terms expressive of great affection and respect, to Mr. Dickinson and Mr. Reed, and believe me, with sincere regard and warm wishes,

You most humble, obedient servant,

JQ

1. In the "Memoir," 2:110–11, QP 46 (reel 6) MHS; and *Memoir,* pp. 119–20. E. S. Quincy copied from the original, which has since disappeared.

2. Quincy quoted Clymer to himself, from his letter of July 29th at supra, pp. 140–41.

"MARCHMONT NEDHAM"

20 December 1773[1]

NEDHAM'S REMEMB'RANCER, NO. I

——THAT, which mischief meant *most harm,*
Shall in the happy trial prove MOST GLORY—
But evil on itself shall back recoil—MILTON.[2]

I HAVE heretofore detected and exposed the political conduct of Governor Hutchinson. His whole deportment on the public theatre, from his first appearance on the stage, ought at this period to be reviewed and *contrasted;* displayed and abhorred. The infirmities of advanced age and ill health have inclined me to the more agreeable duty of contemplation, rather than to the painful task of delineating so hateful a portrait for the public eye. I have kept my tongue with a bridle while the wicked were before me: But even while the royal Psalmist practised this duty, *his heart was hot within him*—and *when the fire burned, he spake with his tongue.*

Whoever considers the *government* and *guidance* which his Excellency hath with two of the Tea-Consignees, and the influence he hath over the rest, must determine him to be answerable for their strange, their unjustifiable conduct. I know, that he disclaims his share in this matter: but I know also, that I confide in him in no instance, where it is *his interest* to deceive; and I know more, that all mankind do, and will disbelieve his affirmation in this matter.

What account the Consignees can give of their trust to those with whom they must account, I leave them to consider. But sure I am, that it was in their power to have saved the property of the East India Company, and that their wantonness and obstinacy promoted that destruction, which they must know would be the consequence of their behavior.

To suppose that they intended the loss of the Teas is to brand them with base ingratitude and breach of trust: to suppose they designed to plunge their countrymen into civil commotion and bloodshed—to gratify resentment *or share in the plunder of forfeitures and confiscations*—is to blast them with THAT SIN, of which *the shedding of their blood is the purchase of remission.*—They will be so happy to find some other alternative.

THE PEOPLE have been mild and considerate: they have been temperate and patient. When their mildness was called timidity, and their consideration want of courage, they did not cease to reason and intreat. When their temperance was treated with insult, and their patience with contempt, they felt the injury tho' they stayed their vengeance. When the situation of public affairs called them to resolve upon their danger and duty, they were unanimous and determined, and when the exigency of the times increased and *resolutions alone* were vain, they proceeded to action with order and discretion and executed; *the only remaining duty,* without unnecessary outrage and intemperate revenge.

If his Excellency had his adversaries as much in his power, as THE PEOPLE have lately had the enemies of their peace, would he have been equally mild—equally sparing and moderate? Let us consider.

A father of his people would admonish and kindly intreat them to consider the consequences of their conduct; and not by insult *in form of law,* exasperate and provoke them, without a possibility of answering one good purpose. A father of his people would look with tenderness on their conduct. If he judged it rash, he would try to soften:—If it called for admonition, his words would be far from opprobrious:—If it called for correction, he would be merciful, and not severe.

But should his Excellency in a time of public commotion observe a very different course; should he to his Council, talk of TREASON, and ATTORNEY GENERALS, of REBELLION, and an ARMED FORCE—what are we to expect—that oil will extinguish fire—or that *big words* will lull the ocean?

I pretend to be no lawyer; but I am sure if to appear for my country is treason, and to arm for its defence is rebellion; like my fathers, I will glory in the name of rebel and traitor, as they did in that of Puritan and Enthusiast.

Indeed I know of no way so likely to drive this people to extremities, as to brand them with these appellations. And I know of nothing, they who use them can have in view, but to accelerate the period, which will never arrive 'till the people are become desperate.

The readiest way to make them so, is to call them hard names.—But let all who do thus remember, that when THIS PEOPLE are driven to desperation, *they who thus abuse them,* will no longer dwell in safety.

MARCHMONT NEDHAM.

[*To be continued.*]

1. *Boston Gazette,* 20 December 1773, p. 2, filling the bottom half of the second column and carrying over to the top third of the third column.

2. From *Comus,* lines 582–84. He had turned to that play on his Southern journey, earlier in the year; in Coquillette and York, eds., *Portrait of a Patriot,* 3:123 and 219.

"MARCHMONT NEDHAM"

27 December 1773[1]

NEDHAM'S REMEMB'RANCER, N. II.

SATAN

Bowed low his grey Dissimulation.

MILTON.[2]

IT is a just observation, that man in nothing seems more to resemble his Creator, than in the utter abhorrence of hypocrisy.—The villain who determines his conduct without reserve, and executes his resolutions with open bravery, seems to irradiate his guilt with a kind of heroism. Attracted with the frankness and splendor of his conduct, we admire the fortitude of the man, while we detest his crime. But to *plot in secret,* discovers malignity without courage, as, the cruelty of a coward displays turpitude of heart without strength of mind. Thus a villain, adventrous and intrepid forces an involuntary applause, while the malicious and wily coward hath nothing to exempt him from our bitterest hatred and indignation.

The various affections of the human breast were implanted for wise and good reasons. It was requisite, that *the most dangerous* wickedness should excite the sharpest resentment. It is just and right, that those, who are the most injurious to the common happiness and security of mankind should be exposed to proportionate detestation & vengeance. The safety of society and individuals could in no way be better secured. The thrust of a duelist may be parried; but who can repel the stab of an assassin? Against the bold and open invader we are in some measure prepared, by the knowledge of our enemy and danger: there is something of generosity in the attack; there is scope for the exertions of virtue. Justice may be present at the combat; the struggle may be glorious and exemplary: the event may be happy—and virtue may be triumphant.—But against the *secret* destroyer, who approaches with smiles of beneficence and professions of regard; who hides his dagger under the veil of friendship or the mantle of religion; innocence is no protection—valour is no adequate defence. Thus disguised, the odious creature wreaths himself into the bosom, and in an unsuspecting moment plunges a poignard[3] to the heart. Having effected his purpose he steals to his covert, and in secret ruminates with malignant joy on the works of his hands.

No wonder that a character of this sort is hateful to all men. As no system of morality hath given a definition of it's guilt, so no code of laws hath assigned an adequate punishment. THE WISDOM OF GOD AND THE POLICY OF MAN SEEM TO RESERVE SUCH INSTANCES OF ENORMITY AND EXTRAVAGANT WICKEDNESS TO BE JUDGED AND AVENGED ACCORDING TO THE RANK OF THE CRIMINAL, AND THE EXIGENCE OF THE OCCASION.

Leaving the truth and application of the preceeding remarks to the wisdom of others, I proceed to pay my attention to his eminence, the governor. A gentleman who owes all that he enjoys, which is *truly honorable,* to the partiality and favor of his countrymen: a man born, bred, and educated among us; and under every moral and religious tie to love, honour and do good to this province: one, who has been unremitted in his pretensions to zeal for it's laws, liberties and religion; profuse of declarations of concern for it's welfare, and lavish of his tears for the errors and delusions of the people. With all this *fine show—what has been this man at heart?* What have been his designs?—What his deeds?—What has he effected?

Have not the council and representatives of the province charged this very man, in the face of the world, with gross misrepresentations and falsehood—with aiming to introduce arbitrary power, and the actual introduction of an armed force,—a force which stained our streets with blood and slaughter;—and finally, with the most *capital* offence against the common wealth—an intent to subvert the constitution?—And have not all these charges been supported by the most conspicuous facts?

Is this THE MAN, who vapours the Attorney-General—TREASON and REBELLION? Surely he has forgot his law and his history. His law books would tell him, what a Finch, a Berkeley and Strafford suffered "for HIGH TREASON against the fundamental laws and introducing arbitrary power."[4]—His history will tell him, that "any treacherous perfidious *attempt* to alter and subvert fundamentally the frame of policy and government, was made (in this colony) a CAPITAL OFFENCE";* and that "A BETRAYER OF THE GOVERNMENT" was by a law of our fathers subjected to the same penalty.+

Who is the Traitor, who the Betrayer of Government? He who *openly* assembles with his brethren to consider of public affairs; who speaks his sentiments freely, and determines his conduct in the face of all men?—Or he who conspires against the very being of the state, and plots the *cutting off individuals;*—who writes *secret and confidential letters* to the enemies of his country, blasts its reputation with calumny, and points the way to its overthrow and ruin?—and while he thus aims the fatal stroke, sneaks like a coward behind the veil of darkness, and supplicates concealment from the face of day?

Surely this is not the period for his Excellency to chaunt of treasons and carrol prosecutions; a lower note is better suited to the day: a softer strain must lull the tumult of the times.

Certain I am, that whenever THIS PEOPLE shall be called to consider THE GREAT DOCTRINES OF CRIMINAL LAW, they will soon cry for justice with a zeal that will not bear restraint, and urge their suit with an impetuosity which will not brook delay.—When A WHOLE PEOPLE present a criminal at the bar of justice, the sword must not *linger* in the hand of the executioner.

MARCHMONT NEDHAM.

[*to be continued.*]

---

* See Hist. Massa: Bay, 1 Vol. p. 412.

+ See same Hist. p. 295. Note.

1. *Boston Gazette,* 27 December 1773, p. 1, the full first column and nearly half of the second.

2. Milton, *Paradise Regain'd,* Book I.

3. French for small, slim dagger; eventually anglicized as poniard.

4. Thomas Wentworth, Earl of Strafford, John (First Baron) Finch, and Sir Robert Berkeley were all caught up in the clashes pitting Crown against Parliament prior to the English Civil War. They sided with Charles I and suffered the consequences. Strafford was executed; Finch and Berkeley, both judges, were impeached and removed from the bench.

"MARCHMONT NEDHAM"

3 January 1774[1]

NEDHAM'S REMEMB'RANCER, N. III.

Stand back, thou *manifest* CONSPIRATOR.
——— Tell me what they deserve,
That do conspire our Death with devilish plots?
————— O conspiracy!
Where wilt thou find a cavern dark enough,
To mask thy monstrous visage? Seek none, conspiracy,
Hides it IN SMILES and AFFABILITY.
SHAKESPEARE.[2]

GREAT pains have been taken to bring his Excellency out of the company with whom he is found, and to save him from sharing the guilt of those with whom he has *openly* and SECRETLY associated himself. This is no doubt renouncing the conduct of *many* as, indefensible to save *one* from his just portion of ignominy and reproach. But it was no doubt good policy to consign the *minor* villains to shame and infamy, if this would reinstate *their leader* in favor and influence.

But I never yet could discern any propriety in judging the conduct of a band of conspirators separate and apart, the one from the other, when all appear, from beginning to end, jointly conspiring to the same purpose, adopting the same measures and acting in the closest union and concert.

If a gang of robbers combine to attack my house, and each agrees upon his separate part; if they unite in *the plot,* and when they come to the time of execution;—one watches my door, another enters my house, a third rifles my family, and a fourth sheds my blood;—while the rest stand without for the purpose of carrying on the *common plan;*—surely they must be *all equally guilty* in the eye of reason and common sense. And what difference is there, between those, who assist in the invasion of a *private* edifice, and they who attack the *public* building of the Commonwealth;—between those who rifle and destroy my house, and those who plunder and overturn the fabrick of the state? Surely none, which makes in favor of *any one* of the assailants, or can exempt from a common abhorrence and punishment, any member of the combination.

Not one of the advocates (base and shameless as they have been) for *the* *chief conspirator* against our laws and liberties hath ever so much as mentioned a word (to my knowledge) in defence or justification of the writings and conduct of Oliver, Hallowell or Paxton.[3] Yet what was this triumvirate without their hero? Oliver was too timid to be formidable, Hallowell too much the man of arms to be an assassin; and Paxton too contemptible to be regarded. Hallowell would have crossed the ocean, harmless & unnoticed as any other seaman, without *a political letter of credit* from the governor; Paxton might have *frothed* the "open rebellion of Boston,"* & remained as little regarded, as when he fawned or flattered, without countenance from the same personage, & a recommendation from his Excellency's brother "as a *good friend*";† and Oliver would have trembled to lisp a "a taking off incendiaries"‡ had not his Excellency talked of "marks of parliamentary resentment to the *province in general* or PARTICULAR PERSONS"—and gave his sanction—that "IT OUGHT TO BE SO."#

THE PRESENT GOVERNOR, therefore, I consider as the great CAPITAL OFFENDER:—To him I look as the origin of all our public calamities—because without his aid, his sanction, his authority and influence, our public enemies would have remained a *paltry few,* a spiritless body, a despicable cabal.

Thus whenever we scrutinize the manoeuvres of the *sub-confederates*—we ought to attend to *their connexions* and *accomplices:*—We shall ever find the grand mover of their mischievous operations *lurking in the dark;*—for in all the more *capital* movements, the *arch agent* keeps himself as much as possible disguised, while, like *the master of puppets,* he holds the political wire, and directs all the motions—*behind the curtain.*

MARCHMONT NEDHAM.

* See his Letter to Whately. [See n. 159 infra.]

† Letter 13th February 1769.

‡ Letter 20th January.

Letter 7th May 1767.[4]

[*To be continued.*]

1. *Boston Gazette,* 3 January 1774, p. 2, taking nearly three quarters of the first column.

2. Quincy blended passages from different Shakespeare plays here, opening with a line from *Henry VI,* Part I, Act I, Scene 3 (hurled by the Duke of Gloucester at the Bishop of Winchester).

The following two lines are from *Richard III,* Act III, Scene 4 (the future Richard III to Lord Hastings). The final four are from *Julius Caesar,* Act II, Scene 1 (Brutus, before Cassius has lured him into the conspiracy to assassinate Caesar).

3. Lieutenant Governor Andrew Oliver, customs commissioner Benjamin Hallowell, and customs inspector Charles Paxton.

4. See *Copy of Letters* (Boston: Edes and Gill, 1773), for all four listed above: Paxton's to Whately of 20 June 1768 (p. 37), Andrew Oliver's of 13 February 1769 (pp. 27–33), Thomas Hutchinson's of 20 January 1769 (pp. 15–16), and Oliver's of 7 May 1767 (pp. 18–24). The title page ended with: "In which (*notwithstanding his Excellency's Declaration to the House, that the Tendency and Design of them was not to subvert the Constitution, but rather to preserve it entire)* the judicious Reader will discover the fatal Source of the Confusion and Bloodshed in which this Province especially has been involved, and which threatened total Destruction to the Liberties of all *America.*" Bailyn, *Thomas Hutchinson*, pp. 221–73 (in a chapter called, fittingly, "The 'Scape-goat'"), reviews the controversy surrounding these letters, within the context of Hutchinson's loss of power in the colony.

"MARCHMONT NEDHAM"

10 January 1774[1]

NEDHAM'S REMEMB'RANCER, N. IV.

——— Think on thy country,
And die in terror of thy *guiltiness.*
SHAKESPEARE.[2]

POLITICALLY speaking, the crime of betraying one's country is—the unpardonable sin. No guilt more deeply poisons the heart and embitters reflection. What pangs must swell in the breast of a man, in the close of life, who looks back and sees himself—laboring to *abridge the liberties of his country,* enslaving it's inhabitants, and procuring the introduction of troops, which insult the civil magistrate and shed the blood of his brethren? What and how exquisite must be his feelings, when he hears young and old imprecate vengeance on his hoary head, and sees his name and progeny blasting with execrations and infamy.

The man who slanders his neighbour with dark insinuations and aims his distruction in secret, is obnoxious to general odium. But what must be our sentiments of him, who with these weapons deliberately renews the same attack on both individuals and the community?

In his excellency's letter of the 18th June 1768, "Mr. Hancock" is first noticed as "a representative of Boston, a wealthy merchant, of *great influence over the* POPULACE," whose sloop being seized, the writer informs, "a mob was *immediately* raised."

As the *populace* ever compose such assemblies, and Mr. Hancock being declared to have *great influence over them,* is there not the plainest insinuation, that this gentleman was the exciter of this tumult? Now as nothing could be more foreign from the truth, and scarce any thing more known to *this informer,* was not his design wicked and his mode of attack base?—

And when we advert to what the same writer says, in a subsequent letter, relative to resentment from Great Britain against PARTICULAR PERSONS, and compare it with a passage in the letter wrote a *few days* after by his brother Oliver, concerning the TAKING OFF *of Incendiaries,* is there not great reason to believe, that this "*wealthy* merchant" was held up as a victim, and that hopes of sharing the plunder of his riches on a confiscation of his estate was the motive of action? Who can doubt that forfeitures and confiscations of this sort were the *penalties* of *another kind,* his excellency thought so *adequate*—so well *adapted* to the purpose.*

But we forget the injuries done the private character, when we contemplate the public.

Whoever reads governor Bernard's letters, of the 16, 17, and 18th of June 1768, Mr. Hutchinson's and Paxton's of the same date, and carefully compares them, can have no doubt, that *they wrote in concert,* and were each apprized of the purport of the other's letter: such a comparison will convince the intelligent reader, that *the conspiracy was joint,* and the guilt of the actors equal, unless the subtlety of Mr. Hutchinson, and his station as chief Justice, aggravate his crime above that of his fellows.[3]

There is one instance of union between Paxton and our chief Justice which I do not recollect Bernard to have shared in. Paxton refers his correspondent to "Mr. Hallowell, the comptroller, to inform of *many particulars*".† Mr. Hutchinson "begs leave to refer to him (Hallowell) *for a more full account.*"‡ To give such a sanction to the stories of a man, who went over heated with party-rage and burning with resentment against this country, is such an instance of *unfairness* and *disingenuity, malice* and *cowardice,* as Bernard with all his enormity could not stoop to practice.#

We find in the 31st page of Mr. Hutchinson's history, that in 1634, Morton the infamous libeller and public enemy of this colony sent his *confidential* letters "by a *convenient* messenger": like principles and views in this and the last century produce similar actions: Thus we find Hallowell is letter-bearer to the chief Justice and Mr. Commissioner in 1768, as Paxton was for *brother* Oliver in 1767.*

His honor Mr. Hutchinson in the above letter, which contains *his* account of a mob on the 10th of June, affirms, that "NO NOTICE was taken of their extravagance in the time of it, NOR ANY ENDEAVOURS *by any authority except the governor,* the next day to *discover* and *punish* the offenders." Now it is most certain, that not only the governor, but the council of this province the very next morning after the riot "agreed that an examination should be made into the affair, in order to the *discovery* and *punishment* of the offenders;" and "appointed a committee of such members of the board as were qualified to act as *justices of the peace in the county of Suffolk* to make enquiry into the facts."†

Surely the council were *an authority*, and their proceedings *a notice* which militate with the account and veracity of this American correspondent.

In what way consistent with either conscience or honor can we acquit this letter writer;—whose station as Chief Justice ought not only to have preserved him from such high crimes, but have kept him perfectly immaculate from the little base views and enterprizes of *party*. But so far was this gentleman from keeping his mind untinctured with the feuds of the times, he enters deeply into party pursuits, and in other passages of this very letter, his heart appears fraught with rancor against the council and the town of Boston, and his writings, *invite the resentment of the British administration.*

I know that it has been said; I know his Excellency has said, "that these were private letters—wrote before he came to the chair—and *expressly confidential!*"‡

That the letters were written when Mr. Hutchinson was *not governor, but chief justice,* that they were *secret* and *confidential,* in my mind, adds a tenfold guilt. The gentleman to whom these writings were addressed was an active member of parliament and a zealous advocate of it's measures with the colonies. There can be no doubt, from many circumstances besides the letters themselves, that they were intended to have an operation against the people of this province. But I have one reason to suppose they *actually had* this effect, from certain resolutions of the house of lords, which I do not remember ever to have seen in print.

Among the Resolves of the Lords, sent by them to the House of Commons in December 1768, I find these following.

"Thirdly, Resolved by the lords spiritual and temporal in parliament assembled, that it appears that the town of Boston in the province of the Massachusetts-Bay, has for some time past been in a state of great disorder and confusion, and that the peace of the said town has at several times been disturbed by riots and tumults of a dangerous nature, in which the officers of his majesty's revenue there have been obstructed by acts of violence in the execution of the laws, and their lives endangered.

Fourthly, Resolved by the lords spiritual and temporal in parliament assembled, that *it appears, that neither the council of the said province of Massachusetts-Bay, nor the ordinary civil magistrates did exert their authority* for suppressing the said riots and tumults.

Fifthly, Resolved by the lords spiritual and temporal in parliament assembled, that IN THESE CIRCUMSTANCES of the province of the Massachusetts Bay, and of the town of Boston, the preservation of the public peace, & the due execution of the laws BECAME IMPRACTICABLE, without the aid of a military force to support and protect the civil magistrate, and the offenders of his majesty's revenue.

Sixthly, Resolved by the lords spiritual and temporal in parliament assembled, that the declarations, resolutions and proceedings in the town meetings at Boston, on the 14th of June and 12th of September, were illegal and unconstitutional, and calculated to excite sedition and insurrections in his majesty's province of the Massachusetts Bay.

Seventhly, Resolved by the lords spiritual and temporal in parliament assembled, that the appointment at the town meeting on the 12th of September, of a convention to be held in the town of Boston on the 22 of that month, to consist of deputies from the several towns and districts in the province of the Massachusetts Bay, and the issuing a PRECEPT* by the selectmen of the town of Boston, to each of the said towns and districts, for the elections of such deputies, were proceedings subversive of his majesty's government, and evidently manifesting a design in the inhabitants of the said town of Boston, to set up a new and unconstitutional authority, independent of the crown of Great Britain.

Eighthly, Resolved by the lords spiritual and temporal in parliament assembled, that the election by several towns & districts in the province of the Massachusetts-Bay, of deputies to sit in the said convention, and the meeting of such convention in consequence thereof, were daring insults offered to his majesty's authority, and audacious usurpations of the persons of government."[4]

It is very observable, that the supposed neglect of council and the civil magistrate, of which Mr. Hutchinson gave information in his *confidential letters,* are *those very circumstances,* which induced the fifth resolution of the peers; in which they appear to be grossly misinformed, as to solemnly resolve upon an impracticability which never existed in nature.

We can no longer doubt that Mr. Whately was of a like spirit with his friend, and made use of his American intelligence with a disposition congenial with his correspondent. And as we know that *previous* to these resolutions, not only the letter of the 18th of June, but divers others of the same hand had reached

England, so we are fully satisfied that the troops quartered in this town, the bloodshed and debauchery they introduced, are all placed to his Excellency's account,—and that in this world and the next he must stand the audit: and let me add in his own words "because *it ought to be so.*"

The introduction and establishment of British land-forces in this province are replete with the worst consequences: if not driven out from among us, they must in the end destroy not only public liberty and security, but all private morality and piety. They, therefore, who were the prime movers and instruments of this measures, are stained with a crime, that this people ought not —*they cannot—they will not* forget or forgive.

MARCHMONT NEDHAM.

[*To be continued.*]

* See his Excellency's Letters in 1769.

† Letter 18 June, 1768.

‡ Letter of the same day.

Hutchinson is guilty of the same mean artifice, by referring to Hallowell for information against Mr. Temple in his Letter in August following.

* See Secretary Oliver's Letter, 7 May 1767.[5]

† See the proceedings and records of Council heretofore published.

‡ Message to the House of Representatives.[6]

* This is another flagrant evidence of the base misinformation sent from people on this side the water to persons in authority on the other.—Does not this whole province know, that no such precept was ever issued, and that there was not even a colour to pretend that there was?—What punishment too great for SUCH INFORMERS against their country!

1. *Boston Gazette,* 10 January 1774, p. 1, filling the first two columns and well over half of the third.

2. Once again showing his Shakespeare expertise, Quincy takes his own line, directed at Thomas Hutchinson—"Think of thy country"—and uses it as a lead to a line from *Richard III,* Act V, Scene 3, the ghost of the Duke of Buckingham appearing to a treacherous and yet troubled Richard III in a dream on the eve of the Battle of Bosworth Field. Other ghosts of those victimized by the King had preceded Buckingham, reminding Richard of his crimes before urging him to "despair, and die."

3. The faces had changed (somewhat), but the issues remained the same. Hutchinson now played the role once filled by Francis Bernard, his predecessor as governor, with letters that Bernard had written being published to embarrass him and rally public support. The letters of June 1768 to which Quincy alluded appeared in *Letters to the Ministry* (Boston: Edes and Gill, 1768), pp. 25–29. Those letters were part of the controversy associated with the *Liberty* affair of 10 June 1768, which is sometimes (wrongly) pointed to as the cause of troops being sent to Boston. The decision to send them had actually been reached before the event even occurred. For details see Hutchinson's version in his *The History of the Province of Massachusetts-Bay*, 3 vols. (Cambridge, Mass.: The Belknap Press of Harvard University Press, 1936), 3:136–40, edited by Lawrence Mayo. Also see Benjamin Hallowell's affidavit of 11 June 1768 in Add. Ms. 38,340, fo. 251 at the British Library (Liverpool Papers) and his testimony before the Treasury lords on 21 July 1768 in the National Archives, Public Record Office T1/468, fos. 338–40; and the overview in George Wolkins, "The Seizure of John Hancock's Sloop 'Liberty,'" *Massachusetts Historical Society. Proceedings* 55 (1921-1922):239–84.

4. The nine resolutions actually passed the House of Commons first, in December 1768, then were concurred in by the House of Lords, after some minor revisions, the following February. They are printed in the *Journals of the House of Commons*, 32:185–86, and were reprinted in various newspapers around the colonies. Edes and Gill added their own emphasis.

5. Drawing once again from the *Copy of Letters*, pp. 18–24, for this one, and the respective pages for the ones above it.

6. On 9 June 1773, which triggered House resolutions a week later in protest. In the *Mass. House Journal*, 50:40–41 and 58–61, resp.

"MARCHMONT NEDHAM"

17 January 1774[1]

NEDHAM'S REMEMB'RANCER, No. V.

Meet it is, I here set down,
That one may *smile, & smile,* and be A VILLAIN:
——- And with this visage sugar o'er
THE DEVIL HIMSELF.
SHAKESPEARE.[2]

SUBTERFUGE and evasion are the true characteristics of a *little* mind; —and so are falshood and cowardice. Such artifices are but temporary expedients which great souls scorn to use: like base coin they may pass currently with the ignorant and incautious for a short time, but the cheat is soon discovered; and the impostor is punished and remains infamous for life. Thus he who practices the low arts of political cunning will in the end be detected and sink into contempt, unless his crimes and his station consign him to an *exemplary* punishment and everlasting infamy.

His excellency, in his message to the house of representatives of the 9th of June, affirms that "there is *not one passage* in them (his letters then lying on the speaker's table) which was ever *intended to respect* the particular *constitution of this government* as derived from the charter."[3]

If his excellency had in contemplation the alteration of our form of government, and committed his sentiments to writing with a view to their being used in derogation of our liberties or annihilation of our charter; I should not be surprized to find *an ambiguity of expression with a plainess of meaning:* he would be too explicit for *his confident* to misunderstand his design, yet would retain a *characteristic* phraseology, which might stand him in stead in case his plan did not take, or his correspondent did not *keep the secret.**

But the most wary knaves, when they enter into deep plots and perplex themselves with many plans, have their conduct attended with certain circumstances which seldom or ever fail to betray their guilt. And even where they have the exquisite caution to use an *intermediate instrument* for the purpose of self-concealment, the connexion between the *master-workman* and *the tool* is commonly discovered, by some *unlucky* accident which subtlety did not provide against.

But to return to his excellency, for whom I am in pain. He explicitly declares to his correspondent, that "there MUST BE an abridgment of what are called ENGLISH *liberties.*"[4]

Now I know of no liberties, emphatically called *English,* but what are as dear, if not more so, than any derived from our charter. Hence I suppose his excellency would not thank any one for *an endeavour to save his veracity,* by suggesting that he designed an excision of those liberties, which are peculiar to us as *Englishmen*, and not the abridgment of those that are recognized by *our provincial charter.* This would be to wreck him on Charybdis in order to deliver him from Sylla.[5]—But, alas! what other subterfuge remains? Neither his excellency or his friends will say, that he did not "*intend to respect*" those subjects to which his reasonings were applied; and to which his words and the whole scope of his correspondence had a direct and plain tendency. Till, therefore, the above expedient—(poor indeed)—is adopted, or his excellency can show "*an abridgment* of what are called *English liberties*" which does *not* "*respect* the particular *constitution of this government* as derived from charter," he must *stand self-recorded* not only odiously wicked, but despicably mean.—Was not the dye of conspiracy against a whole people sufficiently deep, without adding the stain of falshood to the hateful hue?

But in order to determine the truth and sincerity of the preceeding message to the house, let us proceed with our considerations.

In the letter of the 20th of January 1769, Mr. Hutchinson says to his correspondent, that *it is most certain that marks* of PARLIAMENTARY *resentment will* be *placed somewhere,* and affirms that IT OUGHT TO BE *on the* PROVINCE IN GENERAL or *particular persons.* Now I have no doubt that if this resentment had extended to THE TAKING OFF those *particular persons* (which mode his brother Oliver more explicitly pointed out) it had gratified the sanguine appetite of his excellency. But when the writer talks of *parliamentary resentment* to *the province in general* (and this after so much resentment had been shown as to send troops) I have no doubt, that he had "respect" to the "charter of this government," and that he had a more immediate reference to it's annihilation or *abridgment,* by an express act of parliament to that purpose. I am satisfied this was meant, because he soon after proceeds, "but if no measures (that is of parliament) shall have been taken to secure this *dependance,* (of this colony) or NOTHING MORE than some

DECLARATORY acts or resolves, *it is all over with us.*" And I am still more confirmed in this opinion, because with his peculiar hypocrisy he in the same letter soon after adds, "I never think of the measures *necessary* for the peace and good order of the colonies without pain:"—and then subjoins with his characteristic grace, "I wish the good of THE COLONY when I wish to see SOME FARTHER RESTRAINT OF LIBERTY, rather than the connexion with the parent-state should be broken."[6] Now I should be glad to know what parliamentary measures could be taken *to secure our dependance* as a province without injury to our charter? I should be equally glad to be informed what additional *restraint of liberty* would prevent the breach of the before-mentioned connexion; or rather what *new restraint* would not dissolve it? And what *farther restraint of our liberties* could be effected, and especially by a parliamentary interposition, that would not capitally "*respect our constitution of government,*" and destroy our "charter"?—Surely his excellency's *genius* failed him when he penned his message.

But I have not done with the matter yet. The manner in which his excellency and his advocates have endeavoured to *illude* the imputation of a design to subvert our constitution, shows that the guilt of the attempt is apparent. I have in a former number sufficiently intimated, that union of conduct and criminality which took place with the clan of our public enemies. I shall now take occasion to give one specimen (among many) which evinces the justness of my opinion.

It is worthy of notice, that there appears but 24 days difference in the date of the preceeding letter of Mr. Hutchinson, and one from his brother Oliver, which contains a most PREMEDITATED PLAN TO ALTER OUR CONSTITUTION AND ANNIHILATE THE CHARTER. It is far from being certain, that even that time intervened between the periods of the writing those letters: but be that as it may, whoever attends to the purport and expressions of both of them will have little doubt, that they were wrote in close concert, by parties who imbibed each others sentiments by an intimate communion upon the subject, if in fact they were not wrote by the same hand.

Mr. Hutchinson begins his letter to Mr. Whately with an acknowledgment of "very great obligations by a full and clear *account of proceedings in parliament;*" and Mr. Oliver informs the same gentleman that "the lieutenant governor (H.) had communicated to him the letter (of Mr. Whately) containing *an account of the debates in parliament.*" Hutchinson "*expects* to be in suspence for three or four weeks, and then to hear our *fate,*" and Oliver "soon *expects* their *decision*, on American affairs."

Mr. Oliver writes "I have very lately had occasion to know, that be the *determination* of *parliament* what it will, it is the determination of some to agree to no terms that shall *remove us from* OUR OLD FOUNDATION."—Here is a plain intimation that it was then a matter of consideration with the members of that august body to *alter the foundation* of *this government;* and here is a key to what his colleague Mr. Hutchinson means by "marks of resentment the *parliament* will show to the *province in general,*" and confirms my preceeding observation that he intended his "abridgment of English liberties" through the instrumentality of king, lords & commons.

Mr. Oliver directly after mentioning the above resolution to stand on the *old foundation,* immediately adds, "this confirms me in opinion, that if there be *no way* to TAKE OFF the original incendiaries, they will continue to instill their poison into the minds of the people."[7] And his brother (Hutchinson) in league with him against the *community* and *individuals,* gives his sanction as we have before noticed, that *marks of resentment* OUGHT TO BE on the province in general or PARTICULAR PERSONS. The one adhering to his old *cunning,* is not explicit who those *particular persons are,* but from the words of the other, we may easily collect, they were those who wisely *determined not to be removed from their old foundation.*

His Excellency after expressing his "doubt whether it is *possible* to *project* a system of government in which a colony 3000 miles distant from the parent state shall enjoy all the liberty of the parent state," adds "I am certain *I have seen no such projection.*" Now let the reader judge, where the mighty difficulty, nay *impossibility* of such a project for the government of a Colony, without a diminution of the liberties enjoyed by the mother-country, was not sent forward in order to make way for the favorable reception of a *joint projection* of this kind, which in a few days was to be forwarded under the signature of Andrew Oliver. A project which to be sure most notably *abridg'd* those English liberties enjoyed by the parent state; and which *an Englishman* needed some preparation in order to receive without horror, and which he never could read without cursing the projector. The plan transmitted, treated deliberately of proposed "alterations in the charters of the Colonies," and what is called "a reform of them."

Hutchinson begs "*pardon* for his *excursion,*" and Oliver *apologizes* for what he affects to call "his *reveries*";[8] in which there is kept up that similarity of expression and sentiment which runs thro' both the letters; and so characteristically marks them, that few will doubt, they were the work of the same hand; and none will hesitate to pronounce them the *joint project* of two public conspirators against the rights and liberties, the happiness and peace of their native country.

MARCHMONT NEDHAM.

* See his Letter, 20 October 1769.

[*To be continued.*]

1. *Boston Gazette,* 17 January 1774, p. 1, all of columns one and two, and over half of column three.

2. *Hamlet,* Act I, Scene 5, for the first line (Hamlet, upon hearing from his father's ghost how his father was murdered by his uncle, who then married Hamlet's widowed mother Queen Gertrude and took the throne as King Claudius), the second from Act III, Scene 1 (Polonius to his daughter Ophelia, as he and Claudius endeavor to learn what Hamlet is about).

3. *Mass. House Journal*, 5,:40-41.

4. Of all the passages pulled from these letters, this was in some minds, apparently, the most damning (in *Copy of Letters,* p. 15, Hutchinson's letter of 20 January 1769).

5. An allusion from Greek mythology, familiar to at least some of his readers, Scylla was a multi-headed beast and Charybdis a whirlpool, both in the Strait of Messina between Sicily and Italy. They had been sea nymphs, transformed into monsters by angry, jealous gods.

6. Quincy quotes again from the letter noted at supra, n. 4.

7. The references to Hutchinson are from the letter noted above. Those from Oliver are in the letter of 13 February 1769 in *Copy of Letters*, pp. 27–33—with a reference to the *Boston Gazette* as the "vehicle" for poisoning the minds of the people.

8. All of the excerpts that Quincy quoted are from the two letters cited above.

"MARCHMONT NEDHAM"

31 January 1774[1]

NEDHAM'S REMEMB'RANCER, N. VI.

WEAKNESS is thy excuse,
And I believe it. *Weakness* to resist
Philistian gold.—If *weakness* may excuse,
What *murderer,* what TRAITOR, PARRICIDE,
Incestuous, sacrilegious, but may plead it?
All *wickedness* is WEAKNESS.
MILTON.[2]

WISDOM and VIRTUE are not more nearly allied than VICE and *folly.* It falls to the lot of but few villains, among the many, to pass currently through life, with a reputation for sense and judgment. The common herd of rogues and knaves are soon penetrated by the sagacious:—For men of understanding and acquaintance with the world quickly discern *the real character;* while the simple-minded and credulous are later in their discoveries. But in the end the cheat is commonly found out; and, therefore, we may advance it as a general truth, that hypocrites and impostors, *finally* appear *weak and foolish* in proportion as they are *corrupt* and *wicked.*

The truth and integrity of Gov. Hutchinson in his message to the house in their last sessions has already been considered, and I believe his excellency will excuse me from any further illucidations on that subject.

We have already reviewed distinguishing parts of this gentleman's character, in which he appears aiming a fatal stroke at our political freedom and happiness, and in conjunction with his connexions and favourites concerting a plan, which he must know could never be carried into effect, without a waste of much precious blood and a most calamitous oppression of his countrymen.—Be astonished O earth!—This is the man who owed *his* ALL,—his exemption from obscurity and his advancement in honour and wealth, to the partiality of his native land:—And while he was thus ploting and *secretly* conspiring it's destruction, his mouth was as redundant with professions of tenderness and love,* as his heart replete with gaul and malevolence.—But what a singular fatality will attend our hero, if in the subsequent revision, he shall appear as eminently WEAK and RIDICULOUS, as he now does *vile* and *abominable?*

Whoever reads with attention my preceeding numbers, and especially if they consider the observations and resolves of the Council and House on his excellency's letters, will be convinced that *the former* were very lenient when they resolved, that those letters "had a tendency to effect AN "ALTERATION IN THE CONSTITUTION of the province," and that *the latter* were far from being severe. When they so unanimously† declared "that the tendency and DESIGN of said letters‡ was *to subvert the constitution* of this government, and *to introduce arbitrary power* into this province."

And whoever considers his excellency's conduct in publickly affirming "he was *not conscious* of *any letters* which could have such an effect,"# and his express affirmation, that "there was not *one passage* in them *which was ever intended* TO RESPECT *the* particular *constitution of this government* as derived from charter,"* must suppose him given up to the strange delusion to believe a lie, or the more strange infatuation of believing all mankind, *except himself,* were fools and ideots.—But this weakness, with which I am afraid the gentleman is much contaminated, would not be greater than his having recourse to the little, temporary, futile expedient of procuring the following insignificant declaration from an old man. I Wm Brattle do Declare that I heared the Governor read the copies of sundry letters which were wrote by Him to Mr Whately & *the Governor said that those He read were most exceptionable & in them* He read to me *there was nothing more contained than what He had expressed as his sentiments both in Public & Private very often* the letters were wrote *AD* 1768 & were answers to letters wrote by Mr Wately to the Governor that sd Wately first wrote to the Governor WBrattle *there was nothing in either of the letters* as aforesaid *that mentioned any thing relative to a* any *petition of the Council* & to th__ to the King or to the King & council or *to the Parliament* or any Petition of the House or the or of the House & Council to the King or King & Council or to the Parliament.

June 1, 1773. WBrattle†

I am at a loss which to admire most; that his excellency should think such an expedient could do him any good, or that he should prostitute an *old* servant to such a mean office.—But I am not, in the least, surprized to see Brigadier Brattle meanly,—*meanly* stooping to this servility; nor the governor making *this use* of him, when he thought it would *serve his purposes.* It is not easy to say which of *the notable pair,* in this instance, appears the most odious—which the most contemptible.[3]

When *pristine* virtue and *ancient* honour are sullied and disgraced;—when *virgin* purity is *tempted,* or *youthful* innocence *debauched,* sentiments of pity extinguish every other emotion.—But when an *old* TEMPTER *prostitutes* an *hackneyed bawd*—(whether the scene of iniquity is in the lustful recesses of a brothel, or the *political* chambers of state)—compassion takes it's flight, and the bosom of the spectator is alternately filled with scorn and derision, horror and indignation.

How difficult is it, for one who deviates from the way of truth & sincerity not to discover himself? The very windings and doublings practised in order to illude observation exhibit his path to full view.

Was his Excellency so used to dissimulation, that he could not be ingenuous with his friend;—one whom he pitched upon to give a certificate of his character? Why else does he read to him *only* those letters which were wrote *in* 1768, and affirm to *his confident* that *they* were the *most exceptionable?* Now was not this so far from the truth, that every one who saw the letters must discover the falshood? But was it not the design of this certificate, to have a *private operation* with the members to whom it was so industriously shown, previous to the resolves, in order to influence the judgment of the inconsiderate, and then, when it had taken some *little* effect and served some present purpose, to be pocketed or destroyed by this *singular duenna?* With all his weakness the Gov. could not imagine this petty artifice would avail, when his writings should be made public.

As to the Brigadier, he is certainly bound to confess himself imposed on and give up the impostor, or vindicate the truth and honor of his declaration. The general will not hesitate what is the part of a *man of arms.*—His honour is at stake;—the HONOR of a GENERAL must not be stained with impunity;—it must be wiped away by satisfaction—or avenged at *the point of the sword.*

General Brattle has pledged his word and *his honor,* that "there was *nothing more* contained in those letters the governor read to him, than what he had expressed as *his sentiments* both *in public* and private *very often.*" Now it is most certainly incumbent upon the Brigadier—he is *in honor bound*—to inform the world of *one* time out of those *many* in which the *sentiments* contained in the letters of 68, were *expressed in public;* or frankly tell the world, that the governor grossly deceived him, when he said, *those he read to him were the most exceptionable.*—There is no other alternative, General.—And what is more, the work will not end here.

It appears evident that the letter of the 10th of December 1768, gives intelligence of "a long address or *petition* to *parliament,* agreed upon by 8 or 10 of the *council,* & signed by the president—and appearing to be an act of council." The informer goes on to say "that the whole is no more than the doings of a part of the council," whose meeting he declares "irregular and unconstitutional, and ought to be discountenanced and *censured.*" Yet the Brigadier certifies under his hand, that "there was *nothing in either* of the letters as aforesaid, that mentioned *any thing* relative to *any petition of the council* to *the parliament.*" Surely his Excellency must have secreted this letter (tho' he declared he showed *the most exceptionable*) or the general is much impaired in sight and memory. A most unhappy alternative again occurs for the Brigadier's choice. This, this I say, is that very letter which THE COUNCIL have solemnly resolved "had a tendency to effect an *alteration in the constitution* of this province;" and therefore I hope for the sake of his Excellency, he wrote no letter *more exceptionable* in 68: if so, we shall find it impossible to save immaculate and entire the sincerity of his Excellency to the Brigadier, and the Brigadier's veracity in his written declaration. As the general is far advanced in life, it might prevent an unnecessary stain upon his reputation, if he would make his choice of the difficulties before him;—and if the truth is, that *the old game* was played with him, let him now make *one honest* declaration *before he dies:* he need not be afraid that the discovery will *sink his master* much lower in the esteem of all good men, or hope that an affected secrecy will *advance himself* even in the graces of bad men. An honest confession of the truth of fact will in the end certainly serve him more, than any subterfuge or concealment.

MARCHMONT NEDHAM.

*Resolved, that *while* the writer of these letters signed Tho. Hutchinson, has been thus exerting himself by his *secret and confidential* correspondence, *to introduce measures* DESTRUCTIVE *of our* CONSTITUTIONAL LIBERTIES; *he has been practising* EVERY METHOD among the people of this province, to fix in their minds an exalted opinion of *his warmest affection* *for them,* and *his unremitted endeavours* to promote their best interest at the court of Great-Britain.

The house of Representatives in their last session.

† 101 out of 105 members

‡ Meaning those of the whole band of conspirators.

Message to the house of 3rd June 1773.

* Message of 9th June 1773.[4]

† The above we have compared with THE ORIGINAL in the Brigadier's *own Hand writing;* which was most industriously shown to Members of the General Court at their last Session; and it's Purport with equal Industry circulated abroad.

We have made the Copy as exact as is possible to do in Print.

EDES & GILL

[*To be continued.*]

1. *Boston Gazette,* 31 January 1774, p. 1, filling the entire page, except for the last third of the third column.

2. From *Samson Agonistes,* lines 829–33. Garry Wills played off of Milton in *Nixon Agonistes* (Boston: Houghton Mifflin, 1969).

3. There is a sketch of Brattle in Sibley, et al., *Harvard Graduates,* 7:10–23. A Cambridge lawyer and long-time member of the governor's council, he had only recently switched his political sympathies. Once a critic of Hutchinson, placed on the council by Hutchinson's opponents in the House (which Hutchinson chose not to fight), he had decided that the men of Quincy's ilk were widening the divide between mother country and colony. He, like Hutchinson, supported the new policy out of London that paid judges's salaries from proceeds raised through the navigation system rather than by the General Court, as had been the tradition. He differed fundamentally, then, with Quincy over what constituted a more independent judiciary. Perhaps it was a sense of betrayal that caused Quincy to depict the sixty-seven-year-old Brattle as a doddering, superannuated non-entity. Although Brattle was four years older than Quincy's father, he was three years younger than Josiah Junior's uncle Edmund, who was still very active as a justice of the peace in Boston—and a thorough-going patriot.

4. Hutchinson's messages of June 3rd and June 9th, with the House resolution of June 16th, are in the *Mass. House Journals,* 50:29, 40–41, and 57–61 (quotation from p. 59), resp.

"MARCHMONT NEDHAM"

7 February 1774[1]

NEDHAM'S REMEMB'RANCER, N. VII.

Why, he can smile, *and* murder while he smiles;
And cry content to that which grieves his heart;
And wet his cheeks with artificial tears;
And frame his face to all occasions:
Deceive more slily, than Ulyses could;
And, like a Sinon, take another Troy:
Change shapes, with PROTEUS, for advantages;
And set th' asp'rng CATILINE *to school.*
SHAKESPEARE'S HENRY 6th.[2]

IF we did not bear in mind the characteristic features of his Excellency, we should be surprized to find him continue a semblance of regard to this people and making declarations of his services to his country. At the very instant, that he is evading a disclosure of his letters to certain personages in England, the only way in which he could make atonement for his crimes;—at the very time that he must know his *secret and confidential* conduct was detected, and his character stood displayed in the face of all men; at the very moment, when the arrogance of a traitor, above the reach of law, ought to have given place to the humility of a convict;—at the very instant, I say, when the blushes of guilt and contrition ought to have precluded all effrontery and vain-glory;—his Excellency assumes his *wonted character,* shamelessly disavows any design of subverting the constitution of this government, affirms that his letters rather tended *to preserve it entire,* and positively declares he had reason to think they had *not been ineffectual to that purpose.** Is it possible to give an example of an enemy to the Common-wealth, whose public behavior was so devoid of shame, with desperate conspiracies so conspicuous to view? He could never suppose, that a people, remarkable for their discernment and understanding, would be blind to the plenary evidence laid before them, or that so paltry an artifice could renovate their confidence in his professions. It must have been a credulity below the milkiness of infancy, which could induce this people to suffer such declarations *from such a man* to delude them. His Excellency could, therefore, only intend to try the dangerous experiment of braving the scorn of mankind, and by sustaining the pressure of an open conviction, without discovering remorse of conscience, secure his pre-emminence among his fellows. Thus by showing himself as destitute of the sense of shame, as of guilt, he preserved that *darling* prerogative of being *the chief* among *his brethren;* and by pushing a hardy front on this trying occasion, he gave ample testimony, that he was a capable of bearing universal odium and scorn, as of *leading* in secret conspiracies and desperate machinations.

Upon the fourth of June, the House by message desired "that his Excellency would be pleased to order, that copies be laid before them of such letters as he had written (of certain dates) relating to the public affairs of this province; *together with such other letters as his Excellency should think proper,*" Here was a fair opportunity for this gentleman, to discover *some one instance* of friendship to the country in the multitude of his correspondencies. But so far from complying with this rational request, it was slighted with a dexterity and air peculiar to the person to whom it was made.

The Governor in his answer to the Council, on the 17th of June last, informs them that they "could *not possibly* form *a right judgment* of ALL the parts of those letters, unless they should also be furnished with the letters to which his are wrote in answer." But in the name of common sense, in whose power did it lay to furnish these letters, and against whom, and of what does the presumption lay, in case they are not produced? He who wanted *a right judgment to be formed of all parts* of the correspondence would give all the light he was able into the matter;—and he who thought it would be for his advantage, and had it in his power, would speedily give that light. But I have the uncommon happiness to fall in with the gentleman, and in this instance I see other reasons than his word to believe, and, therefore, I credit him. I verily believe that *a right judgment* cannot be formed of ALL PARTS of his excellency's letters, without an inspection into those of his correspondent: and what is more, I believe that the very reason, why the letters of Whately were not produced was because;—being produced & compared;—they would aid us much, not only in *forming a right judgment of the letters,* but also to determine with convincing certainty what were the machinations and views,—the *whole* hearts and souls of *the writers.*

In his Excellency's letter of the 4th of Oct. 68, he acknowledges the receipt of Mr. Whately's letter of the 31st of July, and then proceeds, "*It is not strange* that measures should be immediately taken *to reduce the colonies,*" &c.[3] Now I believe that his Excellency could help us to form a much *better judgment* of what those measures were which he thus acquiesces in, if he would exhibit the letter to which his is an answer. But he prefers leaving the matter to suspicion and conjecture, rather than gratify us with the whole truth of fact:—and manifestly for this reason, because concealment is of more advantage to him than such a discovery. I think he can never have cause to complain, if this people think *the worst* of him, 'till he shall remove their just suspicions by a frank and full disclosure of his whole correspondence.—And as the gentleman chuses to leave us at large to conjecture, I now form one, which will, probably, be not short of truth.

His Excellency had informed his British friend so early as the 18th June, that "the commissioners, *four of them, being destitute of protection,* removed with their families on board the Romney, & there remain and hold their board, and next week intend to do the same, and also open the Custom house at the Castle."[4] Now there can be no doubt, that this letter had reached England, previous to the 31st of July, and resolutions consequent upon it had been taken. If *a Chief Justice* informs that *the Subject,* especially a crown officer, *is destitute of protection,* the representation (however false) will be believed true in fact; and when this is the case, *all the aid which can be given to the officers of the crown* will be afforded; especially if it is credited, that with *all such aid they will have enough to do to maintain* THE AUTHORITY OF GOVERNMENT *and to carry* THE LAWS *into execution.* Now we all know that the extraordinary aid which is in Great Britain ever afforded to the civil power, is that of *the military:*—Tho' it is a solemn truth, that *the civil power,* like every other, which calls in the aid of an ally stronger than itself, PERISHES *by the assistance it receives.*—This military aid was accordingly applied by the British administration to remedy the suggested evils; which from being almost wholly imaginary, became real, and from being trifling and temporary, became fixed and permanent. Of this *warlike*, and *hostile* application, Whately's letter to his Excellency of the 31st of July, no doubt gave full account:—And *these very measures,* there can be as little doubt, were those that *did not seem strange* to his Excellency;—tho' they appeared not only strange, but inhuman and mad, to every other good subject of his Majesty in the province. Instead of reducing the colonies to their former state of government, and order, they confirmed the more modern one of confusion and bloodshed, general oppression and universal murmur and discontent.

If such meaures as these *did not really appear strange* to his Excellency, I can only attribute it to his thorough recollection of what he had done and wrote, and his good opinion of his own influence and weight with the British ministry: So that an *immediate* compliance with his inclinations and desire, was no more than *he expected,* and consequently, that this extravagant measure, which astonish'd all the world besides, was devested of all *strangeness* in the eye of his Excellency.

Thus have I considered Mr. Hutchinson, as degrading the highest station in the law to the lowest office of the inquisition; as descending from the rank of CHIEF JUSTICE to that of a common INFORMER:—An informer against "particular persons" & "the PROVINCE IN GENERAL";—yes,—the *dark* assassin of *private characters* and HIS NATIVE COUNTRY.

Convinced, as I am, that governor Hutchinson, in defiance of every principal of right, every sentiment of honor and gratitude; convinced I say, that HE is the first, the most malignant and *insatiable* enemy of my country;—that he is the chief author and supporter of the severest calamities under which this people labor;—convinced that he has done more general mischiefs, and committed greater public crimes, than his *life* can repair or his *death* satisfy;—and that *he is the man,* against whom the blood of my slaughtered brethren cries from the ground:—I have, and shall, as strength is given me, pursue him. And if at this time of life I am too *old* for an AVENGER OF BLOOD, I am also too *young* to desert the service of my country. But it may be profitable now to leave him to the reflections of his own conscience—the anguish of a *departing* spirit.—And if he be not speedily called to the great bar of the universe; peradventure I shall once more call him—but with no *friendly* voice—to the highest, the most terrible tribunal on earth;—the tribunal of his injured countrymen.

Addressing to the contemplations of his pillow, I close for the present, with the words of a favorite author.

> You have *lived long enough; the way of life*
> *Is fallen into fear,* the yellow leaf,
> And that which should accompany old age,
> As honor, love, obedience, troops of friends,
> You must not look to have: But, in their stead,
> CURSES, BOTH LOUD AND DEEP.[5]

MARCHMONT NEDHAM.

*His message to the House, 9th June last, concludes with these words, "thus much however I may *assure* you, that it has not been the tendency and design of them (his letters) to subvert the constitution of this government, but rather *to preserve it entire;* and I have reason to think that they have *not been altogether ineffectual to that purpose.*"[6]

1. *Boston Gazette,* 7 February 1774, p. 1, taking roughly the same amount of print space as the previous installment. This would be the last.

2. From *Henry VI*, Part III, Act III, Scene 2. Quincy altered the future Richard III's speech from first person to second—"Why, I can smile, and murder whiles I smile," and the lines that follow—to target Hutchinson. Unfortunately, we cannot know how consciously Quincy was mimicking Shakespeare as well as quoting him. Was he attempting to make his Hutchinson the historical Hutchinson, as, over time, Shakespeare's Richard III had become, for many, the historical Richard III?

3. Hutchinson to Whately, 4 October 1768, *Copy of Letters,* pp. 9–12 (quotation from p. 9).

4. Letter of 18 June 1768, ibid., pp. 3–5 (quotation from p. 4).

5. Macbeth speaking, as it begins to dawn on him that he is about be brought down by a fate that he, in his ambition and avarice, made inescapable. Act V, Scene 3 of Shakespeare's *Macbeth.* Quincy changed the first person—"I have liv'd long enough"—to second, to act as commentator on Hutchinson, and he compressed the speech to produce the final line.

6. *Mass. House Journals,* 50:41.

JQ LAST WILL AND TESTAMENT, WITH CODICIL

28 February 1774[1]

Know all Men by these Presents, that I Josiah Quincy Junior of Boston in the County of Suffolk, Gentleman being of sound and disposing mind and memory make publish and declare this my last Will and Testament. Of my Spirit I say the less because I know so little of it, and I make no Disposition thereof, because I am well satisfyed that it is disposed of Already—in a manner perfectly wright upon the whole and altogether unalterable by me. And as to my Creed touching the same it is of no consequence to any but myself and too foreign from my present purpose to be here set forth. Touching the Disposition of my Body I am little solicitous, but extremely averse to any parade in its interment. But if I shall die in New England, I order my Executor to bury or remove it to a new Tomb to be made for that purpose in the burying place of the north parish in Braintree. The Tomb to be dug large enough for the reception of my Wife and her issue by me and also for the containing my Father, if he shall desire it. And I desire the dimensions may be no further extended than is sufficient for these Purposes. I order my Executor, to erect an elegant marble monument over the same Tomb, with such inscription thereon, as to him shall seem best—and order my Executor to pay the Expence, attending the performance of these things as also all my Just Debts and funeral Charges out of my Personal estate.[2]

I give and bequeath unto my Honored[3] and beloved Relations and Friends following namely Josiah Quincy Esq. and Wife William Phillips Esq. and Wife Samuel Phillips Esq, and my Brother and Sister and to all my Brothers and Sisters in Law each a handsome Gold Ring. Those of my Father's and Mother's to be ornamented with an Elegant Stone, not as any compensation for their Goodness but as a Testimony of my Gratitude. I give my good friends James Boies, Perez Morton, Thomas Edwards and Sarah Loring each a Gold Ring. I give to that worthy and good man Richard Cranch of Boston Watchmaker as a small Testimony of my gratitude towards him, an handsome gold Ring. I give to Easther Parker and Mary Walker if they remain in my Service to the time of my Death, one year's advanced Wages to each of them over and above what may be severally due to them for their Services. I give to my Brother in Law William Phillips Junior my Solo-Chaise.[4] I give to my Son Josiah when he shall arrive to the Age of Fifteen Years Algernon Sidney's works in a large Quarto, John Locke's Works in 9 Vol. in Folio, Lord Bacon's Works in 4 Vol. in folio, Gordon's Tacitus in 4 Vol., Gordon's Sallust, Cato's Letters by Gordon and Trenchard, and Miss McCauley's History of England.[5] May the Spirit of Liberty rest upon him. I give also to my said Son, when he shall arrive to the Age of Twenty one years my best Watch and my other Watch I give to my Nephew Samuel Quincy Junr. I give and bequeath unto my beloved Wife Abigail the use and Improvement of all my Household Furniture of what name or Nature soever during her Widowhood and no longer. And all her Wearing Apparell, Linen, Jewels and all other things more especially belonging to her Person and all my Plate I give to her and her assigns forever. I also give her all kinds of Provisions, liquor Stores and such like Things in my House at the time of my Decease to her use forever. I also give to her my House and Chaise forever. I give also to my said Wife forever sixty Books, such as she may chuse for her own Reading out of my Library other than those that treat upon Civil and municipal Law.

My Mind and Will is that the Bequests and Legacies in this my last Will and Testament made to my said Wife shall be in full satisfaction of her Dower and right of thirds in my Estate. I also commit to the care and Custody of my said Wife all my manuscripts of a political and literary Nature, till one of my Sons arise to the Age of Twenty one years at which time I give them to such Son forever. I give to my good friend Mr. Perez Morton the use and improvement of my whole Library belonging to the Office for the Term of seven years; if I dye within three years from the date hereof he signing and delivering unto my Executor an Inventory thereof at the time he shall take the same into his Possession, I give my son Josiah all my wearing apparell, linen and such like Articles forever—I order that the Executor of this my last Will and Testament sell or let out at his Discretion all or any part of my Real Estate, and put the moneys arising from the sale or the rents thereof out at Interest on good Securities by Bond and Mortgage, and that my Executor change all or any of my Bonds and mortgages and other Securities for monies at Interest according to his Discretion without making himself Answerable for bad Debts; trusting to his Vigilance and Fidelity. And my Will and order is that any Executor settle with all convenient Speed my Accounts and collect the Moneys due thereon and all my small Debts upon Notes, and put the Moneys arising therefrom out at Interest on good Securities and that the Executor of this my last Will and Testament hold all my Estate Real, Personal and mixt except what I have and shall in this my last Will and Testament otherwise dispose of, subject to the limitations, restrictions and dispositions in this Will mentioned, in trust for the use therein expressed. I give and bequeath unto my much Beloved Wife, Abigail, if she remain my Widow the whole Interest and Income of all my Estate Real, Personal, not otherwise disposed of in this my last Will and Testament to be anually paid her by my Executor, till my said Son Josiah arive to the Age of Twenty one years for her maintenance and the support and Education of my said Son and other Child or Children, that I may have, in the best manner, and if my said Son Die before his arival to that Age, I order that my said Wife have and enjoy the whole of the same Interest and income during her said Widowhood, unless my said Son leave issue lawfully begotten in Wedlock and in that case I order that such issue take in the same manner as he would if alive. And if my said Son Josiah shall arive to the Age of Twenty one years, then I give and bequeath to him and his Assigns forever one Thousand Pounds Lawfull Money of Great Brittain, to be paid by my Executor out of the capital at Interest and in case my said Wife shall be at such time married, then I give and bequeath to my said Son his Heirs and Assigns forever the whole of my Estate Real Personal and mixt, not otherwise disposed of in this my last Will and Testament.

I order that in case my said Wife marry again that her revinue or Income from my Estate wholly cease and determine on the Day of such her marriage, and that in lieu thereof my Executor pay her one hundred Pounds Sterling and from thenceforth the Interest and income of my Estate be applied, to the support and Education of my said Son Josiah, untill he arive to the Age of Twenty one years and such other Child or Children as I may leave and the surplussage thereof be accumulated and added to the Principal of my Estate and put out to Interest for the uses of this my Will and Testament.

And in case my said Wife do not marry again, then I order that she enjoy what is before bequeathed to her namely, the residue of said Income and Interest, till Death and after her Death, and on the arrival of my said Son to the Age of Twenty one years then I give and Bequeath all the rest and residue of my said Estate Real, personal and mixt not otherwise herein disposed of, to him his Heirs and assigns forever unless he have Brothers and Sisters or a Brother and Sister of the whole Blood, who are then to share equally with him and if he Dye before he arive to the Age of Twenty one years and leave issue I give and bequeath to such issue in the same manner (and so otherwise) as to him. And in case my said Son shall Dye before he arive to the Age of Twenty one years or after he arive to that Age, without issue and without leaving any Brothers or Sisters or Brother or Sister of the whole Blood who are respectively to take as in this Will mentioned, then upon the marriage or Death (which ever shall first happen) of my said Wife I Order and accordingly give and bequeath to the President and Corporation of Harvard Colledge, two thousand Pounds Sterling for the use and purpose of founding a Professorship of Moral Philosophy Law and Oratory and no other; and the desire of my Vanity is, that the Professor thereof be called Quincy—Professor of moral Philosophy Law and oratory. And in case of the Death of my said Son without issue as aforesaid and without leaving any Brothers or Sisters or Brother or Sister of the whole Blood and after the payment of my bequests aforesaid to Harvard Colledge, I give bequeath and Divise all the rest and residue of my Estate to my next of kin of the whole Blood to be equally divided between them share and share alike.

But my mind and Will is (any thing herein contained to the contrary notwithstanding) that if I should leave any other Child or Children (as it seems probably I may) besides my said Son Josiah, that such Child or Children shall take and equally share with my said Son the legacies Gifts and Devises herein made to him and in case of his Death that such Child or Children take as he would if alive provided always that if my said Son leave issue lawfully begotten in Wedlock such issue shall come in for the share of their Father with such other Child or Children as I may leave at my Decease, besides my said Son Josiah.

And last I make ordain and appoint Francis Dane Esqr. Executor of this my last Will and Testament and in case of his Death and Refusal I nominate and appoint Jon. Jackson of Newbury-port merchant Executor thereof; and in case of his Death or refusal I nominate and appoint John Adams Esqr Executor thereof and in case of his Death and refusal I nominate and appoint my Brother in Law William Phillips Junior Executor thereof and in case of his Death or refusal I nominate and appoint Mr. Perez Morton Executor thereof, and in case of the Death or refusal of all the said Executors before appointed to take in succession as aforesaid, I desire that the Judge of Probate would nominate such meet Person, as he shall think proper Administrator with the Will anexed and what sort of a one I should chuse, he may collect from those I have appointed my Executors, but I desire of the Judge, that no Person related to me by Blood may be the Administrator. I desire that the Judge of Probate would make a handsome and generous allowance to the Executor of this my last Will and Testament for his Trouble and not barely give him a Quantum meruit.[6]

In Witness whereof and in Testimony, that this is my last Will and Testament, I hereunto set my Hand and Seal this 28 Day of February, in the fourteenth year of his Majesty's Reign Annoque Domini 1774.

Josiah Quincy Junior [seal]

Signed, Sealed, published and declared by the said Testator to his last Will and Testament in presence of us who in his Presence subscribed our Names as Witnesses–These Words and Wife in the second page and such other Child or Children as I may leave in the fifth Page in this Will is mentioned in the sixth Page first interlined, and the Words say in the first Page and the word aforesaid in the sixth Page first erased by the Testator.

J Quincy Junior
Joseph Warren
William Tudor
John Gill

I Josiah Quincy Junior of Boston in the County of Suffolk Gentleman, the Testator in the preceeding Will named, hereby make this a Codicil thereof and thereto to be anexed and accounted and taken as part thereof—Whereas since the Execution of the same Will I have had born a Daughter named Abigail, who will take by Virtue of the devises and bequests in the same contained a greater Estate and Interest, than I intend or am willing upon further consideration that she should, I therefore do hereby revoke and annul said Last Will so far as it relates to her and what she would or might take (owing her Brother Josiah) by Virtue thereof, but no further and I order that in case her said Brother live to the Age of Twenty one she shall take nothing by force or Virtue of any Devise Gift bequest, clause or paragraph in the same Will contained, my mind and Will however being that in case her said Brother Die before the Age of Twenty one without issue that in such case this Codicil shall be considered as altogether null and void, and that said Abigail shall take as if the same Codicil had never been made. And in lieu of what would go and rest in said Abigail by force and operation of the same Will if not altered by this Codicil as aforesaid, I give and bequeath to her if she shall arive to the Age of Twenty one or marriage the Sum of one thousand Pounds Lawfull Money of Great Brittain and order that from that time till the payment of said Legacy it shall carry Interest. And whereas I have nominated and appointed Mr Perez Morton of said Boston Gentleman to be an Executor of my said last Will and Testament but since the Execution of said last Will and Testament said Morton hath become obligated to me by bond conditioned for the payment of Forty Pounds Lawfull Money and Interest and it is highly probable that before my Death he will become further indebted to me in considerable Sums, I therefore for these and other good reasons Not necessary to enumerate but out of no disrespect of him hereby revoke further said last Will and Testament that is to say so far as relates to said Perez Morton being one of my said Executors and I hereby direct and order that he shall be an Executor of my said last Will or Administrator cum testamento annexo[7] and in the stead and place of said Morton (and to be my Executor in the order and at the time said Morton would have been if this Codicil had never been made) I hereby nominate and appoint John Lowell of Newbury port in the County of Essex Esquire to be executor thereof. And I do hereby order and direct that no Executor of the last Will and Testament of any one of my said Executors shall (ipso facto)[8] be an Executor of my said last Will and Testament, But upon the Death or refusal of all the Executors thereof I hereby pray that the Judge of Probate of Wills and granting of Letters of Administration for the County of Suffolk would grant Administration to some meet Person cum testamento anexo, hoping that he will observe my directions and desires upon this matter in my said last Will and Testament expressed saving that if either of my Children shall at the time of the granting such Administration be arived at the Age of Twenty one years and in other Respects shall in the Judgement of the said Judge be a suitable and proper Person for that office I hereby request the Judge to appoint such Child Administrator with the Will anexed but not otherwise. In Witness whereof I the said Josiah Quincy Junior hereunto set my Hand and Seal this ninth day of September in the fourteenth Year of his Majesty's reign Annoque Domini 1774, hereby ratifying and confirming my said last Will and Testament in all and every part not revoked or annulled by this Codicil hereby publishing and declaring this a Codicil thereto and to be anexed accounted and taken as part thereof the same Day and Year last mentioned.

Josiah Quincy Junior [seal]

Signed Sealed Published and Declared by the said Josiah Quincy Junior the Testator in a Codicil to his last Will and Testament in presence of us who in his Presence subscribed our Names as Witnesses,

Joseph Warren
David Jones
William Venal Jun.

1. QP 51 (and reel 29) MHS.

2. I created the paragraph breaks that follow, added some periods where Quincy continued on, inserted apostrophes where needed, substituted "and" for "&," and filled in abbreviations.

3. He wrote "Hond," after scratching out "Beloved."

4. Light carriage, pulled by a single horse.

5. Quincy, *Memoir*, p. 289, left out both Gordon's *Sallust* and Macaulay's *History*. Bernard Bailyn, in his *The Ideological Origins of the American Revolution* (Cambridge, Mass.: Belknap Press of Harvard University Press, 1967), used Quincy's bequest as the epigraph to Chapter 2, but he worked from the *Memoir* rather than the original, so he did the same–most likely without realizing that Eliza Susan Quincy had made the deletions.

6. The fair amount due a party for services performed, with no formal written contract specifying a fixed total.

7. With the will annexed.

8. A Latin phrase that has passed into common American English usage: "by the fact itself."

"YOUR WELL WISHER" TO JQ

May 1774[1]

Sir ___

I am compelled by the common Principles of Humanity to warn you of the eminent hazard which I consider you to be in, of the Loss of Life, and confiscation of your Estate. It is now become very apparent that the supreme power of Great Britain, viz King, Lords, and Commons, which you sometime since, as I am informed, was pleased to term a transmarine power, to which we were not amenable, hath taken a Resolution to assert its Sovereignty over this his Majesty's Colony of Massachusetts Bay, a Sovereignty which has never been disputed by any of the other Colonies, excepting in the Article of Taxation, and not by this, but a very short time since. Every Measure necessary to carry this Resolution into execution hath been taken. A Force is employ'd for this purpose, to oppose which in our weak forlorn Condition, it would be madness to attempt. This being the case, it cannot be supposed, that if there should be a continuance of those insults and Indignities, which for some Years past have been put upon the Government, and the Servants of it, that the leading promoters of Such Insults and Indignities will escape with impunity. Those Actions and Words, which by the Laws of Great Britain are there determined to be treasonable and rebellious will be considered as such here, and the Authors of them suffer the Pains and Penalties which are inflicted on Traitors, and Rebels in Great Britain, or any other part of the Realm. Of all this you seem to me to be altogether insensible, at which I cannot but express the greatest Supprize, as I consider you to be a person of Quick Discernment, to be well versed in the knowledge of Government, of Law in General, and more particularly of the Laws and Constitution of the Parent State. Your political Enthusiasm, and popular Attachment, must certainly have totally blinded the Eyes of your understanding, otherwise I cannot conceive it to be possible that a man of your good sence instead of promoting such measures at our late town meeting which in our most calamitous condition might have a tendency to soften the resentment of government, and induce his Majesty and his privy Council to remove those evils, which are justly brought upon us for our past Crimes, should endeavour by inflammatory harangues to keep up the Phrenzy of the poor deluded people of this Town to persuade him that they have resourses sufficient within themselves, if they were united and firm, to extricate themselves out of these difficulties, and to obtain a Compleat conquest over Great Britain even without the Assistance of the Neighbouring Towns of this Province, and of the sister Colonies; but if they should join us that our Victory would be beyond a Doubt, that some Cromwell would soon rise, and trample under his Feet; our Enemies, viz. King, Lords, and Commons of Great Britain, for you could mean no other, they being the only enemies you were speaking of. You did indeed in express Terms charge them with Ignorance, and Effrontery, (in another word with impudence) for passing the Late Act which will shut up our Port. Not content with these bold Speeches you was the Principal mover of sundry Votes passed at this meeting, which can be considered in no other Light by Great Britain,than as an hostile attack upon her, as by those Votes the Neighbouring Towns of this Province and all the Colonies from the Floridas to Newfoundland are to be stimulated by Committees of Correspondence to put a force upon her Trade.

Reflect a moment upon this Conduct consider the present Strength of Administration, who have carried their measures against you without the least opposition, consider the power they have at present in their hands (however weak they may be, when your formadable Cromwell steps forth) to bring to Condign Punishment all Offenders against the State, and I am sure you will think with me that your Situation is truly alarming. You will very probably get into the hands of a power, from which no power you can look to will be able to deliver you. You have gone such lengths that I am fearful nothing can save you. I know of but one expedient left you which is that of Acknowledging on Wednesday next to this distressed people that you have been in Error. That you have deceived yourself, that you have deceived them. Employ, for God's sake, those rare talents with which he has blessed you, in convincing them that they have nothing to do but to submit and make their peace with that Government, which they have under the influence of you and other factious Demagogues so long Offended. You may by these means probably make your own peace and ward off the punishment that hangs over your head. It is barely possible that Government may still continue its great Lenity and overlook your Offences. If this should be the Case, permit me to observe there is another danger to which you are exposed. The Inhabitants of this Wretched Town would if proper Measures were taken be saved from total destruction. But if by the mad pursuits of you and others, their Ruin should be compleated, if thousands of the Poor who depend upon their daily Labour for their daily Bread should be in a Starving Condition, if those who now can calculate upon such Incomes from their Real Estates as to be able to live in Affluence should find their Estates to yeild them not sufficient to subsist them, they will begin to look round for the real Authors of their Ruin and wreak their Venjance upon them. They will no longer consider Barnard, Hutchinson, Oliver, Commissioners of the Customs, &c. as their Enemies. They will put the Saddle on the right horse. We shall see an Adams, a Young, a Cooper, a Warren, a Quincy with certain learned Doctors of Divinity either destroyed by, or fleeing in their turn from their Base, and applying to that power which they have so long insulted, for protection.[2] I have conversed with many of the thinking part of this community, and find very few who do not condemn your proceedings. Nothing has prevented a publick protest appearing against you, but the fear of that most formidable tyranny which the ruling part of this town have so long by having the Command of an heated populace, exercised over it. Upon the appearance of any Power that will be sufficient to emancipate them from this terrible Hydra, you will find that Spirit that now vents itself in secret Curses break out into open Violence. I can hear you in almost all Company I go into stiled Villains, Scoundrells, Rascalls, and many wish that the Venjance of Government had been pointed at the Authors of all our Misery; meaning your particular junto, where, it is said, it ought to have fallen, and not upon the whole community a larger proportion of whom are Innocent. Let me conjure you to weigh well what I have offered to your Consideration, and believe me to be

Your well wisher

1. The original note is in QP 51 (and reel 29) MHS; Eliza Susan Quincy transcribed it for her "Memoir," 2:117–20, QP 46 (and reel 6) MHS; and it is reproduced with slight changes in the printed *Memoir,* pp. 131–35.

2. Samuel Adams, Dr. Thomas Young, the Reverend Samuel Cooper, and Dr. Joseph Warren. The author's thinking parallels that of Peter Oliver, who repeatedly decried the "black regiment" of congregational ministers who, he felt, had undercut legitimate imperial authority. See Douglas Adair & John A. Schutz, eds., *Peter Oliver's Origins and Progress of the American Rebellion* (San Marino, Calif.: Huntington Library Press, 1961), pp. 29, 41–45, 53, 63, 106, 163.

JQ TO "YOUR WELL WISHER"

May 1774[1]

Mr. Draper: Boston May 1774

Having this day received (from the British Coffee house) an anonymous letter, in which the author "warns me of the eminent hazard, which he considers me to be in, of the *Loss of Life,* and of *confiscation of my estate.*" I desire through the channel of your paper to acknowledge the receipt of it, and in turn communicate my own sentiments to the Author.

The good or ill design of the writer being problematical, I suspend my censure, and he will surely not expect my thanks. Had he (instead of concealing himself beyond the power of Discovery) desired a conversation with me in person, his frankness would have been an evidence of his sincerity, and my cordiality on the occasion should have testified my gratitude.

The danger and the wrongs of my country are to me equally apparent. In all my public exertions *I feel* a sense of right and duty, that not only satisfies my conscience, but inspires my zeal. While I have this sentiment, *I shall persevere,* till my understanding is convinced of its error:—a conviction that will not be wrought by *the arm of power,* or *the hand of the assassin.*

Threats of impending danger communicated by persons who conceal their name and character ought never to deter from the path of our duty; but exciting contempt, rather than fear, they will determine a man of spirit to proceed with new vigour and energy in his public conduct.[2]

My place of abode is well known, and I am easily found. The author of the letter referred to, if he will favor me, with a visit, shall receive the best civilities of my house; and if he will appoint a meeting I will give him my presence either *alone* or *in company*:—till which time he surely will not expect that I shall endeavour to point out *his* mistakes, or flatter himself that anonymous papers will answer the end he *professes to have in view.*[3]

JQ[4]

1. Original in QP 51 (and reel 29) MHS; printed in the *Massachusetts Gazette,* p. 2, column 3, with various small changes in punctuation and capitalization. Addressed to "Mess'rs DRAPER and BOYLE."

2. Quincy inserted this paragraph after having written a first draft without it.

3. Was Quincy opening the door for a duel—the "in company" a veiled allusion to his second, in such an event?

4. "JOSIAH QUINCY, Jun'r." in the print version.

OBSERVATIONS
ON THE
ACT OF PARLIAMENT
COMMONLY CALLED
THE
BOSTON PORT-BILL;
WITH
THOUGHTS
ON
CIVIL SOCIETY
AND
STANDING ARMIES.

BY JOSIAH QUINCY, JUN'R.

BRITONS *arise!* - - - - - - - - - - - - - - - - - -
And show you have the Virtue to be mov'd.
POPE.

NULLA FIDES, pietasq; viris, qui CASTRA sequuntur,
VENALSQUE MANUS: ibi fas, ubi maxima merces.
LUCAN.

Our necks are under PERSECUTION.
LAM. V. 5

What MAN can do against them, *not afraid,*
Though to THE DEATH; against such CRUELTIES
With *inward consolation* recompene'd:
And oft supported so, *as shall amaze*
Their PROUDEST PERSECUTORS.
MILTON.

They that be slain by THE SWORD are better than they that be slain *with hunger.*
LAM. IV. 9.[1]

To the FREEHOLDERS *and* YEOMANRY *of my Country.*

The virtue, strength and fortitude of a state generally reside in the FREEHOLDERS of the Nation. In you, Gentlemen, as the LANDED INTEREST of the Country, do I place my confidence, under GOD, at this Day.[2]

To you, Gentlemen, therefore, I dedicate THIS *temporary* WORK,[3] as a testimony of that great respect and warm affection, with which,

I am,

Your Friend and Countryman,

JOSIAH QUINCY, jun.

Boston, May 14, 1774.

[1; unpaginated][4]

PREFACE.

THE Statute of the 14th George 3d, received in the last Ships from London (entitled "An Act, to discontinue, in such Manner, and for such Time as are therein mentioned, the landing and discharging, the lading or shipping of Goods, Wares, Merchandize, at the Town, and within the Harbour of Boston, in the Province of Massachusetts-Bay, in North-America,")[5] *gave rise to the following* OBSERVATIONS:—*They will appear thrown together in haste; and as the Writer was out of Town on business, almost every day, the Sheets were printing off, no doubt many Errors of the Press escaped correction.*[6]

The Inaccuracies of a sudden Production from one of infirm health, perplexed with various avocations, will receive a mild censure: more material faults, FRIENDS may be prone to forgive; *but from* Enemies—*public or private—we are never to expect indulgence or favor.*

JOSIAH QUINCY, Junr.

Boston, May 14, 1774.

[2; unpaginated]

OBSERVATIONS &c.

IN times of public calamity, it is the duty of a good citizen *to consider.* If his opportunities or advantages, for knowledge and reflection, are greater than those of mankind in general, his whole duty will remain undischarged, while he confines his thoughts to the compass of his own mind. But if *danger* is added to the *calamity* of the times, he who shall communicate his sentiments on public affairs with decency and *frankness,* merits attention and indulgence, if he may not aspire to approbation and praise.

Whoever attends to the tenor and design of the late act of the British Parliament for the BLOCKADE OF this HARBOUR, and duly considers the extensive confusion and distress this measure must inevitably produce; whoever shall reflect upon the justice, policy and humanity of legislators, who could deliberately give their sanction to such a procedure—must be satisfied, that the man, who shall OPENLY *dare to expose their conduct,* hazards fatal consequences.—Legislators, who could condemn a whole town unheard, nay uncited to answer; who could involve thousands in ruin and misery, without suggestion of any crime *by them* committed; and who could so construct their law, as that enormous pains and pe- [3; unpaginated] nalties would *inevitably* ensue, NOTWITHSTANDING THE MOST PERFECT OBEDIENCE TO IT'S INJUNCTIONS; I say, that legislators, thus *formed as* MEN, thus principled as STATESMEN, would undoubtedly imagine the attainder and death of a private individual, for his public animadversions,[7] a less extraordinary act of power.[8] But all exertions of duty have their hazard:—if dread of Parliamentary extravagance is to deter from public energies,[9] *the safety of the common wealth will soon be despaired of;* and when once a sentiment of that kind prevails, the excesses of present enormities so rapidly increase, that strides, at first appearance, exorbitant, will soon be found—but *the beginning of evils.* We therefore consider it as a just observation, that the weight and velocity of public oppressions are ever in a ratio proportionate to private despondency and public despair. [4]

He who shall go about to treat of important and *perilous* concerns,[10] and conceals himself behind the curtain of a feigned signature, gives an advantage to his adversaries; who will not fail to stigmatize his thoughts, as the notions of an unknown writer, afraid or ashamed to avow his sentiments; and hence they are deemed unworthy of notice and refutation. Therefore I give to the world both my sentiments and name upon the present occasion, and shall hear with patience him, who will decently refute what is advanced, and shall submit with temper to that correction and chastisement which my errors deserve.

The act now under consideration opens with a recital, that "dangerous *commotions and insurrections* have been fomented and raised in Boston—by divers ill-affected persons, to the subversion of his Majesty's Government, and to the utter destruction of the public peace, and good order of the said town; in which commotions and insurrections certain valuable cargoes of Teas, being *the property of the East-India Company*, and on board certain vessels lying within the bay or harbour of Boston, were seized and destroyed: and in the present condition of said town and harbour, the commerce of his Majesty's subjects cannot be safely carried on there, nor the customs payable to his Majesty be duly collected."

Two questions naturally arise out of this preamble: The first, whether *the facts* set forth are *true;* and Secondly, whether *upon a supposition of their truth,* they are a sufficient foundation for the subsequent parts of the statute, or will warrant the disabilities, forfeitures, pains and penalties, enacted and inflicted on the subject?—Both inquiries seem intimately to concern the honour and justice of the British le– [5] gislature. And however unimportant the judgment of Americans may now appear to that august body—yet surely the judgment of Europe and future ages is not unworthy their high consideration. Removed from the eye of royalty, the piety of a Sovereign may cease to pity miseries it doth not behold; remote from the cries of public justice and the efforts of popular despair, Lords and Commons may remain unaffected, for a season, with American convulsions; yet justice and humanity must soon excite those operations in America and Europe, which hereafter will move even the senate of Britain. True knowledge and real virtue perhaps was never more diffused than on this northern continent; refined humanity ('tis boasted) was never more predominant than in Europe at this day:—Can it be supposed, that this virtue will be discordant and inactive; that this knowledge will omit to unfold public wrongs, or that such humanity will cease to interpose?

That commotions were in Boston; that East-India tea was destroyed, are facts not controverted.[11] But that such commotions were natural to be expected; that they were such as *statesmen* must have *foreseen* and A FATHER OF HIS COUNTRY, who foresaw, would prevent, rather than punish, is equally true. The sentiments of all Americans relative to the Tea act are no secret, their fervor in the COMMON CAUSE equally known; and their probable intemperance in consequence of the arrival of India teas, it required no profound skill in men and politics to predict. Nay the British papers were full, and the senate echoed, with the predictions similar to those which are now fulfilled. It was not difficult for *Englishmen in Britain* to tell how [6] *Englishmen in America* would conduct on such occasions. What shall we then say? Shall we impute to those, who are dignified as "the wisest and most august" the barbarous projection—deliberately to ensnare, that they might superlatively punish? The calm deliberation of premeditated malice seems rather more characteristick of a *private* bosom, than a *public body.* But Governor Hutchinson (the representative of his Majesty in this Province) when treating upon an act of *the Massachusetts Government imposing* a tax or *duty* upon goods of the inhabitants of *other colonies*, hath assured us, that "in all ages and countries, by *bodies* and *communities of men* such deeds have been done as most of the individuals of which such communities consisted, acting separately, would have been *ashamed of.*"[12] An observation that his Excellency might have imbibed, from that prince of historians, Dr. Robertson. "To abandon *usurped power,* to renounce *lucrative* error, are sacrifices, which the virtue of *individuals,* has, on some occasions, offered to TRUTH; but from ANY SOCIETY *of men*, no such effort can be expected. *The corruptions of society,* recommended by common utility, and justified by universal practice, are viewed by it's members, *without shame or horror;* and reformation *never* proceeds from themselves, but is *always* FORCED upon them by some FOREIGN hand."[13] "Caesar, Lepidus and Antony, says Plutarch, shew, that no beast is more *savage* than man, when possessed of *power equal to his passion.*"[14] If the sentiments of Dr. Robertson are just, have we not cause to fear from *very powerful* states and legislators an equal ferocity? [7]

And it is an observation of the illustrious Lord Clarendon, that it is the nature of man, rather to commit two errors, than retract one. When elevated characters commit a *second* error, it carries the air of an intended discovery, how little they feel for the *first,* how much they despise *the people,* how much they are above shame, fear and amendment. But to heighten cruelty by wantonness, to render it more pungent by insult, are such exorbitances, as seldom disgrace the records of mankind. But whenever such instances occur, they strikingly verify that eternal truth recorded in the House of Lords—"it is much easier to restrain *liberty* from running *into licentiousness* than POWER from swelling into *tyranny and oppression.*"[15] Can it add dignity to this noble sentiment, or weight to this important truth, to say, that among the illustrious personages who subscribed it with their hands and transmitted it to posterity, we find a "Chesterfield" and "Cobbam," a "Strafford" and a "Bathurst[,] a "Haversham" and "Gower"?

But to return. Are popular commotions peculiar to Boston? Hath not every maritime town in England been repeatedly affected by them? Are they not incident to every commercial and popular city?—whence, then, is it, that BOSTON is devoted to such unexampled treatment? But it may be said, Boston, *as a town,* hath aided, abeted, and participated in these tumults. Where is the evidence of it? I presume the King, Lords and Commons of Great-Britain had none; for they do not *suggest it:* I presume they did not believe it, because they have not *intimated it.* And had they [8] been furnished with such evidence, had they believed the fact, surely it is an imputation unworthy of their dignity, to say, that they would not have given *that matter* in *the preamble* of the statute, as the ground of their extraordinary proceedure. *But the records of Boston, and known facts prove that the inhabitants discountenanced* and *disavowed all riot* and disorder.[16] I am thus warranted in saying, that the *mere occurrences* expressed in the act, is that matter which the British legislature have judged worthy the most unparallelled penal severities. Whether *this judgment* be *right,* is a subject interesting to a citizen of the town to enquire; it is a subject on which *a man* will speak feelingly; on which AN ENGLISHMAN *will* speak *freely* and *openly.*

Previous to further observations, it may be necessary to say, that the town of Boston had as *a town cautiously* and *wisely* conducted, not only without tumult, but with studied regard to established law. This the rolls of the town verify, and a hundred witnesses can confirm.

At the last town-meeting relative to the East-India tea and it's consignees, it was largely debated, whether it should be an instruction to the committee, who were appointed to wait on those Gentlemen, *to insist* on their *preremptory* answer;—whether *they would send back the Tea:* and after long debate on the question, it passed by a very large majority in the *negative.* And the greatest enemy of the country cannot point out any one step of *the Town of Boston,* in the progress of this matter, that was tumultuous, disorderly and against law. This also is an additional reason, why we must conclude that the *mere temporary events which* [9]*took place in Boston,* without any *illegal* proceedure of the town, in the matter of the tea, is in the judgment of the British senate an adequate foundation for the last act received from that powerful body.

The first enacting clause of the statute now in view, annihilates all commercial transactions within two certain points of the harbour of Boston, upon pain of the FORFEITURE of "goods, wares and merchandize, and of boat, lighter, ship, vessel, or other bottom;—and of the guns, ammunition, tackle, furniture and stores, in or belonging to the same:" "and of any barge, hoy, lighter, wherry, or boat into which any goods &c. are laden," &c.[17]

The next paragraph, "in case any wharfinger," &c. or any of their servants shall take up or land, or knowingly *suffer* to be taken up or landed, or shall ship off, or *suffer* to be water-born, at or from any of their said wharves, &c. goods &c." enacts a FORFEITURE and LOSS of such "*goods* &c. and TREBLE the value thereof, to be computed at the *highest* price of such sort of goods, &c. together with the vessels and boats, and all the horses, cattle, and carriages, whatsoever made use of in the shipping, unshipping, landing, removing, carriage, or conveyance of any of the aforesaid goods," *&c.*

The next clause provides, "that if any ship *&c.* shall be moored or lie at anchor, or be seen hovering within said bay, *&c.* or within one league from the said bay, *&c.* it shall and may be lawful for any Admiral, or *commissioned* officer of his Majesty's fleet or ships of war, or for ANY OFFI- [10] CER OF HIS MAJESTY'S CUSTOMS, to *compel* such ship or vessel to depart to SOME OTHER port or harbour, or to SUCH STATION AS THE SAID OFFICER SHALL APPOINT and to use SUCH FORCE for that purpose as shall be found necessary: And if such ship or vessel shall not depart accordingly, WITHIN SIX HOURS *after notice* for that purpose given by *such person* as aforesaid, *such ship or vessel, together with all the goods laden on board thereon, and all the guns, ammunition, tackle and furniture shall be forfeited and lost,* WHETHER BULK SHALL HAVE BEEN BROKEN OR NOT."

Let us here pause for a moment;—let us give time for one single reflection; let us give space for one pulse of the veins—one emotion of the heart. And who can think, but those exalted characters and that generous prince, stiled THE FATHER OF all HIS PEOPLE—who united to this terrible act had many reflections, many feelings of humanity, while they were solemnly consigning thousands—if not millions—to ruin, misery and desperation?

The persons in whom this authority is vested, are not confined to the ports or harbours *on this continent:* the vessel and cargo may be ordered to what harbour, port or station of the whole world, *the officer* pleases—if he appoint a *continental* station, 'tis grace and favour;—and what may be the price of that purchase, who can tell! what scope for malice and ill-will; for pride and haughtiness; for avarice and power to wanton and insult, till the one is satiated and the other wearied![18]

Who are the persons to whom such unbounded, such enormous power is entrusted? Power is [11] known to be intoxicating in it's nature, and in proportion to it's extent, is ever prone to wantoness: power and authority, says Plutarch, awaken every passion, and discover every *latent* vice:[19]—what a cogent temptation is here placed to insnare the most virtuous? But if there be one depraved passion in the bosom, as power gives scope and opportunity, how soon will it be called forth in licentious exercise? Shall I be thought going too far; shall I trespass upon the bounds of truth and decency, if I say, that SOME of his Majesty's *commissioned* officers, in his fleet, or ships of war; SOME officers of his *customs* are *not altogether* worthy of such high confidence and trust? Are there not *inferior commissioned officers* in the King's ships; are there not *many* of the LOWER officers of the customs, who have neither strength of understanding or integrity of heart to weild such a mighty power? Nay, may not I add, that SOME FEW (into whose hands peradventure the estate of *a good* subject and *opulent* merchant may chance to fall) are destitute of all sense, *mental* and *humane?* While contemplating this subject,—while the mind is active, and heart warm—how apt are we to forget, that the illustrious Houses, who gave their sanction to this astonishing law, are dignified as learned and venerable;—and the Prince that gave his *fiat,* denominated—"THE WISEST AND BEST OF KINGS"?

Declining an entrance upon matters heretofore discussed by abler heads, I have omitted all observation on the *right* and *policy* of the claims and laws of Great-Britain over the colonies; upon the same principle, I waive entering that copious field which is presented, by that part of the present act, which provides for the recovery of all forfeitures and penalties in the courts of admiralty—whose extended [12] jurisdiction hath been matter of very great grievance, heart-burnings and complaint; whose judges hold their commissions *by the tenure of will and pleasure;* and whose large salaries are a most powerful incentive to the desire of—*well-pleasing* ALL *on whom they depend.*

Another passage in this statute makes *utterly void* ALL CONTRACTS, "for consigning, shipping, or carrying any goods, &c. *to* or *from* the harbour of Boston, *which* HAVE BEEN *made* or entered into, or which shall be made or entered into, so long as the act continues in force, relating to any ship which shall arrive at said town or harbour after the first day of June".

Jurisprudents and the sages of the law for centuries have taught, that *retrospective* or *post facto* statutes, were not only militant with the principles of sound morals, but those also of political wisdom. But the Parliament, who by the bold figure of common lawyers, are stiled *omnipotent,* here *enforces* a different doctrine. The english colonist, replete with loyalty to his sovereign; the descendant from Britain, animated by love for a mother-country, represses the excursions of his understanding and passions: but the subject or native of another state will feel no such restraint. *He* had *contracted* to send his merchandize to this port, expects his returns in the commodities of the country—in compliance with his obligations, his treasures are moving with hazard upon the ocean, with hopes warm for gain. The ship (in which peradventure he hath risqued his life as well as fortune) after many a toil and jeopardy, reaches the destined port. But how are his hopes baffled—how will he [13] rage and exclaim? vast hath been his expences to prepare for his adventure, and equally great his expectations from the Boston merchant. What guilt hath he contracted, what crime hath *he* committed, that *he also* should be involved in the calamitous consequences of this unexampled statute? Bouyed up for a moment, perhaps, with a vain expectation, that he may have a remedy on his *contract against the merchant here;*—how will this supposed foreigner sink with a ten-fold despondency, how will *he* rise again with adequate indignation, when he discovers all remedy gone;—his contract declared *by the law,* "*utterly void,* to ALL INTENTS AND PURPOSES WHATSOEVER?"—Here again, love of a *parent*-country, love for a *parent*-king checks the current of reason, and restrains the career of passion.

Having taken this view, before we proceed further, it is natural once more to ask, whence arose this extraordinary stride of legislation; what is it, that *the town* of Boston hath done? what new and unheard of crime have the inhabitants committed to justify enacting of such disabilities, forfeitures, pains, and penalties? punishments that descend *indiscriminately on all* ought to have the sanction of *unerring wisdom, and almighty power,* or it will be questioned, if not opposed:—The present vengeance falls *indiscriminately* on the *acknowledged innocent,* as well as the *supposed guilty.* Surely the evil is of a very malignant and terrible nature that can require such an extraordinary remedy. Admit for a moment, that the inhabitants of Boston were charged as high criminals; the highest criminals are not punishable, till arraigned before disinterested [14] judges, heard in defence, and found guilty of the charge. But so far from all this, a whole people are accused, prosecuted by they know not *whom;* tried they know not *when;* proved guilty they know now *how;* and sentenced in a mode, which for number of calamities, extent and duration of severity, exceeds the annals of past ages, and we presume, in pity to mankind, will not mark any future Era in the story of the world.

What will be the *real* consequences of this astonishing measure, and what those *intended and expected by* the *planners* of it are very *different* considerations. A MACHIAVEL may plan, and his schemes prove abortive; an [Duke of] ALVA may be sent to execute, and his army be defeated. The circle of the arts and sciences, like the ball of empire, hath held a *western* course. From Chaldea and Egypt to Greece and Rome, soon after in Italy, and thence to the *western* provinces of Europe. Chaldea and Egypt had their Magi, their law-givers and heroes, when Greece and Rome swarmed with petty feudatories and barbarians; Greece and Rome flourished in literature, when Gaul, Germany, and Britain were uncivilized, rude and ignorant.[20] Wise and sagacious politicians have not been able to stay the rotation of this revolving *scientific* circle, any more than mighty potentates to repel the velocity of the flying ball of empire:—*superior to human powers,* like blazing stars, they hold their destined course, and play their corruscations as they run their race.

The expectations of those who were the fautors[21] of the present measures, must have been to bring down superlative distress, discord, confusion, despair, and perdition upon a multitude. How then [15] will our amazement increase, when we shall hear that the hard fate of this multitude *cannot be avoided?* Let the inhabitants comply with the requisitions of the statute, let them be implicitly obedient to it's injunctions:—what is the evil they will escape? what is the boon they may hope to attain? hope and fear are said to be the hinges of government. Legislators have therefore considered it as sound policy, never to drive the subject into acts of despair, by causing punishments to appear as *inevitable,* on the *first promulgation* of a law. When a legislative body ordaineth *penalties to take* place in cases of performance or non-performance of particular matters, they surely will take due care, that *sufficient notice* is given of *their public will* and *sufficient time to comply* with their mandates; so that obedience may not only proceed from principles of regard to the law-makers, but motives of personal safety to the subject himself. This seems not more consonant to political wisdom, than to nature and equity.—But let us now suppose, that upon the first intimations of the present law, Boston had been as prone to obey the edict of a British Court, as the Turk to comply with the mandate of the Divan;[22] let us imagine them as servile, as fawning as a court dependant to a minister of state;—nay, if there be any thing in nature, yet more humble and more base, let Boston (in idea for a short moment) be that humble, servile base and fawning something: What doth it all avail? The first time the inhabitants of this town had any intimation, of the will of the British Parliament, was on the tenth of may, and the act is to take place on the first of June; and thence to continue in *full force*, "until it shall sufficiently *appear to his Majesty that* [16] *full satisfaction* hath been made *by* or on behalf of *the inhabitants of the said town of Boston to the united company of merchants of England trading to the East-Indies, for the damage sustained by the said company* by the destruction of their goods sent to the said town of Boston, on board certain ships or vessels as aforesaid; AND UNTIL IT SHALL BE CERTIFIED TO HIS MAJESTY *in council* BY THE GOVERNOR, or LIEUTENANT GOVERNOR, *of the said province, that reasonable satisfaction hath been made to the officers of his Majesty's revenue and* OTHERS, WHO SUFFERED BY THE RIOTS AND INSURRECTIONS ABOVE MENTIONED, in the months of November and December in the year 1773, and in the month of January in the year 1774."[23]

Satisfaction could not be made to the East-India company, *if all Boston had the* WILL and POWER[24] to do it, till the town had time and opportunity to call a meeting, assemble, consult and determine upon the measure: great bodies are not calculated for speedy decision, any more than velocity of motion. The resolution formed; time must be given for dispatches to England, application to the East-India company, an adjustment with them upon the nice point of "*full satisfaction*":—that accomplished; time must be given for making the matter "*sufficiently* appear to his Majesty."—Let any one consider but for a moment, what a length of time must inevitably elapse before all this can be accomplished: nay, may it not well be questioned, considering the parties and all persons concern'd and the circumstances of this affair, whether such accomplishment be *practicable?* But is this all that is to be done and effected *before relief can be given to* [17] *this distressed land?* Far otherwise. "The *Governor* or *Lieutenant Governor,* must also first certify to his Majesty, in Council, that *reasonable* satisfaction hath been made to the *officers of his Majesty's revenue,* and OTHERS, *who* SUFFERED *by the riots and insurrections above mentioned*". No person is particularly designated to be the judge between the subject, and the officers of his Majesty's revenue: No provision being expressly made, touching this point, how probable that litigation might arise concerning it? If we say that the Governor, or Lieutenant Governor, is the *implied* judge of this matter: How is the question to be brought before him, how tried, and how adjusted? These also are points not settled in a moment: Long indeed would be the period before the subject in Boston will be capable to ascertain and make such satisfaction, as that *the person here pointed out,* would make his certificate, that it was plenary and *reasonable.* Governor Bernard lately filled the chair of government, while Mr. Hutchinson was second in command: Governor Hutchinson now fills the chair, and the office of Lieutenant Governor is vacant. How long would it be before the inhabitants of Boston would acquiesce in the decision of either of these gentlemen? How little probability is there, considering the sentiments, the past and present conduct of these gentlemen, that they would speedily give the required certificate?—If it hath been found difficult to touch the tender feelings of the *American* and *Native, how long* would it take to excite generous sentiments in the *Briton* and *Stranger?* [18]

But these are *all preparatories* to the obtaining any ease or relief from the pressure of this penal law. The prerequisites to the restoration of public felicity are here not only improbable, but when considered altogether and in the present crisis of public affairs are they not impracticable? But yet worse, being accomplished, it could in no way prevent the misery and calamities of this British edict. The space given for the subject to stay this torrent of evils is so *short,* that it is *impossible* for him, exerting *his* utmost energies, to prevent being overwhelmed. (But what mortals are unable to prevent—HEAVEN may stay or divert.)[25]

An avenue *seems* to be opened by the benignity of our British fathers; but when attempted, affords no way of escape. My veneration for Britain is so great, that I will not suppose the great council of the nation intended to flatter with a false hope, that cruel disappointment might heighten the poignancy of suffering—the anguish of despair. But sure the fathers of a people will consider, what are like to be the sentiments and conduct of *men* driven to distraction by a multitude of *inevitable* evils, and consigned to despair from the terms of their deliverance?

Wonder was excited on the first view of the present law; our astonishment hath been increasing in the progress of our survey.[26] A period is not *yet* put to our admiration. The faculties of sensation are yet to be further stretched.

The civilian and statesman, the moralist and sage had heretofore delivered those maxims of truth and [19] those rules of government, which wise legislators have ever observed, and the bulk of mankind yet honour and revere.—To know the laws of the land *already in force,* previous to the publication of a new code, or in the technical phraseology of a common lawyer "to know how the law stood before we make a new statute", hath been considered as an indispensable accomplishment of a good legislator. But that illustrious Parliament, whose power is distinguished, with the appellation of "omnipotent", seem not to have exercised this important knowledge—tho' we do not hence rashly infer, that they are destitute of information, because all who are vested with *omnipotence of power* are ever inspired with *proportionate* wisdom.

It must again be noticed, that no relief is to be had, "untill full satisfaction hath been made BY or ON *behalf* of the inhabitants of said town of Boston". Now to suppose that any in England or Europe would make satisfaction "*on behalf*" of said Inhabitants was unnatural, if not absurd ; but what is more to the point, it was certainly *unparliamentary.* The remaining alternative is that satisfaction must be made *by Boston.*

Every person knows, that towns in this Province cannot raise or appropriate any monies, but by the express provisions and direct authority of law: it is a matter of equal notoriety that all town assessments of money are expresly confined, by the 4 Wm. & Mar. c. 13. to the "maintenance and support of the ministry, schools, the poor, and defraying of other *necessary* TOWN CHARGES". A law which received the royal approbation, almost a century agone.[27] [20]

Will any now say, that the monies appointed to be paid to the East-India house come within the words of "*necessary town charges*"? When did the town contract the debt, or how are they subject to the payment of it? Had the Parliament seen fit to enact, that monies requisite to satisfy the India merchants, should be so *considered;* two questions (not of quick decision) might then have arisen; the one touching the validity and obligatory force of the statute; the other, whether it would then come within the intent and design of the Province law. For past doubt, our Provincial legislators had no such charge (as the one here supposed) in view, when they made the law of Wm. & Mary; and in this way therefore the matter could not be brought within it's provision. Parliament must then make a *new* act *to enable and impower Boston* to pay the India company, *before the town can comply* with the terms of relief of their trade. In the mean while, what is to be the situation of Boston and the inhabitants of the globe with whom they have such extensive connections?—But, it is very apparent, that the Parliament have not as yet enacted the payment of this satisfaction as a *town charge.* They have only placed it in the option of the town to make that payment, or submit to the consequences. That payment, we affirm, *they cannot pay, without breach of the law of the land.*—New and unheard of therefore is the state of this people. They must sustain the severest afflictions, they must stand the issue of distracting remedies—or—violate one of the most known and practiced laws of the land!—Let us search the history of the world;—let us inspect the records of a Spanish inquisition; [21] let us enter the recesses of an Ottoman court ;—nay, let us traverse the regions of romance and fable—where shall we find a parallel?

"When the Hungarians were *called* REBELS first, they were called so for *no other reason* than this, (says the elegant Ld. Bolingbroke) that they *would not* be SLAVES".[28] But for BRITONS, when they would not venture to *call* their CHILDREN, *rebels,* that they should treat them as worse than REBELS, was reserved to distinguish an age of vaunted light, humanity and knowledge—the Era of a King, who prides[29] himself as *born and bred a Briton!*

To complain of the enormities of power, to expostulate with over-grown oppressors, hath in all ages been denominated sedition and faction; and to turn upon tyrants, treason and rebellion. But tyrants are rebels against the first laws of Heaven and Society:—to oppose their ravages is an instinct of nature—the inspiration of GOD in the heart of man. In the noble resistance which mankind make to exorbitant ambition and power, they always feel that divine *afflatus,* which, paramount every thing human, causes them to consider the LORD OF HOSTS as their leader, and his angels as fellow-soldiers: —trumpets are to them joyful sounds, and the ensigns of war, the banners of GOD; —their wounds are bound up in the oil of a good cause, and their blood flows into the veins of a Saviour; sudden death is to them present martyrdom, and funeral obsequies resurrections to eternal honour and glory:—their widows and babes, being received into the arms of a compassionate GOD, and their names enrolled among [22] DAVID'S WORTHIESS—greatest losses are to them greatest gains; for they leave the troubles of their warfare to lie down on beds of eternal rest and felicity.[30]

There are other parts of the act now before us, which merit notice: particularly that, relative to the prosecution of suits in the ordinary courts of law, "for any thing done in pursuance of the act"; by which the defendant is enabled "to plead the general issue, and give the act, and the general matter, in evidence": whereupon it follows, that if it *shall appear* so to have been done, the jury SHALL find for the defendant"; who, by an after clause, is to "recover *treble* costs". From this passage some have been lead to conclude, that *the appearance* of this matter was to be *to the Judge;* and that if it had *that appearance to him,* and he should direct the jury accordingly; *however it might appear to the jury,* they *must* follow *the directions of the Judge*, and acquit the defendant. But this is a construction, which as the words do not *necessarily* carry that meaning, I will not permit myself to suppose the design of the law. However the late donations of large salaries by the crown, to the justices of our superior Courts, who are nominated by the Governor, and hold their commission, *durante bene placito,*[31] have not a little contributed to the preceeding apprehension.

Another passage makes provision for "assigning and appointing such and so many open places, quays and wharfs, within the said harbour, creeks, havens and islands, for the landing, discharging, lading and shipping of goods, as his Majesty, his heirs or successors, shall judge necessary and ex- [23] pedient" ; and also for "appointing such and so many officers of the customs therein, as his Majesty shall think fit; after which it shall be lawful for any person or persons to lade or put off from, or to discharge and land upon, such wharfs, quays, and places, so appointed within the said harbour, AND NONE OTHER, any goods, wares and mechandize whatsoever".[32] By which the property of many *private* individuals is to be rendered useless, and worse than useless; as the *possession* of a thing, aggravates the misfortune of those who are deprived of a capacity to enjoy. But if the property of *some few* is to be rendered nothing worth, so that of *many others* is to be openly invaded:—But why should we dwell upon *private* wrongs, while those of *the multitude* call for all our attention?

If any should now say—we are a commercial people—commercial plans can *only* save us. If any think that ideas of the merchant are at this day to give spring to our nerves and vigour to our actions; if any say, that *empire* in this age of the world, is only *founded* in commerce:—let him show me the people emancipated from oppression by commercial principles and measures: let him point me, that unexplored land, where *trade* and *slavery* flourish together. Till then, I must hold a different creed; and believe—that tho' commercial views may not be altogether unprofitable; that tho' commercial plans *may* do *much, they never can do* ALL. With regard then, to how much the merchant, the artificer, the citizen and the husbandsman may do, let us no longer differ. But let every one apply his strength and abilities to that [24] mighty burden, which unless removed, must crush US ALL. AMERICANS have one COMMON INTEREST to *unite* them; that interest must cement them. Natural allies, they have published to the world professions of reciprocal esteem and confidence, aid and assistance; they have pledged their faith of mutual friendship and alliance. Not only common danger, bondage, and disgrace; but national truth and honour conspire to make THE COLONISTS resolve—TO STAND OR FALL TOGETHER.[33]

Americans never were destitute of discernment; they have never been grossly deficient in virtue; a small share of sagacity is now needful to discover, the insidious art of our enemies; the smallest spark of virtue will on this occasion kindle into flame.

Will the little temporary advantage held forth for delusion, seduce them from their duty? Will they not evidence at this time, how much they despise the *commercial bribe* of a British ministry; and testify to the world that they do not vail to the most glorious of the antients, in love of freedom and sterness of virtue? But as to THE INHABITANTS OF THIS PROVINCE, how great are the number, how weighty the considerations to actuate their conduct? Not a town in this colony, but have breathed the warmest declarations of attachment to their rights, union in their defence, and perseverance to the end. Should any ONE *maritime* town (for more than ONE I will not believe there can be) allured by the expectations of gain, refuse to lend their aid;—entertaining the base idea of build- [25] ing themselves upon the ruins of this metropolis—and in the chain of future events, on the destruction of ALL AMERICA,—what shall we say?—hours of bitter reflection will come, when their own *feelings* shall excite consideration; when remembrance of *the past,* and expectation of *the future* shall fill up the measure of their sorrow and anguish.—But I turn from the idea, which blasts my country with infamy—my species with disgrace.

The intelligent reader must have noticed, that through the whole of the act of Parliament, there is no suggestion that the East-India company had made any demand for damage done to their property:—if the company supposed they had received injury, it doth not appear whom they considered guilty, and much less, that they had alledged any charge against *the town of Boston.*[34] But I presume that if the company[35] were intitled to receive a recompense from the town until they prosecuted their demand they are supposed to wave it. And we cannot but imagine, that this is the first instance, where Parliament hath ordered one subject to pay a satisfaction to another, when the party aggrieved did not appear to make his regular claim; and much more uncommon is it, for such recompence to be ordered without ascertaining the amount to which the satisfaction shall extend.[36]

But if the East-India company were now made easy, and Boston reduced to perfect silence and humiliation:—how *many* "OTHERS" are they, who would suggest, that they "SUFFERED by *the riots and insurrections abovementioned*" and demand "*reasonable satisfaction*" therefor.—The *singular texture,* uncer- [26] tainty, looseness and ambiguity of this phrase in the statute seems so calculated for dispute, such an eternal bar to a full compliance with the requisitions of the act, and of course to render permanent it's evils, that I cannot speak upon the subject without trespassing upon those bounds of respect and decency, within the circle of which I have endeavoured to move.

Here waiving further particular consideration of that subject which gave origin to this performance; I shall proceed to an equally interesting subject—that of STANDING ARMIES and CIVIL SOCIETY.[37]

The faculty of intelligence may be considered as the first gift of GOD: it's due exercise is the happiness and honour of man; it's abuse his calamity and disgrace. The most trifling duty is not properly discharged without the exertion of this noble faculty; yet how often does it lie dormant, while the highest concernments are in issue? Believe me (my countrymen) the labor of examining for ourselves, or great imposition, must be submitted to; there is no other alternative: and unless we weigh and consider what we examine, little benefit will result from research. We are at this extraordinary crisis called to view the most melancholy events of our day: the scene is unpleasant to the eye, but it's contemplation will be useful; if our thoughts terminate with judgment, resolution and spirit.[38]

If at this period of public affairs, we do not think, deliberate, and determine *like men*—men of [27] minds to conceive, hearts to feel, and virtue to *act*—what are we to do?—to gaze upon our bondage? while our enemies throw about firebrands, arrows and death, and play their tricks of desperation with the gambols of sport and wantonness.

The proper object of society and civil institutions is the advancement of "*the greatest happiness of the greatest number*".[39] The people (as a body, being never *interested* to injure themselves and uniformly desirous of the general wellfare) have ever made this *collective felicity* the object of their wishes and pursuit. But strange, as it may seem, what *the many* through successive ages have desired and sought, *the few* have found means to baffle and defeat. The necessity of the acquisition hath been conspicuous to the rudest mind; but man, inconsiderate, that "in every *society,* there is an *effort constantly* tending to confer on one part *the height of power*, and to reduce the other to *the extreme of weakness and misery*",[40] hath abandoned the most important concerns of civil society to the caprice and controul of those, whose elevation caused them to forget their pristine equality, and whose interest urged them to degrade *the best* and *most useful* below *the worst and most unprofitable* of the species.[41] Against *this exertion,* and the principle which originates it, no vigilance can be too sharp, no determination too severe. [28]

But alas—as if born to delude and be deluded—to believe whatever is taught, and bear all that is imposed—successive impositions, wrongs and insults awaken neither the sense of injury or spirit of revenge. Fascinations and enchantments, chains and fetters bind in adamant the understanding and passions of the human race. Ages follow ages, pointing the way to study wisdom—but the charm continues.[42]

Sanctified by authority and armed with power, error and usurpation bid defiance to truth and right, while the bulk of mankind sit gazing at the monster of their own creation:—a monster,[43] to which their follies and vices gave origin, and their depravity and cowardice continue in existence.

"*The greatest happiness of the greatest number*" being the object and bond of society, the establishment of truth and justice, ought to be the basis of civil policy and jurisprudence. But this capital establishment can never be attained in a state where there exists *a power superior to the civil magistrate* and *sufficient to controul the authority of the laws.* Whenever, therefore, *the profession of arms* becomes *a distinct order* in the state, and *a standing army part of the constitution,* we are not scrupulous to affirm, that *the end of the social compact is defeated,* and *the nation called to act upon the grand question consequent upon such an event.*

The people who compose the society (for whose security the labour of it's institution was perform- [29] ed, and of the toils it's preservation daily sustained) THE PEOPLE, I say, are the only *competent* judges of *their own welfare,* and, therefore, are the only suitable authority to determine touching the great end of their subjection and their sacrifices. This position leads us to two others, not impertinent on this occasion, because of much importance to Americans:—

That the legislative body of the common-wealth ought to deliberate, determine and make their decrees *in places* where the legislators may *easily know from their own observation* the wants and exigencies, the sentiments and will, the good and happiness of the people; and the people as easily know the deliberations, motives, designs and conduct of their legislators, before their statutes and ordinances actually go forth and take effect:—

That every member of the legislature ought himself to be so far subject in his person and property to the laws of the state, as to immediately and effectually feel every mischief and inconvenience resulting from all and every act of legislation.

The science of man and society, being the most extended in it's nature, and the most important in it's consequences of any in the circle of erudition, ought to be an object of universal attention and study. Was it made so, the rights of mankind would not remain buried for ages, under systems of civil and priestly hierarchy, nor social felicity overwhelmed by lawless domination.

Under appearances the most venerable and institutions the most revered; under the sanctity of religion; the dignity of government, and the smiles of [30] beneficence, do the subtle and ambitious make their first incroachments upon their species. *Watch* and *oppose* ought therefore to be the motto of mankind.[44] A nation in it's best estate—guarded by good laws, fraught with public virtue, and steeled with martial courage—may resemble Achilles: but Achilles was wounded in the heel. The least point left unguarded, the foe enters:—latent evils are the most dangerous—for we often receive the mortal wound, while we are flattered with security.

The experience of all ages shews that mankind are inattentive to the calamities of others,[45] careless of admonition, and with difficulty roused to repel the most injurious invasions. "I perceive (said the great patriot Cicero to his countrymen) an inclination for tyranny in all Caesar projects and executes." Notwithstanding this friendly caution, not "till it was *too late* did the people find out, that *no beginnings, however small, are to be neglected.*" For that Caesar, who at first attacked the common-wealth *with mines* very soon *opened his batteries.*[46] —Encroachments upon the rights and property of the citizen are like the rollings of mighty waters over the breach of antient mounds: slow and unalarming at the beginning; rapid and terrible in the current; a deluge and devastation at the end.—Behold the oak, which stretcheth itself to the mountains, and overshadows the vallies, was once an acorn in the bowels of the earth:—Slavery (my friends) which was[47] yesterday engraf- [31] ted among you, already overspreads the land, extending its arms to the ocean, and it's limbs to the rivers:—Unclean and voracious animals under it's covert, find protection and food,—but the shade blasteth the green herb, and the root thereof poisoneth the dry ground, while the winds which wave its branches[48] scatter pestilence and death.

Regular government is necessary to the preservation of private property and personal security. Without these, men will descend into barbarism, or at best become adepts in humiliation and servility: but they will never make a progress in literature or the useful arts. Surely a proficiency in arts and sciences is of some value to mankind, and deserves some consideration.—What regular government can America enjoy with a legislative a thousand leagues distant, unacquainted with her exigencies, militant in interest, and unfeeling of her calamities? What protection of property—when ministers under this authority shall overrun the land with mercenary legions? What personal safety when a British administration—(such as it now is, and corrupt as it may be)—pour armies into the capital and senate-house—point their artillery against the tribunal of justice, and plant weapons of death at the posts of our doors?[49]

Thus exposed to the power, and insulted by the arms of Britain—STANDING ARMIES become an object of serious attention. And as the history of mankind affords no instance of successful and confirmed tyranny, without the aid of military forces, we shall not wonder to find them the *desiderata* of princes, and the grand object of modern poli- [32] cy.—What, tho' they subdue every generous passion and extinguish every spark of virtue—all this must be done, before empires will submit to be exhausted by tribute and plundered with impunity.

Amidst all the devices of man to the prejudice of his species, the institution of which we treat hath proved the most extensively fatal to religion, morals and social happiness. Founded in the most malevolent dispositions of the human breast, disguised by the policy of state, supported by the lusts of ambition, THE SWORD hath spread havock and misery throughout the world. By the aid of mercenary troops, the sinews of war, the property of the subject, the life of the common-wealth have been committed to the hands of hirelings, whose interest and very existence, depend on an abuse of their power. In the *lower* class of life, STANDING ARMIES have introduced brutal debauchery and *real* cowardice; in the higher orders of state, venal haughtiness and extravagant dissipation. In short whatever are the concommitants of despotism; whatever the appendages of oppression, this ARMED MONSTER hath spawned or nurtured, protected or established;—monuments and scourges of the folly and turpitude of man.

Review the armament of modern princes:—what sentiments actuate the military body? what characters compose it? Is there a private centinel of all the innumerable troops that make so brilliant a figure, who would not *for want of property* have been driven from a Roman cohort, *when soldiers were the defenders of liberty?*[50] [33]

Booty and blind submission is the science of the camp. When lust, rapacity, or resentment incite whole battallions proceed to outrage. Do their leaders command—obedience must follow. "Private soldiers (said Tiberius Gracchus from the Roman rostrum) fight and die to advance the wealth and luxury of the great."[51] "Soldiers (said an eminent Puritan in his sermon preached in this country more than 130 years ago) are commonly men who fight themselves fearlessly into the mouth of hell for revenge, a booty, or a little revenue:—a cry of battle is a day of harvest for the devil".[52] Soldiers, like men, are much the same in every age and country.

"Heroes are much the same, the point's agreed,
From Macedonia's madman to the Sweed."[53]

What will they not fight for—whom will they not fight against?—Are these men, who take up arms with a view to defend their country and its laws? Do the ideas or feelings of the citizen actuate a British private on entering the camp?[54] Excitements, generous and noble like these are far from being the *stimuli* of a modern phalanx. The general of an army, habituated to uncontrouled command, feels himself absolute: he forgets his superiors,[55] or rather despises that civil authority, which is destitute of an energy to compel his obedience. His soldiers (who look up to him as their sovereign, and to their officers as magistrates) loose the sentiments of the citizen and contemn the [34] laws. Thus *a will* and *a power* to tyranize become united; and *the effects* are as *inevitable* and *fatal* in the political, as the moral world.[56]

The soldiers of Great Britain are by the mutiny act deprived of those legal rights which belong to the meanest of their fellow-subjects, and even to the vilest malefactor.[57] Thus divested of those rights and privileges which render Britons the envy of all other nations, and liable to such hardships and punishments as the limits and mercy of our known laws utterly disallow; it may well be thought they are persons best prepared and most easily tempted to strip others of their rights, having already lost their own.[58] Excluded, therefore, from the enjoyments which others possess, like Eunuchs of an Eastern seraglio, they envy and hate the rest of the community, and indulge a malignant pleasure in destroying those privileges to which they can never be admitted.[59] How eminently does modern observation verify that sentiment of Baron Montesquieu—a slave living among free-men will soon become a beast.[60]

A very small knowledge of the human breast, and a little [61]consideration of the ends for which we form into societies and common-wealths discover the impropriety and danger of admitting such an order of men to obtain an establishment in the state: the annals and experience of every age shew; that it is not only absurdity and folly—but distraction and madness. But we in this region of the earth have not only to dread and struggle with the natural and common calamities resulting from such military bodies, but the combined dan- [35] gers arising from AN ARMY OF FOREIGNERS, stationed in the very bowels of the land. Infatuated Britons have been told—and as often deceived, that an *army of natives* would never oppress their own countrymen.

But Caesar and Cromwell, and an hundred others have enslaved their country with such kind of forces. And who does not know that subalterns are implicitly obedient to their officers;—who when *they* become obnoxious are easily changed, as armies to serve the purposes of ambition and power are soon new modelled.[62] But as to America, the armies which infest her shores, are in every view FOREIGNERS, disconnected with her in interest, kindred and other social alliances; who have nothing to lose, but every thing to gain by butchering and oppressing her inhabitants.—But yet worse:[63]—their inroads are to be paliated, their outrages are to receive a sanction and defence from *a Parliament* whose claims and decrees are as unrighteous, as *the Administration* is corrupt; as boundless as their ambition, and as terrible as their power. The usurpation and tyranny of the Decemviri of Rome are represented as singularly odious and oppressive: but even they never assumed what Britain in the face of all mankind hath avowed and[64] exercised over the Colonies:—*the power of passing laws merely on her own authority. "Nothing that we propose* (said they to the people) *can pass into a law without your consent.* Be yourselves, ye romans, the authors of those LAWS ON WHICH YOUR HAPPINESS DEPENDS".[65]

"The dominion of all great empires degrades and debases the human species".[66] The dominion of Britain is that of a mighty empire. Her [36] laws waste our substance, her placemen corrupt our morals, and her armies are to break our spirits.[67]—Yes, are they not to do more? "To spoil, to slaughter and to commit every kind of violence; and then to call the manaeuvre by a lying name—GOVERNMENT; and when they have spread a general devastation, call it PEACE."[68] In the barbarous Massacres of France, in the 16th century, *the very hangmen* refused obedience to the cruel mandates of the French monarch, saying *they were legal officers*, and *only executed those the laws condemned.* Yet history bears testimony that *the soldiers performed the office which the hangman refused.*[69] Who then can be at a loss for the views of those who were so fond of introducing and tenacious of obtaining *similar peace-officers* in this obnoxious capital?[70] But let all such—yes, let Great-Britain consider the nature of mankind: let her examine carefully the history of past events, and attend to the voice of experience.[71]

In the same age we have just mentioned, the Low-Countries, then subject to the crown of Spain, being persecuted by the court and church of that kingdom rose up to resist their oppressors. Upon which, in the year 1567, the Duke of Alva was sent, and entered the country with a well-appointed army, ten thousand strong; in order to quell and punish the insurgents. Terrified with these martial operations, the towns [37] suffered the open breach of their charters, and the people submitted to the most humiliating infraction of their liberties; while Alva, being invested with the government, erected the court of twelve, called *the council of blood,* and caused great numbers to be condemned and executed on account of the insurrections. Universal complaints insued on this disuse of the ordinary courts of law and the introduction of the army: but complaints were in vain, and all murmurs despised. The people became enraged; but without a leader, they were over-awed. "The army (says Sir William Temple) was fierce and brave, and *desirous of nothing* so *much as a rebellion of the country.*" All was seizure and process, confiscation and imprisonment, blood and horror, insolence and dejection, punishments executed and meditated revenge. But though the multitude threatened vengeance, the threats of a broken and unarmed people excited contempt and not fear. Alva redoubled his impositions and ravages, *his edicts were published for raising monies without the consent of the state,* and *his soldiers were called to levy the exactions by force.*— But the event shewed, that the timidity and tameness of mankind, like every thing human, will have a period. The patience of the miserable sufferers came to an end; and those commotions began which deluged great part of Europe with blood, and finally freed THE UNITED PROVINCES from the yoke of Spain and the inquisition.—What conflicts too sharp—what horrors too dreadful to endure for such a happy deliverance—such a glorious issue? Thus "the first period of the low-country troubles (says the same ingenious writer) proved to King Philip (of Spain) a *dear experience,* how little the boldest armies and best conduct are able to withstand the torrent of a stubborn and enraged people, *which ever bears all* [38] *down before it, till it be divided into different channels by arts,* or by chance; or till the springs, which are the humours that fed it, come to be spent, or dry up of themselves.[72]

During several centuries, history informs us, that no monarch in Europe was either so bold, or so powerful as to venture on any steps toward the introduction of regular troops. At last, Charles the 7th of France, seizing a favourable opportunity in 1445, executed that which his predecessors durst not attempt, and established the first standing army known in Europe. Lewis the 11th, son, and successor of Charles, finding himself at the head of his father's forces, was naturally excited to extend the limits of his ancestors, in the levies of money and men. Charles had not been able to raise upon his subjects two millions, but the army he left his successor enabled him to levy near five. The father established an army of about seventeen hundred, which "he kept in good order and placed for the defence of the realm"; but this army, though thus disciplined and stationed, enabled the son to maintain "in continual pay a *terrible band* of men of arms, which gave the realm (says the Historian Philip de Commines) a *cruel wound* of which it bled many years."[73] How regular, correspondent and uniform are the rise and progression of *military* calamities in all ages! How replete with instruction—how full of admonition are the memorials of distant times—especially when contracted into the view, and held up in comparison with the present. [39]

Charles and Lewis having set the example, all the neighbouring crowned heads soon followed, and mercenary troops were introduced into all the considerable kingdoms of the continent. They gradually became the only military force that was employed or trusted. It has long been (says the learned Dr. Robertson) the *chief object of policy* to encrease and support them, and *the great aim of Princes or ministers to discredit and to annihilate all other means of national activity or defence*."[74] Who will wonder at this, who reflect, that absolute monarchies are established, and can only be supported by mercenary forces? Who can be surprized, that princes and their subalterns discourage a martial spirit among the people, and endeavour to render useless and contemptible *the militia,* when this institution is the natural strength, and only stable safeguard, of a free country?[75] "Without it, 'tis folly to think any free government will ever have security and stability."[76] A standing army in quarters will grow effeminate and dissolute; while a militia, uniformly exercised with hard labor, are naturally firm and robust. Thus an army in peace is worse than a militia; and in war, a militia will soon become disciplin'd and martial. But[77] "when the sword is in the hands of a single person—as in our constitution—*he will always* (says the ingenious Hume) neglect to discipline the [40] militia[78] in order to have a pretext for keeping up a standing army. 'TIS EVIDENT, (says the same great character) that this is a *mortal distemper* in the BRITISH government; of which it must at last *inevitably perish*."[79] What a deformed monster is a standing army in a free nation? *Free,* did I say? what people are truly free, whose monarch has a numerous body of armed mercenaries at his heels? who is already absolute in his power—or by the breath of his nostrils may in an instant make himself so?

No free government was ever founded or ever preserved it's liberty without uniting the characters of citizen and soldier in those destined for defence of the state. The sword should never be in the hands of any, but those who have an interest in the safety of the community, who fight for their religion and their offspring[80];—and repell invaders that they may return to their private affairs and the enjoyment of freedom and good order. Such are a well regulated militia composed of the freeholders, citizen and husbandman, who take up arms to preserve their property as individuals, and their rights as freemen. Such is the policy of a truly wise nation, and such was the wisdom of the antient Britons.[81] The primitive constitution of a state in a few centuries falls to decay:—errors and corruptions creep gradually into the admini- [41] stration of government—'till posterity forget or disregard the institutions of their remote ancestors. In antient time, THE MILITIA of England was raised *officered* and *conducted* by *common consent.* It's *militia* was the ornament of the realm in peace and for ages continued the only and sure defence in war. Was the King himself general of an army—it was by the *consent of his people.* Thus when the Romans visited the island of Britain, Cassibelan was the Prince and chief commander in war; but it was by *the election of the great Common Council, Summa belli* (says Caesar) COMMUNI CONCILIO, *Cassibelano traditur.* Nor will this seem strange, when we consider that it was the first state maxim of the Druids *ne loqui de republica, nisi per concilium*—not even to speak upon a matter of state but in council.[82] Nor is it to be wondered that such politicians informed Caesar, that they had been so long accustomed to liberty, that they knew not the meaning of *tribute* and *slavery;* and sent him word, that *they had as good blood as he, and from the same fountain.* Surely a message that was received by a *Roman,* may be sent to a British Caesar. There were those *venerable Druids,* who had inspired the Gauls, of whom Caesar reports this memorable boast; *We can call* or appeal to such a *Great Common Council,* as all the world cannot resist. Tacitus, speaking of our Saxon ancestors, relates, *Reges ex nobilitate, Duces ex virtute in iisdem conciliis eliguntur.* The great council, or the parliament of the state, had, not only the appointment of the *principes militia,* but the conduct of all military forces, from the first erection of the standard to it's lodgment in the

Citidel; for as the same noble writer informs, it was their general custom—*not to intrust any man with the bearing of arms, antequam* [42] CIVITAS *suffecturum probaverit.*[83] Such was the security of the people from the calamities of a standing army:—happy indeed if their successors could boast a similar provision—Britain would not now be groaning under oppression—nor her distant children struggling for their freedom.

A spirited nation thus embodied in a well disciplined militia will soon become warlike, and such a people more fitted for action than debate, always hasten to a conclusion on the subject of grievances and public wrongs, and bring their deliberations to the shortest issue. With them "it is the work of but *one day,* to examine and resolve the nice question, concerning the behaviour of subjects towards a ruler who abuses his power".[84]

Artful dissemblings and plausible pretences are always adopted in order to introduce regular troops. Dyonysius became the tyrant of Syracuse, the most opulent of all the Grecian cities, by feigning a solicitude for the people and a fear of his own person. He humbly prayed only *a guard* for his protection: they easily granted, what he readily took—the power of plundering by military force and entailing his sovereignty by a devise of his sword. Agathocles, a successor to the Dyonysian family and to the command of the army, continued the military tyranny, and butchered the enslaved people by centuries.

Cardinal Ximenes, who made the first innovation of this kind in Spain, disguised the measure under the pious and popular appearance of resisting the progress of the Infidels. The Nobles saw his views and excited opposition in the chief towns of the [43] kingdom. But by dexterously using terror and intreaty, force and forbearance, the refractory cities were brought to compliance. The nobles thus, driven to desperate resolutions by the Cardinal's military movements, at a personal interview were warm and intemperate. When the Arch-prelate insensibly led them towards a balcony from which they had a view of a large body of troops under arms, and a formidable train of artillery, "Behold, says he, pointing to these and raising his voice, the powers which I have received from his Catholick majesty." *"With these I govern Castile and with these I will govern it".* Nobles and people discovered it was now *too late* for resistance:—to regret past folly and dread future calamities was the remaining fate of the wretched Castilians. After the Romans quitted the island of Britain, the first appearance of a standing army was under Richard the second. The suppression of his enemies in Ireland calling him out of England, his subjects, seized the opportunity and dethroned him.

Henry the 7th, a character odious for rapacity and fraud, was the first King of England who obtained a permanent military band in that kingdom. It was only a band of fifty archers:—with the harmless appellation of *Yeomen of the guards*. This apparently trivial institution was a *precedent* for the greatest political evil that ever infested the inhabitants of Britain. The ostensible pretext was *the dignity of government*—"the grandeur of majesty":—[85] the alteration of the constitution and an increase of power was the aim of the prince. An early *"oppugnation of the King's authority"*, tho' no doubt his favorite subalterns would have stiled it "ILL TIMED", had easily effected that disbanding [44][86] of the new-raised forces, which being a little while delayed, no subsequent struggles have accomplished. The wisdom of *resistance at the beginning* has been repeatedly inculcated by the wise and liberal-minded of all nations, and the experience of every age hath confirmed their instruction. But no Precept or example can make the bulk of mankind *wise for themselves*. Tho' cautioned (as we have seen)[87] against the projects of Caesar, *the smiles of his benignity deceived* the Roman Common-wealth, till the increase of his power bid defiance to opposition. Celebrated for his generosity and magnificence, his complacency and compassion,[88] the complaisant courtier made his way into the hearts of his countrymen. They would not believe, tho' admonished by the best of men and first of patriots,[89] that the *smiling Caesar* would filch away their liberties, that *a native—born and bred a Roman*—would enslave his country—the land of his fathers—the land of his birth—the land of his posterity.[90] But the ambitious Caesar aiming at authority, and [45] Caesar armed and intoxicated with power, appear in very different characters. He who appeared with the mildness of a fine gentleman, in his primaeval state, in an advanced station conducted with the sterness of a tyrant. Opposed by a tribune of the people *in taking money out of the public treasury against the laws,* Caesar WITH AN ARMY AT HIS HEELS, proclaimed "arms and laws *do not flourish together.*" "If you are not pleased, (added the usurper) with what I am about, you have nothing to do but to withdraw. Indeed war will not bear much liberty of speech. When I say this I am departing from my own right. For you and all I have found exciting *a spirit of faction*[91] *against me* are ay my disposal." Saying this, he approached the doors of *the treasury,* as the keys were not produced, he sent *his work-men to break them open.*[92] This is the complaisant Caesar—renowned for his amiable qualities: by his early address he deceived and by his arts inslaved his countrymen—and prepared the way for a succeeding Nero to spoil and slaughter them.—Singular and very remarkable have been the interpositions of Providence in fa- [46] vour of New-England:—the permission of an early carnage in our streets, peradventure, was to awaken us from the danger;—of being *politely* beguiled into security and *fraudfully* drawn into bondage:—a state that sooner or later ends in rapine and blood.—Shall we be too enthusiastick,[93] if we attribute to the Divine influence, that unexpected good which hath so often in our day been brought out of premeditated evil? Few, comparatively, of the many mischiefs aimed against us, but what have terminated in some advantage, or are now verging to some happy issue.—If the dexterity of veteran troops have not excited envy, if their outrage hath not provoked revenge, their military discipline hath set a well-timed example, and their savage fury been a well-improved incentive. The lusts of an enemy may touch a sensibility of mind and his very pride pique the virtue of the heart.

Fleets which appeared formidable, and armies which threatened destruction have either vapoured away with empty parade, or executed their mischievous designs with rashness and folly. To compensate the insult and repair the injury, Providence hath caused these armaments to scatter much wealth and diffuse abroad a martial passion:—a passion, which hath proved so contagious, that our MILITIA are advanced a century, at least, in discipline and improvements. Where are the people who can compose a militia of better men, more expert in the use of arms, and the conduct of the field, than we can now call forth into action? A militia who a few years ago, knew near as much of the science of Algebra, as of the art military. [47] Thus hostile invasions have roused among us the GENIUS of *War.*—that Genius, which under GOD, will conduct us with safety and honour—with triumph and glory.

Surely we may say of our adversaries;—in the net, which they hid, is *their own foot taken,* and they are snared in the wickedness of *their own hands.*—Our enemies the last ten years, have been employed to *weave a spiders web* and *hatch the eggs of a Cocatrice:—consuming their own bowels by what they have weaved;* and *destroyed* by what they have *brought forth.*—Thus Goliath is killed with *his own sword,* Haman hanged upon *his own gallows.*[94] Marvellous were the doings of GOD in the eyes of our fathers;—nor less astonishing are his works in the days of their progeny.[95]

Charles the 2d. told his Parliament, their "*jealousy,* that the forces he had rais'd were designed to *controul law and property,* was *weak* and *frivolous.*"[96] The cajolement took for a season, [48] but his subjects having been abused by repeated violations of his most solemn vows, at last rouzed from their lethargy; and the King began to dread the severity of their vengeance. He therefore kept up a *standing army,* not only against law, but the repeated resolutions of every Parliament of his reign. He found that corruption without force could not confirm him a tyrant, and therefore cherished and augmented his troops to the destruction of his people and the terror of his senators. "*There go our masters*"[97] was a common saying among the members of Parliament. "No law can restrain these people; houses are taken from us, our lives are in danger" (said one member of Parliament.)[98] "Without betraying our trust, (said Russel) we must vote these standing forces a grievance. There are designs, about the King, to ruin religion and property. Public business is the least of their concern. A few upstart people, making hay while the sun shines, set up an army to establish their interest: I would have care taken for the future, that no army be raised for a cabal-interest. A Gentleman said the last session, that this war was made rather for the army, than the army for the war. *This government, with a standing army, can* NEVER BE SAFE: *We cannot be secure in this house; and some of us may have our heads taken off.*"[99]

Patriots harrangued in vain—the Commons voted the Keeping up the army illegal and a grievance—but while they thus did, they openly betrayed a dread of *that army.* "I would not give an [49] alarm to those *who have arms* in their hands" said one member; "I cannot but observe that the House of Commons is now in fear of the army", said another.[100] Plain as it was for what end the army was kept up, the people slumbered.

The exigencies of the times called for something more than votes and *paper-resolutions.* What was the consequence of this national cowardice and inactivity? "England saw herself engaged in the expence *of* 600,000 Pounds sterling, to pay an army and fleet, which *certainly* (says Rapin) had not been prepared TO *make war with France* OR FOR THE SECURITY OF ENGLAND"[101] —Spirited resolves may please the ear; senatorial eloquence may charm the eye, but these are not the weapons with which to combat standing armies: (these was not those,) which freed this Capital from stationed regiments;—they are not those, which will ultimately—But I forbear: time will unfold, what I may not foretell.

The British Court, never destitute of plausibilities to deceive, or inventions to enthrall the nation, appropriated monies, raised by Parliament for the purpose of disbanding the army, to their countenance,[102] and uniformly pursued similar measures, till in the year 1684, "the King in order to make his people sensible of their *new slavery,* affected to muster his troops, which amounted to 4000 well-armed and disciplined."[103] If Rapin denominated so small an armament, *the slavery of the subject* under Charles the 2d:—what would he call the state of Britons under George the third? With 4000 troops the kingdom it seems was reduced to servitude: but the spirit of the nation soon after [50] rose. In 1685 complaint was made in Parliament, "that the country was weary of the oppression, and plunder of the soldiers"; "the army (it was said) debauched the manners of *all the people,* their wives, daughters and servants."[104] The grievance became intolerable—and what was happy, it was not too mighty for opposition. James the second, had only 14, or 15,000 troops,—and no riot act. The barbarities of a Kirk, and the campaign of a Jefferies, could not pass with impunity. THE REVOLUTION succeeded and James abdicated his throne.—Such was the fate of one, who vainly affected to play the despot with about fifteen regiments: had he been encircled with an hundred, no doubt, he had reigned an applauded tyrant—flattered *in his day,* with that lying appellation—"*the wisest and the best of Kings.*"[105]

The army of the present king of great Britain is larger than that with which Alexander sub- [51] dued the East, or Caesar conquered Gaul. "If the army, we now keep up (said Sr. John Phillips 30 Years ago, in the House of Commons) should once be as much attached to the Crown as Julius Caesar's army was to him, I should be glad to know where we could find a force superior to that army."[106] Is there no such attachment now existing?[107] Surely the liberties of England, if not held at will, are holden by a very precarious tenure.

The supreme power is ever possessed by those who have arms in their hands and are disciplined to the use of them. When the Archives conscious of a good title disputed with Lysander about boundaries, the Lacedemonian shewed *his sword,* and vauntingly cried out, "he that is *master of this* can best plead about boundaries."[108] The Marmotines of Messina declined appearance at the tribunal of Pompey, to acknowledge his jurisdiction, alledging in excuse, *ancient priviledges, granted them by the Romans*—"Will you never have done (exclaimed Pompey) with *citing laws and priviledges to men who wear swords.*"[109] What boundaries will they set to their passions, who have no limits to their power? Unlimited oppression and wantoness are the never-failing attendants of un-[52] bounded authority. Such power a veteran army always acquire, and being able to riot in mischief with impunity, they always do it with licentiousness.

Regular soldiers, embodied for the purpose of originating oppression or extending dominion, ever compass the controul of the Magistrate. The same force which preserves a despotism immutable, may change the despot every day. Power is soon felt by those who possess it, and they who can command will never servilely obey. The leaders of the army, having become masters of the person of their Sovereign, degrade or exalt him at will.[110] Obvious as these truths may seem, and confirmed as they are by all history,[111] yet a weak or wicked Prince is easily perswaded, by the creatures who surround him to act the tyrant. A character so odious to subjects, must necessarily be timid and jealous. Afraid of the wise and good, he must support his dignity by the assistance of the worthless and wicked. Standing armies are therefore raised by the infatuated Prince. No sooner established, than the defenceless multitude are their first prey. Mere power is wanton and cruel: the army grow licentious and the people grow desperate. Dreadful alternative to the infatuated monarch! In constant jeopardy of losing the *regalia* of empire, till the caprice of an armed Banditti degrade him[53] from sovereignty,[112] or the enraged people wreak an indiscriminate and righteous vengeance. Alas! when will Kings learn wisdom, and mighty men have understanding?

A further review of the progress of armies in our parent-state will be a usefull, tho' not a pleasant employ. No particular reason or occasion was so much as suggested in the bill which passed the Parliament in 1717, for keeping on foot a standing army of 30,000 men *in time of peace:* (a number since amazingly encreased.) An act justly recorded in the Lord's Journal to be *a precedent* for keeping the same army *at all times,* and which the protest of that day foretold "MUST INEVITABLY *subvert the antient constitution of the realm, and* subject the *subjects to arbitrary power.*"[113] To borrow the pointed turn of a modern orator—what was once *prophecy,* is now *history.*[114]

The powers given by the mutiny act which is now constantly passed every year was repeatedly in former times "opposed and condemned by Parliament as repugnant to MAGNA-CHARTA, and inconsistent with the fundamental rights and liberties of the people."[115] In this statute no provision is made for securing the obedience of the military to the civil power, on which the preservation of our constitution depends. A great number of armed men gover- [54] ned by martial law,[116] having it in their power, are naturally inclined not only to disobey, but to insult the civil Magistrate:[117] The experience of what hath happened in England, as well as the memorials of all ages and nations have made it sufficiently apparent, that wherever an *effectual provision* is not made to secure the obedience of soldiers to the laws of their country, the military hath constantly subverted and swallowed up the civil power.—What provision of this mind can the several Continental legislatures make against British troops stationed in the Colonies? Nay, if the virtue of one branch of government attempted the salutary measure, would the first branch ever give it's consent? A Governor must—he will obey his master: the alternative is obvious. The armies quartered among us *must be removed,* or they will in the end overturn and trample on all that we ought to hold valuable and sacred.

We have[118] authority, to affirm, that the regular forces of Great Britain consist of a greater number than are necessary for the guard of the King's person and the defence of government, and therefore dangerous to the constitution of the kingdom.[119] What then do these armaments, when established *here,* threaten to our laws and liberties? Well might the illustrious members of the house of Peers, in 1722, hold forth the danger of "*a total* alteration of the frame of our constitution from a legal and limited monarchy to a despotick" [55] and declare, they were "induced to be of this judgment, as well from the nature of armies, and the inconsistency of great military power and martial law with civil authority, as from the known and *universal* experience of other countries in Europe, which, *by the influence and power of standing armies, in time of peace, have from limited monarchies, like ours, been changed into absolute.*"[120] The taxes necessary to maintain a standing army, drain and impoverish the land. Thus exhausted by tribute, the people gradually become spiritless, and fall an early sacrifice to the reigning power.

Spirits, like Britons, naturally fierce and independent are not easily awed or suddenly vanquished by the sword. Hence *an augmentation* of forces hath been pushed, when there was no design of bringing them into action against

Englishmen in an *open field.* New forces have oftener than once been raised in England more for *civil* than *military* service; and as elections for a new parliament have approached, this door has been opened to introduce a large body of *commissioned Pensioners.*[121] What hath been the consequence? A constant majority of placemen meeting under the name of a Parliament, to *establish* grievances instead of *redressing* them—to approve implicitly the measures of a court without information—to support and screen ministers they ought to controul or punish—to grant money without right and expend it without discretion? Have these been the baneful consequences? Are these solemn truths? Alas! we tremble to think:—but we may venture to say, that when this is true of that legislative autho [56] rity, which not only claims, (but *exercises)* "full power and authority to make laws and statutes to bind the colonies and people of America IN ALL CASES whatsoever";[122]—the FORMS of our constitution, creating *a fatal delusion,* will become our greatest grievance.

The FORMALITIES of a free and the ends of a despotic state have often subsisted together. Thus deceived was the Republick of Rome:—Officers and Magistrates retained their old names:—the FORMS of the antient government being kept up, the fundamental laws of the Common-wealth were violated with impunity, and it's once free constitution utterly annihilated.[123] He who gave Augustus Caesar the advice "that to the officers of state the same names, pomp and ornaments, should be continued, *with all the appearances of authority, without the power,*[124] discovered an intimate acquaintance with mankind. The advice was followed, and Caesar soon became Senate, magistracy and laws. Is not Britain to America, what Caesar was to Rome?

It is curious to observe the various acts of imposition, which are alternately practiced by the [57] great and subtle of this world on their subordinate and simple-minded brethren. Are a people *free, new* oppressions are introduced or shrouded under *old names;*—are they in *present bondage,* and begin to grow turbulent; *new* appellations must be adopted to disguise *old burthens.* A notable instance of this latter kind we find in the Parliament of Great Britain, (in 36 Edw: 3.ch:2) upwards of four hundred years ago. The royal prerogative, called *purveyance,* having been in vain regulated by many preceeding statutes, still continued so intolerably greivous, that fresh murmurs and complaints called for a more adequate or better adapted provision. The British legislature, for this valuable purpose, therefore passed this very remarkable law; which by way of remedy, enacted as follows, viz.—"That the *hateful* NAME of *purveyor*, shall be changed into that of *Acator*." Thus the nation were to be made to believe, that the oppression ceased, because, *the name was altered*.—For the honour of government, as well as mankind, it is devoutly to be wished,[125] that our laws and history contained no other record of such disgracefull practices.—If any late acts of the British parliament carry strong marks of a similar policy, it is surely, not altogether unworthy the consideration of the members of that august body;—how far, such disingenuous practices are consistant with the honour of their private characters, or the dignity of their public station.[126]

The magic of sounds and appellations hath not ceased, and they work as much deception and abuse as ever. What valuable purpose does a *wholly subordinate* legislative serve, (except to amuse with the *shadow*, while the *substance* is departed) if [58] a remote state may legislate for and bind us "*in all cases*"? To what end doth an American house of Representatives go through *the forms* of granting away monies, if another power, full as familiar with our pockets, may annihilate all they do; and afterwards, with a modern dexterity, take possession of our purses without ceremony, and dispose of the contents with modesty;—without controul, and without account?[127]

It is curious and instructive to attend the course of debate in the British Commons for keeping up the army. At first even the highest courtiers would argue—that a standing army, *in time of peace*, was never attempted;[128] Soon after the Court-speakers urged for continuance of a numerous army for *one year* longer. At the end of several years after, the Gentlemen throw aside the mask, and boldly declare such a number of troops *must always be kept up*. In short, the army must be continued till it be- [59] comes part of the constitution, and in later times members of the house have ventured to harangue for measures, none would have dared to lisp a few years before. The wise foresaw this, and the honest foretold it. "If we continue the army but a little while longer (said a celebrated member upwards of forty years ago,) it may be in the power of some Gentlemen to talk in this house[129] in terms that will be no way agreable to the constitution or liberties of our country. To tell us, that the same number of forces must be always kept up, is a proposition full-fraught with innumerable evils, and more particularly with this, *that it may make wicked ministers more audacious than otherwise they would be in projecting and propagating schemes which may be inconsistent with the liberties, destructive of the trade, and burthen-*

some on the people of this nation. In countries governed by standing armies, the inclinations of the people are but little minded, the ministers place their security in the army, the humours of the army they only consult, with them they divide the spoils, and *the wretched people are plundered by both.*"—Who that now reconsiders this prophetic language, in conjunction with the events of his own time, but will cry out—the speaker felt the impulse of inspiration!"

"Whoever (says the justly celebrated Dr. Blackstone) will attentively consider the English history may observe, that the stagnant abuse of *any power,* by the crown or it's ministers, has always been productive of a struggle, which either dis- [60] covers the exercise of that power to be contrary to law, or (if legal) restrains it for the future."[130]

The ingenious commentator seems here to have particular reference to periods prior to the revolution. But will the learned judge say, that, since that era there have been *no flagrant abuses of power by the crown or its ministers?* Have not repeated struggles arose in consequence of such abuses, which did not terminate in the happy issue so characteristic of Englishmen? Let any one peruse the journals of parliament, especially those of the house of peers: let him carefully review the British and American annals, of the present century, and answer truly to those questions.—The natural enquiry will be—whence then is it—that such abuses have become so numerous and flagrant, and the struggles of Britons so unsuccessful? Will not the question receive an ample solution in the words of the same great lawyer?—"There is a newly acquired branch of (royal) power; and that not *the influence only,* but THE FORCE OF A DISCIPLINED ARMY, paid indeed ultimately by the people, but *immediately by the crown; raised by the crown, officered by the crown, commanded by the crown.*"[131]

We are told, by the same learned author, that "whenever the unconstitutional oppresssions, even of the SOVEREIGN POWER, advance with gigantic strides and threaten desolation to a state, mankind will not be *reasoned* out of the *feelings* of humanity, nor will sacrifice their liberty by a scrupulous adherence to those political maxims, [61] which were established to preserve it."[132]—But those who *cannot be reasoned* out of their *feelings,* are easily repressed by *the terror of arms* from giving tokens of their sensibility; and states antient and modern—(yes Britain will bear me witness!)—who would disdain to *sacrifice* their freedom to *political institutions* have tremblingly stood alooff, while it was dragged to the altar under the banners of a royal army.

The policy and refinements of men cloathed with authority often deceive those who are subject to it's controul; and thus a people are often induced to waive their rights, and relinquish the barriers of their safety. The fraud, however, must at last be discovered, and the nation will resume their antient liberties, if there be no force sufficient to screen the usurper and defend his domination. *The sword* alone is sufficient to subdue that spirit which compells rulers to their duty, and tyrants to their senses. Hence, then, though a numerous standing army may not be absolutely requisite to depress a kingdom into servitude, they are indispensably necessary to confirm an usurpation.

A large army and revenue are not easily and at once forced upon a free people. By slow degrees and plausible pretences, as we have seen in England, the end is accomplished. But when once a numerous body of revenue and military men, entirely dependant on the crown,[133] are incorporated, they are regardless of any thing, but it's will: and where *that will* centers and what such power can effect is a matter of no doubtfull disputation. [62]

The *present army* of a prince is always composed of men of honour, and integrity, as the *reigning monarch* is ever *the best of kings.* In such an army, it is said, you may trust your liberties with safety: in such a king you may put your confidence without reserve:—the good man has not a wish beyond the happiness of his subjects! Yet let it be remembered, that under *the best of kings,* we ought to seize the fleeting opportunity, and provide against *the worst.* But admitting that from this rare character—a wise and good monarch—a nation have nothing to fear;—yet they have every thing to dread from those who would cloath him with authority, and invest him with powers incompatible with all political freedom and social security.[134] France, Spain, Denmark, and Sweden, in modern times, have felt the baneful effects of this fatal policy. Tho' the latter state are said to have this excellent institution; that the commissions to their military officers all run *quamdiu se bene gesserit:*[135] a regulation which ought to be the tenure of all offices of publick trust and may be of singular utility in states which have incorporated[136] a standing army as part of the constitution of government.

An invasion and conquest by mere strangers and foreigners are neither so formidable or disgraceful as the establishment of a standing army under co-[63] lour of the municipal law of the land. Thus *Roman armies* were more terrible to the *Roman colonies,* than an "enemy's army."[137] Valor has scope for action against an open enemy, but the most precious liberties of a kingdom are massacred in cold blood by the disciplined Janizaries of the state, and there is little hope of a general resistance. The natural inherent right of the conquered is to throw off the yoke, as soon as they are able; but subjects enslaved by the military forces of their own sovereign, become spiritless and despondent; and scaffolds and axes, the gibbet and the halter, too often terrify them from those noble exertions which would end in their deliverance by a glorious victory or an illustrious death.

Yet *in full peace* without any just apprehensions of insurrections at home or invasions from abroad, it was the mischievous policy of the English ministry, in 1717, to procure an allowance of near double the forces to what had ever before been established by the sanction of parliament in times of public tranquillity. Well might many of the nobility of Britain[138] conceive, that as so many forces were no ways necessary to support, they had reason to fear danger to the constitution, which way never entirely subverted but by a standing army.[139] The English military bands have since been much augmented;—and whether this disgraceful subversion has already taken place, or is still verging to it's accomplishment, may be resolved, after a further inspection into memorials of the present age. [64]

More than half a century since, the discerning members of the house of Lords discovered the tendency of these extraordinary armaments to be no other, than *to overthrow the civil power of the kingdom, and to turn it into a military government.*[140] A very short period after this, many of the same noble house, bore open testimony, that they were "justly jealous from the experience of former times, that *the crown itself,* as well as *the liberties of the people* might be found *at the disposal of a standing army at home.*"[141]

But as if one standing army was not enough to ruin a nation of *Englishmen,* a new kind of forces was raised against the Common-wealth. The officers employed in the customs, excise, in other branches of the revenue, and other parts of the public service compose in effect A SECOND STANDING ARMY *in England,* and in some respects are more dangerous, than that body of men properly so called. The influence which this order have in the elections of members to serve in parliament, hath been too often felt in Great Britain to be denied. And we have good authority to say, "that examples are not hard to find, where the military forces have withdrawn to create an appearance of a free election, and the *standing* CIVIL *forces of this kind have been sent to take that freedom away.*"[142]—Is a house of commons thus chosen the representative of the people,—or of the administration,—or of a single minister?[143] [65]

As Lewis, the 11th of France, was the first monarch in Europe, who reduced corruption to a system, so the era of it's establishment in England may be fixed at the reign of Charles the second. Britain, then for the first time, saw CORRUPTION, like a destroying angel, walking at noonday.—Charles pensioned his Parliament, and by it extinguished not only the spirit of freedom, but the sentiments of honour and the feelings of shame. Since the age of Charles, the science of bribery and corruption hath made amazing progress. Patriots of the last century told their countrymen what it threatned—the Worthies of this day ought rather to tell what hath been effected.[144]

Nearly fifty years ago, there were more than two hundred persons holding offices or employments under the crown in the house of commons.[145] Since that time this body like the military (and for the same purposes) have received very notable additions.—Is it to be wondered, then, as we verge nearer to our own times, we should hear the most august assembly in the kingdom declaring to the whole world that "the influence of the crown is *almost irresistable,* being already overgrown and *yet increasing.*"[146]—that "the *most valuable rights* of the nation are *subverted by arbitrary and illegal proceedings:*—"[147] that "*a flagrant usurpation*" (is made upon the subject) *as highly repugnant to every principle of the constitution,* AS THE CLAIM OF SHIP-MONEY BY KING CHARLES THE FIRST, *or that of the dispensing power* [66] *by king James the second*"?[148] Finally, considering all that we have seen in the course of our review, could any thing else be expected, than what forty of the house of Lords openly protest they "have seen with great uneasiness,—*a plan* for a *long time* SYSTEMATICALLY *carried on,* FOR LOWERING ALL THE CONSTITUTIONAL POWERS OF THE KINGDOM, rendering the house of Commons "odious and the house of Peers contemptible"?[149]

Here let us pause (my fellow citizens) and consider:—hath the execrable plan thus *systematically and for a long time* pursued, at last, *taken effect?* Are *all the constitutional powers* of Great Britain *so lowered* in the estimation of the people, that *their representatives are detested, and their nobility despised?* Is their King possessed of power sufficient to make fear, a substitute for love? Has he *an army at his absolute command,* with which no force in his empire is able to cope?—judge ye, my countrymen, of these questions, upon which I may not decide:[150]—judge, for yourselves, of the political state of that kingdom, which claims a right of disposing of OUR ALL;—a right of laying every burden that power can impose;[151]—a right of over-running our soil and freeholds with mercenary legions, and still more mercenary placemen and dependants. Thus luxury and riot, debauchery and havock are [67] to become the order and peace of our cities, and the stability and honour of our times. To this and like hopeful purposes—we find "the fullest directions sent to the several officers of the revenue, that all the produce of the American duties, arising or to arise, by virtue of any *British* act of Parliament, should from time to time, be paid to the deputy pay-master in America to defrey the subsistence of the troops, and *any military* expences incurred in the Colonies."[152] Highly favoured Americans! You are to be wasted with taxes and impositions in order to satisfy the charges of those armaments which are to blast your country with the most terrible of all evils—*universal corruption, and a military government.*[153]

The reigns of past and present great monarchs when compared, often present a striking similitude. The Emperor Charles the fifth, having exalted the royal prerogative (or *the influence of the crown)* on the ruins of the privileges of the Castilians, allowed the name of the Cortes (or the Par- [68] liament to remain; and the *formality*[154] of holding it thus continued, he reduced it's authority and jurisdiction to nothing, and modelled it in such a manner, that *it became* (says Dr. Robertson) *rather a junto of the servants of the crown, than an assembly of the representatives of the people.*[155] The success of Charles in abolishing the privileges of the commons, and in breaking the power of the nobles of Castile, encouraged an invasion of the liberties of Aragon, which were yet more extensive.

Attend *Americans!* Reflect on the situation of your mother country, and consider the late Conduct of your Brethren in Britain towards this Continent. "The Castilians (once high spirited and brave in the cause of freedom) *accustomed to subjection themselves,* ASSISTED (says the same illustrious historian) IN IMPOSING THE YOKE *on their more happy and independent neighbours.*"[156]—Hath not Britain (*fallen from her pristine freedom and glory)* treated America, as Castile did Aragon? Have not Britons imposed on our necks the same yoke which the Castilians imposed on the happy Aragonese? Yes!—I speak it with grief—I speak it with anguish—Britons are our oppressors:—I speak it with shame—"I speak it with indignation—WE ARE SLAVES."

As force fixes the chains of vassalage, so cowardice restrains an inslaved people from bursting in sunder their bands. But the case perhaps is not desperate till the yoke has been so [69] long borne, that the understanding and the spirits of the people are sunk into ignorance and barbarism, supineness and perfect inactivity. Such, I yet trust, is not the deplorable state of the land of my nativity.[157] How soon it may be—we shall tremble, when we reflect[158] that the progress of thraldom is secret and its effect incredibly rapid, and dreadful.[159] Hence we see nations once the freest and most high-spirited in Europe, abject in the most humiliating condition. The oath of allegiance to their king, exhibits the true standard of all just subjection, to government, and testifies a genuine sense and spirit. "We, who are each of us as good, and *who are altogether more powerful than you, promise obedience to your government,* IF YOU MAINTAIN OUR RIGHTS AND LIBERTIES; IF NOT, NOT."[160] When a people, endowed with such understanding, sentiments and virtue have fallen into a disgraceful vassalage—what have WE in this land, *at this time,* reason to fear?—The same *Athenians* who insulted and bid defiance to a Phillip of Macedon crouched and cowled at the feet of an Alexander. ROMANS who with righteous indignation expelled royalty and the Tarquins bore with infamy and shame the ravages of succeeding kings and emperors. ENGLISHMEN who rose with a divine enthusiasm against *the first* Charles, disgracefully submitted to the usurpation of a Cromwell, and then with unexampled folly and madness restored that odious and execrable race of tyrants, the house of Stewart.[161] Examples, like these, ought to excite [70] the deepest concern;—*at this day;*[162] they ought to do more—to inspire fortitude and action.

Providence from the beginning hath exercised this country with singular trials. In the earliest periods of our history, New-England is seen surrounded with adversaries, and alternately vexed with foes foreign and domestick. Fierce as her enemies were from abroad and savage as the Natives of America were within,—her worst enemies will be found those of her own household.—

Our fathers "left their native country with *the strongest assurance* that they and *their posterity* should enjoy the priviledges of *free* natural born *English subjects.*"[163] Depending upon these assurances, they sustained hard-ships scarcely parralled in the annals of the world.[164] Yet compassion natural to the human breast did not restrain *internal* foes from involving them in new calamities, nor did that disgrace and contempt which suddenly fell upon the conspirators damp the ardour of their malignity.[165]

So early as 1633, (not fourteen years after the first arrival at Plymouth) "the new settlers were in perils *from their own countrymen.*"[166] In this, the infant state of the country, while exposed to innumerable hardships, vexed with hostilities from Europe and the depredations of savages, there existed men, who "beheld the Massachusetts with an *envious eye:*"[167] The characteristicks of the first conspirators against this province were *secrecy and industry:* they had [71] effected the mischief before *the people* knew of their danger. Morton in his letter to Jefferies of the first of may 1634, writes, that "the Massachusetts patent by an order of Council was brought in view and the privileges well scanned."[168] But by whom? Very like some of more modern fame:[169] An archbishop, and the privy council of Charles the first! Excellent essay-masters, for New-England priviledges,—most renowned judges of the rights and liberties of mankind!—They first discover the Charter ("to be void,")[170] and then no doubt advise to the issuing of the commission found by my lord Barrington in the 31st volume of Mr. Petyt's Manuscript, "a commission directed to the archbishop of Canterbury, the Lord chancellor, and other Lords of the privy council, by which they are impowered to prepare laws, for *the better government of the Colonies*", "which were afterwards to be *enforced by* THE KING'S PROCLAMATION."[171]

This was considered as a master-stroke of policy, and the public conspirators of the day display'd the plumage of triumph with that spirit and ostentation[172] which have descended to their successors. But how easy is it, with Providence, to disappoint the projects and humble the pride of man! Laud and his master in the subsequent periods of history are found too busied with their own concerns, to attend much to those of others. Hence this extraordinary Commission was never executed and the plan set on foot within three years after, "for revoking the patent of the Massachusetts,"[173] [72] proved abortive. Literary correspondencies inimical to the Province, commenced with Archbishop Laud,[174] in 1638.[175] But in the pious language of our fathers, "the LORD delivered them from the oppressor,"[176] "against all men's expectations they were encouraged, and much blame and disgrace fell upon their adversaries."[177] Yet notwithstanding, "a spirit full of malignity against the country (not very long after, much endangered both it's civil and religious liberties."[178]

More than a century agone[179], "the great priviledges of New-England were matter of envy,"[180] and accordingly complaints multiplied to Cromwell,[181] no doubt for the benevolent purpose of *abridging* (what were called)[182] *English Liberties.* "All attempts to the prejudice of the colony being to no purpose"[183] with the Protector, the adversaries of the province were despondent, untill the restoration of Charles the 2d. gave new hopes; when "petitions and complaints were prefered against the Colony to the king in council, and to the Parliament."[184] [73]

"False friends and open enemies" now became the terror of the country,[185] while new foes brought new charges to render it obnoxious.[186] "The *great men and muses of the country,* made their complaints also to the king."[187]—The consequences were such as might be expected. "Four persons were sent over from England, *one of them the known and professed enemy of the country,* with such extraordinary powers (that our ancestors with grief complain) they were to be subjected to the *arbitrary power of strangers* proceeding not by any established law, but their own discretion."[188] How astonishingly uniform, how cruelly consistent has been the conduct of Britain from that day to the present?

Amid all these severe trials,[189] the inhabitants of New-England, conducted with a virtue and piety worthy [of] remembrance and imitation. "They appealed to GOD, they came not into this wilderness *to seek great things* for themselves, but for the sake of a poor and quiet life"—they testified to their Sovereign that "*their liberties were dearer to them than their lives.*"[190] "Evilminded men continue (however) to misrepresent them"[191] and what is a most incredible, "the difficulties of the Colony, during a war, which excited compassion in some, yet those very distresses were improved by others to render the Colony more obnoxious."[192] [74]

Although "this is certain, that as the Colony was at first settled, so it was preserved from ruin without any charge to the mother country";[193] yet "in the height of the distress of war, and whilst the authority of the Colony was contending with the natives for the possession of the soil: complaints were making in England which struck at the powers of government."[194] With what ferocity have Americans been pursued from the earliest times? That Daemon of malevolence, which went forth at the beginning, still spirits up our adversaries and persecutes the country with unabated malice.

"Randolph, who, the people of New England said, went up and down seeking to devour them,"[195] was the next active emisary against the province. "He was incessant and *open* in endeavouring the alteration of the constitution."[196] In his open enmity, he appears far less odious than those who have been equally inimical and equally indefatigable to the *same purpose,* with more cowardice, dissimulation, and [75] hypocrisy. Eight voyages were made across the Atlantic in the course of nine years by this inveterate spirit, with hostile intentions to the government.[197] Nor will it be surprising to find him thus expose his life upon the ocean, when such services acquired "new powers".[198] Have we not seen in our own day, a similar policy adopted, and the same object operating as a motive to the like execrable conduct? Such has been the strange, tho' unhappily consistent, conduct of our mother-country, that she has laid temptations and given rewards and stipends to those who have slandered and betrayed her own children. Incited probably by the same motive, Cranfield rose up in league with Randolph, and "infamously represented the colony as rogues and rebels."[199]

Libels and conspiracies of this nature called for the interposition of authority: express laws were enacted for the prevention of like treasonable practices for the future and death being deemed the proper punishment for an enemy to his country, traitors to the constitution were to suffer that penalty. Thus a "*conspiracy* to invade the commonwealth, or *any treacherous attempt to alter and subvert fundamentally the frame of polity and government was made a capital offence.*"[200] Did our laws now contain a like provision, public conspirators and elevated parricides would tremble for their heads, who do not shudder at the enormity of their crimes.[201] There are characters in society so devoid of virtue and endued with ferocity, that nothing [76] but sanguinary laws can restrain their wickedness. Even the distress and cries of their *native* country excite no compassion: reverence for fathers and affection for children cause no reluctance at measures which stain the glorious lineage of their ancestors with infamy, and blast their spreading progeny with oppression.—that emanation from the Deity which creates them intelligents, seems to cease it's operation, and the tremendous idea of a GOD and futurity, excites neither repentance or reformation.

Thus my countrymen, from the days of Gardiner and Moreton,[202] Gorges and Mason,[203] Randolph and Cranfield[204] down to the present day, the inhabitants of this Northern region have constantly been in danger and troubles from foes open and secret, abroad and in their bosom. Our freedom has been the object of envy, and *to make void the charter of our Liberties* the work and labor of an undiminished race of villains. One cabal having failed of success, new conspirators have rose, and what the first, could not make "void", the next "humbly desired to revoke."[205] To this purpose one falshood after another hath been fabricated and spread abroad with equal turpitude and equal effrontery. That minute detail which would present actors now on the stage is the province of HISTORY:—She, inexorably severe towards the eminently guilty, will delineate their characters with the point of a diamond:—and *thus blazoned in the face of day,* the abhorrence and execrations of mankind will consign them to an infamous immortality. [77]

So great has been the credulity of the British Court, from the beginning, or such hath been the activity of false brethren, that no tale inimical to the Northern Colonies, however false or absurd, but what hath found credit with administration, and operated to the prejudice of the Country. Thus it was told, and believed in England, that we were not in earnest in the expedition against Canada at the beginning of this century, and that the country did *every thing in its power to defeat the success of it, and that the misfortune of that attempt ought to be wholly attributed to the northern colonies.* While nothing could be more obvious, than that New-England had exhausted her *youngest* blood and all her treasures in the undertaking; and that every motive of self-preservation, happiness and safety must have operated to excite these provinces to the most spirited and persevering measures against Canada.[206]

The people who are attacked by bad men have a testimony of their merit, as the constitution which is invaded by powerful men, hath an evidence of it's value. The path of our duty needs no minute delineation:—it lies level to the eye. Let us apply then, like men sensible of it's importance and determined on it's fulfillment. The inroads upon our public liberty call for reparation: The wrongs we have sustained call for—justice. That reparation and that justice may yet be obtained by union, spirit and firmness. But to divide and conquer was the maxim of the Devil[207] in the garden of Eden—to disunite and inslave hath been the principle of all *his* votaries from that [78] period to the present. The crimes of the guilty are to them the cords of association, and dread of punishment, the indissoluble bond of union. The combinations, of publick robbers ought, therefore, to cement patriots and heroes: and as *the former* plot, and conspire to undermine and destroy the common-wealth, *the latter* ought to form a compact for opposition—a band of vengeance.

What insidious arts, and what detestable practices have been used to deceive, disunite and enslave the good people of this Continent? The mystical appellations of loyalty and allegiance, the venerable names of government and good order, and the sacred ones of piety and public virtue have been alternately prostituted to that abominable purpose. All the windings and guises, subterfuges and doublings, of which the human soul is susceptible, have been displayed on the occasion. But secrets which were thought impenetrable are no longer hid; characters deeply disguised are openly revealed: the discovery of gross impostors hath generally preceeded, but a short time, their utter extirpation.[208]

Be not again, my country-men, "EASILY *captivated with the appearances* ONLY *of wisdom and piety—professions* of a regard to liberty and of a strong attachment to the publick interest."[209] Your fathers have been explicitly charged with this folly by one of their posterity. Avoid this and all *similar errors.* Be cautious against the deception of appearances. *By their fruits ye shall know them,* was the saying of ONE who perfectly knew the human heart.[210] Judge of affairs which concern *social* happiness *by facts:*—Judge of man *by his deeds.* For it is very certain, that pious zeal *for days and times,* for [79] mint and cummin[211] hath, often, been pretended by those who were infidels at bottom; and it is as certain, that *attachment to the dignity of Government, and the King's service,* hath often flowed from the mouths of men who harboured the darkest machinations against *the true end of the former,* and were destitute of every right principle of loyalty *to the latter.* Hence then, care and circumspection are necessary branches of political duty. And as "it is *much easier* to restrain liberty from running into licentiousness, than power from swelling into tyranny and oppression,"[212] so much more caution and resistance are required against the over-bearing of rulers, than the extravagance of the people.

To give no more authority to any order of state and to place no greater public confidence in any man, than is necessary for the general wellfare, may be considered by the people as an important point of policy. But though craft and hypocrisy are prevalent, yet piety and virtue have a real existence: duplicity and political imposture abound, yet benevolence and public spirit are not altogether in sheep's-cloathing, so superlative knaves and parricides will assume the vesture of the man of virtue and patriotism.

These things are permitted BY PROVIDENCE, no doubt, for wise and good reasons. Man was created a rational, and was designed for an active being. His faculties of intelligence and force were given him for use. When the wolf, therefore, is found devouring the flock, no hierarchy forbids a seisure of the victim for sacrifice; so also, when [80] dignified impostors are caught destroying those, whom their arts deceived and their stations destined them to protect,—the sabre of justice flashes righteousness at the stroke of execution.

Yet be not amused, my Countrymen!—the extirpation of bondage, and the reestablishment of freedom are not of easy acquisition. The worst passions of the human heart, and the most subtle projects of the human mind are leagued against you; and principalities and power have acceded to the combination. Trials and conflicts you must, therefore, endure;—hazards and jeopardies—of life and fortune—will attend the struggle. Such is the fate of all noble exertions for public liberty and social happiness.—Enter not the lists without thought and consideration, lest you arm with timidity and combat with irresolution. Having engaged in the conflict, let nothing discourage your vigour, or repel your perseverance:—Remember, that[213] submission to the yoke of bondage is the worst that can befall a people after the most fierce and unsuccessful resistance. What can the misfortune of vanquishment take away, which despotism and rapine would spare? It had been *easy* (said the great law-giver Solon to the Athenians,)[214] to repress *the advances* of tyranny, and prevent it's establishment, *but now it is established and grown to some height* it would be MORE GLORIOUS *to demolish it.* But nothing glorious is accomplished, nothing great is attained, nothing valuable is secured without magnanimity of mind and *devotion of heart to the service.*—BRUTUS-LIKE, therefore, dedicate yourselves at this day to the service of your Country; and henceforth live A LIFE OF LIBERTY AND GLORY.—"On the [81] ides of March" (said the great and good man to his friend Cassius just before the battle of Philippi) "On the ides of march I DEVOTED MY LIFE *to my Country, and since that time, I have lived* A LIFE OF LIBERTY AND GLORY".

Inspired with public virtue, touched with the wrongs and indignant at the insults offered his Country, the high-spirited Cassius exhibits an heroic example:—"Resolved as we are", (replied the hero to his friend) "resolved as we are, let us march against the enemy, for *tho' we should not conquer, we have nothing to fear.*[215]

SPIRITS and GENII, like these, rose in Rome—and have since adorned Britain: such also will one day make glorious this more *Western world.* AMERICA hath in store her BRUTI and CASSII—her Hampdens and Sydneys—Patriots and Heroes, who will form a BAND OF BROTHERS:[216]—men who will have memories and feelings—courage and swords:—*courage,* that shall inflame their ardent bosoms, till their hands cleave to their swords—and their SWORDS to their Enemies hearts.[217]

FINIS

The Author has *felt exquisitely* while writing upon the subjects of his consideration; and the multitude and perplexity of his private business have denied him sufficient time to revise this publication. Under these circumstances, (and being also several years on this side the meridian of the age of man) there will be found, no doubt, many indiscretions and faults for those of *riper* years and cooler judgment to correct and censure.—The great Lord Chan. Bacon hath told us of *wise legislators* who have made *their law* upon *the spur of the occasion:*—a good citizen, deeply pricked by *the spur of the times,* is very apt to start with an over-hasty speed.—The only excuse of the writer is;—that as he at first assumed his pen from the impulses of his *Conscience,* so he now publishes his sentiments from a sense of duty to GOD and his Country.[218] [82]

1. Quincy's epigraphs came from a range of sources. Those from Lamentations are of course from the Old Testament. The passage from Lucan's *Pharsalia,* Book 10, lines 407–8 (on Caesar), condemns soldiers who have become mercenaries, fighting for money rather than duty or honor. Quincy could have taken those lines from any one of several Latin editions published in London in the 18th century. The Alexander Pope passage is from the prologue that Pope wrote for Joseph Addison's play *Cato.* The longer passage by John Milton is from *Paradise Lost,* Book 12, lines 493–97. Quincy owned copies of the *Works* of both Milton and Pope. See Coquillette and York, eds., *Portrait of a Patriot,* 5:892 (no. 28) and 5:901 (no. 312), resp., in the posthumous "Catalogue of Books." Of the five epigraphs on the printed page, only the passage from Lucan is in the original manuscript.

2. He changed the order of the two sentences in this paragraph, to put the freeholders first, the landed interest second.

3. He had written "the first fruits of my pen," then changed it–at the printer's?–to "this temporary work."

4. Pamphlet pages are set within brackets. Edes and Gill placed those numbers at the top of each page; here, they should be considered as at the bottom. Reprint editions were published in both Philadelphia and London, the former by John Sparhawk, the latter by Edward and Charles Dilly (which was also sold by John Almon in his Piccadilly shop). The Dillys removed the epigraphs from Lamentations on the title page and made other, smaller changes as well–not unusual when printers reset type and made editorial choices as they went. See the listings for the *Observations* in Thomas R. Adams, *American Independence: The Growth of an Idea* (Providence, R. I.: Brown University Press, 1965), pp. 101–2; and idem, *The American Controversy*, 2 vols. (Providence, R. I.: Brown University Press, 1980), 1:228–29.

5. That is to say the Boston Port Act, in Danby Pickering, ed., *The Statutes at Large,* 46 vols. (Cambridge, Eng.: Joseph Bentham, 1762–1807), 30:336–41 (24 George III c. 19). Quincy included at the bottom of this page the following "ERRATA: Page 6, line 13, for 'was' read were—page 8, line 25, for "popular" read populous—page 13, line 20, for lawers, read lawyers—page 21, line 26, for 'pay' read *make—D*ele[te] the word 'king' in the 8th Page 4th line from the bottom." I have made the changes in the text itself. There were other errors that Quincy did not note, and perhaps did not catch; these too I have corrected silently in the text.

6. Quincy altered this paragraph somewhat, noting in the original version that the Boston Port Act had been published in Draper's paper (the *Massachusetts Gazette*), which had prompted him to write the pamphlet. He also crossed out: "If the author appears warm, it is to be remembered that he is a native of Boston, and that what he delivers is the language of his heart."

7. He deleted "the destruction of power" after "animadversions."

8. Quincy deleted "as an inferior species of parliamentary extravagance" in the manuscript copy, and added this footnote to the print version: "Since this treatise was advertised in the public papers, as being in the press, the author hath received, from the British Coffee-House, an anonymous Letter, in which he is represented as being 'in eminent hazard of THE LOSS OF LIFE *and confiscation of estate:*' It is said, that 'I shall very probably get into the hands of a *power,* from which no power I can call to will be able to deliver me.'—There is (says the writer) 'but one expedient left to save me:'— 'Employ, for GOD's sake, those rare talents, with which (saith the artful flatterer) he hath blessed you, in convincing THE PEOPLE that they have *nothing to do, but to* SUBMIT, and make their peace WITH GOVERNMENT:—You may, (continues he) by this means probably make your peace, and ward off the punishment that hangs over your head. It is barely possible, THAT GOVERNMENT may still continue IT'S GREAT LENITY, and overlook your offences.'" On a separate line Quincy added: "The Reader is left to his own Reflections." See Coquillette and York, eds., *Portrait of a Patriot,* 1:33–4 for context. The source of the "threat" is not clear, though it seems likely that Quincy knew the author's identity. The letter to Quincy, and Quincy's response (which was printed in the *Massachusetts Gazette),* are reproduced at supra, pp. 180–84.

9. Quincy crossed out "exertions" on the manuscript.

10. Quincy deleted after "concerns" the passage "will lose much of" and also "find what he delivers desperately to the swift."

11. For which see the brief overview in Robert J. Allison, *The Boston Tea Party* (Beverly, Mass.: Commonwealth Editions, 2007); Benjamin L. Carp, *Defiance of the Patriots* (New Haven, Conn.: Yale University Press, 2010); Harlow Giles Unger, *American Tempest* (Cambridge, Mass.: Da Capo Press, 2011); and what remains the standard study, Benjamin Woods Labaree, *The Boston Tea Party* (New York: Oxford University Press, 1962).

12. Most likely taken by Quincy from his commonplace book, p. 177, in York and Coquil-

lette, eds., *Portrait of a Patriot,* 1:165, which Quincy had copied from Mr. [Thomas] Hutchinson, *The History of the Colony of Massachusetts-Bay,* 2 vols. (Boston: Thomas and John Fleet, 1764, 1767), 2:156, the first two of what eventually were three volumes. Hutchinson's *History* is not in Quincy's "Catalogue of Books." It is most accessible in the three-volume version published by Harvard University Press in 1936, as edited by Lawrence Shaw Mayo.

13. Also from the political commonplace book, p. 9, in ibid., 1:105, which Quincy had copied from William Robertson, *The History of Scotland,* 4th ed., 2 vols. (London: A. Millar, 1761), 1:167; listed in the "Catalogue of Books," ibid., 5:897, at no. 210.

14. He inserted this sentence in the left margin, perpendicular to the text, presumably at some later point before going to press. Quincy did not indicate his source here, perhaps because he just went to his commonplace book, p. 47, for it. See Coquillette and York, eds., *Portrait of a Patriot,* 1:121, Quincy having originally found this passage in John and William Langhorne, eds., *Plutarch's Lives,* 6 vols. (London: Edward and Charles Dilly, 1770), 5:323 (Cicero). This is almost certainly the set listed in the "Catalogue of Books" in Coquillette and York, eds., *Portrait of a Patriot,* 5:207.

15. This time Quincy did cite his source–*A Complete Collection of the Lords' Protests,* 2 vols. (London, 1767), 2:140–41, a protest made in 1735–as taken from the political commonplace book, p. 198, in ibid., 1:172. The first volume began with a protest lodged in 1242, during the reign of Henry III; the second ended with a protest against rescinding a dividend granted to the East India Company in June 1767. A *Supplement to the Last Edition of the Lords' Protests* (1770) added protests made through May 1770, and was added to volume 2 when a new printing of the *Protests* was done in 1772.

16. Quincy inserted this sentence in between lines already written.

17. Pickering, ed., *Statutes,* 30:337 (24 George III c. 19).

18. Most of this paragraph is squeezed into the left margin, again running perpendicular to the text, after beginning between lines—Quincy changing his mind about what he going to write before settling on it? He had already written the next paragraph, then came back to the one inserted here.

19. Quincy copied this passage into his political commonplace book, p. 48–see Coquillette and York, eds., *Portrait of a Patriot,* 1:121, but, once again, he did not include a footnote referring readers to where he had found it–in this instance the Langhornes' *Plutarch's Lives,* 5:329 (Demosthenes and Cicero Compared).

20. Another case of drawing from the political commonplace book, p. 212. See Coquillette and York, eds., *Portrait of a Patriot,* 1:176; from an "An Essay upon the *Ancient and Modern Learning*" found in Sir William Temple, *The Works of Sir William Temple,* 2 vols. (London: A. Churchill, et al., 1740), 1:159–60. Temple is not in the "Catalogue of Books."

21. A supporter or abettor.

22. Quincy provided no citation, but the passage is from a speech made by Sir John Phillips in the House of Commons, 29 January 1744, as copied into the political commonplace book, p. 114, in Coquillette and York, eds., *Portrait of a Patriot,* 1:144, from *The Debates and Proceedings of the British House of Commons,* 8 vols. (London: J. Almon, 1766–1772), 23:48. This is most likely the set listed in Quincy's "Catalogue of Books," at no. 268 (see Coquillette and York, eds., *Portrait of a Patriot,* 5:899).

23. Again, as quoted from the Boston Port Act, in Pickering, ed., *Statutes,* 30:340 (24 George III c. 19).

24. Quincy was going to add a line to his footnote, but then crossed it out: "This will be explained presently."

25. This sentence was inserted between the lines.

26. Quincy crossed out the next sentence, which is now barely legible. In it he continued his sarcastic tone, saying that it had been "the design of some" not to "excruciate" the "body" with "uncommon misfortunes," but to "excruciate" it nonetheless.

27. Passed by the General Court in 1692; printed in *Charters and General Laws of the Colony of Massachusetts Bay* (Boston: T. B. Wait, 1814), pp. 243–45.

28. A passage from Hector St. John , Viscount Bolingbroke, *Letters on the Study and Use of History,* 2 vols. (London: A. Millar, 1752), 1:278; copied into the political commonplace book, p. 129, in Coquillette and York, eds, *Portrait of a Patriot,* 1:149. Bolingbroke is not listed in Quincy's "Catalogue of Books."

29. Substituted for "boasts."

30. G. B. Cheever thought this paragraph moving enough to include it in his *The American Common-Place Book of Prose* (Boston: Carter and Hendee, 1832), 37–38, but he encountered it in the appendix to Quincy's *Memoir,* where it was reprinted (at pp. 386–87 in the original 1825 edition), not in the pamphlet itself.

31. Meaning, during or at pleasure (as opposed to good behavior). In the manuscript Quincy had written "quamdiu se bene gesserit," another phrase in legal Latin that said the same thing a different way, in specifying the terms of an appointment.

32. Quoting (and paraphrasing) again from the Boston Port Act, in Pickering, ed., *Statutes,* 30:340 (24 George III c. 19).

33. Quincy inserted the phrase after "disgrace," and moved "Here waiving . . . and civil society" to p. 27 in the print version, to end this first section of the essay.

34. Quincy deleted, after "Boston," the phrase "as being trespassing against them."

35. He deleted "if an individual or any body of men have a claim," after "company."

36. He changed around the wording in this sentence before settling on the final form.

37. For the English background (and a passing reference to Quincy) see Lois G. Schwoerer, *No Standing Armies* (Baltimore, Md.: The Johns Hopkins University Press, 1974). For how those issues played out in the colonies (with a fair amount on Quincy's pamphlet) see John Phillip Reid, *In Defiance of the Law* (Chapel Hill, N.C.: The University of North Carolina Press, 1981).

38. After crossing out this entire paragraph, Quincy inserted: "Set the following for the press, notwithstanding the X."

39. Quincy quoted here, repeated on the next page, from Marquis Beccaria, *An Essay on Crimes and Punishment* (London: J. Almon, 1767), published in Italian three years before, a sentiment too often thought to be original to Jeremy Bentham in his explication of "utilitarianism." Quincy quoted other passages in his political commonplace book and the title is listed in the Catalogue of Books. See Coquillette and York, eds., *Portrait of a Patriot,* 1:121–22, 127 and 5:898 (no. 232) resp.

40. Quincy went to Beccaria's *Essay* for this particular passage (from p. xi), which he had included in the political commonplace book, p. 51; see Coquillette and York, eds., *Portrait of a Patriot,* 1:122.

41. Quincy included a footnote, drawing again upon the political commonplace book, at p. 196 (in Coquillette and York, eds., *Portrait of a Patriot,* 1:171), to quote from Catharine Macaulay's *Observations on a Pamphlet Entitled, Thoughts on the Cause of the Present Discontents,* 5th ed. (London: Edward and Charles Dilly, 1770), p. 10: "The modes of government which have been imposed on credulous man, have been not only deficient in producing the just ends of government; viz, the full and impartial security of the rights of nature; but also, have been rather formidable and dangerous cabals against the peace, happiness and dignity of society." Macaulay's pamphlet is not in Quincy's "Catalogue of Books."

42. This sentence replaces another that Quincy crossed out.

43. Quincy added this footnote: "This (standing army) is a monster, that will devour all your liberties and properties—there is a time for all men to speak, and now, when our liberties are at stake, duty to GOD, our Prince and country forbid [him; left out, presumably a printer's error] to be silent." He drew this from a 1673 speech by Sir John Hotham in the House of Commons, as recorded in Anchitell Grey, *Debates of the House of Commons, From the Year 1667 to the Year 1694,* 10 vols. (London: D. Henry, R. Cave and J. Emonson, 1763), 2:391. He also tapped Grey's *Debates* for his commonplace book, though he did not include this particular passage. Grey's *Debates* are not listed in the "Catalogue of Books."

44. Quincy may have gleaned this phrase from Trenchard and Gordon's *Cato's Letters (*no. 83, 30 June 1722) or from a number of other sources. It was common enough by then that he saw no need to cite it, if indeed he was aware himself of where he first heard or read it. He did leave his set of *Cato's Letters* to his son in his February 1774 will (see supra, p. 174), although that set is not listed in the Catalogue of Books–yet another reminder of how incomplete our knowledge of Quincy's intellectual world is.

45. Quincy went back and inserted "inattentive to the calamities of others" after writing the sentence without it.

46. Quincy entered three separate footnotes for just one source in this paragraph–the essay on Caesar in Langhorne, *Plutarch's Lives,* 4:328–29, 331. Those passages are also in the political commonplace book, pp. 44–45; see Coquillette and York, eds., *Portrait of a Patriot,* 1:119–20.

47. Quincy had "but" in the manuscript, after "was."

48. Replacing "foliage."

49. Quincy included a footnote: "All this, and much more, hath Boston been witness to."

50. Quincy referred readers to Jean Jacques Rousseau, *The Social Contract,* p. 202, and turned to the 1764 London edition printed by T. Becket and P. A. De Hondt for the political commonplace book, though he did not include this passage there, and Rousseau is not listed in the "Catalogue of Books."

51. From Tiberius Gracchus in Langhorne, *Plutarch's Lives,* 5:194, presumably taken from the political commonplace book, p. 47, in Coquillette and York, eds., *Portrait of a Patriot,* 1:120–21.

52. Quincy did not tell readers his source here, which was the printed version of William Hooke's 1640 sermon, *New Englands teares, for old Englands feares* (London: T. P. For John Rothwell and Henry Overton, 1641), p. 12. It was not cited in the political commonplace book nor is it in Quincy's "Catalogue of Books."

53. Quincy offered no attribution for these lines from Alexander Pope's "An Essay on Man,"which he squeezed between lines that he had already written. Quincy did not include anything from Pope in his political commonplace book, but he did own a copy of Pope's works (which edition is unclear). See Quincy's "Catalogue of Books" in Coquillette and York, eds., *Portrait of a Patriot,* 5:901 (no. 312).

54. Quincy referred readers to William Blackstone's *Commentaries,* 1:307. Quincy did not cite the *Commentaries* in his political commonplace book, but he did own a set—presumably the second edition published in Oxford at the Clarendon Press between 1766 and 1767. See the "Catalogue of Books," Coquillette and York, eds., *Portrait of a Patriot,* 5:893 (no. 67). The four volumes of *Commentaries* went through several editions very quickly, and there were Dublin and Philadelphia printings as well. Naturally there are variations in pagination. The p. 307 in that first volume fell within Chapter VIII, "Of the King's Revenue." Since Blackstone was discussing the problematical nature of customs duties, their impact on trade, and prosecution of those who violated them on the page in question, it is not clear what the connection is, beyond Quincy's own mind, or he miscopied the page number.

55. Quincy added this footnote: "It is grown a principle among the army (an ill nursery for

young men) that Parliaments are roots of rebellion." He cited "Sir John Hotham in the house of commons 1673," once again from Grey's *Debates,* 2:203.

56. The portion of the paragraph beginning at "The general of an army" was added later, with Quincy carrying the insertion over the left margin to fit it in the text.

57. Quincy cited the *Lords' Protests,*1:280, from a February 1718 protest against excluding the provision in a mutiny bill that would have forbade court martial courts from passing a death sentence. Quincy used this source in his political commonplace book (though not this particular protest) and it is listed in his "Catalogue of Books." See Coquillette and York, eds., *Portrait of a Patriot,* 1:172 and 5:898, resp.

58. Quincy again referred readers to the source above.

59. Quincy quoted from Blackstone's *Commentaries,* 1:416 and referred readers as well to Charles de Secondat, Baron de Montesquieu, *The Spirit of the Laws,* presumably the two-volume second edition published in London by J. Nourse and P. Vaillant in 1752 that he listed in the very next note, although the two numbers that he entered here, 12 and 15, seem to connect to Book XV, Chapter 12 ("Danger from the Multitude of Slaves"), rather than page numbers in either volume. He may have used another edition for this particular allusion, though it is not likely. The 1752 printing is what he turned to for the political commonplace book; the "Catalogue of Books" does not specify. See Coquillette and York, eds., *Portrait of a Patriot,* 1:109 and 5:894 (at no. 112), resp.

60. Montesquieu, *Spirit of the Laws*, 1:348. Quincy paraphrased this passage: "Nothing more assimilates a man to a beast, than living among freemen, himself a slave."

61. In the manuscript copy Quincy crossed out "affection or" before "consideration."

62. Quincy did not inform readers that he was paraphrasing the political commonplace book, p. 79, here, copied from comments that Thomas Gordon had made in his translation of *The Works of Tacitus*, 2nd ed., 4 vols. (London: T. Woodward and J. Peele, 1737), in Coquillette and York, eds., *Portrait of a Patriot,* 1:132, and 5:898 (no. 231) for the listing in Quincy's "Catalogue of Books," which simply says "Tacitus."

63. Inserted in the margin after the passages before and after had been written.

64. Quincy added "hath avowed and" after dropping "has" before "exercised."

65. Quincy quoted from Rousseau's *Social Compact,* p, 65, but he did not cite it for his readers.

66. Quincy referred readers to William Robertson's *History of the Reign of Emperor Charles V,* 3 vols. (London: W. and W. Strahan, 1769), 1:3, which was used for the political commonplace book, p. 9, and was listed in the "Catalogue of Books," in Coquillette and York, eds., *Portrait of a Patriot,* 1:105 and 5:897 (no. 206), resp.

67. He crossed out this question: "What is there valuable among us that remains to extirpate?"

68. Quincy: "Part of a noble speech recorded by Tacitus (vita [see] Agricola) of an old Briton to his followers, exciting them to free their country, when a Province of Rome, from the yoke of bondage." The passage was taken from Thomas Gordon's *The Life of Agricola. By Tacitus* (Glasgow: Robert Urif, 1763), p. 59, or some other edition of Tacitus edited by Gordon–perhaps the 1737 four-volume *Works* (see n. 62 supra).

69. Quincy sent readers to [Sarah Scott], *The Life of Theodore Agrippa D'Aubigné* (London: Edward and Charles Dilly, 1772). It is not cited in the commonplace book or listed in the "Catalogue of Books."

70. Quincy to the reader: "Whoever wants information of the spirit, cruelty and rapine of soldiers quartered in popular cities, let them peruse the first book of the elegant and instructive history, written by the masterly hand of Tacitus."

71. This sentence and the entire next paragraph appear to have been inserted in the manuscript later, squeezed onto the bottom of one page and then carried over to the left margin of the one following.

72. Quincy wrote: "See Temple's obs[ervations] upon the united Provinces, pp. 15, 16, 17, 19." See the previous note for how this paragraph was inserted into the text; and p. 234, n. 20 for Temple.

73. Quincy cited Philip De Commines, *The History of Philip De Commines* (London: John Bell, 1614), p. 206, a passage he altered somewhat. He alluded to *The History* in the political commonplace book, p. 99 (see Coquillette and York, eds., *Portrait of a Patriot,* 1:139) but it is not listed in the "Catalogue of Books." Robertson, *Charles V,* which is in both, covered much of the same ground, with the same tone (see p. 237, n. 66 supra).

74. Quincy cited Robertson, *Charles V,* 1:95; and also included Catharine Macaulay's *The History of England From the Accession of James I to the Elevation of the House of Hanover,* 5 vols., 3rd ed. (London: Edward and Charles Dilly, 1769–1772), 2:165; and a 1744 speech by Sir John Phillips in the House of Commons, in the *Debates,* 2:61.

75. Quincy quoted John Milton's *Eikonoklastes,* as most likely taken from one of the many editions of his collected *Works* then in print.

76. Here Quincy cited David Hume, "Idea of a perfect Commonwealth" in *Essays and Treatises on Several Subjects* (London: A Millar, 1758), p. 278, the passage one of many from Hume that he included in the political commonplace book (in this case, p. 59), from a volume also listed in the "Catalogue of Books." See Coquillette and York, eds., *Portrait of a Patriot,* 1:125 and 5:898 (no. 220), resp.

77. Quincy inserted the previous two sentences, writing them in the margin, then added the "But" as well.

78. Quincy slipped "(a)" into the text, to refer readers to a footnote, which read: "Of a like opinion was Sir Thomas Lee in Charles the 2d's reign. See Grey's debates 2 vol. 391. In order to discourage the *train bands* in Charles the first's time, the court found means *to enhance the price of powder;* and it was accordinly complained of in Parliament as 'a great grievance.'" Quincy urged readers to consult Rushworth, *Historical Collections,* 1:33, and then admonished: "Let us not be surprized, if any like artifice should be practiced in our day." Quincy drew on Rushworth's *Collections* for the political commonplace book; they are also listed in the "Catalogue of Books." In Coquillette and York, eds., *Portrait of a Patriot,* 1:181–82 and 5:892 (no. 35), resp.

79. Citing again Hume's "Idea of a Perfect Commonwealth," in *Essays,* 279. Hume deleted this last sentence from subsequent editions–his own form of political correctness, the philosophical skeptic as political moderate?

80. He inserted this phrase to replace "pro aris et focis" [idiomatically, for hearth and home], a favorite Latin phrase, one that he had used as the nom de plume for his 11 September 1769 piece in the *Boston Gazette* (see pp. 32–35 supra).

81. The rest of the paragraph, beginning with this sentence, appears to have been inserted later, written as it was on two smaller sheets of paper. The sentence beginning "A spirited nation," originally part of this paragraph, was afterward set apart as the start of a new paragraph (see p. 211, supra).

82. Quincy owned a copy of Caesar's commentaries, as indicated in the "Catalogue of Books" no. 117 ("Caesar's Comment"), mislabeled as "Caesar's Government" in Coquillette and York, eds., *Portrait of a Patriot,* 5:895. He did not copy excerpts from it for the political commonplace book. He may have owned and used the version translated and edited by Johnson Towers, *C. Julii Caesari, Commentaria De Bello Gallico,* 2nd ed. (London: L. Hawke, et al., 1768); or, given his Latin proficiency, he may well have owned–and used–an untranslated copy. In Towers' edi-

tion, the comment about Cassibelan (Cassivellaunus) is at p. 248 (Book V, paragraph 11) and the Druids at p. 344 (Book VI, paragraph 20).

83. It appears that Quincy went to an edition of Tacitus in the original Latin, not Gordon's translation, to quote from "Germania," the first passage referring to kings being chosen by birth, generals for merit by a popular council; the second, finishing the thought expressed in the first part of the sentence: not being called to bear arms, unless capable of doing so.

84. Quincy referred readers to Robertson, *History of Scotland,* 1:204–5; a passage that he had copied into the political commonplace book, p. 11 (in Coquillette an York, eds., *Portrait of a Patriot,* 1:106).

85. Quincy wrote in a footnote: "See Rapin"—Paul de Rapin de Thoyras, whose history of England had circulated in various editions since its first appearance a half century before, first printed in French but long since reprinted in English.

86. Quincy added this now seemingly cryptic note, but clear to readers at the time: "See the Late Gover. Bernard's Speeches." He meant *Letters to the Ministry* (Boston: Edes & Gill, 1769), which included official reports from General Thomas Gage and Commodore Samuel Hood as well as Bernard to London. Those reports were intended to discredit administration critics in Boston; supporters of those critics published them to return the favor, with the hope that Whitehall and Westminster would reconsider the Townshend program and the stationing of troops in Boston.

87. "See before p. 31." Quincy again sent readers to the collection noted above, and a letter from Bernard dated 25 June 1768 to the Earl of Hillsborough in particular. The letter is in diary form, with entries for June 28th and July 1st as well as June 25th. It is one of many where Bernard complained of the intransigence of his political opponents, most especially in the Massachusetts House of Representatives. For dissident Bostonians, this was proof that Bernard was behind the dispatch of soldiers there. It was more complicated than that, however.

88. "See Sallust." Quincy owned Thomas Gordon's *The Works of Sallust* (London: T. Woodward and J. Peele, 1764). He cited it in the political commonplace book and it is listed in the "Catalogue of Books." See Coquillette and York, eds., *Portait of a Patriot,* 1:159–64 and 5:893 (no. 70), resp.

89. "M T Cicero. See Plu. Life of Caesar." Quincy had copied the line about "*smiles of his benignity*" from Plutarch into his political commonplace book, p. 44—see Coquillette and York, eds., *Portrait of a Patriot*, 1:119–20.

90. Quincy's note: "A similar infatuation hath, oft[e]ner than once, prevailed in this Province: an instance of which we have in the time of Governor Dudley. This Gentleman 'after he had been agent for the Country, tacked about, and joined with the instruments that overthrew the charter, and accepted an illegal and arbitrary Commission from King James, by which he held the Government, until the arrival of Sir Edmund Andross; and then was, (as *president* of the Council, and *Chief Judge* of the territory,) a *chief tool* of all the insuing, barbarous and infamous administration.' After his appointment to the Government, his conduct was of the same texture with his former life: (it was his Son Paul, who wrote to England, that this Country would never be worth living in, for lawyers and Gentlemen, till THE CHARTER IS TAKEN AWAY.")—yet such was the dulusion at that day, 'Some of the Council would *firmly believe* charitably of him because *his family* and *interest* were here, and therefore thought it unreasonable to believe he would do any thing that should hurt his Country." He added "See a Book published in London, about 1708, intitled 'The deplorable state of New-England, by reason of a *covetous* and *treacherous* Governor and *pusillanimous* Counsellors." Quincy quoted from the title page for this last sentence, and from p. 3 for the one before it. Sir Henry Ashurst, a London merchant and onetime member of the House of Commons who acted as agent for the

Massachusetts General Court, authored the piece anonymously. Quincy added a second part to this note, but then moved it to a later page–see p. 241, n. 112, infra.

91. "Justice was *faction* in antient Rome as well as modern Britain," wrote Quincy in a footnote. He referred readers to Macaulay, *History*, 405; and Montagu's *Rise and Fall of the Antient Republicks,* a source that he turned to for his political commonplace book, which is also listed in the "Catalogue of Books." See Coquillette and York, eds., *Portrait of a Patriot*, 1:101–2 and 5:898 (no. 230), resp.

92. Quincy quoted here from the Langhornes' *Plutarch's Lives*, 4:365, the essay on Caesar, which he had copied into the political commonplace book, p. 46 (in Coquillette and York, eds., *Portrait of a Patriot,* 1:120).

93. Quincy crowded much–too much–onto this page of the original manuscript, so the rest of this sentence and the larger paragraph, plus the paragraph that follows, were written on separate, smaller sheets as insertions.

94. Quincy observed in a note: "Thus also the Bishop of Verdun, who was the modern contriver of a new species of State-prison (for which, many have cursed him) was by the righteous dispensation of providence, *first* put it into himself and confined 'in the cruel prison' fourteen years." He gave as his source Commines' *History,* p. 216. The tales of Goliath and Haman came from 1 Samuel 17 and Esther 7 in the Old Testament.

95. Quincy commented: "It was an observation applied by the first settlers of New England to their great consolation, that when *wicked men are nearest their hopes, godly men are furthest from their fears,* because the *insolence* and *cowardice* of the wicked *usually* engage GOD to defeat their design." Quincy may have had in mind Proverbs 10:24, which would have been familiar to the province's Puritan fathers: "The fear of the wicked, it shall come upon him: but the desire of the righteous shall be granted."

96. He cited the King's speech to Parliament of 5 February 1673, as recorded in Grey, *Debates,* 2:1–2.

97. *The Works Of the Late Reverend Mr. Samuel Johnson* (London: John Darby, 1710), p. 312.

98. William Harbord in the House of Commons, 3 November 1673, in Grey, *Debates,* 2:219.

99. William Russell in the Houe of Commons, 7 February 1674, in ibid., 2:393.

100. Ibid., 7:72 and 73, Sir William Coventry and William Sacheverell, resp., in the Commons on 1 April 1679.

101. Quincy only referred to Rapin parenthetically in the text. The lines that began this paragraph, and to this point, were actually written in the left-hand margin of the manuscript–on the very crowded page alluded to at n. 93 supra. Most of what is written in these pages actually came as insertions–smaller sheets of paper slipped into the larger, as Quincy decided at that moment–not coming back later, it appears–to revise his text, even as he wrote it.

102. Quincy's note said simply "See King's Speech October 1678" (it is in Grey, *Debates,* 6:112–13, 21 October 1678). There, Charles II contended that the continued fighting in Flanders made it necessary to keep troops in the field, and he expected Parliament to provide funding for them.

103. "Rapin" was all he entered as his footnote.

104. Grey, *Debates,* 8:365–66, Edmund Waller and Thomas Coningsby, resp. in the Commons, 16 November 1685. Quincy squeezed this sentence and the next into the top margin, above "Such was the fate . . . ," which had started a new paragraph.

105. Quincy's long note: "Patriae Patri, *Regum optimo* [essentially father of the country, best of kings] was part of an inscription on the marble statue erected to Charles the second, as worthless and odious a Prince as any in the history of England. See Rapin 1734. Fol. Edit.—Even Richard (the third) generally represented, both as a monster in person and disposition, hath however had panegyrists who affirm, that he was remarkably genteel, and *the best of Kings*. See

Barrington's Obs. on the more antient statutes. p. 392, 3" [meaning Daines Barrington, *Observations upon the Statutes,* 2nd ed. (London: W. Bowyer and Nichols, 1766)]; cited in the political commonplace book, pp. 300–1, and listed in the "Catalogue of Books," in Coquillette and York, eds., *Portrait of a Patriot,* 1:185, 186 and 5:893 (no. 69). Quincy continued, at a new paragraph: "Thus that insolent tyrant, Hen. 8th, who disgraced his species by repeated violations of his most solemn vows and the practice of open debauchery and riot; a despot, who, lost to the common feelings of humanity made his laws more bloody than those of Draco or Dionysius, and caused a greater number of executions, than any other King of England, is characterized on the Journals of the house of Lords, as a *Prince of wonderous goodness and wisdom.* See the same Observations 461, 2 and 472. Surely He who calls the REIGNING MONARCH '*the wisest and best of Kings*' ought always to be suspected of burlesque and sarcasm, or something worse."

106. Sir John Phillips in the House of Commons, 29 January 1744, in *Debates,* 2:56–58; quoted in the political commonplace book, 119–20 (in Coquillette and York, eds., *Portrait of a Patriot,* 1:146).

107. Quincy answered his own question in a footnote that alludes to another speech made soon after that delivered by Sir John Phillips (see supra, p. 195): "By a numerous army and a severe riot act, you may indeed prevent mobs and riots among the people; but if this method be pursued for a long time, *you will make your ministers tyrants and your people slaves.*" Noting that Sir John Bernard stated this in the Commons (on 12 February 1744), in the *Debates,* 2:118, Quincy added this "Qu: [query] If this method hath not been thus pursued? and Qu. Whether the prophecy is fulfilling, or already accomplished in Great-Britain?"

108. From the Langhornes' *Plutarch's Lives,* 3:198 (Lysander), quoted in the political commonplace book, p. 40 (in Coquillette and York, eds., *Portrait of a Patriot,* 1:117–18.

109. Also from the Langhornes' *Plutarch's Lives,* 4:126 (Pompey); in the political commonplace book, p. 43 (and in Coquillette and York, eds., *Portrait of a Patriot,* 1:119).

110. Quincy's note: "Whoever uses a mercenary army (says the good Ld. Chancellor Bacon) tho' he may spread his feathers for a time, he will mew them soon after: and *raise them with what design you please,* yet, like the *West-India* dogs, in Boccaline, *in a little time they will certainly turn sheep-biters.*"

111. Quincy sent readers to Francis Stoughton Sullivan, *An Historical Treatise on the Feudal Law, and the Constitution and Laws of England* (Dublin: Thomas Ewing, 1772), 56, which he paraphrased here. Quincy quotes a different passage from Sullivan in the political commonplace book, p. 213, and a copy is listed in the "Catalogue of Books," at no. 68. See Coquillette and York, eds., *Portrait of a Patriot,* 1:149 and 5:893, resp.

112. Quincy's note: "Sir Robert Atkins (afterwards Ld. Ch. Justice of the Common Pleas in England) said in Parliament, (anno 1667)—'Six Emperors in five years had their heads tumbled down by a military government." Quincy cited Grey, *Debates,* 1:23; it was actually a statement made by Edmund Waller, entered ten pages earlier, on 29 October 1667.

113. *Lords' Protests,* 1:273, from a formal dissent signed by six peers to the passage of a mutiny act in the Lords, 32 to 9, on 25 March 1717.

114. Quincy cited no source here. It seems unlikely that he simply reworked it from a phrase that appeared in Edward, Earl of Clarendon, *A Complete Collection of Tracts* (London: C. Davis, 1747), p. 396 ("Some have undergone this Fate literally, as if it had not been a History, but Prophecy;"). He had included the same passage in the political commonplace book, p. 116 (in Coquillette and York, eds., *Portrait of a Patriot,* 1:145), and he appears to have slipped it into the *Observations* manuscript as a second thought. See too the comment he made as Marchmont Nedham on 6 July 1772 about Hutchinson's behavior boding ill for the Bay Colony: "How far this prophecy is, or will be, history others are left to consider." (At supra, p. 109.) John Adams

used a variation of this phrase when commenting as "Novanglus" for the *Boston Gazette*, 23 January 1775, on punitive British policies: "The people had been warned" but they "could never be persuaded to believe, until prophecy, became history." Did Adams do so because he had read Quincy's tract? And if so, did it simply cause him to recast sentiments he had expressed in an earlier piece for the *Boston Gazette*, 13 January 1766 ("Are we not to prophesy the future by the experience of the past?")–that he signed "Clarendon," interestingly enough?

115. *Lords' Protests*, 1:279, from a protest against a bill passed by the House of Lords on 20 February 1718 that did not prevent a military court from imposing the death sentence for desertion in time of peace. Forty-one peers signed it.

116. Quincy quoted from another protest made by peers less than a week later, against setting the peacetime army at over 16,000 men.: "A law unknown to our constitution, destructive of our liberties, *not indured by our ancestors*, and never mentioned in any of our statutes, but in order to condemn it." Ibid. 1:283.

117. "Very notable instances of this have been seen in this Province—which will be recorded to the eternal infamy of those who brooked the insult."

118. Substituted for the thicker-tongued "We are not destitute of."

119. Originally he had "dangerous to our laws and liberties."

120. From a protest of 16 February 1723 signed by twenty peers, once again against the content of a mutiny bill, in this case one that proposed to augment the size of the peacetime army. In *Lords' Protests*, 1:377.

121. See *Lords' Protests*, 2:162, a protest signed by twenty-four peers, questioning the financial and political wisdom of raising yet more troops that would ultimately result in "commissioned pensioners" in the officer corps.

122. Quincy: "See the declarative act of the British Parliament Anno 1766. From that period (Sir Robert Walpole's day) to the present time (1762) has proved a very remarkable one in the history of the British constitution:—*no one instance can be produced in which the royal business has been retarded*, through the scrupulousness of the people's representatives. From the revolution to this day (1762) the *measures of the crown have* UNIVERSALLY been *the measures of the Parliament*." The date 1762 is a misprint by Edes and Gill. Quincy quoted from [Arthur Young], *Political Essays Concerning the Present State of the British Empire* (London: W. Strahan and T. Cadell, 1772), 31, a passage that he had copied into the political commonplace book, p. 137; Young's treatise is no. 126 in the "Catalogue of Books." See Coquillette and York, eds., *Portrait of a Patriot*, 1:152 and 5:893 (but misidentified on p. 920). For Parliament's attempt at evasivenesss by leaving the word "tax" out of the Declaratory Act see Neil York, "When Words Fail: William Pitt, Benjamin Franklin and the Imperial Crisis of 1766," *Parliamentary History* 28 (2009):341–74.

123. "See hereafter," wrote Quincy in a footnote.

124. "Eadem Magistratuum vocabula, sua consulibus, sua paretoribus species," Quincy's take in the text above on the translation in Gordon's *Works of Tacitus*, 1:3 (wth Gordon actually relying on John Dryden).

125. Was Quincy consciously slipping in a bit of Shakespeare (from Hamlet's soliloquy in Act III, Scene 1 of that eponymous play)? Sadly, his Shakespeare commonplace apparently did not survive. Quincy compressed this paragraph into the left margin (perpendicularly) and then along the bottom, in the same direction.

126. In the manuscript copy, this paragraph comes before the one now preceding it. The order was switched perhaps at the printer's, as type was being set, since there is no indication on the manuscript itself that Quincy had made that decision.

127. Quincy entered this long footnote: "If the king could at pleasure levy the necessary sums of money (for the expences of government &c.) he being sole Judge of the necessity, both as

to measure and quantity, as Charles the first claimed, in the case of ship-money, the state of the subjects would be precarious, and *the king would be as absolute a monarch as the present king of France or Spain.* Dr. Sullivan's lectures on the laws of England 189. What is it to America, whether *the King* or *the Parliament* of Great-*Britain* or any other body natural or political *is absolute master over her,*—and where is the difference between French, Spanish, and English Dragooning?—In the reign of Charles the 2d. *a wooden shoe,* such as the Peasants wear, in France, was laid near the chair of the Speaker of the Commons-house:—the arms of *England* drawn at one end of it, and those of *France* at the other, with these words in the interval, *utrum horum mavis accipe.* Grey, *Debates,* 2:220 [which could be translated as "take whichever you prefer"].

128. Quincy: "See Sir Robert Carr's Harangue in Parliament." 3 November 1673. Grey, *Debates,* 2:220.

129. Quincy's footnote said simply "Commons of Great-Britain." He was quoting from a speech in the Commons on 2 February 1734 by Sir William Wyndham, and he could have gone to a number of sources for it–such as *The Bee: Or, Universal Weekly Pamphlet*, 3:157.

130. Blackstone, *Commentaries,* 3:135 (Book III, Chapter 8).

131. Ibid., 1:325 (Book I, Chapter 8).

132. Ibid., 1:238 (Book I, Chapter 7).

133. Quincy added this clause between the lines.

134. Quincy's note: "Galba had *the greatest integrity of heart:* but in the court of Galba appeared all the extortion of Nero's reign:—and as the rapacity and other excesses of his ministers were imputed to him, Galba was no less hated, than if he had committed them himself." Quincy drew this from the Langhorne's *Plutarch's Lives,* 6:198–228 (Galba). And he sent readers as well to Gordon's *Tacitus,* 3:19, 35, 38, 79. He added: "A Monarch justly dignified with the appellation—'of the wisest and best of kings'—will surely receive some advantage by attentively contemplating an instance so replete with instruction." He crossed out: "What an instructive lesson. How replete with instruction is this anecdote to a British monarch."

135. That is to say, during good behavior.

136. Replacing "made."

137. Quincy refers readers to Gordon's *Sallust,* 3, 6, 128.

138. With "of Britain" replacing "of the land."

139. *Lords' Protests,* 1:282.

140. Ibid., 1:315. From a December 1721 protest, signed by fifteen peers, against a bill funding a standing army during peacetime.

141. Ibid., 2:80. From a dissent, signed by twenty-three peers, in March 1733 over failure to pass a bill that would have limited the army to 12,000 men.

142. Ibid., 2:83, in response to a failed March 1732 bill that would have kept customs collectors from being involved in House of Commons elections. Signed by twenty-two peers.

143. Quincy referred readers to a January 1730 protest in the Lords against a treaty with Spain (at ibid., 2:56–61), signed by twenty-four peers, and a protest against the failure to pass a March 1730 bill restricting pensioners from sitting in the House of Commons (ibid., 2:63–68).

144. He inserted most of this paragraph, written on another sheet, here, then he added material from an insertion in the left margin (beginning with "Since the age . . .")

145. In reference to the "dissentient" lodged by twenty-six peers on 21 March 1729 when a bill that would have blocked placemen and pensioners from sitting in the House of Commons failed to pass in the House of Lords–overwhelmingly, 86–31. In the *Lords' Protests,* 2:63–68. Quincy took the two hundred figure from the fifth of eight particulars enumerated there (on p. 66).

146. See *Lords' Protests,* 8 February 1768. Supple. to *Lords' Protests,* p. 9. In this instance, eleven peers (the Duke of Richmond, the Marquess of Rockingham, the Earl of Dartmouth

and Earl Temple among them) protested an act where Parliament intervened in the affairs of the East India Company, bolstering dividends, "which was a pure act of power," not in the public's interest.

147. Quincy quoted here from a protest of 15 January 1770 signed by eleven peers (including Richmond, Rockingham, Temple), in ibid., pp. 11–14. It was prompted by the lingering results of the Wilkes crisis. There were peers who had protested against Wilkes being expelled and then, after an election,being denied his seat in the House of Commons. One of those was Lord Camden, then the lord chancellor, and rumors were that he was going to be removed by the king because of it. The protesting peers wanted to go on record that a member of the ministry should not be removed from office simply because he took a stand against what the king and his men preferred. Grafton's ministry, already shaky, fell soon after, and North replaced him—which did not solve the deeper-seated problems.

148. This protest of 2 February 1770, ibid., pp. 17–24, from which Quincy quoted, was signed by forty-two peers–an unusually large number (which included the three noted above, plus William Pitt, Earl of Chatham–whom Quincy admired greatly). Superficially, it dealt with a fairly narrow issue: the reasons that the House of Commons used to expel one of its members. The protesting peers did not question the Commons' authority over its own membership; they did, however, question removal that seemed to be based on personal politics rather than a matter of law, thus turning out someone chosen by the people to represent them.

149. This protest was made the same day as the one noted above and carried forty signatures (including, again, those of Richmond, Rockingham, Temple and Chatham). It was in response to a resolution that carried, declaring that the House of Lords should not insert itself into the internal affairs of the House of Commons. In ibid., pp. 24–32.

150. Quincy wrote the material following "consider" in the left margin, and inserted it here, through "decide:"

151. Quincy's footnote, quoting a printed source: "It will be *proper* to lay on the Americans EVERY BURDEN which the hand of power can impose, if they should *attempt* to become manufacturers." *The Conduct of the Administration* (London, 1767; reprinted by Edes in Gill in Boston, also 1767), p. 62. Quincy admonished: "THUS Americans are to be treated for *an attempt* only to do, what is their duty as soon as possible to effect, and what no Power on earth can restrain without violating the laws of GOD and nature."

152. *Lords' Protests,* 2:291. 17 March 1766. By the twenty-eight peers who entered their protest against repeal of the Stamp Act.

153. Quincy: "Englishmen in the reign of Henry the 4th had the virtue and courage to 'declare it in Parliament as the *undoubted right* of the Kingdom, not to be charged *with ought*, for the defence of the realm, or safeguard of the seas, *but by their own will and consent in Parliament.*' [John Sadler], *The Rights of the Kingdom* (London: J. Kigdell, 1682), p. 146. Quincy cited different pages from this tome in his commonplace book, pp. 224–25 (see Coquillette and York, eds., *Portrait of a Patriot,* 1:180–81). He added: "Had Britons in the age of Geo. 3d. been as considerate of the spirit of their laws and constitution, or attentive to that old rule—*to do as you would be done by*—they would not have charged America with a large revenue for '*the subsistence of troops and military expences*, without consulting *it's local Parliaments*, and against the will of *it's Commons;* more especially since it was the position of that able, tho' most arbitrary prince, Edward the first of England, touching martial affairs—*Quod omnes tangit, ab omnibus approbetur*" [What touches all, must be approved by all].

154. Quincy directed readers to pages 56–57, 58, 65 of his pamphlet.

155. Here he sent readers to Robertson, *Charles V,* 3:434, and to pp. 56–57 and 65 of the pamphlet.

156. Robertson, *Charles V,* 3:434.

157. Originally "my Country."
158. Replacing "consider."
159. Quincy's footnote: "The loss of liberty (says that sagacious politician Tacitus) is *ever* accompanied with the loss of spirit and magnanimity. Vita Agricola."
160. Robertson, *Charles V,* 1:153.
161. The sentence beginning "The same Athenians" and ending here was an insertion, from the lower part of the page.
162. These three words were apparently added for emphasis.
163. See Hutchinson, *History,* 1:iv; preface.
164. Ibid., 1:19, 45; Appendix, p. 558.
165. In the manuscript this paragraph, and the one before it, actually follow the next one ("So early as . . .")
166. Hutchinson, *History,* 1:31.
167. Ibid.
168. Hutchinson, *History,* 1:31n.
169. This opening portion of the sentence was inserted between the lines.
170. Hutchinson, *History,* 1:31.
171. Barrington, *Observations,* p. 146 note c. Quincy included this passage in the political commonplace book, p. 303. There he followed it with a sarcastic comment: "The Colonies must be prodigiously well governed by such legislators and with such an Administration."
172. Quincy's note stated simply "See Morton's Letter before cited" (in Hutchinson, *History,*1:31n).
173. Hutchinson, *History,* 1:51 (with Quincy paraphrasing from this page).
174. Quincy: "Laud was the favourite character selected for a correspondent by the American letter-writers of the last century; in the next age mankind will be as well acquainted with the genius and spirit of some more modern British correspondents, as they now are with the temper of that renowned prelate." This comment and eight of the preceding references were on a separate sheet of paper, with Quincy numbering them for the printer to locate.
175. Hutchinson, *History*, 1:86.
176. Nathaniel Morton, *New-England's Memorial* (Newport, R.I.: S. Southwick, 1772; orig. ed., 1669), p.15.
177. Ibid., 1:35. Quincy also referred readers to [Thomas Hutchinson], *A Collection of Original Papers Relative to the History of the Colony of Massachusets-Bay* (Boston: Thomas and John Fleet, 1769), pp. 52–53. The document he referred to was a letter from Governor John Winthrop of the Bay Colony to Governor William Bradford at Plymouth, expressing relief that their patents would not be vacated and joy that the Lord still smiled upon them. Winthrop copied for Bradford the finding of the privy council in January 1633 not to proceed against either colony, despite the request by Sir Ferdinando Gorges and others, who were rival claimants to both. Quincy drew upon this collection for his political commonplace book, pp. 5 and 203–204, though not this particular document (in Coquillette and York, eds., *Portrait of a Patriot*, 1:103 and 173–74, resp). It is not in the "Catalogue of Books."
178. Morton, *New-England,* pp. 96, 187.
179. Simply "ago" in the manuscript.
180. Hutchinson, *History,* 1:194, with Quincy altering the phraseology only slightly.
181. Ibid.
182. A parenthetical insertion, written into the margin.
183. Ibid., 1:194.
184. Ibid., 1:211.

185. Ibid., 1:220n. Hutchinson was quoting a letter from William Pynchon to John Davenport of 26 March 1662, so he was not necessarily expressing his opinion on the subject–though, ironically, even if unintentionally–Hutchinson's history reinforced the views of those who decided that the empire had failed from the beginning, that it was never a family, never a community.

186. Ibid. 1:224–25.

187. Ibid., 1:535–36 (Appendix, No. 15; the 1664 royal commission). Quincy: "Another *native of New-England* in (we have seen adopt) the year 1705, wrote to England, that "this country, would never be worth living in for Lawyers, and Gentlemen, *until the* CHARTER *was taken away.*"

188. Hutchinson, *History,* 1:232.

189. Substituted for "conflicts."

190. Hutchinson, *History,* 1:542 (Appendix, No. 16, 1664 Massachusetts General Court appeal to Charles II), Quincy mixing quotation with paraphrase; 1:537–43 for full document.

191. Ibid., 1:242–43.

192. Ibid., 1:318. Quincy noted also: "Anno 1676."

193. Ibid. 1:310. Quincy added: "See also in confirmation of the above: same history, 1: 93–114 and 2:130, 204."

194. Ibid. 1:310, 311. "The dominion of the crown over this country before the arrival of our predecessors was meerly ideal. Their removal hither realized that dominion, and has made the country valuable both to the Crown and Nation, *without any cost to either of them from that time to this.* EVEN IN THE MOST DISTRESSED STATE *of our Predecessors, when they expected to be destroyed by a general conspiracy and incursion of the Indian natives* THEY HAD NO ASSISTANCE FROM THEM. The answer of the Council of the Province to Governor Hutchinson's Speech 25th of Jan. 1773." Quincy wrote this note in two parts, at the bottom of one page (the first sentence) and on a separate slip of paper (the rest). Hutchinson's debate with the Council and House, spread over January-March 1773, was printed contemporaneously as *The Speeches of His Excellency, Governor Hutchinson to the General Assembly of the Massachusetts-Bay* (Boston: Edes and Gill, 1773), but it is most accessible in John Phillip Reid, ed., *The Briefs of the American Revolution* (New York: New York University Press, 1981), with Reid's invaluable commentary.

195. Hutchinson, *History,* 1:319.

196. Ibid., 1:335–36.

197. Hutchinson, *History,* 1:329. Randolph had become the great bogeyman of colonial Massachusetts history. See Michael Garibaldi Hall, *Edward Randolph and the American Colonies, 1676–1703* (Chapel Hill, N.C.: University of North Carolina Press, 1960); Richard R. Johnson, *Adjustment to Empire* (Leicester, Eng.: Leicester University Press, 1981) for context; and Robert M. Bliss, *Revolution and Empire* (Manchester, Eng.: Manchester University Press, 1990), for a broader context still.

198. Hutchinson, *History,* 1:329. Hutchinson actually put it "fresh orders and powers."

199. Ibid. 1:337. Edward Cranfield, who as governor of New Hampshire tried to secure the Mason family's proprietary interests there.

200. Ibid., 1:442. Quincy added: "See too pp. 295, 336."

201. The second clause (after "provision") read originally: "many would tremble for their heads, who seem to feel no remorse at their crimes."

202. Hutchinson, *History,* 1:31, 32. Anno 1632. Sir Christopher Gardiner and Thomas Morton, both of whom were troublesome for the first generation of Bay Colony leaders.

203. Ibid., 1:51. Anno 1636. Sir Ferdinando Gorges and John Mason, members of the Council for New England determined to undercut the 1629 charter rights and land patents of the Bay Colony.

204. Ibid., 1:337; "and *Collection of Original Papers*, :&c., p. 477, &c."

205. Ibid., 1:31, and 48–53 passim (in requests for the Massachusetts charter to be revoked).

206. This paragraph was added later, from two slips of paper, as was a footnote reference to Jeremiah Dummer's *A Letter to a Noble Lord, Concerning the Late Expedition to Canada* (London: A. Baldwin, 1712). Craig Yirush, *Settlers, Liberty, and Empire* (New York: Cambridge University Press, 2011), discusses Dummer in detail and calls his pamphlet "the most comprehensive case for settler rights in the empire to date." (p. 98)

207. Quincy did not include a footnote here, but he was drawing on the same source that he used in his political commonplace book–"Divide and conquer is the maxim of Satan," which is from Archbishop Robert Leighton's *Expository Works,* 2 vols. (Edinburgh: David Wilson, 1748), 1:470; in Coquillette and York, eds., *Portrait of a Patriot,* 1:117.

208. This sentence was apparently inserted later, after Quincy had moved on to the next paragraph.

209. Hutchinson, *History,* 1:53.

210. Quincy borrowing Christ's admonition from the Sermon on the Mount, as found in Matthew 7:20 (KJV).

211. "Woe unto you, scribes and Pharisees, hypocrites! for ye pay tithe of mint and cummin, and have omitted the weightier matters of the law, judgment, mercy, and faith: these ought ye to have done, and not to leave the other undone." (Matthew 23:23 (KJV)

212. *Lords' Protests*, 2:140–41 (1735), which Quincy had copied into the political commonplace book, p. 198; in Coquillette and York, eds., *Portrait of a Patriot,* 1:172.

213. Quincy inserted this now first part of the sentence later.

214. Langhorne, *Plutarch's Lives,* 1:140 (Solon). Quincy had copied this passage into his political commonplace book, p. 36 (in Coquillette and York, eds., *Portrait of a Patriot,* 1:116).

215. Ibid., 6:88 (Brutus); in the political commonplace book, p. 50 (Coquillette and York, eds., *Portrait of a Patriot*, 1:122).

216. Quincy, Shakespeare devotee, slipped in these lines from Henry V, Act IV, Scene 3, the young king, seemingly on the verge of defeat, about to lead his men ("We few, we happy few, we band of brothers") to glory at Agincourt. For Hampden and Sydney and their appeal to the Revolutionary generation see Karsten, *Patriot-Heroes in England and America.*

217. This was not Quincy's original final paragraph. That one read: "When the spirit of patriots & heroes, like these, shall arise, & form into a band of brothers; when such firmness shall compact, & such intrepidity go forth with us against our enemies, our fathers will then cry to us, as one of them did to his Countrymen, who were in arms for their Law and Liberties: 'Go on, brave Englishmen [Renowned Gentlemen, in the actual text], fall on resolvedly, till your hands cleave to your swords, your swords to your enemies hearts, your hearts to victory, your victory to triumph, your triumph to the praise of him, that giveth your spirits to offer yourselves willingly, & to jeopard your lives in high peril, for his name & service sake…Your words shall be furthered & sharpened, by HIM who made their metal;—your wounds bound up with the oil of a good cause, and sudden death shall be present martydome & life. Your greatest losses are greatest gains, where you leave the troubles of an earthly warfare, to lye downe in beds of eternal rest.'" Quincy quoted from Theodore de la Guard [Nathaniel Ward], *The Simple Cobler of Aggawam in America* (London: John Dever & Robert Ibbiton, 1647), pp. 70 and 71, resp. He had turned to the first passage, though not the second, for his political commonplace book, p. 87, in Coquillette and York, eds., *Portrait of a Patriot,* 1:135.

218. This postscript was composed on separate sheets of paper.

SAMUEL QUINCY TO JQ

1 June 1774[1]

Dear Brother Boston, June 1st 1774. Wednesday Morning

The Pamphlet you presented me yesterday was doubly acceptable, as the billet that accompanied it, assures me of your desire to live in amity with an *only* Brother. Such a testimony of your respect I cannot fail of remembering with pleasure.

The Convulsions of the times is in nothing more to be lamented, than the interruption of domestic *Harmony*. We have hitherto, I trust, happily seconded the Friendship of *Blood,* by the Friendship of the *Heart* and *Affections;* and though our Intercourse is not so free or frequent as it could be wished, yet the caution we have preserved when together, in conversing on the Subject of *Politicks,* will continue to prevent a clashing of the fiercer *Passions.*

Our natural Frame and Constitutions, though cast in the same mold, are not in all respects alike; nor is a difference in the turn of mind, among branches of the same Family an uncommon appearance. A love of Ease and Retirement (though not idle, nor unemployed in the valuable purposes of life) may be the predominant passion in One, while another, carried out by the Zeal and Fervor of Imagination, Strength of Genius, and love of Glory, shall snatch at the Wreaths of Fame through the Turmoils of *public action*. Both of these may nevertheless, be actuated by the purest principles of Virtue, and Integrity; nay more, equally *serviceable,* in that Community wherein providence has assigned them a Being.

A State of Inaction, among Philosophers the *Vis inertia*, is in some degree a State of criminality. But *Innocence* ought never to be condemned, whether the Gem lies uncultivated in a dunghill, or is found polished in the Courts of princes. *Ignominy* cannot sully *Virtue,* which is the same in all conditions, and must ever challenge *Respect.* A consciousness therefore of having done his Duty, will support every Man against the Attacks of Obliquy and Reproach, even though he should meet with the *Frowns* and *Contempt* of the World, at a time when he ought to inhabit its *Praise* and *Admiration.*

Our notions both of Government and Religion, may be *variant,* but perhaps are not altogether *discordant.* The Complexion of our external Conduct as *Men* and *Citizens,* may have it's Cast from such Variance, but I hope cannot fairly be imputed to Either of Us, as a defect of *Conscience* or *Uprightness* of *Intention.* Want of Communication often produces a contrariety of Opinion, and is sometimes a Source of *disquietude* and *division.* Should we at any time *disagree upon matters that require an Explanation,* it will be my Study to obviate the Effect of such an Infelicity.

God preserve you in health and longevity, the *Friend* and *Patron,* and at length the *Father* of your Country; and the Eclat of your own times record you with honor to the memory of the latest ages. And especially (the prayer nearest my heart) may you continue, and have reason to continue, the *Friend* and *Companion* of

Your most cordially affectionate Brother,
Saml. Quincy

1. QP 51 (reel 29) MHS; also in the "Memoir," 2:123–125, QP 46 (reel 6) MHS; and the *Memoir,* pp. 138–40.

GEORGE CLYMER TO JQ

13 June 1774[1]

Dear Sir Philadelphia June 13 1774

The Business I have been ingaged in almost ever since I had the Pleasure of seeing you has in a great Measure prevented me from improving a Friendship and Correspondence, in which I expected the greatest Satisfaction. Knowing how much you have at heart the Welfare of your Country, the Character you sustain and your circle of Connexions, any Information from you respecting the true Springs and Motives of Action in your People, on many late Occasions would have been extremely agreeable to me, finding myself much interested in every Thing that can affect them. I have ever been an Advocate for the political Conduct of the People at Boston wherever it has been made the Subject of Conversation; but Manners dissimilar to those of many of the more southern Colonies, and perhaps some other Causes, have most undoubtedly contributed to fix Prejudices which nothing but a clear Knowledge of Circumstances can possibly remove. I firmly believe that fair Representations of Things would always have freed them from any Suspicions of an Impatience of good Order, and of just Authority. Those among Us of the most enlarged Sentiments, and who have elevated Ideas of Liberty, are unwilling to censure any Irregularities or even Extravagancies which a Zeal for her Cause may have produced, but narrow Minds can scarcely, in any Case, be brought to approve, where domestick Oeconomy and good Order seem to be disturbed. I would willingly hope the Number of such short sighted Censurers is diminished, and that the Distress now so unjustly inflicted upon the Town of Boston has fixed their Attention more upon the Danger which so fatal a Precedent has made common to all the Americans. At present I believe this to be the Case, and that almost everyone amongst Us sees the Necessity of checking the Progress that arbitrary Power is making.

Would to God your Relief could be speedily effected by the Means pointed out by the Vote of your Town, but the Minds of Men, at least in two of the principal Colonies cannot yet be brought to combat with the most powerful Principles in human Nature—I mean self Interest, which must be so generally renounced during a Suspension of Trade. Many indeed who are not swayed by Selfishness are for offering the Olive Branch to the Mother Country, unaccompanied by the Threats or Menaces implied in that Measure, and professing through a general Congress such Terms of Accomodation as will leave Us the essential Rights of Englishmen, and suffering her at the same Time to reap those Advantages in Trade which some suppose she had in Contemplation in first settling the Colonies, notwithstanding the Opinion which old Charters or many early Transactions justify, that the absolute Independence of the Colonies was intended. If these two Ideas are not to be fairly reconciled in Theory, they think, perhaps a temporary Compromise, that should leave any determinate Principles out of the Question, may be effected. Our People seem bent upon first trying this Experiment—the Necessity of Harmony and perfect Unanimity, which all seem sensible of, has reconciled very different Interests among Us, and by yielding to each other the Quakers and Presbyterians and other contending Sects have met in this Point.

A Measure of this kind seems calculated rather as a general Barrier against the encroaching Power of Parliament, than to give immediate Relief to Peoples in your Situation. We all wish however that your Firmness should remain unshaken untill the Remedy to be applied shall have had its Operation, but this seems hardly possible. Patriotism assailed by Poverty and Want has seldom stood its Ground. The general Subscription to be opened here, which I hope will be followed in other Places, show that your Neighbours have not absolutely forsaken you in the Day of Distress. It will in some Measure alleviate the Wretchedness of the Poor and stifle their Clamours for Bread. Would to Heaven this proposed Charity may be in the least adequate to the Occasion, that the hard Necessity of complying with dangerous and disgraceful Terms might be utterly taken away.

It is said there is a Crisis in political, as well as natural disorders. This may be when the apprehensions of any great Evils shall have made such Progress as to incline Men to make the strongest and most decisive Efforts to avoid them. I believe we are not yet ripe for these Efforts. The two Bills before Parliament for taking away the peculiar Privileges of your Province, and making the Soldiery Masters of your Lives, will probably quicken and mature our Resentments and give Us a greater Certainty of approaching Tyranny.[2]

But I have to ask your Pardon for this tedious Letter. I expect in a few Weeks to see you at Boston with a Brother of Mr. Dickinson.[3] We take our Wives with Us, whose want of Health makes such a journey necessary.

My best Compliments to Mrs. Quincy.

I am dear Sir,
Your most obedient Servant
Geo Clymer

1. QP 51 (and reel 29) MHS; also "Memoir," 2:125–28, QP 46 (reel 6) and *Memoir*, pp. 144–47, with the usual changes in spelling, capitalization and punctuation; and also reprinted in Force, ed., *American Archives*, 4th series, 1:406–7, the first of over a dozen pieces of Quincy correspondence that would appear there. Force and Clarke, needless to say, worked from the original 1825 edition of the *Memoir* (on pp. 164–68) rather than the 1874 edition used here. In places they added their own emphasis, italicizing words that were not in the printed text.

2. He referred to two of the so-called "Coercive" or "Intolerable" acts, the Massachusetts Government Act that passed Parliament in mid-May (in Pickering, ed., *Statutes*, 30:381–90, 19 George III c. 45) and a new quartering act in early June (ibid., 30:410, 19 George III c. 54). The Government Act was an attempt to change the balance of power in the colony and restore imperial authority. It altered the selection of members of the governor's council, judges, justices of the peace, and sheriffs, and restricted the calling of and agenda for town meetings, all in an effort to check the growing oppositionism on both the local and provincial levels. The act, not surprisingly to some, had the opposite effect. The new quartering act renewed and extended what had been in place since 1765 (see ibid., 26:305–18, 5 George III c. 33), which took on new significance with the return of troops to Boston and the appointment of General Thomas Gage, who retained his position as commander of the British army in North America, to succeed Hutchinson as governor. This, again as many astute observers at the time understood, was a particularly volatile mix in the minds of dissident colonists, and not just in Massachusetts. Gage had arrived the month before but he was still in the midst of implementing changes, as he would be through the summer.

3. Presumably his younger brother Philemon, who lived in Trenton. He would serve as a New Jersey militia general during the war and eventually sat in the Continental Congress.

JOHN DICKINSON TO JQ

20 June 1774[1]

Dear Sir Fairhill June 20th 1774

I sincerely thank you for your kind Letter and the present attending this, without flattery, I think highly valuable; and it gives Me inexpressible Pleasure to find Myself addressed in so friendly a manner, by a Gentleman I so heartily wish to call a Friend.

As far as I have been able to collect the sense of the Colonies, they are very unanimous in the Measure You mention of a Congress. You and your worthy fellow sufferers would receive a Glimpse of Joy amidst your Distress to know, with what sympathy, the Inhabitants of this province consider your Case. What never happened before, has happened now. The Country people have so exact a knowledge of Facts, and of the Consequences attending a surrender of the Points now in Question, that they are if possible, more zealous than the Citizens who lye in the direct Line of Information. Doubt not, that every thing bears a most favorable aspect. Nothing can possibly throw Us into a pernicious Confusion, but one Colony's breaking the Line of Opposition, by *advancing* too hastily before the rest. The one that dares to betray the Common Cause by rushing forwards, contrary to the Maxims of Discipline established by Common Sense and Experience of Ages, will *inevitably* and *utterly* perish.

May God Almighty bless you, and my beloved Brethren of Boston and Massachusetts Bay. My heart is full. The time will come, I *hope,* when I may congratulate them on a more stable Security of their Liberty than they ever yet have enjoyed.

I am, Sir, with Truth, your very affectionate and very humble Servant,

John Dickinson

Our Country People appear to Me, to be very firm. They look to the last Extremity with Spirit. It is right they should—if they will submit their Resentments to the Guidance of Reason.[2]

1. QP 51 (reel 29) MHS; "Memoir," 2:128–29, QP 46 (reel 6) MHS; *Memoir,* pp. 147–48; and Force, ed., *American Archives,* 4th series, 1:434. Quincy had met Dickinson on his Southern journey in April 1773—see Quincy's journal entries in Coquillette and York, eds., *Portrait of a Patriot,* 3:294–306. He had been a longtime admirer, quoting the third of Dickinson's "Pennsylvania

Farmer" letters during his opening arguments in the soldiers' defense during the "Massacre" trials (see Wroth and Zobel, eds., *Adams Legal Papers,* 3:164–66). Samuel Adams had written Dickinson from Boston on 27 March 1773 that Quincy, "a young Gent but eminent here in the profession of the law," should be arriving in Philadelphia, and he would appreciate it if Dickinson would meet with him and introduce him to Joseph Reed as well. "His Conversation m[igh]t not be unentertaining even to them," Adams wrote Dickinson. Printed in Harry Alonzo Cushing, ed., *Writings of Samuel Adams,* 4 vols. (New York: G. P. Putnam's Sons, 1904–1908), 3:14. Milton Flower's *John Dickinson: Conservative Revolutionary* (Charlottesville, Va.: University of Virginia Press, 1983), which mentions the Dickinson–Quincy connection only in passing, remains the standard biography. Dickinson's political thinking was more recently assessed in Jane E. Calvert, *Quaker Constitutionalism and the Political Thought of John Dickinson* (New York: Cambridge University Press, 2009). Quincy is mentioned there in connection with his letter to Dickinson of 20 August 1774, which is reproduced infra at pp. 262-63.

2. Dickinson inserted this paragraph, opposite his closing lines, apparently as an afterthought.

MILES BREWTON TO JQ

12 July 1774[1]

Dear Sir Charlestown 12th July 1774

I this day only received your polite favor of the 27th May, and can only say I wish it had been in my power to have shown more Civility to a Gentleman I so much Esteem as I do Mr. Quincy. You must give the Madeira time to Mellow and I dare say it will be good, or Fernandez has for the first time disappointed me. You have my best Thanks for your Pamphlet. Too many cannot step forth at this alarming Crisis in defence of the much Injured Rights of America, and those that do, should, and no doubt have the united Thanks of the friends of America. Those pamphlets inclosed I have forwarded as directed.[2]

Your situation at this time is truly hazardous and trying. But you will not fall for want of Friends, because all British America are your freinds. For Godsake be firm and discreet at this time. The good people of this Colony have sent for you one sloop load of Rice, and we shall send more soon.[3]

The 6th, 7th and 8th Instant we had the greatest assembly of the Inhabitants of this Colony I ever saw. After much debate and discussion of matters it was determined that Henry Middleton, John Rutledge, Thomas Lynch, Christopher Gadsden, and Edward Rutledge should meet the general Congress at Philadelphia at the 1 Sept. Their powers are unlimited. I hope the other Colonies will do the same and place entire Confidence in their Deputies; they can do nothing effective without such powers. Our Deputies project being at Philadelphia by the middle of August.

I should suppose the first step taken by the Congress would be to Remonstrate and petition King, Lords and Commons. Our Grievances should be all stated in the way of a Bill of Rights. The sore should be probed to the bone. The Deputies or a large part of them should go to England with the petition. Agents should not be trusted in this important affair. I should suppose this would bring us Relief, but if Redress did not come, then all to enter into both a Non Importation and Non Exportation Agreement; and I think this to be the Sence of almost all the Colonies and such a measure would place America in such a consequential point of View as would astonish all Europe. I think we have the Cards in our own hands, but if we do not play them with Caution we shall be juggled out of the Game.[4] Our Fears are only about you, that you may despond and give up, for I am sorry to see you have so many adders in your own Bosom, who may sting you to death. We have our share in this plan also of internal foes. Pity it was that Hutchinson should have gone home with so many names to petitions. It will do you no good, but much harm I fear.[5]

I have quited Trade and am now winding up my Labor for 21 years past. I long for shelter—which once I get under the shade it is not a little thing that will bring me out again. Out of the reach of my friends I wish never to be, for I can never give up my Rights to the affection of those I call my friends. I will strain a point to pass the next summer among the Northern Colonies. It is a Country I long to see, and I shall agreeable to your polite request give you Notice.

I beg to hear as often from you as your Business will permit. It is not trifling to write or speak on public affairs at this time of eminent danger. Politicks should be the Theme of the day, and our Dreams at night should be of the hapless Situation of our Country. However bad as it is, if Boston does not persevere and be prudent, her Sisters and Neighbours will work out her Salvation without taking the Musquett. Unanimity must be the great leading Star.

I am with much regard,
Your most obedient and obliged Servant
M Brewton

1. QP 71 (reel 29) MHS; printed in the *Memoir*, pp. 151–53; reprinted in Force, ed., *American Archives*, 4th series, 1:534. For Quincy meeting Brewton in March 1773 during his stay in Charleston, see Coquillette and York, eds., *Portrait of a Patriot*, 3:185–86. Brewton used dashes to end his sentences; I substituted periods. I also added most of the commas, and extended shortened names to full length. Eliza Susan Quincy wrote a note opposite her transcription of Brewton's letter (having deleted the sentence about the Madeira, among others), lamenting that Brewton had been all but forgotten as a leading patriot because he died early on in the contest. Roughly a year after he wrote this letter, he and his family perished at sea while sailing for England. ("Memoir," 2:129)

2. What they were, I cannot say; they are not in the Quincy Papers at the MHS.

3. In response to the closing of the port of Boston to private traffic. See Pickering, ed., *Statutes*, 30:336–41 (14 George III c. 19); and David Ammerman's overview, *In The Common Cause* (Charlottesville, Va.: University of Virginia Press, 1974).

4. For the first Continental Congress see Jack N. Rakove, *The Beginnings of National Politics* (New York: Alfred A. Knopf, 1979); and Jennifer Greene Marston, *King and Congress* (Princeton, N.J.: Princeton University Press, 1987). Also see my "The First Continental Congress and the Problem of American Rights," *Pennsylvania Magazine of History and Biography* 122 (1998):353–83.

5. Proof that news circulated the colonies fairly quickly, Brewton was aware of the two "farewell testimonials"—as Bailyn, *Thomas Hutchinson*, p. 273 put it—presented to Hutchinson before he departed for London, that were printed in a broadside dated 30 May 1774, *Addresses &c. to the Late Governor Hutchinson.* One was from lawyers in the province, the other from "gentlemen" in general. Samuel Quincy was among the twenty-four lawyers whose names were listed in the former testimonial. The names and addresses of sixty of those in the latter (just under half the total) were printed in another broadside "so that every Friend to his Country may know who is Assisting to carry the execrable Purposes of the British Administration into Execution." (*. . . a true LIST of those Persons . . .*)

JQ TO SAMUEL ADAMS

20 August 1774[1]

Dear Sir, Boston Augt. 20th 1774

The matter is closed. I have taken my passage and sail (God willing) for London in 18 days certain. The master with whom I go, will not know who is his passenger till he is 3 Leagues below the Light house. Nay he is not to know that any one sails with him as a passenger, and it is to Leave too far to receive the orders of the owner who is our friend William Dennie (otherwise to favor the plan all in his power).

I must request your most strenuous endeavours to obtain letters recommendatory from as many members of the Congress as possible. Mr. Lynch, I am inclined to think, will lend all in the assistance he can. Mr. Edward Rutledge I had a *transient acquaintance* with in Charleston, and having lately returned from the Temple, can (if made willing) give much aid.[2] I shall write to Mr. Dickenson and Mr. Reed on the subject; but pray you and my other good friends would back the matter with them. Desire all the Gentlemen who write in my favor to inclose their letters under cover to the house of Messrs. Henry and Thomas Bromfield, merchants in London.[3] By this means all miscarriages may be prevented.

You know my friend, that we all have our bright and our weak side; you know, better than I, which side I shall show most to advantage. Let my friends present me in that point of view. I do not want to be out sight at the Court of Great Britain. *Sat verbum sapti*.[4]

I think you may inform those, whom you sollicit for the above favor, that my education has been liberal, my profession the noblest on earth, and the partiality of my countrymen hath pushed me from among the lowest of its practitioners. I have relinquished a very lucrative employment, I have left endearing friends and relatives, from a good motive—you will say the best.

You see that I shall have embarked, before this reaches you. Let there be no delay in forwarding my letters. I depend Dear Sir more upon you, than any one as to this matter, because previous to your Departure you thought it important and promised *your activity*. Dr. Shippen junior[5] I believe will cheerfully give a Letter, if requested.

I take my departure execrating the assassins and traitors of my Country: if I join also, the odious band, remember that *Old clause is still good.* I shall deserve the Curses of my fellow citizens—and Americans may rightfully say let him be anathema.

Enough of my poor self.[6]

It is very difficult to keep our poor in order: those who have least reason to complain are most clamorous. Mr. Phillips hath done wonders among them. I don't know what we should do without him.[7] Molineux hath resigned his seat at the Committee of ways and means nobody is troubled at it.[8] We are in good spirits but tremble for fear of the storms.

Remember our disease will not do to be *tampered with:* Mr. Harnett says any thing short of a non-importation and non-exportation will ruin all. A large circle of friends join with him.[9] But we are in great expectation here that the Congress will raise on *their own Authority* £100,000 sterling at least for the dismay of some, and *the temptation of others.* There are European Potentates who would long for the provisions we sell. It will make you, as a body, and the Colonies in general, very respectable.

Our new Council are more ignominiously treated than any among Us. A Gentleman from Taunton tells us, that *The Green* is already (or on notice will be) adorned with a 3 legged Gibbett. Colonel Murray's family have begged he would not think of returning to his House. We expect, that the Congress will not fail of blasting *with a vengance* the *SWORN* Enemies of our Peace.[10] You will do great mischeif if you disappoint our righteous expectation.

NB. It is expected here that you will resolve that the Port Bill is a mere act of Power, and that the two acts for altering our Charter and the Impartial Administration of Justice[11] are violations of the rights and liberties of the Subject—and therefore not binding on the People.

To return to myself,[12]

Urge as many Southern friends as you can to give me intelligence from their several Provinces the Ensuing Winter: you may assure them of my gratefull notice of their favors and a reciprocal information. Don't let want of Acquaintance be a bar. I shall make a good Use of all Intelligence I receive, for I shall dedicate my whole soul to the Service of my injured Country.

I expect great aid from you and Brother Adams, and our friend Cushing while in London. They shall hear often from me, if they behave like Good soldiers and good Brothers toward a poor fellow-laborer.

I am unwell. In much hurry of writing and business, but with my whole heart

Your friend and servant,
In the Cause of God and my Country,
Josiah Quincy, Junior

PS. The Letter that you will see in our next Monday's Paper was from Dr. Lee to Mr. Speaker. The Blanks you will find no difficulty of filling up. Your name fills two. 'Tis your plan he speaks of. Mr Speaker is directed to show the Letter to you, but it bears so hard upon his friend Lord Dartmouth, I doubt he will omit it. Keep this PS a profound Secret—for I also indulged in passing the Speaker's Letters in his Absence.[13]

Post PS. I desire that my sailing for London may be kept a secret as long as possible. All our friends join in the Utility of such secrecy.[14]

1. From the Samuel Adams Papers, New York Public Library; most of it is printed in the *Memoir*, pp. 155–57. In this letter (as in some others), Quincy would end a phrase with a colon, then continue with the first letter of the next word in lower case. I changed those colons to periods, to end the sentence, with the first letter of the next word being capitalized as the first word in a new sentence.

2. Edward Rutledge, younger than Quincy by five years, had studied at Oxford and, like his older brother John, had been admitted to the English bar after studying law at the Middle Temple. Quincy spent some of his time in Charleston copying reports on cases that Rutledge had recorded while practicing the law in Charleston, which can be found in QP 60 (also on reel 4) MHS. Rutledge was fast rising as a patriot leader and would be one of South Carolina's delegates to the first Continental Congress. He is among those listed in E. Alfred Jones, *American Members of the Inns of Court* (London: St. Catherine's Press, 1924), pp. 187–88. No Quincy, incidentally, ever followed that track into law during the colonial era. Josiah Junior of course knew that Adams would be leaving soon for Philadelphia to attend Congress, and that Rutledge and others he mentioned would be there as well.

3. Eliza Susan Quincy wrote this note in the *Memoir*, p. 407: "Thomas Bromfield, born in Beacon Street, Boston, New England, 1733," moved "to England in 1760, and was established as a merchant in London, until his death in 1816, aged eighty-three years. His sister, Abigail Bromfield, married William Phillips, of Boston; and their daughter, Abigail Phillips, married Josiah Quincy, Junior, 1769." Thomas's brother Henry carried on the business with him on both the London and the Boston sides of the Atlantic.

4. Verbum sat sapienti: "a word to the wise" [is sufficient]. This paragraph is not in the printed *Memoir*.

5. William Shippen Jr., on the rise as a Philadelphia physician with an interest in politics, who trained at Edinburgh.

6. This sentence and the brief paragraph above it were also left out of the *Memoir*.

7. Referring to his father-in-law, William Phillips, prominent Boston merchant and political ally of Thomas Cushing and others in the town meeting, and thorn in the side of Thomas Hutchinson, who refused to allow him a seat on his council when he was nominated for it by the House. He had begun as an apprentice to the merchant Edward Bromfield, eventually marrying his daughter and becoming his business partner.

8. William Molineux, referring to his position with the town of Boston. Though English-born and an Anglican, Molinuex, a merchant of modest income, was associated with the more outspoken elements in the Boston town meeting. He died in October 1774 before independence became the primary political objective. Whether he would have joined others in determining that the quest for rights within the empire had to be abandoned for something more ambitious must therefore remain moot, his "radical" politics and involvement in political street theatre regardless.

9. The rest of the paragraph was not included in the *Memoir.*

10. Adams referred here to the new "mandamus" council set to replace the old governor's council, as stipulated under the Massachusetts Government Act. John Murray of Rutland, one of those named to the council, was, like all of the others, pressured to resign. Failure to ever get a full set of thirty-six council members was an indicator that royal government was being eclipsed by a rival shadow government, as Massachusetts Patriots became subconscious revolutionaries long before they decided on independence as the only solution to the problems of empire. See my "Imperial Impotence: Treason in 1774 Massachusetts," *Law and History Review* 29 (2011):657–701; and Ray Raphael, *The First American Revolution* (New York: The New Press, 2002). This paragraph is also not in the *Memoir.*

11. The Administration of Justice Act was, like the Massachusetts Government Act, designed to bolster imperial authority in the colonies, allowing imperial officials—civilian or military—to request a change of venue, even to a court in England, if accused of a capital crime in the colonies. In Pickering, ed., *Statutes*, 30:367–71 (14 George III c. 39).

12. Not included in the *Memoir.*

13. Neither Arthur Lee nor Thomas Cushing are identified in this "Extract of a Letter from a Gentleman of Distinction," dated 1 June 1774, London, that appeared on the front page of the *Boston Gazette,* 2 August 1774. It derided the laws affecting the colonies then coming out of Parliament and lumped the pending Quebec Act with them—all being part of the same legislative program designed to strip the colonists of their liberties.

14. The *Memoir* reproduces this sentence as the "PS" rather than the "Post PS," and excludes the "PS" above it altogether. In the original letter both were sandwiched into the margins of different pages, as was the "NB" (to "note well").

JQ TO JOHN DICKINSON

20 August 1774[1]

Much respected and Dear Sir Boston Augt. 20th 1774

Your cordial approval of my poor work communicates a happiness surpassed only by your kind invitation of me into your Circle of Friends. Believe me, Sir, that I recollect no feeling which would give me more solid heartfelt satisfaction, than being considered by you an honest friend, unless I except a consciousness of deserving that rank and confidence.

Your sentiments relative that "Colony which shall *advance too hastily* before the rest, contrary to the maxims of discipline" &c. are no doubt just.[2] Yet, permit me, Sir, to use a freedom, which your partiality seems to invite, and observe: That those maxims of discipline are not universally known in this early period of Continental warfare; and are with great difficulty practiced by a people under the scourge of public Oppression. When time shall have taught wisdom, and past experience have fixed Boundaries to the movement of a single Colony, its intemperate and over-hasty strides will be more unpaid. But, if we should unfortunately see one Colony under a *treble* pressure of public oppression, rendered impatient by the refinements, delays, and experiments of the Philadelphians, of their less oppressed and therefore more deliberate Brethren: I say, if a Colony thus insulted, galled from without and vexed within, should seem to advance and break the line of opposition, ought it to incur the heavy sense of "betraying the Common Cause"? Though not to be just, may not its fault be considered as venial?

Believe me, Dear Sir, you know not all of our patriotic trials in this Province. Corruption (which *delay* gives time to operate) is the Destroying angel, we have most to fear. Our enemies wish for nothing so much as our tampering with the fatal disease. I fear much that timid or lukewarm Councils will be considered by Our Congress as prudent and politic: such Councils, will inevitably *enslave Us.* We subjugated—how rapid and certain the fall of the Rest? Excuse my freedom of telling what I dread, though seeming to differ from those I honor and revere.

We are at this time calm and temperate; and partiality to my Countrymen aside, I question whether any antient or modern State can give an instance of a whole people so severely suffering with such dignity, fortitude and true spirit. Our very enemies are dismayed, and though they affect to sneer at our Enthusiasm, yet they so far catch the noble infirmity, as to give an involuntary applause.

I see no reason to apprehend our advancing before our Brethren, unless the plans they should adopt should very avidly be too languid and spiritless to give any rational hopes of safety to Us in our adherence to them. *Sobrius esto* is our present motto.[3]

At the urgent solicitation of great number of warm friends to my Country and me, I have agreed to relinquish business and embark for London—and shall sail in 18 days certain. I am flattered by those, who perhaps place too great a confidence in me, that I may do some good the ensuing winter at the Court of Great Britain. Hence I have taken this unexpected resolution. My design is to be kept as long secret as possible, I hope till I get to Europe. Should it transpire, that I was going Home, our public enemies here would be indefatigable and persevering to my injury, as they have been to the Cause in which I am engaged heart and hand; perhaps more so, as personal pique would be added to public malevolence.

I would sollicit earnestly intelligence from you, Sir, *while in our Modern Babylon.*[4] I shall endeavour to procure the earliest information from all parts of that Country, as I propose dedicating myself wholly to the service of my Country. I shall stand in need of the aid of every friend to America; and believe me, when I say, that I esteem no one more capable of affording me aid, than those who inhabit the fertile banks of the Delaware.

If you can lead me to any channel of doing real service to the Common Cause, I flatter myself you are not disinclined; and though it should never be in my power to cancel the Obligation, it will ever be my study to remember it.

I am &c.

1. QP 51 (reel 29) MHS; "Memoir," 2:131–33; and *Memoir,* pp. 149–51; and reprinted in Force, ed., *American Archives,* 4th series 1:725–26. The original was obviously a rough draft, with more than the usual number of words in shorthand, and perfunctory punctuation.

2. Quincy quoted from the letter that Dickinson had written to him on June 20th, reproduced at p. 253, supra.

3. Be sober; be calm.

4. Eliza Susan Quincy excised the reference to London as modern Babylon from the printed *Memoir,* but not her transcribed "Memoir."

JQ TO JOSEPH REED

20 August 1774[1]

Most respected and dear Sir, Boston Augt. 20th 1774

At the earnest solicitation of a number of warm friends to my Country and me, I have engaged to remand my business and repair to London for the coming year. I sail in 18 days from this time. Whether I shall be able do any good is altogether problematical. I think I have *the will.* It is a great measure within the compass of others to give me *the power.*

I am using my best endeavours to procure a stated correspondence with all parts of the Continent. On this head I now trouble you, Sir. If my intelligence is regular and *early,* and my *whole* soul is devoted to that Common Cause, I shall have the means and opportunity to do some good. Permit me, Sir, to solicit the favor of information from you, while I am in London. If reciprocal intelligence will in any degree compensate the trouble, you may depend on my fidelity in this respect. It must, it will, be a very important [occasion?] in Britain the next session of Parliament. Your friend Mr. Cushing will be able to confirm this opinion by communicating some intelligence I have sent him by this post.

It is the desire of my friends here, that my sailing for England may be kept a profound secret as long as possible. Should it transpire, that I was going Home, our public Enemies here would indulge a malignant pleasure in doing me, and the cause in which I am embarked some great injury.

I shall stand in need of all your aid while in London. The *Genii* on the Banks of the Delaware are as capable of inspiring and protecting me, as any in the Americas would.

If you can lead me into any channel doing good to the Common Cause, I flatter myself you are not disinclined; and though it should never be in my power to cancell the Obligation, it will ever be my study to remember it.

With great respect
And most cordial esteem
Your obliged and most humble Servant,
JQuincy jun.

PS. Please to cause all Letters for me, to be put under a cover, directed to Messers Henry and Thomas Bromfield, merchants in London. This will frustrate any endeavours to stop your favors.

1. Joseph Reed Papers, New-York Historical Society manuscripts. Quincy met Reed while passing through Pennsylvania on his overland return trip from South Carolina. For tidbits about their meetings see Quincy's Southern journal in Coquillette and York, eds., *Portrait of a Patriot*, 3:294, 298–99. Reed had met Josiah's father and wrote the senior Quincy to tell him how impressed he had been by his son—see his undated letter in QP 51 (also reel 29) MHS, written shortly after Josiah Jr. resumed his journey north. Reed expressed great pleasure at the stands taken in the Bay Colony in defense of colonial rights. "It is truly surprizing that the two most remote Colonies, Massachusetts and Virginia, differing in every Point of Religion and domestick Policy, should thus harmonize in the Essentials of American Liberty," he wrote Quincy Sr., adding, "some spark of the sacred Fire, it is hoped, will in Time warm the intermediate Provinces." On 6 May 1773 Reed wrote Josiah Jr. a letter of introduction to William Smith to open doors in New York, as Quincy made his way back home, still eager to meet potential political allies and correspondents. Quincy had carried with him for Reed a letter of introduction from Thomas Cushing, speaker of the Massachusetts House. Both are in QP 51 (reel 29) MHS.

CHARLES LEE TO JQ

23 August 1774[1]

Dear Sir, Newport August 23rd

I have sent you a copy of the letter to Lord Percy but I must intreat that you will copy it, and send this to Major George Clerk of the 43rd Regiment. He is an old Freind. It was He who delivered it, and to him I promised a copy. I think of setting out through Connecticut the day after tomorrow. When you have idle time on your hands you will make me happy in letting me hear from you. You must direct to me at Mr. Davis Barber corner of dock Street New York. Adieu Dear Sir, my respects to Mrs. Quincy, Dr. Cooper, Warren, Young, Mr. Jannot, in short to the whole white Tribe.

Yours most sincerely,
Charles Lee
Newport August 23rd

My Lord ,

Were your Lordship only a common Colonel of a Regiment, I certainly should not have given myself the trouble of writing nor you the trouble of reading this letter. But as you hold so high a rank, and will one day hold a still higher I conceive it will not be improper to address you, and in some measure to apologize for my seeming want of respect. As I have not waited upon the General—for reasons which He cannot, I think disapprove, I was not certain whether you might, in your military capacity, consider my visit as proper. But as you are not merely a Soldier, but a Citizen of the first class and importance, from your illustrious family and fashion, your vast property and from being born to be a Counsellor of the Nation, I think some explanation of my conduct not only proper but necessary, and I flatter myself that some time or other Your Lordship will not simply approve my conduct, but become a friend to the same cause.[2] My Lord, I will venture to say that it is the cause of Great Britain as well as of America; it is the cause of Mankind. Were the principle of taxing America without their consent admitted, Great Britain would that instant be ruined: The pecuniary influence of the Crown and the Army of Pensioners and Placemen would be so increased, that all opposition to the most iniquitous Measures of the most iniquitous Ministers would be for ever borne down.

Your Lordship, I am sure, must be sensible that this pecuniary influence is already enormously too great, and that a very wicked Use is made of it. On these principles every good Englishman (abstract of any particular regard for America) must oppose her being taxed by the Parliament of Great Britain, or more properly by the first Lord of the Treasury, for in fact the Parliament and Treasury have of late years, been one and the same thing. But, My Lord, I have besides a very particular regard for America. I was long amongst them,[3] and I know them to be the most loyal affectionate zealous Subjects of the whole Empire. General Gage himself must acknowledge the truth of what I advance. He was witness through the course of the last war of their zeal their ardor their Enthusiasm for whatever concerned the welfare the interests and the honour of the Mother Country. When I see, therefore, the extreme of calamities attempted to be brought upon such a People by the intrigues of such a couple of Scoundrels as Barnard[4] and Hutchinson and their profligate associates; when I see a Minister violent and tyrannical like North mowing down whole communities merely to indulge his hereditary hatred to Liberty and those attached to her, I think it the duty of every honest Man and Freind to humanity to exert his utmost to defeat the diabolical purpose. That these People have been totally misrepresented at home, that they have been most unjustly and cruelly treated, your Lordship will, I have no doubt, sooner or later be convinced.

But as from your present situation and many little mistakes you will not probably fall into the way of truth so soon as I could wish, I beg leave to recommend to your perusal a sort of pamphlet lately sent from England. It is intitled a true State of the proceedings in the Parliament of Great Britain and in the Province of Massachusetts Bay.[5] Mr. Josiah Quincy will furnish your Lordship with it if you will make use of my name. It is a fair and candid relation of the whole process from beginning to end. When your Lordship has read it, you will be struck with compassion and horror, and I have great hopes not a less warm (but more powerfull) freind of this much injured Country than myself. I take the liberty of recommending this method to your Lordship, as it is impossible that you should gather any thing but misinformation from those Men who I find surround head quarters. The Scovels and Paxtons[6] are not only interested to misrepresent and calumniate but to exterminate their Country: There is no medium. Their Country must perish or They meet with the desert of impious Parricides.

It was the misfortune of General Gage from the beginning to fall into such hands as these. Had He not been deluded by miscreants of this stamp, We should never have seen him acting in a capacity so incompatible with the excellence of his natural disposition. I must now, My Lord, intreat that as Fools and Knaves will from misunderstanding and malice probably disfigure my conduct, you will not suffer them to make any wrong impressions; that you will be persuaded that Fact not from any pique and disappointment (as will, I conclude be thrown out) but from principle. I think My Lord, that an English Soldier owes a very great degree of reverence to the King as first Magistrate and third branch of the Legislature appointed to the high office by the voice of the Nation. But I think He owes a still greater to the rights and liberties of his Country. I think his Country is every part of the Empire; that in what ever part an flagitious Minister manifestly invades these rights and liberties, whether in Great Britain, Ireland or America, Every Englishman (Officer or not Officer) ought to consider their cause as his own, and that the rights and liberties of this Country are invaded every man must see who has eyes and is not determined to shut them. These, My Lord, are my principles. From these, I swear by all that is sacred and tremendous, I purely and solely act, and these I hope will rather serve than prejudice me in your Lordship's opinion. I flatter myself still farther, I flatter myself that you yourself, will, before it is long, adopt them that you will at least in your letters to your Father (whom I have always been taught to esteem an honest man and freind to humanity) endeavour to undeceive the People at home. If the delusion is too strong, I will venture to assert that you will feel some consolation amidst the calamities, ready to fall upon your Country, in the reflection that you had attempted to avert them.

I shall now finish, My Lord, with intreating that if you find any thing impertinent either in the matter or length of this letter, you will attribute it to an intemperate zeal in an honest cause, and that you will be persuaded that I should not have addressed it to a man of whom I entertained an unfavourable opinion.

I am, My Lord, your most obedient

1. QP 51 (also reel 29) MHS. In the note to Percy that follows, I added the paragraph breaks and altered some of the punctuation, to make the reading less awkward. Lee used dashes to serve all his punctuation needs. Lee had left active duty in the British army as a major but

went on to become a general in the Polish army, fight against the Turks, return to England, and go from thence to the colonies in 1773. By then a retired lieutenant colonel on half-pay, Lee identified increasingly with the critics of empire; hence his letter to Earl Percy. He would enter the lists as a pamphleteer for the American cause with *Strictures on a Pamphlet Entitled, A Friendly Address to All Reasonable Americans, on the Subject of Our Political Confusions* (Philadelphia: William and Thomas Bradford, 1774), which responded to the pamphlet of that title written (anonymously when published) by Thomas Bradbury Chandler. Not identifying himself as the author, Lee sought to reassure Americans (and warn Britons) that they were right in objecting to Parliament's presumed authority to tax them, and that they should be confident they could defend themselves against any attempt to impose policies on them by force. He would have a stormy wartime career as a major general in the Continental army. John Richard Alden's *General Charles Lee, Traitor or Patriot?* (Baton Rouge, La.: Louisiana State University Press, 1951) is largely sympathetic.

2. Hugh, Earl Percy, son of the Duke of Northumberland, was a brigadier posted with the British army in Boston, who by then had also held a seat in the House of Commons for over a decade. Although he believed that crown and parliament had been far too lenient for far too long when dealing with opposition leaders in Boston, he was not particularly enthusiastic about the use of force to quell political protest. Still, he did not think the locals would be "mad" enough to resist and on 19 April 1775 he commanded the relief column that saved the expeditionary force sent out to Concord. He served honorably, going where duty took him, but he was happy to leave the American war behind and return to England in 1777. See Charles Knowles Bolton, ed., *Letters of Hugh Earl Percy* (Boston: Charles E. Goodspeed, 1902); and the brief sketch of him by Stephen Conway in the *Oxford Dictionary of National Biography,* 60 vols. (Oxford: Oxford University Press, 2004), 43:754–55.

3. Lee almost invariably wrote "'em" rather than "them."

4. Francis Bernard, Hutchinson's predecessor as governor, who was popular enough when he arrived in 1760 but was reviled among Boston's leaders by the time he left in 1769. For his controversy-riddled years in the Bay Colony see Colin Nicolson's excellent *The 'Infamas' Governer* (Boston: Northeastern University Press, 2000).

5. A reference to Arthur Lee's anonymously published *A True State of the Proceedings in the British Parliament and In the Province of Massachusetts Bay* (London: W. Bingley, 1774). In the space of twenty-four pages, Lee reviewed imperial policy, from the governorship of Francis Bernard through that of Thomas Hutchinson, to show how both men had fed the unrest caused by foolish, insensitive imperial policies coming out of London. The good people of Massachusetts, he contended, were loyal subjects of the crown, willing to accept parliamentary authority within proper constitutional limits, but their motives and actions had been misrepresented by those seeking to cause contention.

6. Daniel Scovil and Charles Paxton.

JOHN ADAMS TO JQ

18 September 1774[1]

Dear Sir Philadelphia Sept. 18. 1774

I am to acknowledge the Receipt of your kind Letter, and to thank you for it, and then Seal my Letter.

Business, Ceremony, Visits and a thousand Ideas take up my Time so entirely that I can scarce find half enough for sleep.

I have spoken to several gentlemen concerning you and shall to more.[2] I wish you a prosperous voyage and much of the exalted Pleasure of serving your Country.

You are surrounded with active scenes in our Province at present: We are not idle here. But how long it will be before the World will know our Meditations I cannot say.

Our Country is in the Post of Honour, and of Danger and she behaves in Character. The Congress is sensible of it, and will act in Character too, I hope and believe.

Adieu,
John Adams

1. QP 51 (reel 29) MHS; transcribed in the "Memoir," 2:135; printed in the *Memoir,* p. 154. Adams and Quincy were well aware of their family tie by marriage—John's wife Abigail being connected to the Quincy line through her mother Elizabeth Quincy Smith, whose father John Quincy was a first cousin of Josiah Sr. John Adams, famously, felt slighted in national historical memory. Josiah Junior, by contrast, is even more in his shadow than Adams was in that of Franklin or Jefferson. It is often forgotten that Josiah Junior, nine years younger than Adams, served alongside the future president as defense counsel in two of the three "Massacre" trials, and that, as Josiah told it, the jailed Preston asked for him first. See Josiah Junior to his father, 26 March 1770, at supra pp. 51–52.

2. For efforts to spread the word of Quincy's trip and make connections in England, see Charles Chauncy to Samuel Adams, 26 August 1774, Samuel Adams to Charles Chauncy, 19 September 1774, and Chauncy's letter of introduction for Quincy to Dr. Thomas Amory of 13 September 1774, for Quincy to use in London, all in QP 51 (reel 29) MHS; and the latter two in the "Memoir," 2:136 and 134; and *Memoir,* pp. 155, and 159–60, resp.

JQ TO COLONEL LEONARD

September 1774[1]

Sir Boston Septr. 1774

Before this will be delivered to you, I shall be on my passage to Europe. My intended tour hath occasioned my calling in monies, which would otherwise have remained at interest; and having not been able to collect the sum wanted, I am obliged to ask the discharge of your note. I have been offered the money or bills for it, but supposing a negotiation would be disagreeable to you, I declined that measure; and would not trouble you with this request, did I know of any of my debtors more able, (or as I believe more willing) than yourself to make payment.

If a compliance with my desire will be inconvenient, or my having made the request at *this time* will give any uneasiness, I shall be very sorry; but if it shall happen (as I trust) that discharging the note will be both convenient and agreable, your compliance with my request will confer a favor on

Sir, your humble and obedient servant,
Josiah Quincy junr.

PS I have ordered the note to be delivered to our mutual friend Ezekiel Goldthwait Esqr who will receive the money, and deliver up the note.

1. Presumably Ephraim Leonard, by then just over seventy years old, who had been a militia colonel in the French and Indian War, a judge, and was still a prominent resident of East Mansfield. Unlike his son Daniel of Taunton, a future loyalist who wrote as "Massachusettensis" in a newspaper essay debate with John Adams (who wrote as "Novanglus") in 1774–1775, the elder Leonard remained attached to the patriot cause and lived to see American independence. In the Ferdinand J. Dreer Collection #175, American Statesmen, Historical of Pennsylvania [hereafter HSP] manuscripts. The postscript was written along the left edge of the letter, perpendicular to it.

JAMES LOVELL TO JQ

10, 25, 28 October 1774[1]

My Dear Sir Boston Octr. 10th 1774

Though a slavish Confinement to one single Spot prevents my being able to acquire a Knowledge, especially an early one, of such Articles of Intelligence as you ought to receive, yet it is by no Means so severe as to become a full Excuse for my intire Silence after having made you a Promise of Writing. Besides, if I was utterly unable to furnish you with a single Line of political Information, or deterred by the Fear of Death from speaking my Opinion upon the Times, yet Nature will not suffer me to be so unfaithful to the sincere Feelings of my Heart as not to let my Pen tell you it's most affectionate Wishes for your Health, Safety and Prosperity.

You will receive Facts from the Gazettes, and your numerous intelligent Correspondents, peculiarly in the Way of ascertaining them. The latter will also doubtless make a Variety of Judgment upon each Particular. But be sure to stand ever aware that such Judgment depends in general very much upon the Constitution of the Air and its Influence upon the Nerves of your Correspondent at the Date of his Epistle. For my own Part, being sensible that my nervous System must have had a severe Shock, since my dear Friend Joseph Gardner was induced to wish me dead in the Paroxisms of my Disorder, I determined early in my Recovery to fortify my Mind in such a Manner that my Comfort should not be hazarded by every political Breeze.[2] I lay'd it down therefore as undoubted Truth that all the Plots of all the Enemies to our heaven descended Rights would prove abortive in the final Issue. By this Faith I have escaped the Pain of Fear even under Appearances where I have yet been led to counteract traiterous Operators. From this Sketch perhaps you will mark me down as a *presumptuous* Correspondent. Be it so; I here finish my Porch.

You will see by the Papers that immediately after you sailed a Proclamation was issued to discharge the Members from Attendance upon that General Court for which Precepts you know had been given out. They judiciously slighted this, sticking to Charter-Rule; and upon finding Mr. Gage did not attend to his proper Duty, they resolved themselves into a Provincial Congress to meet at Concord Tomorrow. They will be strenuous, I expect, in pressing the General to desist from his Fortifications.[3] What can the poor Soul do?

He cannot declare in plain English that he is only striving to make the Minds of his Officers and Men easy, and yet I believe that to be the Truth and the whole Truth.

October 25th

I told you at parting that if I was deceived in my Countrymen and found they turned out Poltroons I would not inform you of it, though such was your Request. Let not that Speech detract from my Credit when I tell you they rise every Day in Character. It is become a downright Task for the warmest Patriots of our Town and County to confine the Spirit of the other Counties to an Attention to the *Causes* rather than to the *Executors* of our Wrongs. I am really pained at finding that the Wickedness of ministerial Conduct has brought the Province so generally to make the Idea of an Engagement between fellow Subjects so familiar to their Minds. How would such a Thought have shocked us all a few years go! But the insolent Appearance of the Works upon the Neck has roused the Inclination of the vigorous country Youth to play over again the Niagaral Game of filling Trenches with round Bundles of Hay, under which they advanced as securely as under the Vines of old, though in a more lowly Posture. The Folly and Weakness of the Works may easily be proved to be fully equal to the Insolence. Our Besiegers, sensible how much Nature is against them, talk of employing constantly great Numbers of their Soldiery to break the Ice of the two Bays; little knowing, however, what mighty Reparation will be made in only one of our clinking Nights; and little considering also the non Importance of it's being broken in Bays which are a dead Flat upon every Ebb. I wish again and again that the Temptations to chastize the Insult were not so glaring; as the Provincial Congress, with all their Efforts to confine the inland Spirit solely to the *Defensive,* will assuredly fail upon Notice of ministerial Determination to continue hostile. Nothing, I think, but speedy Knowledge of a Change of Measures in England can prevent a capital winter Stroke. They press us to leave the Town in the strongest Manner. Many are for doing it, and others for sending off their most valuable Articles, to be in a Readiness. All agree it is better to sell the Town to the Continent than to have it preserved for a Slave-Pen of Great Britain.

I have just received a Letter (dated the 13th) from Doctor Loring who lodges in the same House at Philadelphia with our Members. Though every Thing is conducted with Secresy, yet he is satisfied from their uniform Cheerfulness than every Thing goes on to their Wishes.

Our Friend Molineux overplied in the good Cause and was last Evening laid to rest, where the incomperable Mayhew, and the Brother patriots Dana and Thatcher await the Morning of a glorious Resurrection; and where you and I had nearly gone to rest before him.[4] May it not prove unimportant to ourselves and to the Publick that a gracious Providence has been pleased to mark down for *us* some later Date!

October 28th

I am informed that a Letter was Yesterday read in Provincial Congress from Mr. Samuel Adams purporting that Things went in the Continental Congress, without any motion of our Members, as perfectly to his Liking as if he was sole Director, and that in a very few Days he doubted not his Friends here would receive the most Satisfactory Intelligence. Though the King's fisher has orders to sail, yet the Weather being bad I had Thoughts of risquing the Chance, that I might gain some further Lights concerning this Matter; but finding a general Suspicion of the Insecurity of Conveyance by a King's Ship, I am led to think most of your Friends will wait other Opportunity. Therefore I close for the present, that you may not think yourself neglected, in Consequence of what I really think an *ill-grounded* Suspicion. We have London-News so late as Sept. 2d . If the *People* of England, our *Fellow-Subjects* will cease obstinately to shut their Eyes upon the Justice of our Cause, we ask no more; Conviction must be the Consequence of a bare Admission of the Light.

God preserve you, my Friend. I think it will be the Fashion in London to speak well of us long before this reaches you; and when once it is the Fashion, I doubt not it will be in Proportion to its opposite lately prevalent there.

Your. Friend and obliged humble Servant,
Jas. Lovell

1. QP 51 (reel 29) MHS; *Memoir,* pp. 161–65; reprinted in Force, ed., *American Archives,* 4th series, 1:948–49.

2. Lovell may have been under the care of Dr. Joseph Gardner for some sort of gastrointestinal disorder, which Quincy probably knew—and which was why Lovell could engage in a bit of sarcasm; at least, that is my reading of the tone, reinforced by the insights of J. L. Bell, the man behind the ingenious "Boston 1775" blog.

3. The provincial conventions that sprouted up in 1774 are the best evidence of shadow governments that were the result of changing loyalties, a revolutionary subconscious taking root months before the shooting war started, and well over a year before independence would be declared. Jackson Turner Main reviews these developments in *The Sovereign States, 1775–1783* (New York: New Viewpoints, 1973), pp. 123–42. *The Journals of the Provincial Congress of Massachusetts in 1774 and 1775* (Boston: Button and Wentworth, 1838) provide an excellent case study of the phenomenon. The fortifications to which Lovell referred were being erected on Boston Neck.

4. For Molineux see p. 261, n. 5 supra. Jonathan Mayhew, who died in 1766, was revered as one of Boston's most influential congregational ministers. John Adams considered him in some sense an intellectual father of American independence, with his emphasis on immutable, God-given rights, and the right to resist if they were trampled upon. Higher truth comes from God, not man, Mayhew emphasized, but man had the rational capacity and moral obligation to act on it. His was a bully pulpit, from which he denounced imperial policies that he considered oppressive, the Stamp Act heading the list. Oxenbridge Thacher, who died the year before Mayhew, was a prominent Boston lawyer, under whom Josiah Jr. trained. Quincy essentially inherited Thacher's practice, which helps to explain his quick rise in the profession. Richard Dana had also been a prominent Boston lawyer, a Son of Liberty and protestor against British policies that were thought to infringe on American rights. He died in 1772.

CHARLES CHAUNCY TO JQ

21 October 1774[1]

Dear Sir, Boston Oct. 21st 1774

Not knowing of this opportunity of conveying a letter to you but a few minutes since, and being told that I must in a few minutes write, if at all, I have time only to inclose part of a newspaper, which contains some things of importance, which you will be glad to see; and also to inform you, that Mr. Revere, who came from the Grand Congress last week informs me, that it was supposed that Congress would break up, at least for the present, this week. Probably, you will hear from there, and read the result of the proceedings sooner by some vessel from Philadelphia, than from these parts.

I saw your good wife yesterday, as she came from our Thursday-lecture. She and those you are most concerned for are well. I am, hoping to hear from you by the first opportunity,

Your assured Friend and humble Servant,
Charles Chauncy[2]

1. QP 51 (reel 29) MHS; also printed in Mark Antony DeWolfe Howe, ed., "Letters to Josiah Quincy, Jr." *Proceedings of the Massachusetts Historical Society* 50 (1917):471–96. The letter above was the first of seventeen gathered by Howe, all taken from the originals. They were printed as an appendix to Quincy's London journal (on pp. 433–71), also taken from the original at the MHS. I offered a new edition of that journal in Coquillette and York, eds., *Portrait of a Patriot,* 1:223–69. I also commented there (on pp. 219–21) on Howe, a prolific writer and Pulitzer Prize-winning biographer some years later, and what led to his involvement with things Quincy.

2. Chauncy, nearly seventy, was the oldest of Boston's prominent congregational ministers who proved such a frustration to Thomas Hutchinson. The First Church provided him a bully pulpit to harangue against foolish policies and the foolish men who passed and attempted to enforce them. There is a good sketch of him in Sibley, *Harvard Graduates,* 6:439-467.

JOSEPH REED TO JQ

25 October 1774[1]

Dear Sir Philadelphia. Oct. 25.1774

I hope this will find you safely arrived in Great Brittain a Country wherein I have spent many happy Hours before she began to play the Tyrant in America. The Cloud which hung over the Colonies at the Time of your Departure begins to disperse. Instead of divided Councils and feeble Measures which at one Time there was too much Reason to apprehend, all now is Union and Firmness and I trust we shall exhibit such a Proof of publick Virtue and enlightened Zeal in the most glorious of all Causes as will hand down the present Age with the most illustrious Characters of Antiquity. I have with great Difficulty procured you the Proceedings of the General Congress which is now rising, but your Delegates from whom I received it beg you will not make any publick Use of it as the Copy is incorrect. Your Friend Mr. John Adams has written something to this Effect in the first Page. As the Proceedings of this great Assembly are so important and interesting I could not think of this Vessels going without carrying them to you. Another Ship will sail in a few Days by which I shall send you what remains, being the List of Grievances and Claim of Rights. The Congress would not adjourn but have recommended another to be held the 10th of May at this Place. They part with each other on Terms of the utmost Friendship; it will have the most happy Effect in cementing the Union of the Colonies, not only by the Ties of publick Interest but of private Friendship. This Ship will carry you the Account of the Destruction by Fire of both Ships of Cargo which arrived at Annapolis. The Owners of both to avoid a more dreadful Punishment for their Presumption and Folly offered to set Fire with their own hands, which they did. These Proofs of the Spirit of the People will I trust be of some Service to Boston. The People of England must see that Opposition to Parliamentary Tyranny is not local or partial. It will also have a happy Effect on the Non-Importation Agreement resolved by the Congress as the Owners of Ships will not abuse to hazard them with the forbidden Wares.

I congratulate you my dear Sir upon the rising Glory of America; our Operations have been almost too slow for the accumulated Sufferings of Boston but I trust they will prove effectual for their Relief. Should this bloodless War fail of its Effect an infinite Majority of all the Colonies will make the last Appeal before they resign their Liberties into the Hands of any ministerial Tyrant.

I shall be allways happy in hearing from you by every Opportunity and you may rely upon my sending you a speedy and faithful Account of every Transaction here. I have wrote to an old Correspondent of mine, a Mr. Hugh Baillie,[2] a true Friend to Liberty and the Cause of America that if he will call on you, You will show him the Proceedings of the Congress which I have failed in procuring for him. I salute you with much Esteem and wishing you Health and Happiness , I am Dear Sir

Your most obedient and obliged

J. R.

I only put the Initials of my Name, as I believe you remember my Hand writing or if not you will recollect to whom you wrote on this Plan first before you embarked.

1. QP 51 (reel 29) MHS; also in the "Memoir," 2:142–44 the *Memoir*, pp. 165–67; and reprinted in Force, ed., *American Archives*, 4th series, 1:892. Either this letter, or the one following, was misdated. I divided a few sentences that ran on for too long, with Reed quite possibly composing as he wrote.

2. Quincy would become acquainted with Hugh Baillie once he arrived in London, and a letter from Baillie of 28 January 1775, is at infra pp. 371-74.

JOSEPH REED TO JQ

27 October 1774[1]

Dear Sir Philadelphia Oct. 27th 1774

When I wrote you yesterday the Captain of the Vessel which carrys this had resolved to sail immediately but having been induced to wait in Order to carry the Address of the Congress to the King gives me an Opportunity of sending you the Additions which we have since had from the Press of their Proceedings. I congratulate you my dear sir on the Spirit[,] Firmness and Unanimity of this great Assembly, the most respectable ever known in this Country. I am with real Regard

Your Affectionate and obliged,
Sincerely,
Jos. Reed

1. QP 51 (reel 29) MHS.

JOHN DICKINSON TO JQ

28 October 1774[1]

My dear Sir, Fairhill Octr. 28th 1774

I should have answered your last Letter before You left Boston. I had not imagined from what You said in it, that You must have sailed before it could have reached that Place.

I now congratulate You on the hearty Union of all America from Nova Scotia to Georgia in the Common Cause. The particulars, You are, no Doubt, acquainted with. The Congress broke up the Day before Yesterday; and if it be possible, the Return of the Members into their several Countries, will make the People still more firm. The most peaceable provinces, are now animated, and a Civil War is unavoidable, unless there be a quick Change of British Measures. The usual Events, no Question, will take place, if that happens—Victories and Defeats. But what will be the *final* consequence? If she fails, immediate Distress, if not Ruin. If she conquers, Destruction at last. But from the best Judgment I can form, she will not wait long for her fate. Several European Powers, it is probable, will fall on, as soon as she is entangled with Us. If they should not, what can she affect at 3000 Miles Distance against at least four hundred thousand freemen, fighting pro aris et focis?[2]

I cannot but pity a brave and generous Nation thus plunged in Misfortune by a few worthless persons: but, it may be said, how can she retreat with Dignity, in the present position of Affairs? I answer, *her* Dignity is not at all concerned, unless it be, to punish those who have abused and betrayed her into Measures inconsistent with her Welfare. Is a Nation bound in Honor to support every mad or villainous Step of a Ministry? It is mean to persist in Errors because *We* have committed them; but what is to be said of those, who talk of asserting *their own* Dignity, by vindicating the errors of *others?*

The present Cause, is that of Bute, Mansfield, North, Bernard, Hutchinson and not of Great Britain. Let her renounce their detestable projects, which point at her as their ultimate Object, and reconcile herself to her Children, while their Minds are capable of Reconciliation. "Oh for a warning voice,"[3] to rouse them to Conviction of this important truth that—the Reconciliation depends on the passing Moments—and that the Opportunity will in a short time be as irrecoverably past as the Days beyond the flood. Every thing may *yet* be attributed to the *Misrepresentations* and *Mistakes* of *Ministers,* and universal Peace be established throughout the British World, only by a general Acknowledgment of this Truth, that—half a dozen Men are Fools or Knaves. If their Character for Ability and Integrity is to be maintained by wrecking the whole Empire, Monsr. Voltaire may write an addition to the Chapter on the Subject of little things producing great Events, that will be very entertaining to *Readers.*[4]

As to your Complaint against an Expression in a late Letter, know, Dear Sir, I wrote in agonies of Mind for my Brethren in Boston. I trembled, least something might have happened, which I could not only forgive but applaud, but which might have been eagerly and basely seized by others, as a Pretence for deserting them—This was the desire of Men in Philadelphia the most devoted to them—and under this apprehension, We agreed to make use of the strongest Expressions.

May the Father of Mercies, bestow every Blessing upon You, is the fervent Prayer of, my dear Sir, your faithful and affectionate Friend

John Dickinson

1. QP 51 (reel 29) MHS; "Memoir," 2:149–51; *Memoir,* pp. 168–70 ; Force, ed., *American Archives,* 4th series, 1:947–48.

2. Was this Dickinson's way of telling Quincy he knew Quincy wrote the piece under that nom de plume for the *Boston Gazette,* 11 September 1769 (see supra, pp. 32–35) or could his use of the phrase—common enough among Dickinson's contemporaries—have just been a coincidence?

3. Quoting Milton's *Paradise Lost,* Book IV, beginning at line 1: "Oh For the warning voice, which he who saw Th' Apocalypse heard in heav'n aloud . . ."

4. Quincy was familiar with Voltaire but the "Catalogue of Books" does not include Voltaire's *Philosophical Dictionary* which would have been translated into English and published in London in 1765. Dickinson was referring to Voltaire's chapter on "Chain of Events."

JOSIAH QUINCY SR. TO JQ

26 October[?]–3 November 1774[1]

Dear Son

It is now four Weeks since you sailed, and if my Prayers are heard, and the Petition of them granted, your Health is restored; your Voyage comfortable and your Arrival safe: News! that would be almost as joyfull and reviving to your aged Father, as to hear that, through your Mediation, Peace and Harmony were restored, between the Parent State, and her injured and oppressed Children upon this Continent.

I have not, nor shall forget to inform you of facts, as they have taken, or may take Place since you left us; but my retired Situation wont permit my gratifying you so much as I should, otherwise, be glad to.[2]

All the Tories and some of the Whigs resent your clandestine Departure. Many of the Former say, that as soon as your Arrival is known, you will be apprehended and secured. One in particular offered to lay 10 Guineas you were not gone to London, provided another 10 Guinea were laid, that you would not be hanged when you got there. Some say, you are gone to Holland, and from thence to the south of France. Others say, the general Congress have appointed, and Commissioned you their Agent at the Court of Great Britain, and that you had your Credentials and Instructions from them before you went away. Your Friends say, your principal Motive is the recovery of your Health, which if Providence should please to restore, they rest assured of your best Endeavours to procure, a Redress of the Grievances, and a speedy Removal of the intolerable Burthens, with which your native Country is, and has been long oppressed. I had almost forgot to tell you, that your Sister Quincy, who is here upon a Visit, says, she heard a Gentleman say, you loved money too much, to be trusted at a Court where every thing is bought and sold: That if they could not refute your Arguments in Defence of your Country, they would offer invincible Arguments to induce you to betray it. Thus you see, how much you are a general Subject of Conversations: Perhaps, there never was an american, not even a D[ickinson] nor a F[ranklin], whose Abilities have raised the Expectations of their American Brethren more than yours.[3] God Almighty grant, if your Life and Health is spared, that you may exceed them in every Respect.

I last Monday, dined with your Wife at her Fathers where I had the Pleasure of seeing and caressing both my dear grand Children. The lovely *Bouy* and his Mamma, I expect, the Week after next, will come and spend a Month or two with us.[4] When in Town I found two political Productions:—An Essay on the Constitutional Power of Great Britain over the Colonies in America, &c." and a Letter from Lord Lyttleton to Lord Chatham on the Quebec Bill.[5] They are each of them esteemed masterly Performances, by their respective Partizans. Before this reaches you, I doubt not you will have received the *Former* from its Author, whose distinguished Abilities shine through this equally, if not superior to his former Productions: however I regret his allowing Great Britain a Revenue from the Colonies, whilst she persists in her Claim of an exclusive Trade with them, which appears to me to be an over Ballance for all the Protection she has, or can afford us especially when it is considered that all the Profits resulting from the immense Extent of Territory, ceded to her at the treaty of Paris, remains solely to her. At the same Time we are restrained from the profitable whale and cod Fishery in the Bay of St. Lawrence, and straights of Belisle which we formerly enjoyed without Interruptions. But perhaps I am mistaken and therefore submit to his better Judgments.

If I am not greatly mistaken, there is not a single Argument in Lord Lyttleton's letter, whereby he endeavours to prove the Justice, Wisdom, Benevolence, and Policy of Parliament in indulging the Canadians with this french Law, which wont much more forcibly conclude in Behalf of these Colonies, that their respective Constitutions and Laws should remain inviolate, and thus Rights and Privileges secured by them upon no Pretence whatever be abridged.[6] Where then is the wisdom, the Benevolence and Justice of Parliament; and what besides low Cunning and left handed Policy could induce them to their past and present Violent Measures, which must ultimately be as injurious to them as they are, or can be, to us? But his Lordship in the Close of his Letter tells us it is necessary to conciliate the Affections of the Canadians and thereby induce them to assist Administration in *coercing* America. Read this Passage, attend to the meaning of it; and then, if you can, suppress your Indignation.

What! Have we Americans spent so much of our Blood and Treasure in aiding Britain to conquer Canada, that Britons and Canadians in Conjunction may now subjugate Us? Forbid it Heaven! Surely the Heart of a Canadian Savage would recoil at the horrid Thought.[7]

Is this the Policy, which he recommends as best calculated to unite natural born and adopted Subjects, in one common Bond of Interest, Affection and Duty? His Lordship's Letter, I own, has given me both Pleasure and Pain: Pleasure to find him emerging from the Follies and Dis[si]pation of heedless Youth to become a Man of Business and Importance: Pain to think his first political Essays should be opposed to the Sentiments of his Illustrious Uncle whose meaning, whether relatively to the Quebec Bill or this coercing America I apprehend he has intirely mistaken: Whose attachment to the natural and civil Rights of Mankind, as well as his friendly Disposition to his american fellow Subjects are too deeply impressed upon their Minds to be effaced by any thing Lord Littleton has said or can say to the contrary.[8] But I must quit the Subject[9] to tell you that the Boston news Papers are just come to hand with an Account of his Lordship's sudden Death. Had he lived I doubt not he would soon have viewed things in a very different Light.

By the same Conveyance came to hand a Letter from your Sister Lincoln, who ever since you left us, has been rambling to the Eastward as far as Portsmouth, and but just returned. The enclosed bit of Paper, contained in her Letter, will (I doubt not) afford you as much and more heartfelt joy, than it gave me; for which reason I transmit it to you. Your dear Sister Nancy will not be persuaded but that the inclosed Letter of her own inditing and writing will be some amusement to you.

I forgot to tell you that Sister Betsey had a hearty crying Spell to think she was not worthy to be trusted with the secret of your going: however, she desires to be remembered to you, with her best Wishes for the Recovery of your health, success in your Business and a speedy and safe Return.

The New Papers will inform you of the Death and Character of Mr. Molineaux who to the last Breath was anxious for the publick safety and it is more than probable, you will hear also of the premature Death of poor Tommy Gray, who a few Days since returning from Plymouth, was overset in his Carriage, broke both the Bones of one of his Legs, and other one bruised so as that his Life is dispaired of.[10]

The Reputation of our Friend Mr C—g,[11] is greatly and I hear deservedly suffering, on Account of his applying the money he received out ot the Treasury to be remitted for the brass Cannon, to the Discharge of his private Obligations, which, if true, is an infamous breach of Trust.

Mr. Bowen, who preached to us last Sunday, and lodged with us the ensuing Night, said, Mr. Gordon of Roxbury[12] shewed him a Paragraph of a Letter from his Friend in Philadelphia, wherein he tells him, they thought their Speaker Mr Galloway a man of learning and a fine orator, but, that 50 such Heads compounded, would not make a John Adams.[13] I hope, for his sake, such an hyperbolical Encomium will never come to his Knowledge. Thus, I have filled my Pages with Currency, down to the 3d of November; and have only Room to add, the affectionate Regards of your good Mamma, joined to those of

Your unalterably fond Parent J Quincy

1. QP 51 (reel 29); "Memoir," 2:138–41; *Memoir,* pp. 160–62; Force, ed., *American Archives,* 4th series 1:952; Howe, "Letters," pp. 479–82. Josiah Sr. may have begun the letter on October 26th, but he did not complete it until at least November 3rd, as he stated in the letter itself. Eliza Susan Quincy transcribed the full letter for the "Memoir," 2:138–41, but deleted portions from the *Memoir,* pp. 160–62, and inserted "Braintree October 1774" at the top. Force worked from the printed *Memoir* and dated the letter October 31st. Howe worked from the original and may have deduced the start date that he used, October 26th ("four weeks since . . .").

2. Eliza Susan Quincy could not resist adding "do" in the *Memoir,* p. 160, to better end the sentence.

3. Eliza Susan Quincy excised everything after the sentence ending "oppressed" until this point in the *Memoir.*

4. She also deleted the first two sentences of this paragraph.

5. [John Dickinson], *An Essay on the constitutional power of Great-Britain over the colonies in America* (Philadelphia: William and Thomas Bradford, 1774); *A Letter from Thomas Lord Lyttelton, to William Pitt, Earl of Chatham, on the Quebec Bill* (Boston: Mills and Hicks, 1774).

6. Quincy Sr. referred to the anonymously authored *A Letter To The Earl of Chatham On The Quebec Bill* (London: T. Cadell, 1774), which, at the time, was assumed by some (including Josiah Sr.) to have been written by Thomas, the second baron Lyttelton. See Adams, ed., *American Controversy,* 1:224, for the suggestion that Sir William Meredith may have been the actual author. Thomas Lyttelton had succeeded his father, George, the first baron, just the year before. While his father chose to keep out of the limelight and not be too tied to any particular faction, his family connections to the Grenvilles and William Pitt notwithstanding, the younger Lyttelton cut a more rakish figure. Pitt (Chatham) was the "Illustrious Uncle" Quincy Sr. alluded to later in the letter. Lyttelton supported the Quebec Act, despite disagreeing with North over Parliament's authority to tax the colonies (he leaned more toward Pitt), proof, again, that constitutional differences did not necessarily determine political positions. For his part, Lyttelton supported the use of force in 1775, then changed his position to oppose the war, just before he died suddenly in 1779.

7. This last sentence does not appear in the *Memoir.*

8. Everything after the sentence-ending "Duty" to this point was left out of the *Memoir.*

9. Everything from this point was jumped over in the *Memoir* until the closing that begins "I have filled . . ."

10. See infra, p. 292.

11. Thomas Cushing, speaker of the Massachusetts house of representatives.

12. The Reverend William Gordon, who crossed over from England before the war erupted, served as the pastor of a congregational church in Roxbury, then returned to England after the war and wrote a three-volume history of the American Revolution, published in London in 1788 and in an American edition the next year.

13. Joseph Galloway of Pennsylvania, onetime political ally of Benjamin Franklin, whose proposal at the first Continental Congress to save the empire by restructuring it along the lines that Franklin had first suggested twenty years before, went down to defeat. Embittered by what he considered the conspiratorial actions of the "radicals" there, Galloway eventually went into exile. For his failed plan see Julian Boyd, *Anglo-American Union* (Philadelphia: University of Pennsylvania Press, 1941); and John E. Ferling's *The Loyalist Mind* (University Park, Pa.: Pennsylvania State University Press, 1977).

JAMES LOVELL TO JQ

3 November 1774[1]

Dear Sir Novr. 3d 1774

For the same Reasons which I have given already for writing by Dundass (be the Name of the Vessel what it will) I add a few Lines. You will receive the Proceedings of our Congress which is adjourned to the 25th and of the general Congress which is adjourned till May, from the gazettes. Indeed you will know more of the last than I can give you as you will know the Contents of the *Petition* to the King, and the *Address* to the *Inhabitants* of Britain,[2] if you do not of that to the Inhabitants of North America and Canada in particular. The non Importation and non Exportation and non Consumption will fly by the Birds of Heaven doubtless.

We are in a little Snarl which I hope will be settled at this Day's Town Meeting. Jemmy Richardson and Thomas Crafts having often had Conversation with Major Sheriff and sometimes with Mr. Gage were hereby induced to propose and carry, at a very *small* late Adjournment, a Committee to confer with said Gage upon a Mode of keeping Peace and Quiet with 8 Regiments and more scattered among us this Winter, which you will fully conclude impossible. They received Proposals such as might naturally be expected from a Man who cannot possibly remember in the Hurry of his great military Employment, that he is at the Head of our mangled civil magistracy. These Proposals were received in a proper Light and debate had upon them, in which Mr. Otis spoke cool and consequently up to the Hub, but Church's Keeness raised such a Warmth that the Meeting was adjourned till Today.[3] When I hope the Committee will resign all Care of the Town back into the Hands of the Select Men. This Proceeding has had too much the Air of Coalescence with the Idea of a garrisoned Town, and wounded that Delicacy which had hitherto been observed upon that stead. I said the General forgot the Government you are not to think he will not put *Soldiers* under Guard, and thereby *satisfy* the grossest Abuse of *Officer*s upon the civil magistracy. Wiswall[4] whose first Wife died any how at Cambridge, and whose second the Brigadier's Doctor gave an Affidavit the Devil did *not* run away with, and whose third kept a Dram- and Bawdy-House near the Ferry, by which the Guard there was always intoxicated more or less, in particular one Evening the whole being drunk wounded one of the Ferrymen badly, and were *all put under Guard.* This same Wiswall and Wife were ordered out of Town sec. Leg.[5] last May and upon fresh Complaints she was carry'd to Charlestown by a Constable the Day before Yesterday, but Lt. Col. Boquet of the 5th,[6] upon Complaint of the flying Husband that he was persecuted for Connexion with Camp, sent a Party who pursued to Charlestown and seized the Woman from the Constable before the Charlestown People could afford him Aid against Men who with loaded musquets & Bayonets fixed threatned to destroy all Opposition. The General yesterday being pressed by our Select-Men ordered *Col. B.* to put the *Soldiers* under Guard, and I suppose will do the same as often as M B or Capt C. or Corporal D. shall abuse to call the Lives of the Inhabitants to Risque, and if Death is the Consequence of that Call, he will *send them under Guard* to Lord North who will most cordially thank them for their Services.

The *Owners* of a Quantity of Tea at Maryland have burnt Ship and Cargo of Tea after taking out other Things,[7] as much of their *own Accord* as some Counsellors on Mandamus have resigned. I wish one of Today's Papers may reach you, that you may see whether the Fugitives regard the Stigma of the Congresses this being the last Day of Grace. Adieu—James Lovell——

Capt. Trumbull the Governor's oldest Son is now with me and I have a Letter from Major Parsons.[8] Nothing can exceed the Spirit of that Colony in their military Aims. A Priest *Peters,* whom you will have seen before this reaches, has wrote such Threats of the mighty Things he would do against their Charter that they are determined to be perfectly ready. However, the Episcopal Clergy his Brethren there were in Convention, and drawing up his infamous Character to send to the Society whose Servant he is for Propagating the Gospel in that *heathenish* Land.[9] Pray get some Knowledge of the Part *Caner*[10] has taken, and compare it with what shall be given from Connecticutt where the man is truly known. Judge Auchmuty and Mr. Troutbeck[11] are ashamed of being even supposed to have taken Part with him, though you will find he has used their Names in his published Letters.

There has been an Uneasiness at Newport in which there had nearly been broken Heads upon a Design of some to furnish Blankets. Maryland refused their Flour till the Congress advised them to send it to Lloyd for the Army. Such is the Sand-Rope. I might mention no more Lumber can they get from the Eastward. If no other Correspondent obeys you, I am sure you must allow I write according to Order, *any thing* and perform it *any how*.

I imagine the Ministry will receive Letters by this Opportunity which will embarrass them more than how to get the Port open, which God grant may be never unless the other Acts dye with the Port-Bill. How are the obstinate miscreants who continue yet in this Town to be secured from Inquiry without a Garrison? You will receive the highest Paintings from them of Danger to their Lives and Property. The first they know in their Consciences are secured by the Education of this Country, and as to the other they must take their Chance. I believe myself that their grain may rot in the Field for Want of Reapers, more than they can muster in their own Family. This and a long &c of that Kind they may look for. They esteem themselves of such Importance that the Ministry must keep up the Discontent of whole Continents upon their Accounts only though their personal Security is evident by the Rides they take to Cambridge and other places, and their passing and repassing from their Card Clubs at all Hours in the Dark as well as by Day Light.

1. QP 51 (reel 29) MHS; Howe, "Quincy Letters," pp. 472–73. On 2 April 1771, at the Old South meetinghouse, Lovell delivered the first oration commemorating the Boston "Massacre." By the time of Quincy's trip abroad, the Harvard-educated schoolmaster and member of the Sons of Liberty had become a leader in patriot politics. Waiting too long to leave Boston once the fighting erupted, he was taken as a prisoner to Halifax when the British evacuated, was exchanged, returned to patriot politics and served in the Continental Congress.

2. Which are printed in Worthington C. Ford, *Journals of the Continental Congress*, 34 vols. (Washington, D.C.: Government Printing Office, 1904-1937), 1:115–22 and 1:82–90, resp.; and widely reprinted in the colonial press.

3. Dr. Benjamin Church, not yet exposed as a traitor—the appellation by which he is most remembered. Inoculation enthusiast, Son of Liberty, deliverer of the "Massacre" oration the year before, Church was apparently already reporting to Thomas Gage on the activities of his associates in the patriot cause. His treachery would not be discovered for many months, well after the shooting had started and he was heading the medical department for the Army of the United Colonies under Washington. There is a brief essay on Church in Sibley, *Harvard Graduates*, 13:380–98. David James Kiracoffe revisits Church's case and the difficulty of determining when treachery constitutes treason under law in "Dr. Benjamin Church and the Dilemma of Treason in Revolutionary Massachusetts" *New England Quarterly* 70 (1997):443–62.

4. Daniel Wiswall.

5. That is, "according to law."

6. Howe, ed., "Letters," p. 473, changes the identity to that of Lieut. Col. William Walcott.

7. The brigantine *Peggy Stewart* docked at Annapolis in October 1774 with a cargo of East India Company tea. The local owners paid the duties but were put under intense pressure not to unload and sell the tea. So, instead, they allowed the ship to be burned, with the tea still on board, in the harbor.

8. Jonathan Trumball stayed in Cambridge after completing his studies at Harvard and found a place as a staff officer in the army under Washington. After two years in the field he would return to Boston, where he halfheartedly pursued a career as a merchant. His deeper desire was to be an artist, so he crossed over to England, with the war still going, to study under Benjamin West, an expatriate who had made a name for himself in London society. It would take Trumball a decade to become modestly successful as a portraitist, and another two decades before he embarked on his commissioned work to capture dramatic moments from the history of the American Revolution on canvas.

9. Samuel Peters. His letter, dated October 1st, Boston, was printed in the *Boston Evening-Post,* 24 October 1774. In the paragraph leading into the letter he was derided as a "diabolical Incendiary" and a "detestable Parricide."

10. The Reverend Henry Caner, rector of King's Chapel, the center of the Anglican Church in Boston. He would be among those who fled Boston with the British evacuation in March 1776.

11. Robert Auchmuty had become a vice-admiralty judge, after success as a lawyer in Boston (including as a defense counsel with Adams and Quincy in the Preston trial). Siding with the empire, he would eventually be obliged to flee Boston with other loyalists. The Reverend John Troutbeck was associated with the King's Chapel Anglican congregation in Boston. He too would go into exile.

CHARLES CHAUNCY TO JQ

3 November 1774[1]

Dear Sir, Boston Novr. 3d 1774

The inclosed letter I wrote with a view of its going by the first vessel that went from us since you embarked for London. But the vessel unhappily sailed before it got to Marblehead. The special reason of my writing was, that you might see a few resolves of our continental Congress, as I supposed this would give you the first sight of them.

The fortifications at the neck are nearly finished; the troops sent for from Philadelphia, New-York, and Canada are mostly, if not wholly, arrived. The Grand Congress, it is supposed, are broke up, either by dissolution or adjournment. Our delegates are expected in town next week. Our provincial congress is likewise adjourned to the 13th of this instant November. You will see what has been done by both the congresses, so far as what they have done is known, by the news-papers; the whole of which, from the time of your leaving us till this day, are sent with Mr. Hyslop by this opportunity; and he will, as he had been desired, let you have the use of them that you desired, and they have not been sent to you. Poor Molineux is dead, and died suddenly. Mr. Thomas Gray, in coming from Plymouth was thrown out of his chaise, by which means he dislocated his shoulder, was bruised in his body, and had one of his legs broken and gravely shattered. He is thought to be very dangerous, and more likely to die than to live. Our sufferings in the town increase as the winter comes on; and our situation is the more distressingly difficult, as we are so guarded both by sea and land, that we may be restrained from going out of town and may lie at the mercy of those who are sent on purpose to distress us. Would our circumstances permit it, the town would be immediately evacuated of its proper inhabitants; and this will certainly be the case should administration determine to proceed in an hostile manner against us. It may be depended on, that the Colonies are marvellously united, and determined to act as one in the defence of this town and Province, which they esteem the same thing with defending themselves. We are impatient to hear, what is likely to be the result of administration upon their knowing, as they do by this time, the union there is in the Colonies in their resolution to defend their rights and liberties even to the utmost. The spirit in the Colonies, especially the four New-England ones, instead of being lowered since you went from us, is raised to a still greater height; insomuch, that there may be danger of a rashness and precipitancy in their conduct. I hope all prudent care will be taken to govern its operations by the rule of wisdom. It is the wish of every sober understanding man among us, that harmony, love and peace may be restored between Great Britain and the Colonies. They dread nothing more, *slavery* only excepted, than a bloody conflict for the security of their liberties; and yet this, so far as I am able to judge, they will readily and universally go into, rather than submit to such cruelly hard and tyrannical measures as are imposed on them.

I trust you are, by this time, in London. The weather has been uncommonly clear and mild from the time you took your departure from us. We have had scarce a foul day from that time to this.

Wishing you prosperity in all your affairs, especially in your endeavours to serve your Country, I am,

Your assured friend and humble Servant,
Charles Chauncy

1. QP 51 (reel 29) MHS; "Memoir." 2:152–53 ; *Memoir,* pp. 170–72; Force, ed., *American Archives,* 4th series, 1:958.

CHARLES CHAUNCY TO JQ

4 November 1774[1]

Dear Sir, Boston Novr. 4th 1774

I wrote you yesterday, and delivered what I had wrote, with two pamphlets, to the care of Capt. Cal[e]f, who promised he would with his own hands, give what I had by him to Mr. Thomas Broomfield for you.

Last night the Continental Congress's non-importation and non-exportations, and non-consumption agreement came to town, and were printed this morning.[2] As it is highly important that this agreement should be known in England, I could not refrain taking this first opportunity of sending it to you. In the utmost hurry, as you see by my writing, I am

Your Friend and humble Servant,
Charles Chauncy

1. QP 51 (reel 29) MHS.

2. Chauncy appears to be referring to a broadside printed by the Fleet brothers (publishers of the *Boston Evening-Post)*, laying out the component parts of The Association, approved by Congress on October 20th.

JQ TO ABIGAIL QUINCY

5, 8 November 1774[1]

Dear Partner of my Life, At Sea. About Latitude 49° 45m N

1774 Nov. 5. 2 in the morning

We generally estimate the value of our possessions by their loss, and the worth of our friends is seldom better realized, than in their absence. As therefore when removed from you I most sensible *feel* how dear you are to me, I cannot resist the impulse of my heart to impart my affectionate emotions. And I the rather transmit to you the pleasing intelligence, that I look towards you as my most valuable treasure; because in the former periods of my affection I was never given to flattery, and in the present stage of our Love (being both useless and unfashionable), I shall not be suspected of it.[2]

Believe me my Dear wife, you cannot think with how much tender solicitude I look towards you and my Little Ones. My Country, my friends and family occupy my whole thoughts, and while I see myself blessed with a promising prospect of doing some little service to the One, and of being returned in safety to the others, it inspires me with sensations I must leave you to realize. And why should I detain you with reflections and sentiments, while to a Bosom friend (who is absent) nothing can be more gratefull, than to tell you how *I have been* and *where I am.*

After an agreeable and very refreshing ride to Salem, We sailed from thence about X in the morning and was clear of the Land about 2 in the afternoon. Though the weather was fine, yet in less than an hour I was confined to my cabin, but was happy in finding my sickness neither so violent or unremitting as in my former voyage: and more peculiarly so, in finding my spasms and pains so far from returning, that all symptoms of them left me from the moment of being ill.[3]

Five and twenty days rolled away with much of the uninteresting vacuity and sameness of a sea-life. I had however the pleasure of perceiving a gradual daily advantage from my voyage, and my retired moments were gratefull in reflecting upon the many prayers and benisons which were breathed toward me by my American friends.

Such was the unremitted favor of the winds during the whole of the preceeding period as that we never failed of being able to lay one course, which was a circumstance no one on board had ever known for so long a time, except in the Latitudes of the trade-winds. But this felicity was in a great measure destroyed by the poor improvement we were able to make of it. Our ship was deep laden and as bad a sailer as was ever navigated by a Dutch commander. Not a skiff in the ocean but what passed by Us, as if we had been at anchor. Had we been only in a tolerable-going ship we should in all probability been at the Land's-end in one or two and twenty days. Instead of which, at the end of about eight and twenty the winds set in strong at SouthEast, while they have continued ever since, and seem at this time as likely to continue as ever. These circumstances at Sea are a little more vexatious, than those at land easily imagine. But as for myself I had less reason, than any one on board to be uneasy. Every day hath surprisingly added to my health. The benefit from *the sea* is far beyond any thing experienced in my voyage to South Carolina. Ever since the day I left land I have never had one symptom of my former complaints. They did not leave me by degrees, but entirely and at once. So that while writing this, no one on board appears freer from disorder, and none most certainly in better spirits. Indeed if it were not for my concerns about America and my friends there, I should not feel one uneasy sensation. They frequently rally me on ship-board about my appetite and encreasing *size,* but though I don't think they have any great occasion for this, yet I am satisfied my colour and complexion have so wholly changed since my departure, as that my friends who saw me leave land would now scarce know me. But enough about *myself.* My only excuse for which is that among near friends, the *minutiae* of their concerns are interesting and acceptable.

All on Ship-board are well, except Old Mr. Hyslop, who this two or three days just past has complained of much weakness. Indeed he is too old a man for such a tour, and he I believe begins to suspect it himself. He has a fetid disorder upon him which is an incessant vexation, and will undoubtedly in the end prove too much for him. Dr. Paine of Worcester hath had considerable of the bloody flux, but is now I think well recovered of it.[4]

Tell my American friends, that I see more reason than ever that they should write me minute states of facts. Tell them the period to false representations of American affairs is not yet come. I shall probably enlarge on this head in another Letter, and if I should write under a new signature, you must not be surprised.

I know not by what opportunity I shall send this. The season is so far advanced, and the winds have of late been so favorable for the departure of American-bound ships, it is probably I shall have no very speedy conveyance. However, as there is a possibility of meeting some vessel bound to one of the Colonies, either in the Channell or Dover, I write at this time, so as to be able to embrace the opportunity on the shortest notice.

Kiss my Little ones for me and tell all my friends I remember them—I hope as I ought. As for my wife, I can tell her nothing so expressive of my Love toward her, as that I am her

J.Q. jr.

1774 November 8 10 c'clock in the morning. Just stepping aboard a Pilot Boat and going up to Falmouth 202 miles distant from London. I take a stage or Post Chaise for London—In very great haste—equal health and Spirits.

Yours as before

JQ——y

P.S. I think I was never better, if so well in my life.

1. QP 51 (reel 29) MHS; "Memoir," 2:166–69; *Memoir,* pp. 187–89. This is the first of Josiah Jr.'s (surviving?) letters to Abigail written on this journey. At the time Josiah Jr. wrote, they had two children, the son born in 1772 and named for him, and the daughter born not long before he left, named for her. The son, of course, lived a long life; the daughter died not long before her father. Part of Eliza Susan Quincy's objective in keeping her grandfather's memory alive was also to pay tribute to her grandmother. Theirs, she felt, was a true partnership built on mutual love and respect. See the grieving Abigail's letters to her father-in-law and sister-in-law of 18 September and 11 November 1775, resp., at infra, pp. 396–97 and 401–2, and the brief comments in Coquillette and York, eds., *Portrait of a Patriot,* 1:44–45.

2. The rest of this paragraph, after the sentence ending with "absence," was not included in the printed version.

3. Quincy scratched out the paragraph following this so completely that is now impossible to read.

4. Boston merchant William Hyslop and Dr. William Paine of Worcester.

JOSEPH REED TO JQ

6 November 1774[1]

Dear Sir Phila. Nov. 6th 1774

I wrote you the latter End of last Month, expecting it would be the first Advice you would receive of the Proceedings of the American Congress. But by a Delay of the Vessel and her being obliged to put into New York in Distress it is probable my well intended Efforts will fail. The Congress broke up soon after and your Boston Brethren returned in high Spirits at the happy and harmonious Issue of this important Business. Since that Time there has been a Stagnation of publick Intelligence and Advices. On Saturday next agreeable to the Directions of the Congress a great Committee is to be chosen in this City to carry The Association of the Congress into Execution. The Quakers who you know form a considerable Part in this City act their usual pusillanimous Part. They have directed their Members not to serve on the Committee, and mean to continue the same undecisive neutral Conduct untill they see how the Scale is like to preponderate; then I doubt not they will contribute to the Relief of Boston and appear forward in the Cause, but American Liberty in the mean Time must take her Chance for them. However there is no Danger of the Enemy being let in through this City. There is a Band of staunch chosen Sons of Liberty among some of our best Families who are backed by the Body of the People in such a Manner that no discontented Spirit dare oppose the Measures necessary for the publick Safety. I am more afraid of New York there has been a strange Delinquincy and Backwardness during the whole Summer and though their Delegates came into all the Measures, yet it was not untill they perceived they should be nearly alone and win ashamed of their Singularity in the glorious Cause.[2] If you have any Correspondence there I wish you would endeavour to animate them, while they are attending to the little paltry Disputes which their own Parties have produced. The great Cause is suffering in their Hands. There is too much Reason to fear the powerful Rhetorick of Corruption in which the present Administration is too well versed has not been used in vain. Their publick Papers are the vilest Collection of publick Invective upon the Cause of every private Character that appears in suppport of it and are so replete with Falshoods invented to mislead and deceive that we have little Doubt they are bought by some Agent of Administration and applied to promote the infamous Purposes. You must therefore hear and read from there with some Caution. You see by the Example I set you of writing by every Vessel that you cannot oblige me more than by letting me hear often from you. I heartily wish you Health and as much Happiness as the Situation of your suffering Country will allow you to take and am with much Esteem, Dear Sir,

Your very obedient and Affectionate Humble Servant,
J. R.

P.S. I have inclosed you a News Paper containing a Letter from the Congress to the Canadians which was published after I wrote you last. The villainous Tricks of the Post office against which we are cautioned from your Side the Water induce me only to put the Initials of my Name but I trust you will be at no Loss to determine who this Letter is from.

1. QP 51 (reel 29) MHS; "Memoir," 2:154–55; *Memoir*, pp. 172–74; Force, ed., *American Archives*, 4th series, 1:963–64. For the problems that beset New York see Joseph S. Tiedemann, *Reluctant Revolutionaries* (Ithaca, N.Y.: Cornell University Press, 1997); and Carl Becker's classic *The History of Political Parties in the Province of New York, 1760–1776* (Madison, Wis.: University of Wisconsin, 1909).

2. The sentence is ended at "Summer" in the printed version—Eliza Susan Quincy and her father not wanting to include a passage so critical of New Yorkers ostensibly united in the common cause?

JQ TO ABIGAIL QUINCY

8 November 1774[1]

Dear — Falmouth, Great Britain Nov. 8 1774

I have already wrote[2] you this day. I shall therefore write nothing very material at this time.

I am now on shore; everything around me happy and agreeable as *to myself.* The people crowd round me eager to hear about American affairs. I gratify their itching ears.

This place in situation is delightfull; the Country and cultivation surpass description. I long to paint the Scenes around me. All things are heightened by my uncommon health and spirits. I am almost afraid I shall meet with a damper, but I was never better prepared to conflict with adversity.

Since writing the above I have been regaled with the profusions of Great Britain to *those who have money.* We had a most delicate desert of Portugal grapes.

I have read also about 20 of the Late London Papers. I would have sent them, but could not procure them for money. They contain the resolves of the Congress relative to the Suffolk Proceedings.[3]

They also seem to breathe a spirit favorable to America. I am in some pain on finding that six Men of War sailed for Boston on the 26 of October.

I have conversed with several sensible people here. I have not yet met one, but what wish well to the Americans and one or two expressed great veneration for "the Brave Bostonians."

We have a report that the Congress have agreed upon a Non importation agreement and also upon a non exportation agreement to commence the first of august next.

I have also been informed that Lord North had desired leave of his Majesty to resign; to which the King replied "Your Lordship's policy hath made an American snarl, and your Lordship's dexterity must untie it, or it must *be cut*—And when Englishmen once begin *that work,* they will probably go much further."

I have no room for more, except that tomorrow I proceed towards Plymouth by Land.

Adieu,

JQuincy

1. QP 51 (reel 29) MHS; *Memoir*, pp. 190–91.
2. Which Eliza Susan Quincy converted to "written" for the *Memoir.*
3. Ammerman, *Common Cause,* discusses Congress's response to the Suffolk Resolves, pp. 74-75, 90–92 and passim; the Resolves themselves are in Ford, ed., *Journals of Congress*, 1:32–39.

NATHANIEL APPLETON TO JQ

15 November 1774[1]

Sir

When I parted with you I fully intended to have wrote you before this time. Be assured I have not been unmindfull of you, but public and private business have intirely engrossed my time.

Your leaving this Country so privately has been matter of generall speculation. Some say you went away through fear, others that you went to make your peace, others that you went charged with important papers from the Continental Congress. Many conjecture you were gone to Holland. Upon the whole it was a nine days wonder. Since you left us there has been a Provincial Congress which consisted of about 250 members, in which matters of the greatest importance were debated. All their proceedings, which I have liberty to communicate, you will see in the prints.

The Town continues to meet from time to time without molestation and indeed they determine to; there has been frequent affrays between the Inhabitants and Soldiers which have generally ended to the mortification of the latter. The Selectmen and towns' Committees have frequent interviews with the General. He declares he has no expectations that this People will ever submitt to the late Acts. He converses much freer with the Inhabitants than Hutchinson did on matters of a public nature, though we are not off our guard[,] knowing that it is the part of [a] Generall to deceive. The Inhabitants persisted in refusing to build Barracks for the Soldiers, but have in some measures assisted them in refitting old houses and stores.

This Fall has been remarkably moderate so that the soldiers are but now entering their Winter quarters. The Main Guard is kept at George Lorings Warehouse in King's Street. Almost the whole soldiery in America are now collected in this Town. The new erected Fortifications on the Neck are laughed at by our old Louisburgher soldiers as *mud walls* in compare with what *they* have subdued, and were it necessary they would regard them no more than a Beaver's dam.[2] The Spirit of the Inhabitants both in Town and Country are as firm as ever, determined to defend their Rights to the utmost. The Grand Continental Congress broke up 26th ultimo and our Members all returned safe last wednesday evening. The Bells rang the whole Evening; an Extract of their proceedings you will doubtless have before this reaches you. It is the universal Voice of this People that they will sacredly observe the injunctions and recommendations of the Grand Congress.

The Provincial Congress meet by adjournment 23 instant. The Neighbouring Towns and Colonies continue to send in their generous Donations to the Poor of this town. We have our Woolen manufactory in good forwardness, having compleated a considerable quantity of Baizes; and should it be necessary we see that we could easily carry on any branch of woolen or Linnen manufactures.

We have great expectations from your abilities and attachment to the Rights and Liberties of your country. We are sure you will not be an idle spectator, but will with your usual spirit (if you have health) be an active advocate for *truth* and *justice,* which is all we wish to take place in our present unhappy disputes with great Britain. It is said the ministry cannot receed now they have gone so far. I wish they would consult the good Bishop of Asaph who I am sure could put them into an honorable way.[3]

W. Molineaux died after short illness about 3 weeks past. All friends that I recollect are well, presume you will receive several Letters from your friends by this opportunity which will doubtless be more entertaining than I can be. Depending upon a line from you as soon as your leisure will permit. I conclude at present with great respect

Your sincere friend and Humble Servant,
Nathaniel Appleton

1. QP 51 (reel 29) MHS; *Memoir,* pp. 174–76; Force, ed., *American Archives,* 4th series, 1:980. Nathaniel Appleton was a Boston chandler who was very active in town politics, joining with those who protested attempts to raise revenue from the colonies through new navigation laws and sought to strengthen their hand through non-importation agreements. He was close to James Lovell.

2. Louisbourg fell to a combined colonial and British force in June 1745, the colonists providing most of the funding (for which there was some reimbursement by London) and men, and the Royal Navy a small fleet. It fell more easily than most had anticipated, its high stone walls insufficient protection for an undermanned, undersupplied garrison cut off from aid and reinforcements. Since Massachusetts provided most of the men and much of the funding, and William Pepperrell of the Maine country commanded the land forces, Bay Colonists consid-

ered the victory somehow primarily theirs. That Louisbourg and all of Cape Breton Island were returned to the French at the end of the war in 1748 proved an irritant to them at the time, turned into an underlying cause of revolution later—as proof that colonial needs were always secondary to those of the mother country, that the empire was not an effective community of interests, much less a true family.

3. Jonathan Shipley, Bishop of St. Asaph, a Welsh diocese, who often sided with Chatham in the House of Lords in opposing the North ministry's policies toward the American colonies. Paul H. Smith, ed., *English Defenders of American Freedom, 1774–1778* (Washington, D.C.: Library of Congress), pp. 9–14, discusses Shipley before reproducing one of his sermons and a speech he had written to deliver in the Lords.

JQ TO ABIGAIL QUINCY
17 November 1774[1]

My amiable and Dear Friend London 13th [17th] Nov. 1774
9 O'Clock in the Evening

About 10 hours ago I arrived in this great City, and am now snug at my lodgings near the Hay-market.[2]

With you and my real friends, the first object of enquiry will be about my health and spirits. In one word (for just now I am a man of too much business and importance to use many) they are both surprisingly fine, rather bordering upon extravagance, than under par. Indeed how could they be otherwise? From *sea* I landed in fine health, and have now finished a delightfull—a surprisingly delightfull journey of 300 miles. The scenes of Plymouth Docks, Stonehenge, Wilton House (containing the Statues, the Paintings, the furniture of the Earl of Pembroke on which volumes have been published to the world) beggar all description: nay, I will venture to say, that the imagination stretched to its utmost limits can't form any idea of their grandeur &c without a view. It wrecks my mind even in contemplation. The same may be said of Exeter and Salisbury Cathedrals. But why do I waste time upon any other subject, than my country?

I have spent about 2 hours today with Dr. Franklin. He appears the staunch friend of America, and confident of the ultimate success of its friends. He has promised me his patronage, and I have reason to believe him sincere. He enquired particularly after "his old friend" my Father, and rejoiced "at his happiness."

Young Mr. Jonathan Williams hath waited on me and treated me with great ability and politeness.[3] He lives with Dr Franklin, and told me, that on his waiting on him with intelligence of my arrival, he asked, if it was the author of the "Observation," &c, and being answered in the affirmative, He replied "I am very glad of it." You will discern a little vanity in the communication of this anecdote, but you have seen so many of my foibles before, I thought I would not hide this from you. Take care lest this communication don't infect your heart with its contagion.

Your Uncle B [Thomas Bromfield] hath showed me every mark of respect. He is a very amiable man. He told me, that when it was known today at the

New England Coffeehouse, that I had arrived, *certain* Americans made a great wonderment—"what I had come for."

One of the friends of Liberty in this City came to him also, and told him, that a certain Gentleman in the Coffee Room said—"Yes Q has been *blowing up* the *seeds of* sedition in America, and has now come to do the same here." I returned my compliments, and sent word, that, if I had done nothing but *blow up seeds,* they would probably be very harmless, as they would never take root, but if I should have the good fortune to *sow* any *here,* and they should afterwards *ripen,* He or the ministry *might blow them about* at their leisure.

I am well informed, that the friends of America increase here every day. In the West of England a very considerable manufacturer told me, that if the Americans stood out "we must come to their terms."

I find Our friends here dread nothing so much, as lest the Congress should *petition.* Should they adopt that mode it will be injurious to Our Cause.

The ministry have carried their men at the late election, but the people seem to be rousing.[4]

You see I have been a short time in London. I can as yet communicate, but little intelligence. A large field is opening to me. I am preparing for the course, with *feelings,* which render me careless whether I shall be *pursuing* or *pursued.*

Tell my political friends I shall soon write to them, and that when I informed Dr. Franklin of the pains I had taken to establish an extensive correspondence he rejoiced at it much. Let their intelligence be as frequent and as minute as possible. Let them *all* direct to Messrs Bromfield or Messer. Dilly.

This is the third Letter to you and 1 to Mr P[5] makes 4. Not a *line* as yet from America.

Salute all my friends with due respect, and accept of mine with the affection and sincerity of an antient lover.

JQ—y jr.

PS. Present my Compliments to Mr. Jonathan Williams,[6] and inform him of the health and happiness of his son, and those marks of respect and utility with which he has obliged me.

1. QP 51 (reel 29) MHS; *Memoir,* pp. 195–97. Quincy misdated this letter December 13th; Eliza Susan Quincy corrected it to the 17th. On the 13th Quincy was in Exeter, still four days out of London. It being a Sunday, he attended communion services at the cathedral there as well

as toured the city. See Coquillette and York, eds., *Portrait of a Patriot,* 1:226–27, from Quincy's journal of his journey to England.

2. He rented rooms from a Mrs. Lawrence at Arundel Street on Panton Square, in the Haymarket district, which put him about a ten-minute walk from Benjamin Franklin's lodgings on Craven Street.

3. After attending Harvard, Jonathan Williams traveled to London in 1770 to live with and assist his great-uncle Benjamin Franklin. He spent well over a decade in Europe, at various enterprises, before recrossing the Atlantic to become a military engineer, and eventually superintendent of West Point.

4. Bernard Donoughue, *British Politics and the American Revolution* (London: Macmillan, 1964), pp. 177–200; and Peter D. G. Thomas, *From the Tea Party to Independence* (Oxford: Clarendon Press, 1991), pp. 143–49 discuss the implications of the fall 1774 election for the Americans, when North obtained a more solid majority and, it is argued, better secured the hard-line policies that had been decided upon in the spring.

5. It is not clear to whom Quincy refers; perhaps his father-in-law, William Phillips. As such, it is yet another example of a lost letter in the very incomplete correspondence passed on to the present.

6. Boston merchant and the father of Franklin's grandnephew (see supra n. 3) and husband of Franklin's niece Grace, who was the daughter of Franklin's sister Anne.

JOSEPH WARREN TO JQ

21 November 1774[1]

Dear Sir Boston November 21st 1774

As Nothing interesting which I am at Liberty to communicate has taken place since your departure from hence, except such matters as you could not fail of being informed of by the publick papers, I have defered writing to you, knowing that upon first arrival in London, you would be greatly engaged in forming your Connections with the friends of this Country, to whom you had been recommended. Our friends, who have been at the Continental Congress, are in high spirits on account of the union which prevails throughout the Colonies. It is the united voice of America to preserve their freedom or lose their lives in defense of it. Their resolutions are not the effects of inconsiderate Rashness, but the sound result of sober inquiry and deliberation. I am convinced that the true Spirit of Liberty was never so universally diffused through all ranks and orders of People, in any Country on the face of the Earth as it now is through all North America.[2] The provincial Congress met at Concord at the time appointed; about 260 Members were present. You would have thought yourself in an Assembly of Spartans or ancient Romans, had you been a witness to the Order which inspired those who spoke upon the important business, which they were transacting. An injunction of secrecy prevents my giving any particulars of their transactions, except such as by their express order were published in the Papers; but in general you may be assured that they approved themselves the true Representatives of a wise and brave people, determined at all events to be free. I know I might be indulged in giving you an account of our transactions, was I sure this would get safe to you; but I dare not as the times are, risque so important intelligence. Next Wednesday the 23rd Instant, we shall meet again according to adjournment. All that I can safely communicate to you shall be speedily transmitted. I am of opinion that the dissolution of the british Parliament, which we were acquainted with last week, together with some favourable Letters received from England, will induce us to bear the inconvenience of living without government until we have some farther Intelligence of what may be expected from England; it will However require a very masterly policy to keep the Province for any considerable time longer in the present state. The town of Boston is by far the most moderate part of the Province. They are silent and inflexible. They hope for relief, but they have found by experience that they can bear to suffer more than their oppressors, or even themselves thought possible. They feel the Injuries they receive; they are the frequent subject of Conversation, but they take an honest pride in being singled out by a tyrannical Administration as the most determined enemies to arbitrary power. They know that their merits, not their crimes, have made them the objects of ministerial vengeance. We endeavour to live as peaceably as is possible with the soldiers; but disputes and quarrels often arise between the Inhabitants and the Troops. General Gage has made very few new manuvres since you left us; he has indeed rendered the Entrenchments at the entrance of the Town as formidable as he possibly could. I have frequently been sent to him on Committees and have several times had private conversations with him. I have thought him a man of honest, upright principles, and one desirous of accommodating the difference between great Britain and her Colonies in a just and Honorable way. He did not appear to be desirous of continuing the quarrel in order to make himself necessary, which is too often the case of Persons employed in publick affairs; but a copy of a letter via Philadelphia, said to be written from him to Lord North, gives a very different cast to his character. His answer to the provincial Congress which was certainly ill judged, I suppose was the work of some of that malicious group of Harpies whose disappointments make them desirous to urge the Governor to drive every thing to extremes.[3] But in this letter (if it be genuine) he seems to court the office of a Destroyer of the Liberties, and Murderer of the People of this province: but you have doubtless read the paper and thought with Indignation on the contents. I wish to know of you how affairs stand in great Britain, and what was the principle motive of the dissolution of Parliament. If the late acts of Parliament are not to be repealed the wisest Step for both Countries is fairly to separate, and not spend their blood and treasure in destroying each other. It is barely Possible that Britain may depopulate North America; but I trust in God she never can conquer the Inhabitants and if the cruel experiment is made, I am sure whatever fortunes may attend America that Britain will curse the wretch, who to stop the mouths of his ravenous pack of dependants, bartered away the wealth and Glory of her Empire. I have not time to say more at present, than to assure you that from this time you may expect to hear from me, news or no news by every vessel, and that my earnest wish is that your abilities and integrity may be of eminent service to your Country.

I am dear Sir you most obedient Servant,
Joseph Warren

1. QP 51 (reel 29) MHS; "Memoir," 2:156–59, QP 46 (reel 6) MHS; *Memoir,* pp. 176–79 ; Force, ed., *American Archives,* 4th series, 1:990–91. Dr. Joseph Warren is best remembered for having fought and died at Bunker Hill. Modest background notwithstanding, he had worked his way up in society, as a scholarship student at Harvard and as a successful physician in Boston–with Josiah Quincy Junior among his many patients. Most of his papers have not survived; John H. Cary's *Joseph Warren* (Urbana, Ill.: University of Illinois Press, 1961) remains the standard biography, the vague portrait painted there a reflection of that lack of sources.

2. This sentence and the one above it ("It is . . .") were turned into a "facsimile" for a page tipped in between pp. 176–77 of the *Memoir,* with a "facsimile" of Joseph Warren's signature added, along with Josiah Quincy Esq. as the addressee. A copy of it is also in the Simon Gratz Autograph Collection, #250B, Case 8 Box 16, HSP.

3. This letter, inferred to have been from Gage to North, had also purportedly been printed in the *London Chronicle,* 13 September 1774 (actually for September 13th–15th),which is why Warren assumed Quincy had seen it. It had been printed in both the *Boston Evening-Post* and *Boston Gazette* for 21 November 1774 (the same day that Warren wrote to Quincy), and Isaiah Thomas would reprint it in his *Massachusetts Spy* for November 24th. All three papers reported that the letter had been forwarded to them by yet another missive dated November 9th from Philadelphia. The Fleets later printed a retraction in their *Boston Evening-Post* on 28 November 1774, claiming that they had since learned that the letter was spurious and that it had not appeared in the London paper (they were right; it was not printed there). It is still not clear how the "letter" came into being in the first place. As forgeries went, it was not far off from what Gage was actually writing to the Earl of Dartmouth about his difficulties as governor and his frustrations with those in the Bay Colony who opposed him.

GEORGE GREEN TO JQ

23 November 1774[1]

Dear Sir, Wednesday Evening
23d Nov.

The next Saturday afternoon at 4 o'Clock is appointed by Mr. Keen and my Lady Huntingdon[2] for your drinking Tea with her Ladyship at her apartments near the Tabernacle, Moor fields; and I am desired to show you the way, which I will do with pleasure.

If you are not engaged to Dine on that day it is Mr. Keen's desire that you will Dine with him and myself at Islington, at a public house which he frequents there. I beg your answer directly by the penny post. You have nothing to do but write a few lines and give it to *Nelly* with a penny and order her to put it into the penny post office in Coventry Street, directing it agreeable to my Card No. 55 Northside St. Pauls and it will come safe to me in a few hours. If you can Dine there be with me at my Lodgings by 12 oClock on Saturday. If to drink Tea only be with me one hour before the time, my Lodgings being all in the way.

I am with much Affection, Your very Sincere friend and humble Servant

G. Green

For Salem. Capt. Coues, next Saturday
For N. York, Capt. Bussell—Ditto[3]

If you wish to get into the house of Lords next Tuesday to hear the King's Speech, and do not depend on any body else, let me know and I believe I can procure you a birth, though it is become immensely Difficult, Members of the House of Commons being frequently refused to bring in a friend with them.

I cannot be Easy before I put in writing what I hastily said by word of mouth last time I saw you, Vizt., That the person who *cautioned* you must have been wholly ignorant of my true Character, Spirit and Disposition, and of the nature of the application I had made, which is for a place perfectly agreeable to and paid by the people and without us we know they could not exist as a Government. That I am not asking favours myself but two Noble souls, particular friends of Lord Dartmouth, have taken the request wholly upon themselves and made it a matter of their own, as a favor to be done themselves. If I have occasion to do anything in the asking way I shall now ask it as a matter of right on account of the great and unmeritted injury I sustain by the Shuting up of the Port and Harbour of Boston, but it is not probable I shall have any such occasion. Lord Dartmouth does not approve of all the measures of Government. That I know for certain and I believe he is at heart really a friend to America, though officially obliged to do some things that are not quite agreeable, but he never approves of little tittle tattle or scandalous information, and if he did he would never have it from me even if it was necessary to obtain my desire. But as that is far from being the case it would be folly to the last degree in me, in every view of the matter, to do any such thing.[4]

1. QP 51 (reel 29) MHS; Howe, ed., "Quincy Letters," pp. 476–77. Originally from Boston, Green was by then living in London. The note was addressed to "Mr. Quincy, At Mrs. Laurence's, Arundel Street, Panton Square, Haymarket."

2. Howe, "London Journal," p. 445, suggested that "Keen" might have been Winstead Keene, whose wife was the sister of the Earl of Dartmouth (and therefore the half-sister of Lord North). Selina Hastings, widow of Theophilus Hastings, 9th Earl of Huntingdon, was a fixture in London society and close friend of Dartmouth, who shared her Methodism.

3. Quincy appears to be indicating the captains of the vessels by which he would be sending letters.

4. The Earl of Dartmouth, who succeeded the Earl of Hillsborough as secretary of state for American affairs, had a much less confrontational style than his predecessor. Colonists frustrated by what they deemed Hillsborough's inflexibility looked to Dartmouth to intercede on their behalf against the Coercive Acts. They misunderstood their position at Whitehall, and his views as well. B. D. Bargar, *Lord Dartmouth and the American Revolution* (Columbia, S.C.: University of South Carolina Press, 1965) remains the best starting point. I reviewed desperate attempts to stave off confrontation that were directed at Dartmouth in "Federalism and the Failure of Imperial Reform, 1774–1775," *History* 86 (2001):155–79.

JQ TO ABIGAIL QUINCY

24, 27 November 1774[1]

My very dear friend London Novr. 24th 1774

Having wrote[2] you many Letters, since my landing on this Island, as my Bosom friend, I now assume a new character, and address you as my political confidant.

Ever since my arrival here, I have been an object of much more attention and respect than I had any right to claim. However these circumstances have not flattered my vanity, because I know that it was not my merits that procured this distinction.

The first principle I laid down to regulate my conduct was to make no appearance in any noted Coffeehouses, and no very conspicuous figure in any public place. This contributed (especially after the daily papers noticed my arrival) to make me more enquired and sought after. The next rule I observed was, to wait upon no public Character, though ever so much sollicited, till the complements of a request to see me were first paid.

Lord North was the first who desired my attendance. Mr. Commissioner Morris next requested my dining with Him; and Lord Dartmouth, as soon as he arrived in Town appointed an hour for my attending him. With neither of these Gentlemen had I less than 2 hours conversation.[3]

I long to communicate the substance of these interviews, but I have not time to transcribe them from my Journal. Indeed I have not an hour's time to myself: the friends of liberty and the friends of the ministry engross my whole time. I am in a delicate situation. I have a very difficult task. Each party make great professions of friendship, with what views or sincerity you may conjecture.

Governor Pownall hath detained me several hours in conversation on American affairs, and is now writing on that subject.[4]

Dr Franklin and Mr. Sheriff Lee[5] with very many others appear my staunch friends. With these I spend, and shall spend, almost every day , considerable portions of time.

Critical as my situation is, yet (save the concern I feel for my country) I have high pleasure. My health is good beyond example and my spirits are truely American.

In *all* companies I have endeavoured to give a true state of the affairs of the Continent, and the genuine sentiments of its inhabitants. I find many things I advance are said to be novel, but I have openly and repeatedly declared (even to the Characters before mentioned) my willingness to meet and controvert *face to face* with *any* who dispute the justice of my opinions or the truth of what I relate. Whether it be a good or ill omen, my friends may judge, but certain it is, that all (even the highest with whom I have conversed) declare they have no doubt, but that my coming over will be of great service to both Countries. To a great officer of state who conveyed this sentiment, my reply was: "there is a certain *influence* which will counteract all I can possibly do." I was understood *not* to mean a *British* influence, and the reply was "perhaps not."

America hath none to fear so much as her own children. Some of these are inveterate and persevering beyond example or conception.

Seeing I have not time to give you a regular detail of all I have heard and seen, you will probably enquire, what is the substance of what you collect? What is your own private opinion? To gratify my friends on these heads was the cause of my snatching this hasty moment and transmitting my opinion.

The minds of people are strangely altered in this island. *The many* are now as prone to justify and applaud the Americans, as but a little while ago, they were ready to condemn and punish. I have conversed with almost all ranks of people for this fifteen days past; and having been in very large circles of the sensible part of the Community during that time, my opportunity for information was the more fortunate.

I came among a people, I was told, that breathed nothing but punishment and destruction against Boston and all America. I *found* a people who revere, love and most heartily wish well to Us. Nor is it strange, that it should be so. For abstracted from the pleasure that a good mind takes in seeing truth and justice prevail, it is *the interest*—the *highest private interest* of this whole nation to be our fast friends. And strange as it may seem, when you consider the conduct of the nation as represented in parliament, *the people* know it. Hence the following language hath been reiterated to me in various companies, and re-ecchoed with approbation and warmth.

"This nation is lost. Corruption and the influence of the Crown hath led Us into bondage, and a Standing Army hath rivetted our chains. To America only we look for our salvation. Tis there, and there only, that true virtue and genuine spirit is to be found. America can alone effect the removal of our oppressors; America alone is the place to which *we must fly.* Here we have no public virtue, but what is divided and destroyed *by party.* All opposition to Administration hath failed from this cause. Division among the friends of liberty is a curse of the Land. We do, and we must look toward America with infinite anxiety. 'Tis America only can save England! We are afraid of nothing but your division, and your want of perseverance. Unite and persevere [and] you must prevail, you must triumph."

This and similar language hath been held to me with a zeal that bespoke it came from the heart, with *a frequency,* that proved such sentiments dwelt upon the mind. I could name you the first characters for understanding, integrity and spirit who have held this language. But it would be indiscreet to name those, who might perhaps be discovered through *the indiscretion* of *American friends,* or the *prying* villainy of public conspirators. Bowdoin, Winthrop, Chauncey, Cooper, Warren &c can recollect who they introduced me to, and thence conjecture of those *few,* whose British hearts are thus *in America.*

Vast is the distress here,[6] lest the Congress should petition or remonstrate. In the acts of negotiation your adversaries are infinitely your superiors. If that mode of proceedure is adopted by the Congress, many, very many friends, will sink. They will desert your cause, from despondency. At present (as I am assured, and as I verily believe), could the voices of this nation be collected by any fair method, twenty to one would be in favor of the Americans. You wonder and say, then, whence is it, that they do not exert themselves? One American phrase will give you the true reason. *The people* are *cowed* by oppression. 'Tis amazing, tis incredible how much this is the case. Corruption, baseness, fraud, exorbitant oppression never so abounded as in this Island. As will you believe me, when I say, that *Englishmen,* that boasted race of freemen, are now sunk, are sunk in infamous submission.

From parliament, therefore, expect no favor but what proceeds from fear. From the people here expect no aid. 'Tis yourselves, 'tis yourselves, must save you. *And you are equal to the task.* Your friends know this, and your very enemies acknowledge it. But they believe you are as corrupt and as corruptible, as themselves; and as destitute of union, spirit and perseverance as the friends of freedom in this country.

For your country's sake! depend not upon Commercial plans for your safety.

The manufacturers *begin to feel,* they know, *they acknowledge,* they must feel severely, and if you persevere, they must be ruined. But what are these men, what are the body of this people? The servants of their masters. How easy [is] it for the ministry to frown or flatter them into silence? How easy to take the spoils of the nation and *for a season* fill the mouths of the clamorous? T is true *your persevrance* will occasion in time, that hunger, which will break through stone-walls. But how difficult is it, how impracticable is it for *mere commercial virtue* (if indeed it have any existence) *to persevere.* I repeat, therefore, depend *not* upon this scheme for your deliverance. I do not say renounce it, I say continue it, but look towards it, in vast subordination to those noble, generous and glorious exertions which alone can save you.

Before I came among this people, the friends of Liberty desponded, because they believed the Americans would give up. They saw the irretrievable ruin of *the whole cause* lost in that fatal yielding. I feel no despondency myself. I am sanguine my country must prevail. I feel the ardour of an American. I have lighted up the countenances of many. I am speaking conviction every day to more. In short I am infected with an Enthusiasm which I know to be contagious. Whether I have caught or spread the infection here, is no matter needfull determine.

[November 27th]

Since writing the above I have spent three hours in private conversation with Governor Pownall. He confirmed [to] me, that the People of Boston are not mistaken in *the man* who they have most reason to curse of all others. I have his very words down in my journal, but they are too many here to transcribe.

Tomorrow I am to see Lord Chatham.[7] In the afternoon I am to dine with Lady Huntingdon. On Tuesday I am to go to the House of Lords at the opening of Parliament, and on the same day shall converse with Lord George Saville.[8] My whole time is dedicated to the Common cause; my heart and soul are engaged in it.

Be carefull of what parts of this Letter you publish: without *absolute* necessity don't publish any. I shall be known here upon its coming over. That knowledge will destroy my future means of information, and do a great injury to my usefullness.

Dr. Franklin and others complain much of their Letters being made publick; 'tis fear of that prevents him and many more writing to you.

Dr. Franklin is an American in heart and soul. You may trust him. His Ideas are not contracted within the narrow limits of exemption from taxes, but are extended upon the broad scale of total emancipation. He is explicit and bold upon the subject and his hopes are as sanguine as my own of the triumph of Liberty in America.

It would entertain you if I could spare time to relate all that is said of me and my designs. But I have no leisure for amusements of this kind.

Not a line yet from America. Judge of my impatience to hear of your wellfare. Collect all the intelligence possible, and transmit accounts by *every* conveyance.

This is my 6th Letter. My last went inclosed to Mr. Mason. This I shall convey to Mr. Benjamin Clarke, but without any signature. Don't forget to pay the postage to him.

I have not time to correct or peruse this Letter.

Adieu! the support and blessing of Heaven be with you
and your assured friend,

Henry Ireton[9]

PS You are desired to let no part of this Letter be printed, but what Mr. Phillips[10] should advise to.

You may communicate a sight of it to all candid friends. And if it should fortunately happen, that a whole circle should be present, desire them to let one of the Company set down and *in their presence* give me their joint sentiments and *council.*

I yesterday heard two eminent bankers and three very wealthy merchants say, that as soon as America shall free herself from the tyranny of this Country they would take *their all* and remove to New England. And they affirmed, that they knew many more resolved to do the same.

Post PS. In the last ships sailed for Pennsylvania, under the Auspices of the Great Dr. Franklin, two very wealthy farmers (from the County of Norfolk) with their families to settle. If these should succeed hundreds will follow from that fertile county, which contains *the best husbandsmen* on the Island.

1. QP 51 (reel 29) MHS; transcribed in the "Memoir," 2:190b–97. QP 46 (reel 6) MHS (where she dated it simply November 27th); printed in the *Memoir*, pp. 205–12.

2. Once again changed to "written" by Eliza Susan Quincy in both the *Memoir*" and the *Memoir.*

3. North has long been one of the bogeymen of Revolutionary American history, his disrepute among American patriots only being matched by that of George Grenville. Even though North, like Grenville, believed that Parliament had the authority as well as the need to tax the colonists directly, he did not seek confrontation and did not take any sort of hard-line stand until after the Tea Party, over four years after he formed his ministry. Evenhanded biographies include Peter D. G. Thomas, *Lord North* (London: Allen Lane, 1976); and Peter Whiteley, *Lord North* (London: Hambledon Press, 1996). Corbyn Morris sat on the board of customs, capping a thirty-year career with the customs service. A mercantilist who supported the navigation system, he also saw the need for imperial reciprocity, wrote thoughtfully about issues concerning trade within the empire, and had been named a fellow of the Royal Society.

4. Thomas Pownall, an Englishman, had been a popular governor of Massachusetts during the French and Indian War. The more that difficulties arose between the Bay Colony and Britain, the more longing there was among a few in the Bay Colony for someone like him to play that role once again. He was a public advocate of imperial reform. Whether the changes he had in mind, if implemented, would have changed the destiny of Massachusetts in the empire must remain an unknown, a speculation in counterfactual history. John A. Schutz, *Thomas Pownall, British Defender of American Liberty* (Glendale, Calif.: A. H. Clark, 1951) is the only full-length biography. Pownall's ideas for reform are reviewed in G. H. Guttridge, "Thomas Pownall's *The Administration of the Colonies:* The Six Editions," *William and Mary Quarterly,* 3rd series 26 (1969):31–46.

5. William Lee and his brother Arthur had both gone to England over a decade before to make their reputations and restore their family fortune. William established himself as a merchant and became part of the opposition political movement associated with John Wilkes. He was successful in being named a sheriff of London but unsuccessful in a bid to win a seat in the House of Commons. He and his brother figure prominently in the escapades of their fellow expatriate from the colonies in London, *Stephen Sayre,* as told by John Alden (Baton Rouge, La.: Louisiana State University Press, 1983). Also see John Sainsbury, *Disaffected Patriots* (Kingston, Ont.: McGill-Queen's University Press, 1987).

6. Which Eliza Susan Quincy (or her father or even the printer?) changed to "Great is the anxiety . . ." in the *Memoir;* it is not rewritten in the "Memoir." This is one of several instances of such changes in just this one letter. Similar changes had been made in earlier letters, as they would be in later epistles.

7. Quincy had long admired Pitt, the "Great Commoner," who by this point had been sitting in the House of Lords as Earl of Chatham for eight years. Pitt styled himself a friend to America and in some sense he was: he denied that Parliament had the authority to tax the colonists directly, he thought the use of force to impose policies he deemed foolish even more foolish, and he was willing to work with the Continental Congress, if that is what it took to placate dissident Americans and restore a lost sense of community. Nonetheless, he believed that Parliament had to be supreme even if its constitutional powers were limited, and that Britain must reign sovereign over the empire, which meant that Americans had to accept their subordination once their rights were secured—if indeed he or anyone could have clearly delineated what those rights were. The best introduction to Pitt and his complexities and inconsistencies on such matters is Marie Peters, "The Myth of William Pitt, Earl of Chatham, Great Imperialist. Part II: Chatham and Imperial Reorganization, 1763–1778," *Journal of Imperial and Commonwealth History* 22 (1994):393–431.

8. Quincy was still learning the ropes of British politics. Sir George Savile, not a peer, was tied to the Marquis of Rockingham and had long sat for Yorkshire in the House of Commons. The baronet supported Wilkes in his quest to be seated there and he disagreed with policies aimed at coercing the colonists, from Grenville's ministry through North's, though he resisted taking too strident an opposition.

9. Ireton does not turn up in Quincy's other writings, but he was obviously a heroic figure to Josiah Jr. Originally from the Nottinghamshire gentry, he had attended Trinity College, Oxford, and studied law at the Middle Temple, but without becoming a barrister. Elected to the House of Commons because of his valor in the New Model Army during the civil war, he married a daughter of Oliver Cromwell. Pious, a Puritan not given to ostentatious display nor enriching himself by public service, Ireton had many admirers on the Roundhead side. Initially reluctant to depose Charles I and bring an end to monarchy, he eventually joined with the regicides. While sympathetic to those Levellers who wanted more radical political and social change, he tried to keep the army subordinate to Parliament. Even though he died in 1651 while campaigning in Ireland, that did not stop supporters of the Restoration a decade later from disinterring his remains to disgrace him posthumously.

10. Abigail's father.

JAMES LOVELL TO JQ

25 November 1774[1]

Dear Sir Boston Novr. 25th 1774

I imagine I may by this Time congratulate you upon a general Change in the Prejudices of the People of England with Regard to us Americans and our Claims. Be that as it may, I can certainly call on you to rejoice at the firm Continuance of that heaven-inspired Union of the Colonies, which you saw formed before you left us. I think it would not now be in the Power of the whole mercantile Interest of America, joined together in Devotion to the ministerial System of Tyranny, to beguile the country Yeomanry. The Multiplication of Committees out of the Sea-Ports, to see to the Execution of the Resolutions of the General Congress, gives a finishing Damp to the Spirits of Messers. the Importers under the former Combination. When Jackson and Taylor[2] can't see a Door of Escape open, we may safely conclude that the Eye of every other Son of Trafick will search in vain even for a Crevice.

Our private Accounts are such from Quebec as to make us think that Administration cannot possibly receive even from Governor Guy,[3] such strong Assurances of the blood thirsty Disposition of the Canadians as at least Lord North's Heart longs for.[4] Heaven appears to continue its Patronage of our Cause, and to defeat the Expectations of our Enemies in every Quarter.

Sewall,[5] Auchmuty and such like have led the General to pursue the stupid Thought that the People have no Right to attempt the Preservation of the publick Liberty but just in that Road which is effectually blocked up by the late Mandamus. Hence an Attack upon the Provincial Congress by a ridiculous Proclamation, which will prove as impotent as a former one respecting the nonConsumption Covenant, or as H. Gray's Advertisement in Regard to the Treasury.[6] The Congress are again together at Cambridge to receive the Report of Messrs. the 4 Delegates, who, except J. A. Esq. are Members of this Assembly. A Voice more familiar to the Ears of 7/8th of them than Dr. Warren's will I dare say often try its Efficacy upon them this Session.[7]

Cowardice and Insolence hold a divided Empire in the Breasts of Tyrants.[8] I have it through so direct a Channel as a Colonel that, in the Heat of the County and Provincial Remonstrances against the Work on the Neck, as the probable Cause of provoking the Spirits of the People to an immediate violent Decision, it was determined to stop Hands and to compleat the Work in the

Spring. But just at that critical Period the Advice of the continental Congress came to restrain Violence except upon downright Necessity; which Necessity was known to mean the taking up of Individuals. Upon this the Works went on magnanimously even to polishing off with Whitewash; and now tis boasted they are as strong as those of Gibralter. Nor will it be strange if you see displayed in London an Account most pompous of the military Genius of Gage in Return for the following Compliment upon, somebody in England, in a Letter which the Philadelphians say is damned as authentic, and which we here believe to be so, from its exact Conformity to the whiffling Conduct we were Witnesses of at G[age]'s first Arrival.* Here must have been Cash to such poor Wretches as Nat[haniel] Ray, and Promises of Place to other Traytors.

You will make yourself Master of the strenuous Efforts that some Villains will make by this Opportunity for the Continuance of a Garrison in Boston. How could London, Bristol or any mercantile City there endure the Fife and Drum of 11 Regiments in its Streets at several Times each Day?[9] Here they are, mangled by Twenties for Drunkeness, while Virginia is going through all that bloody Scene which the Massachusetts's sustained a Century upon their Frontiers without the least Aid from England. We had not indeed *then* the Mortification of thinking the english Ministry set the Savages upon us, because we had not *then* such a Foundation to build upon as the stirring up of the french catholicks of Canada against us. We *used* to conclude both moved by the same Agents; and *was* not that a natural Conclusion?

I appeal to the Framers of the Quebec Bill.[10] Do, my Friend, be very attentive to the plausible Pretences which may be formed for fixing Troops here in Case of Relief in other Matters. Englishmen will lose their Priviledges, *only* when they are in good Humour. My Fears for America have always been greatest when Britain appeared most condescending. A Courtier Minister will be likely to do more with us than all the Bullies on both Sides the Tweed united. But I will hope even the former cannot accomplish our Ruin at this Period of our Society; for it is not analogous to the divine Proceedings to destroy growing States but to spare them till they reach mature Corruption like that of Rome or ________. I wish you Health and all Happiness, being your affectionate Friend

and very humble Servant,

Jas. Lovell

*Extract: "I have, my Lord, to the utmost Extent of my Power, executed those *private* Matters given to me in Charge by your Lordship and by *their success* am still more confirmed in your Lordship's profound political Researches and extensive Knowledge of Mankind in general."[11]

1. QP 51 (reel 29) MHS; transcribed in the *Memoir*, pp. 180–81; printed in Howe, ed., "Quincy Letters," pp. 477–79.

2. He probably had in mind William Jackson and William Taylor, Boston merchants who refused to support non-importation and, as Loyalists, eventually left Massachusetts.

3. Guy Carleton, who as wartime governor of Canada would turn back the rebel invasion of 1775–1776 and, as Sir Henry Clinton's successor as commander-in-chief of the British forces in North America in 1782, would preside over the formal British withdrawal from an independent United States. Four years after that he would return to govern Canada as a baron in the peerage, capping an interesting career reviewed in David Paul Nelson, *General Sir Guy Carleton, Lord Dorchester* (Madison, N.J.: Fairleigh Dickinson University Press, 2000).

4. Everything after the sentence ending "Combination" in the previous paragraph to this point was not printed in the *Memoir*.

5. Jonathan Sewall, though older than John Adams, had risen in the legal profession with him. Politically they took different roads and Sewall, as attorney general, chose to defend the empire. He left the Bay Colony during the 1775 siege. See Sibley, *Harvard Graduates*, 12:306–25; and Carol Berkin, *Jonathan Sewall* (New York: Columbia University Press, 1974).

6. Gage's proclamation condemning the Provincial Convention that met in Cambridge in October as an unlawful assembly was printed as a broadside, and reprinted on the first page of the *Boston Evening-Post*, 14 November 1774, which was satirized in some anonymous doggerel on the third page of the *Boston Gazette* for that same date. Harrison Gray was the Bay Colony's treasurer and, in the battle for control of tax monies being paid into the towns–should they go to the crown, or be held in reserve–Gray, not surprisingly, sided with the crown. See resolutions passed in York County (the Maine country) on November 16th that determined Gray had lost his mind; printed in the *Boston Gazette*, 5 December 1774.

7. The delegates appointed by the Massachusetts House in June to attend the Continental Congress, before Gage could dissolve it, were Thomas Cushing, Samuel Adams, John Adams, and Robert Treat Paine. James Bowdoin had been selected as well, but did not attend.

8. In a second sizeable excision, everything following "a former one" in the previous paragraph to the sentence following this was left out of the *Memoir*.

9. There is no more of this letter in the *Memoir* after this point, except for Lovell's closing and signature.

10. The Quebec Act is in Pickering, ed., *Statutes*, 30:549–54 (14 George III c. 83); and discussed thoroughly in Gustave Lanctot, *Canada & the American Revolution, 1774–1783* (London: George G. Harrap & Co., 1967); and Philip Lawson, *The Imperial Challenge* (Montreal and Kingston: McGill-Queen's University Press, 1989).

11. See Warren's letter to Josiah Junior of 21 November 1774, supra at p. 310, n. 3.

JQ TO JOSIAH QUINCY SR.

27 November 1774[1]

Honored and Dear Sir, London 27 November 1774

I snatch my pen to pay you that tribute of rememberance and duty which I owe.

Having wrote many letters to Mrs. Q I must refer you to her for information relative to my health and spirits and the occasion of my present brevity.

Your friend Dr. Franklin is a truely great and good man. Please to write to him and transmit the letter to me.

Please to thank Mr. Goldthwait[2] for his Letters, which have been of service to me and inform Mr. Jona[than] Williams[3] (should you see him) that he has a very worthy son in this City, who is in health and much beloved.

If the affairs of America should terminate speedily in the freedom and peace of the Country, I can send over very substantial yeomen with their families who will settle your Lenox land in a very short time. If you should think of such a plan, I must know the soil, the distance from a market and the best terms of settlement.

My health and spirits were never better. My friends and well-wishers never more.

Give my unfeigned affection to my Mama and sisters and present me to my brother in the bonds of love.

After you have perused my letter to Mrs. Q. of this date, you will not wonder, at that haste with which I am obliged to subscribe.

Your very affectionate and dutiful

J Q Junr.

1. QP 51 (reel 29) MHS; transcribed in the "Memoir," 2:190a, QP 46 (reel 6) MHS. A note at the bottom of the letter indicated that it had been received on 28 February 1775.

2. Possibly Ezekiel Goldthwait, the same age as Josiah Sr. He had once served as the Boston town clerk and had been prominent in the town meeting.

3. The father of Franklin's grandnephew (see supra p. 307, n. 3).

RICHARD PRICE TO JQ

6 December 1774[1]

Dear Sir Newington Green Dec. 6th 1774

Dr. Franklin has agreed to dine at Mr. Hollis's in Great Ormond Street next tuesday, on the 13th.[2] It will be an additional pleasure to Mr. Hollis to be favoured at the same time with your company; and I wish to be able to introduce you then to him. I likewise wish you would allow me to introduce you to Lord Shelburne.[3] I have mentioned this to him; and he has told me that he will be glad to see you. May I hope to see you at the Society which meets at the *London* Coffee House next thursday night? I shall be glad then to settle these things with you.

With much regard, I am, Dear Sir, your most obedient and Humble Servant

Richd. Price

1. QP 51 (reel 29) MHS; transcribed in the "Memoir," 2:200a, QP 46 (reel 6) MHS; and printed in Howe, ed., "Quincy Letters," pp. 482–83.

2. Thomas Brand Hollis was the friend and heir of Thomas Hollis. He added the Hollis to his name as a tribute to his benefactor. Brand Hollis was a supporter of parliamentary reform and John Wilkes, an admirer of William Pitt and critic of the North ministry's hard-line policies. Thomas Hollis had been a business associate of Josiah Jr.'s deceased older brother Edmund. He died less than a year before Josiah Jr. arrived in London and had continued a tradition of giving to Harvard College begun by his great-uncle, also named Thomas Hollis. Books were among his most important bequests, including the writings of John Milton and Marchmont Nedham. There is a letter from Thomas Brand Hollis to Quincy of 2 March 1775, at infra, p. 375. The Hollises are discussed in Robbins, *Eighteenth-Centutry Commonwealthman,* passim. Also see W. H. Bond, *Thomas Hollis of Lincoln's Inn* (Cambridge, Eng.: Cambridge University Press, 1990).

3. William Petty, Earl of Shelburne in the Irish peerage, Baron Wycombe in Britain, was a leading Pittite. He had long taken an interest in American affairs, dating back at least to when he was on the Board of Trade, and, in Chatham's ministry, when he was the secretary of state for the Southern Department. Political allies thought him clever; political opponents thought him devious. He believed better policies devised in London could have headed off confrontation. Heading his own ministry in 1783, he saw through the preliminary treaty recognizing American independence, but reluctantly, out of necessity; he would have preferred some sort of informal postwar federation with the Americans, tapping into the two nations' cultural and trade connections. For Shelburne and American affairs see John M. Norris, *Shelburne and Reform* (New York: St. Martins Press, 1963).

JQ TO ABIGAIL QUINCY
7 December 1774[1]

My very dear friend London 7 December 1774

There never was a time in which I wished more "to speak without a tongue" and "to be heard without ears:"—"then", as Shakespeare expresses it, "in despight of broad-eyed *watchful* day, I would into thy bosom pour my thoughts."[2]

This kingdom never saw a time in which the minds of *all ranks* were more upon the wreck[3] with expectation. And when I tell you, that yesterday in the Coffee Room adjoining the House of Commons, one of the ministerial members offered to lay a wager of 75 Guineas to 25 that *Boston was now in ashes*, you,will not think my own bosom free from anxiety. 'Tis now more than two months since any advices have been received from America of the state of things in your province. The subalterns of the ministry give out that the most peremptory orders went to General Gage last October to proceed *to extremities* with vigour. They therefore, vapor with much vaunting upon the expectation of hearing in a few days you are all subdued and *in deep humiliation.* Should *the reverse* of this this prove true (as God grant it may!) you[r] enemies will sink—and sink—forever.

Let me here tell you a great truth. The people of this country have too generally got an idea, that Americans are all cowards and poltroons. This sentiment is propagated and diffused with great industry and success. Now, it is *agreed on all hands*, that *your courage*; *your courage,* I repeat it, will be *brought to the test.* Should it prove answerable to your ostentations—worthy your Ancestors—your friends will *amazingly* increase, your *hearty* friends will be in raptures, and your very *enemies will embrace you.* I could easily explain to you, the reason of all this, but I must leave you to consider of that yourself. Read the paragraph again, and make your own reflections.

Will you believe me, when I tell you, that your letting a certain character *escape* from your justice is imputed to you *on all hands* as a fault? Your enemies impute it to your *cowardice,* your friends to your want of political sagacity. Certain it is, that from *one man*; from *one man* I say, (and he neither a Bute, a Mansfield, a North or a Bernard) are all your miseries supposed to flow.[4] This supposition is not made by those alone who are sanguine in your Common Cause. It is the General Sentiment of all parties; and were[5] I to show you my journal, in which I enter the sentiments and expressions of those with whom from time to time I converse you would find (unexpected) characters intimating speaking out the same ideas. "Tis his Advice that dictated the steps of Administration, and 'tis his present opinion and assurances that keep up the spirits and measures of the ministry" were the very words uttered to me not 20 minutes ago by a Gentleman in office in the Customs.[6]

I should take a satisfaction in naming to you those who are my informants; but a fear lest your indiscretion in publishing what I write, should discover the author of your intelligence denies one that indulgence. Remember in whatever you publish; to beware *you do not print* something that may betray the writer. Not that I am conscious of any wrong, but I am here surrounded with great villains who have *will and power* to injure, but want a pretext.

Apropos, this leads me to speak of your friend Quincy who lately arrived in this City. In the House of Lords last week when the Address to the King was in debate, Lord Hillsborough said that there were then men walking the streets of London who ought to be in Newgate or at Tyburn. Upon which the Duke of Richmond rose, and said, that he was surprised, that *that* Gentleman should cast such a heavy reflection on his Majesty's ministers, by suggesting a matter which, if true, they were guilty of gross neglect of Duty; and called upon his Lordship for an explanation of who and what he meant. Upon which Lord Hillsborough rose, and pointed out, though not in words, yet so as every body knew who he meant Dr. Franklin and Mr. Quincy: the latter gentleman he mentioned as author of a late publication called "Observations on the Boston Port Bill and Standing Armies."[7]

The Character of your Mr. Samuel Adams runs very high here. I find many who consider him the first politician in the World. I have found more reason every day to convince me that he has been right, when others supposed him wrong. But why should we spend time in looking back. Look forward.[8] God grant you penetration that you may all see the great duties which lay before.[9] May you have fortitude to *suffer*—courage to encounter—and activity and perseverance to press forward.

Prepare, prepare I say, *for the worst.* I fear your delays have been your ruin. I know that your energies may already or in future, bring upon you *many and great* calamities; but I am from my own observation and the judgment of very many others, most sure that your forbearance, your delays, your indecision—in short, what your enemies call your arrant cowardice hath or will bring upon you *many more* and *greater* evils. These are important truths. Weigh—*commune*—consider and act as becomes your former professions and your highest duty.

You see my heart gets the better of my head. My feelings rise paramount to [my] discretion. Thus it will always be with those who are warm in the Cause of their country. Their zeal banishes caution. You see, however, I still retain some discretion: but even *that,* I had rather lose, than be "unpregnant of my causes or lack gall to make oppression bitter."[10]

GOD knows whether this Letter will ever reach you. Was I sure it would I should write a volume.

I have lately wrote largely to you on political matters. Tell me what my enemies write of me from this side the water: write me what my friends *think* of me on your side the ocean.

My whole time is taken up in my duty. I never was more *busy,* I never was more *talkative.* I wrote you fully relative to my health in former letters. I have as yet had no symptoms of taking cold since I have been in London; but incessant application—incessant *talking* with several members of Parliament and others this four days past hath brought on a little fever and some spitting of blood. But otherwise I was never better in my life; certainly I never was in better spirits.

Don't be concerned about this circumstance. I would not have mentioned it, but in fidelity to one, from whom I cannot conceal anything which concerns my wellfare.

I am urged by Dr F. to go down with him and spend Christmas with the Bishop of St. Asaph: I have not yet given my answer. On Friday I expect to see Lord Shelburne, and have very lately conversed several hours with Sir George Saville.

By the way, you must know, that many of your friends here in both houses will not take a *decisive* part, till they see how you act in America. For should they take a *determined* part now in favor of that country, and in a short time America should give back, their hopes of rise into power and office (which is the hopes of *all British* Statesmen) would be forever at an end. Therefore, till the Colonists discover that union and spirit, which all parties here agree must *force* success, you are not to expect any great exertions in your favor. But when once there is a conviction that the Americans are in earnest; that they are resolved to endure all hazard with a spirit worthy the prize for which they contend, then (and not till then) will you have many firm, active, persevering, and powerfull friends in both houses of Parliament. For let me again tell you, that strange as it may seem, there is a great doubt here, among many, whether you are *really in earnest* in the full force and extent of those words.

I am called out. Peace be with you. Salute my friends—embrace—[11] and remember *in antient* love

Your most affectionate
and fast friend
Henry Ireton

1. QP 51 (reel 29) MHS; transcribed in the "Memoir," 2:201–7, QP 46 (reel 6) MHS; printed in the *Memoir,* pp. 216-20.

2. Quincy, paraphrasing as well as quoting lines from Shakespeare's *King John*, Act III, Scene 3, the King to his chamberlain, Hubert.

3. Changed to "upon the rack" in both the "Memoir" and the *Memoir.*

4. Meaning Thomas Hutchinson, who of course had left Massachusetts for England well before Quincy.

5. Quincy wrote "where," by mistake no doubt.

6. Presumably Commissioner Morris.

7. The sources for the House of Lords on 30 November 1774 in Simmons and Thomas, eds., *Proceedings and Debates,* 5:237-39, do not allude to this exchange.

8. Italicized, with an exclamation point for emphasis, in the *Memoir,* but not in the original, or as transcribed for the "Memoir."

9. "Lay before" being changed to "lie before you" in the *Memoir.*

10. From *Hamlet,* Act II, Scene 2. Quincy repeats these lines, plus more from the same soliloquy, in his letter to Joseph Reed of 17 December 1774 (see infra, p. 340). Hamlet is on the eve of staging the play-within-the-play that he hopes will expose his uncle as the killer of his father. He knows that Polonius, acting for Claudius, has a plot of his own involving Hamlet's old, and unwitting, friends Rosencrantz and Guildenstern.

11. "Embrace" is left out of the *Memoir,* though Eliza Susan copied it into the "Memoir."

JQ TO ABIGAIL QUINCY
7 December 1774[1]

Dear, Dear one[2] London Dec. 7th 1774

You will form a poor idea of my feelings for you and my country, if you do not consider that I have had no tidings of you, since I sailed. Not only my breast, but the breast of ministers and kings, nations and empires, are big with expectation of American events—That 'tide'—but I forbear.

I this day wrote you very largely and a few days ago more &c, and prior to that again, very full. These letters were all signed by a new political signature. The last mentioned (the first wrote) went directed under cover to Mr. Jonathan Mason; the other two were inclosed to Mr. Benjamin Clarke; and these both go by the Packet, the mail for which is made up tonight. And the chief design of my writing is to let you know this, by sending the present letter by some other ship.

I would have transcribed my letters but have not time to write duplicates; and I have yet found no body who I dare trust to copy for me.

My whole heart is with you; my whole time is employed in endeavouring to serve my country. It is now three weeks since I came to this city, yet I never dedicated but two evenings to the entertainments of the Town. And though Garrick hath acted four nights I have seen him but one.[3]

You will wonder how I spend my nights and days in serving my Country. But in one word—I find every body eager to hear—most people willing to be set right—and almost all grossly ignorant of the American world. I have been taught to believe, that I have spoke conviction to many sensible minds.

My friends are many, my spirits excellent, my health as I mentioned in my last.

Make it your business to enquire for the December packett, and do not rest till you get the letters I sent by it.

Believe me I know not when to leave writing, and was I sure of a safe conveyance I should write a volume.

My heart feels for you all very exquisitely when I think of you, which is 18 hours out of the twenty four.

Adieu, my best friend.

JQ———y

PS. Give me the earliest intelligence of the Dates of those letters which you receive.

1. QP 51 (reel 29) MHS; "Memoir," 2:208–9, QP 46 (reel 6) MHS; *Memoir,* pp. 221–22.

2. Changed to "My dear wife" in both the "Memoir" and the *Memoir.*

3. Quincy saw Garrick perform as Hamlet at the Drury Lane theatre–no doubt a thrill for him, since there was as yet no theatre in Boston. Still, he was not uncritical, writing in his journal: "He is certainly the Prince of Players, but most certainly not without his faults as an Orator." In Coquillette and York, eds., *Portrait of a Patriot,* 1:241. He had first seen Garrick at the Drury Lane in George Farquhar's "Beaux' Stratagem" two weeks before. "He was a surprising fellow," Quincy noted cryptically then (at ibid., 1:237). Garrick had been on the London stage for well over thirty years by that point. He would play Hamlet ninety times, in the later years casting himself even if he was past his prime and long in the tooth for the part.

RICHARD PRICE TO JQ

9 December 1774[1]

Dear Sir Newington Green Dec. 9th 1774

I am much obliged to you for the letter with which you favoured me by Dr. Franklin. It would have given me much pleasure to have met you at the London Coffee-House last night. I am to be at Lord Shelburne's in Berkeley Square next monday morning; and, if convenient to you, I shall be very glad you would call upon me there any time between half an hour after ten and eleven o clock, that I may have the pleasure of introducing you to his Lordship. I am very glad you can give my friend Mr. Hollis the pleasure of your company to dine with him on tuesday. He goes to dinner at about half an hour after three, and lives in great Ormond Street, Bloomsbury. With the best wishes and much regard, I am, Sir, your very obedient and Humble Servant

Rich:d Price[2]

1. QP 51 (reel 29) MHS; Howe, ed., "Quincy Letters," pp. 482–83.

2. Richard Price—often called Dr. Price in recognition of his doctor of divinity degree—was the longtime pastor of a presbyterian congregation at Newington Green, on the north edge of London. By the time Quincy met him he had become friends with Franklin, and was part of a small circle of intellectuals that revolved around the Earl of Shelburne that also included Jonathan Shipley, Bishop of St. Asaph, and Joseph Priestley. Price had also been named to the Royal Society. His public fame would come a couple of years later, with his pamphlet on the nature of civil liberty, which included a defense of the American patriot cause. For this side to Price see William Bernard Peach, ed., *Richard Price and the Ethical Foundations of the American Revolution* (Durham, N.C.: Duke University Press, 1978); Cal B. Cones's somewhat dated biography, *Torchbearer of the Revolution* (Lexington: University of Kentucky Press, 1952); and two briefer pieces—chapters on Price in Robert E. Toohey, *Liberty & Empire* (Lexington, Ky.: University of Kentucky Press, 1978) ; and Jerome R. Reich, *British Friends of the American Revolution* (Armonk, N.Y.: M. E. Sharpe, 1998).

JAMES LOVELL TO JQ

9 December 1774[1]

Dear Sir, Dec. 9th 1774

Several Days after Callahan had sailed the inclosed was returned to Mr. Bromfield with some of his own, which had been given to the Care of a negligent Salemite. I hope your other Friends here have not been careless of writing by Mr. Blowers,[2] who will certainly have had Honor enough to deliver any Charges of that Kind, however widely he may differ from you in political Sentiment or the Intentions of his Voyage. We do not expect any great Favor from his or the immense Mr. Bliss's Representations.[3]

The Scarborough's and the Asia's Arrival have not given those tip Top Spirits to the traitorous Band now Prison-cooped in this Town, which on many late Occasions they had discovered. They appear to be beginning to conceive that Great Britain will not maintain a Resolution to hazard the Profit of all nor commercial Intercourse with America barely on their Account.

It is certain that Gage himself is in great Complacency on his past Conduct being approved by the Ministry; and, we know, that very Conduct has fallen vastly short of the bloody Expectations of those Villains who surround him, in a mock Council and as fugitive *Martyrs in the Cause of Government,* so they count themselves. If any Credit is to be given to the public Assertions of a General sent on so vile an Errand as Gage was when he professes a benevolent mediational Intention, we are intitled to believe from his Pleasure upon the late Pacquet that he finds he may exercise his benevolence with Safety to his Commission. All his past Conduct proves that he judged the Dispute cannot be settled by a Coup de Main,[4] and he must be an Idiot indeed to desire to beat the Bush for some future General's Profit and Glory. You will readily see that such Secresy is observed upon the Scarborough's Errand that we go wholly upon Conjecture, and you may have Sagacity enough to pick out of the confused Manner in which I have expressed myself, that I do not believe the Ministry have signified an Intention to oblige us to take the Field. But, while such is *my* Belief, I assure you the general Current is otherwise, and especially in the provincial Congress now sitting. And I further assure you that there appears as full and cool a Resolution to draw the Sword upon Necessity as to celebrate a Day of Thanksgiving upon our happy Reunion; but I cannot add "*either* with *equal* Pleasure"; no, I cannot cast such a Slur upon common humanity, much less can I upon that habitual Affection of Englishman to Englishman, which some notoriously abandoned Men-in-Power have done so much of late years to destroy utterly, though, God be praised! they have done it hitherto in vain. What an Aceldama[5] would this Province have now been, had no more Humanity ruled in the Hearts or Prudence in the Heads of some of the Executors than what Those can possibly pretend to who were Framers of the late execrable Acts? Perhaps it may be some Solace to those vile Spirits to know that, if the Sword they have sent among us is not vigorously executive, this abused City will *in the Spring* be filled with Pestilence and a consequent Degree of Famine.

You know it has even been the Progress of the Small Pox to lurk through the Winter and make rapid Strides in the Spring. Besides those mentioned in the Gazettes Colonel Hamilton (too good a Man and Christian for the present vile Expedition) has given Notice *Today* of a fresh Eruption and the Soldier is sent to the Pest House at the Westward of the Town. But the most alarming Circumstance is that a regimental Doctor said if the Soldier who was moved *Yesterday* had the true small Pox 40 others had been thoroughly exposed. He has it, and, Sexton Barret says, he cannot live through it.[6]

The most resolute Determinations are made here as well as in the other Colonies to execute the grand Association Plan.[7] We have a large Town Committee but Salem and Marblehead will give us no Opportunity to act, unless the polite and sagacious Graves should make this Harbour the Asylum of refugee Ships, as the General has made the Town one for refugee Traytors.[8] Mr. Solicitor and his Like at Club last Evening thought Shayler would be admitted, being refused the Use of any Wharfe at Salem. They will conduct themselves at the said Port in respect to Arrivals between December 1st and February 1st as directed by the Congress, though they will continue every palliative till January 1st.

Some busy Enemies will doubtless expose the Quiet of this Town by importing in the Transports by which you receive this. The Captain has offered his Assistance to one or two of his Friends as I am *well* informed, and probably to more. If you cannot give us a Clue to trace the Importers by, the Country Committees will in Time do it, and I think great Woe will be all the Profit of such clandestine Importations.

While the Tories here say "the Congress have not made any Offers on the Part of the Colonies, so that it is quite impossible for the Ministry to alter their late Plan",[9] I feel confident that their Moderation will surprise both Enemies and Friends in Great Britain after the many misrepresentations that have been made of our Designs. I am far from certain that it will not surprise *you.*

Health and Happiness attend you,
Yours sincerely,
Jas. Lovell

1. QP 51 (reel 29) MHS; Howe, ed., "Quincy Letters," pp. 482–84.

2. Sampson Salter Blowers, a few years younger than Quincy and from a far more modest background, had assisted Quincy and John Adams with the soldiers' defense in 1770. Tied to Hutchinson from the time he had decided to study law after finishing at Harvard, it would not have surprised Quincy to see Blowers in London; he set sail just a couple of months later. He eventually was named chief justice of Nova Scotia.

3. Quite likely Daniel Bliss, a Concord lawyer who had been close to Hutchinson, reported on local affairs to Gage and fled, never to return, with the outbreak of fighting. See Sibley, *Harvard Graduates,* 14:563–66. For Bliss in the context of how the coming revolution transformed one Massachusetts town see Robert A. Gross, *The Minutemen and Their World* (New York: Hill and Wang, 1976).

4. In the military sense, to make a decisive strike, deliver a quick blow.

5. A field outside of Jerusalem where, according to some traditions (see Acts 1:18–19), Judas Iscariot suffered a miserable death, his bowels "bursting asunder" after he betrayed Jesus Christ; thus Aceldama, or "the field of blood."

6. What Lovell described presaged a wider outbreak of "variola," as examined in Elizabeth A. Fenn, *Pox Americana: The Great Smallpox Epidemic of 1775–1782* (New York: Hill & Wang, 2002).

7. The Association, as called for by the Continental Congress, laid out in Ford, ed., *Journals of Congress,* 1:75–81, and discussed in Ammerman, *In the Common Cause*, pp. 73–87.

8. Admiral Samuel Graves, relatively new commander of the North American station, a position he would hold through the end of 1775 and into early 1776 during the siege of Boston.

9. Lovell may have been offering a generic catchphrase rather than a direct quotation.

JQ TO ABIGAIL QUINCY
14 December 1774[1]

Dear, Dear friend[2] London Decr. 14.1774.

I have lately wrote you by the Packett two very long Letters and by some other ships three or four more, upon Politicks. I , therefore, shall not now resume the subject any further, than to say—*Be true to yourselves.*

There is not a sensible man of either party here, but acknowledge your ability to save your country, if you have but union, courage and perseverance. But your enemies pretend to be sanguine, that your avarice of commercial riches will dissolve your union and mutual confidence; that your boasted courage is *but vapor;* and that your perseverance will be as the morning cloud. Let me tell you one very serious truth, in which we are all agreed: your countrymen *must* seal their cause *with their blood.*[3] You know how often and how long ago I said this.[4] I see every day more and more reason to confirm my opinion. I every day find characters, dignified by science, and *station** of the same sentiment. Surely my countrymen will recollect the words I held to them this line this time twelvemonth. "It is not, Mr Moderator, the spirit, that *vapors* within these walls that must stand us in stead. *The exertions of this day will call forth events* which will make a very different spirit *necessary* for our salvation. Look to the end. Whoever supposes, that shouts and hosannas will terminate the trials of the day entertain a childish fancy; we must be grossly ignorant of the importance and value of the prize for which we contend; we must be equally [in] ignorance of the powers of those who have combined against us; we must be blind to that malice, inveteracy and insatiable revenge which actuate our enemies, public and private, abroad and in our bosom, to hope we shall end this controversy without the sharpest, the sharpest conflicts; to flatter ourselves that popular resolves, popular harangues, popular acclamations, and popular vapor will vanquish our foes. Let us consider the issue—let us look to the end—let us weigh and consider before we advance to those measures which must bring on the most trying and terrible struggle this country ever saw."[5]

Hundreds I beleive will call these words and many more of the same import, to remembrance; hundreds, who heretofore doubted, are long ere this convinced I was right.

The popular sentiments of the day prevailed; they advanced with resolutions to hazard and abide the consequences. They must now stand the issue; they must *persevere a consistency of character; they must not delay;* they must __________ or be trodden down into the vilest vassalage, the scorn, the spurn of their enemies, a by-word of infamy among all men.

In the sight of GOD and all just men, the cause is good. We have the wishes of the wise and humane, we have the prayers of the pious, and the universal benisons of all who seek to GOD for direction, aid and blessing. I own I feel for the miseries of my country; I own I feel much desire for the happiness of my Bretheren in trouble. But why should I disguise: I feel, ineffably for the honour—*the honour* I repeat it—*the honour* of my country. Need I explain myself further? When you shall act agreable to your past ostentations, when you have shown that you are, what Englishmen once were, whether successfull or not, your foes will diminish, your friends amazingly encrease and you will be happy in the peacefull enjoyment of your inheritance; or at least your enemies will in some measure stay their intemperate fury from a reverence of your virtue, and a fear of reanimating your courage. But if in the trial, you prove (as your enemies say) arrant poltroons and cowards, how ineffably contemptible will you appear; how wantonly and superlatively will you be abused and insulted by your triumphing oppressors!

Will you believe it? I took up my pen with a design only of saying, that the mail for the December Packett was staid from Wednesday to Saturday for no apparent reason, because Parliament had not the Affairs of America under consideration. Therefore it is generally beleived, that it was to inspect all letters. If so, two of mine, very long, are in the hands of the ministry. They were inclosed to Benjamin Clarke, and Nathaniel Appleton &c. Another went sometime before inclosed to Mr. Mason. I sent a long letter from Mr. Bollan to Mr. Bowdoin to William Dennie.[6]

I have received your Letter of the 17th of October and your worthy Papa's of the same date. Write me word what letters you from time to time receive. Lord North has, I hear, given out that I have my price. Tell my father that Dr. Franklin is my great friend and daily companion. Tell your dear parents that they have my gratitude and warmest thanks.

Adieu, Henry Ireton

*By the way, Lord _____ said to me yesterday: "It is idle, 'tis idle Mr (Ireton) this country will never *carry* on a civil war against America: *we cannot.* But the ministry hope to carry all by *a single stroke*." I should be glad to name the Lord, but think it not best.[7]

PostPS. I am in health and spirits.

1. QP 51 (reel 29) MHS; "Memoir," 2:211–14, QP (reel 6) MHS; *Memoir*, pp. 224–27.

2. A salutation changed to "My dear wife" in the "Memoir," and "My Dear Friend" in the *Memoir*.

3. See Quincy's letter to Joseph Reed of three days later, p. 343 infra, where he repeats the sentiment.

4. See, for example, his "Hyperion" essay for the *Boston Gazette*, 5,October 1767, lines that Daniel Webster would repeat at the fiftieth anniversary commemoration at Bunker Hill (see supra pp. 7–11).

5. Quincy quoted himself here, from the speech that he gave at the Old South meetinghouse on 16 December 1773, just as men disguised as Indians went to dump tea into Boston harbor, tea in the holds of three ships that could not leave (Governor Hutchinson would not grant permission for them to sail away) nor could they land their cargoes (local protestors patrolling the docks as an informal posse comitatus made that impossible). These passages have been reprinted elsewhere, such as in Richard Frothingham, *The Life of Joseph Warren* (Boston: Little, Brown, & Company, 1865), p. 276; and Francis Drake, *Tea Leaves* (Boston: A. O. Crane, 1884), p. lx. Frothingham may have seen Quincy's letter. The 1825 first edition of the *Memoir* included it (as did the later two editions). In our own generation, Quincy's words were even recorded and repeated in a taped dramatization provided to headphone-wearing visitors to the Old South.

6. William Dennie and James Bowdoin were ardent patriots, prominent in Boston politics. William Bollan had once served as the agent for the Massachusetts General Court in London, then for the governor's council, and, with Franklin and Arthur Lee, would try (and fail) to get Parliament to deal formally with the Continental Congresss.

7. Shelburne, perhaps?

JQ TO ABIGAIL QUINCY

16 December 1774[1]

My very dear friend, London Decr. 16. 1774

Permit me to congratulate my Countrymen on the integrity and wisdom with which the Congress have conducted. Their policy, spirit and union have confounded their foes and inspired their friends. All parties agree in giving them a tribute of honour and applause.

I have this moment attended a desultory, despicable, because trifling, debate in the house of C_____ s, relative to America. My Lord North apologized for and endeavoured to explain away his expression "I will have America at my feet".[2] The important Questions relative to Our Common Cause will not be agitated till after the holidays are over.

There is great talk and much hope and fear about you; and your friends seem to intend pressing a suspension for three years of all acts made since 1764 relative to the Colonies. Your staunch friends say "if they are unjust, repeal[3]; we then shall treat with you as friend. At all hazards recall your troops, for we will *not treat* with the sword at Our Breast." Be the event as it may—continue true to yourselves, and the day is your own.

If they only *suspend* don't, for Heaven's sake, think of relaxing your agreements, while you are treating. Beware of the act of negotiation. The ministry are all adept in them; at least they are skilled in the science of Corruption.

By the way, there is no doubt, but the ministry sent large sums to New York in order to bribe your Continental Delegates. It was openly avowed and vindicated and great boast was made of ministerial success in this way with the Delegates from New York. It was said that they had affected a disunion, which would be fatal to the Cause of all America.

You can't well imagine the chagrin with which the ministry received the results of that glorious body. They are viewed as the Northern constellation of glorious worthies, illuminating and warming the new world.

I feel a pride in being an American. Neither my affection or zeal is any degree abate in the cause of my injured country.

I have just supped and spent the evening with a circle of about a dozen of the influential members of the House of Commons. But whether I see them in the House or out of it, they appear ——— not fit to *represent the inhabitants of North America.*

I should be glad to be informed, whether, in case a suspension of the acts takes place, my friends would chuse my continuance on this side the Water. If they chuse me to be with them I will repair to my standard, when they shall command.

Had the Congress made application to Ireland to join them in Congress in May next, it would [have] been a most capital stroke of policy. Your friends have intimated such an invitation as having actually been voted, and, the measure is now pursuing.[4] It has had great effect. Few political *finesses* have alarmed more. The matter takes well: it properly affects friends and foes.

The Watchmen remind me that it is morning, but the Lamp of my Affection burns as bright as ever; and towards you with a warmth that ever characterises

Your
Henry Ireton

1. QP 51 (reel 29) MHS; "Memoir," 2:216–18, QP 46 (reel 6) MHS; *Memoir*, pp. 229–31.

2. North was responding to comments made by George Johnstone; in Simmons and Thomas, eds., *Proceedings and Debates*, 5:256 (North) and 5:253 (Johnstone).

3. Eliza Susan Quincy added "them" in the "Memoir," which was carried into the *Memoir*.

4. Congress would in fact approve a message to the people of Ireland in July 1775, after it had reconvened—see Ford, ed., *Journals of Congress*, 2:212–228—the next year. Congress, still professing to want reconciliation, did not call for Ireland to join in rebellion, however, and it appears that the provision for Ireland to join in an expansive political union drawn up by Franklin at about that time, but never formally proposed, was left out. For more on Ireland and the American Revolution see my *Neither Kingdom Nor Nation* (Washington, D.C.: Catholic University of America Press, 1994), pp. 74–108; and Vincent Morley, *Irish Opinion and the America Revolution, 1760–1783* (Cambridge, Eng.: Cambridge University Press, 2002).

JQ TO JOSEPH REED

17 December 1774[1]

Respected and Dear Sir London Decr. 17th 1774

Your favor of the 4th of November came to hand this moment; and to show my sense of the obligation without any delay, I transmit an answer with thanks. The importance of a great cause and the rising events of every day demand a mutual and unremitting intercourse of intelligence[,] sentiments and councils among the friends of America and mankind. Believe me, Sir, there is a very culpable negligence in this regard on both sides [of] the water, and I know of no excuse but what betrays a want of zeal and timidity unworthy of men engaged in so glorious a contest. "Unpregnant of our cause, we are pigeon-livered", but I hope that neither you or I shall ever "lack gall to make oppression bitter."[2]

The information you give relative to the New York Deputies was the least we expected. The ministry (it is confidently said and universally believed) had been lavish of monies in that quarter to foment discord. Nay, their setters and tools have made great amounts of unexampled success with the great men of that city. Our Coffee houses were lately filled with scoffs at American virtue, and they boasted of success in creating a fatal disunion in our great Sanhedrim with a confidence that gained much credit. Did you know the chagrin that took place on the arrival of the result of the Congress, it would gratify your keenest sensations. Be assured that august body have done a lasting service to their country, and that they are paid the well-earned tribute of honour and applause even by their rankest enemies. They are considered as a constellation of the first worthies of our Hemisphere: their influence is not confined to the circle of an American world, but they burn with a splendor that illuminates and warms the Continent of Europe. GOD grant that many such glorious luminaries may shine in everlasting the honour and blessing of mankind.

Did the inhabitants of New York, and especially their delegates know of what easy virtue they have been represented in this city, they would begun patriots from indignation, if not from virtue. What greater blast could be thrown on the reputation than to suggest that a little gold had made Americans sacrifice their country to the worst men in the worst of times? But when you hear this suggestion extended to the elevated character of men appointed guardians of the people—Good GOD how hatefull the idea!

Did our worthy Bretheren of New York know all that is daily said of them in this great world, and the confidence with which the tale is told, they would be singularly touched; they would be carefull to have all party-spirit cease, and let their conduct give the lie to their defamers. Sure I am, that the ministry have no where such sanguine hopes of a defection as from that quarter: their *influence* is no where so *forcibly* extended, and it is certain they will be astonishingly disappointed if they do not find a *sensibility* to their *touch*. Our Bretheren of New York have an opportunity to display more virtue and do more real service to the great cause of liberty and their country, than perhaps any Americans on that side [of] New England. But New England, I take it, is the *great field* for the *first and most heroic virtues*. Should Administration be disappointed in exciting discord and defection in New York, they will sink with shame and despondency.

There was last Friday *a little play* in the house upon American subjects. I attended to see *the actors* and was confirmed in nothing more, than that *English players* are *not representatives* of American heroes. However this might be only *the rehearsal,* and at the exhibition soon after the holidays, *the actors* may display their talents to more advantage. But brilliant as imagination can figure the *splendid actors* on this *August theatre,* I shall not substantially alter my opinion of the heroes of the Drama.[3]

The ministry had never so difficult a task before: they are plunged. The emotions of chagrin and resentment most conspicuously mark their countenance and conduct. The nation are viewing the present crisis with equal anxiety as the Americans. All Europe have their eyes fixed on the important conflict. How elevated, then, must be the feelings of an American who sees his countrymen distinguish themselves as wise and virtuous, calm and brave, rising in the estimation of all mankind as the illustrious remnant of the Sons of freedom?

You see, my worthy friend, that the glitter of a Court hath not yet fascinated me, with its splendor, nor the corruption of Britain, made me an apostate from the cause of my country. That pageantry which I see here makes me every day more attached to the simplicity of my native soil; and while I hourly survery the extended miseries of enormous wealth and power I swell with a more enthusiastic fervor in the cause of freedom and my country. And in what cause ought the pulse of man to beat with a more full and genial current? If intemperance is at any time a venial fault, it must be when mighty oppressors, shielded with the forms of law and defend[e]d by the arm of power, spread misery over a happy land, with wantoness and insult.[4]

But I desist from the contemplation of this hatefull subject, lest the contagion of intemperance prove infectious to my friend.

Lord North on Friday last had hard work to apologize for and explain away his vapouring expression "*I will have America at my feet.*"[5]

Lord Cambden in the house of Lords on the day before said—"were I an American I would resist to the last drop of my blood."[6]

Let me tell you a great truth which ought at this, and every future day, to have much weight and influence in America. Few men are more ill disposed towards the Continent than those who are under the greatest obligations to it: thus the *commercial* world like the *political* world gives us striking instances of favorites of America, who have become among the most sanguine conspirators against her public happiness. Nay some who ought to have America inscribed in their furniture and equipage, and gratitude towards that country written on their hearts, have uttered the bitterest things against it with licensed freedom and insidious industry. 'Tis true they are *now* about calling a meeting to petition Parliament in favour of the Colonies. But is an idiot at a loss to discern the motive?

The manufacturers also are on the move. If Americans continue to firm themselves they will not only have the honour and reward of emancipating themselves; but even a whole kingdom roused by their example, brought to feel by American oeconomy, and fired by a thousand wrongs may, peradventure, be brought once more to think a little of those great subjects: national justice, freedom and happiness. But by no means entertain an idea that *commercial* plans formed on *commercial* principles are to be engines of your freedom or the security of your felicity. Far different are the weapons with which oppression is repelled; far more noble the sentiments and actions which secure liberty and happiness to man.

The Friends of America in the house of Commons are now consulting a plan for carrying a *suspension* of all acts, made since 1764 relative to America, for three years: in which time, it is said, both sides may cool, and they may then think seriously of negotiation and compromise. I think it was Hannibal who said "*We* treat with *arms in our hands.*"[7] Now whether the weapons of our warfare be commercial or carnal, methinks we should not suddenly lay them down, lest we not only lose use of them, but become *so broken* for want of daily discipline, as that we shall not easily embody again in so *united* and *formidable* a band. Besides the arts of negotiation are much better understood in Europe than America. And great statesmen sometimes pretend to *negotiate,* while they only mean to *corrupt.* And the oeconomy or religion of British ministers will not restrain them from an essay upon those Colony virtues, which should they prove of easy impression might hazard mighty blessings.

Let Our countrymen, therefore, well consider how much a British ministry, as well as themselves have at stake. No arms, no acts, no plots or conspiracies will be thought unlawful weapons: let them look all around them, and be on their guard at every point.

The blessings of the wise and the prayers of the pious universally attend you, even throughout this nation. Will you believe it, Englishmen have become of that tame temper as *avowedly* to look to the virtue and spirit of a distant people for salvation. Like an aged parent, Britain looks to her children for support and defence. And were the voices of this people this day to be fairly collected, a vast majority would emancipate and bless All America to the extent of her warmest wishes.

My dear Sir, before I close, I cannot forbear telling you, that I look to my country with the feelings of one, who verily believes they must yet seal their faith and constancy to their liberties *with blood.* This is a distresssing witness indeed! But hath not this ever been the lot of humanity?[8] Hath not blood and treasure in all ages been the price of Civil Liberty? Can Americans hope a reversal of the laws or our nature, and that the best of blessings will be obtained and secured without the sharpest trials?

Adieu my friend! My *heart* is with you, and whenever *my countrymen* shall *command* my *person* shall be also.

Tell your worthy friend Mr Dickenson I flattered myself with hopes of his council while in this world of trials. Tell that good man George Clymer, if I did not love him too much, I should call him an apostate from his professions and promises.

Believe with great truth, and equal esteem
(Your obliged and affectionate Servant)
JQ

PS. When I receive your first Letter you shall hear from me again.

1. Draft copy in QP 51 (reel 29) MHS; a cleaner version is in the Joseph Reed Papers, New-York Historical Society. Also transcribed in "Memoir," 2:219–25, QP 46 (reel 6) MHS, and printed in the *Memoir,* pp. 231–37.

2. *Hamlet,* Act II, Scene 2; see p. 327 supra, Josiah Junior to Abigail, 7 December 1774.

3. "Last Friday" referred to debates in the Commons just the day before, on December 16th; in Simmons and Thomas, eds., *Proceedings and Debates,* 5:250–56.

4. In the original draft Quincy went back and deleted this unfinished closing sentence to the paragraph: "Whenever we survey the odious havock and devastation, the feelings of the man rise paramount we are apt to rise paramount the dictates"

5. See supra, p. 338.

6. Quincy may have been reporting what he heard firsthand. Charles Pratt, Inner Temple trained barrister, owed his rise in public life to William Pitt, and Camden never strayed politically far from his patron's side. By the time of Quincy's trip to England he had served as attorney general, left his seat in the Commons to become chief justice of the Court of Common Pleas, been elevated to the peerage as Baron Camden and took the post of lord chancellor in Pitt's ministry formed in 1766. He survived the ministry's fall in 1768 but by 1770 had been pressured to step down because of his vocal opposition to policies the king supported, including those toward the colonies. His was a leading voice in the House of Lords, second only to that of Chatham, against any sort of punitive policies against the Americans. He and Shelburne, Chatham's other leading ally in the Lords, kept their distance from each other.

7. I have not been able to find a source for these lines being spoken by Hannibal, if indeed Quincy remembered correctly.

8. These lines were excerpted to serve as the frontispiece for the *Memoir* in its second and third editions. They are reproduced as if they were in facsimile; they are not. It is not clear who wrote them for the printer to reproduce in this fashion. There is also a copy of this "facsimile" in the Simon Gratz Autograph Collection #250B, Case 8 Box 16, HSP.

JQ TO ABIGAIL QUINCY

19 December 1774[1]

My very dear friend London Dec. 19.1774

I have so much to do, that instead of writing to you, or any of my friends I transmit the rough draught of my Letter to Mr. Reed. It contains all I wish to say to you at this time on political subjects.

Gratitude, love and affection fill my heart towards my country and so many of my personal friends, that I must transmit my whole soul to them before I should do justice to myself. Therefore in one word to all of my friends say that I love, honour and revere them as much as ever; that I am the same man as when I abode with them beyond the great waters. And as to you my dear, I trust that nothing will ever be more acceptable to you, than to be assured that I am still

The same JQ——y

1. QP 51 (reel 29) MHS; "Memoir," 2:226, QP 46 (reel 6) MHS; *Memoir,* pp. 237–38.

JQ TO ABIGAIL QUINCY

22 December 1774[1]

My very dear friend, London Decr. 22d 1774

I have wrote you lately so many Letters, that there is the less need of my now reassuming the pen, but the ship by which I have written several Letters being unexpectedly delayed, I embraced the opportunity of saying a few words more.

I this day have spent six hours with four very influential members of the House of Commons. I have as yet heard or seen nothing to alter my sentiments of the duty of my Countrymen, since I so fully wrote my opinion of the part they ought to act. But the facts which the before mentioned gentlemen assured me of, were the infinite perplexities of the ministry and the general connection now beginning to take place among the merchants and Manufacturers. Indeed, if it was not for the treachery and base designs of certain merchants trading to the Colonies, the manufacturers would long ago have been clamorous in your favor. I was shown two Letters to two of the first manufacturing towns written by three members now in Parliament, which I have his promise to give a copy of in a few days. As soon as I receive,[2] I shall transcribe the copies; they will give you great insight into the commotions now beginning to take place.

Only be men of common sense and common integrity, and you can do wonders. People here have no idea, that any body of men can be virtuous, but surely you have common sense. And if you have, pride will keep you from any infraction of your agreements.

You see I write so much in haste,[3] that I can only hint a sentiment, and must leave you to collect the full of what, if I had time and leisure, I would be glad to say. But I would be glad my friends would be deliberating (and *corresponding)* upon what part to take in case Parliament *suspend* all the Acts enumerated by the Congress, or *repeal* the Tea Act and the three acts relative to the Massachusetts bay and Boston.

Your *Parliamentary* friends say, snatch the opportunity for peace and reconcilliation. Your sanguine and warm partizans say, You are united and inspired now: circumstances that may never happen again. Seize the happy, glorious opportunity for establishing the freedom and social felicity of all America. There is a tide in the affairs of men.

GOD direct you,
Henry Ireton

PS. If you should hear of any *honourable* and advantageous offers to induce my *settlement* in this Island, don't be concerned. My heart and happiness are as much centered and bound up in America as ever. My health was never better.

1. QP 51 (reel 29) MHS; "Memoir," 2:227–28, QP 46 (reel 6) MHS; *Memoir,* pp. 239–41.

2. Eliza Susan Quincy added "these copies" in the "Memoir," which she carried into the *Memoir.*

3. Which Eliza Susan rendered as "in so much haste" in both the "Memoir" and *Memoir.*

THOMAS CUSHING TO JQ

30 December 1774[1]

Dear Sir, Boston Decr. 30th 1774

While at Philadelphia I received your Favors of the 20th and 25th August last, and agreable to your Request I spoke to divers Gentlemen to favor you with Letters and with Intelligence and amoung the rest to Mr. John Dickinson and Mr. Joseph Read from whom I doubt not you have heard ere this time.[2] I should have wrote you from Philadelphia but I was so engaged that I had not a moment's time and as Mr. John Adams and Mr. Read told me they should write you by the same Conveyance, that I wrote Dr. Franklin, I knew you would be, by them, favoured with the Proceedings of the Congress and the necessary Intelligence, and therefore that my writing would at that time be needless. Since I have returned home I shall have had nothing of Importance to Communicate. The Proceedings of the Continental Congress are universally approved and will be Sacredly adhered to. The Inhabitants of Canada are much dissatisfied with the late acts relative to that Province and instead of aiding the Administration in carrying the late acts relative to this Province into Execution, they will unite with the Continent in measures to obtain their Repeal. When you left the Province it was in a Convulsed State. They had a Complication of difficulties and distresses to Encounter. Under these Circumstances it was necessary to have a Provincial Congress to Consent upon measures to save themselves from Impending Ruin and to preserve their inestimable Liberty. They met in October last. If in any of their Proceedings they have gone beyond the true line marked out by the Constitution, certainly People of Candor and Consideration will excuse it and make all due allowances for a People in such an alarming perplexed and critical situation and under the dreadfull apprehensions of having their dearest Rights and Liberties torn from them by the Hands of Violence. You are fully acquainted with the distressed situation. You doubtless have been furnished with the Proceedings of the Provincial Congress in October last, and as you are capable, so I doubt not you will be disposed to make the most favourable representation of our Conduct during this time of Perplexity. The Provincial Congress adjourned from October 29 to November 23, when they met at Cambridge and on the 20th Instant they Dissolved. Their Proceedings or the most of them you have in the Public Papers. The late order of the King in Council prohibiting the Exportation of Powder or any sort of arms and ammunition from Great Britain unless by special Licence, has alarmed the People in America. It forebodes the most vigorous exertions of Martial Force. They are therefore adopting the most Effectual Methods to defend themselves against any Hostile Invasions of the Enemies to America. The People of Rhode Island have used the precaution to remove their Powder, Cannon and other Military Stores from the Fort at Newport into the Country. The People at Portsmouth in New Hampshire have done the like by their Cannon and other military Stores at the Fort at New Castle at the Entrance of their Harbour.[3]

I remain with strict truth
Your Friend and humble Servant
Thomas Cushing

PS. Pray let me hear from you how it is like to fare with my dear Country.

1. QP 51 (reel 29) MHS; "Memoir," 2:160–62, QP 46 (reel 6) MHS; *Memoir*, pp. 181–83; Force, ed., *American Archives*, 4th series, 1:1080.

2. The sentence is ended at "Intelligence" in the "Memoir" and *Memoir*.

3. David Hackett Fischer recounts the details of this episode in *Paul Revere's Ride* (New York: Oxford University Press, 1994), pp. 52–57. As with the so-called "powder alarm" in Cambridge the previous September, and the near confrontation between townsfolk and regulars in Salem the following February, the seizing of munitions at Fort William and Mary in Portsmouth raised questions about whether "public property" belonged first and foremost to the crown, or to the people of the province.

JOSIAH QUINCY SR. TO JQ

3 January 1775[1]

Dear Son, January 3d 1775

I have wrote two long Letters to you since your Departure, the last of which, for want of a safe Conveyance is I suppose now in Boston.

Yesterday your Fathers Partners, after keeping us in Suspence about an hour and half, presented Us with the most valuable (the Spanish Prize[2] not excepted) and therefore the most welcome new years Gift, I ever received: The doubly joyfull News of your safe Arrival in England, and your Health restored; confirmed by two Letters to your Wife (but not a Line to your dear Papa). May that all perfect Being who has bestowed such inestimable Blessings upon Us, impress our Minds with a correspondent gratefull Sense of them, manifested by a constant Exertion of our rational Powers, in Pursuit of their *proper Objects.*

It is now about 6 Weeks, since your Wife, and my dear little grandSon returned to Boston, after a short Visit of 3 or 4 Weeks. If I thought the Relation could entertain you, as much as the Action did me, I would fill the Remainder of this Sheet, with a minute Detail of those little Tricks and Arts, by which he discovered such natural Endowments, both of Body and Mind, as if duely cultivated, by a *truely* liberal Education, bid fair to render him an eminently usefull Member of Society, which he certainly will be, if the Petition of my Prayers is granted.[3]

No sooner were the Results of the Continental and provincial Congresses published to the World, than the Presses from South to North, have labored and been delivered of ennumerable Productions in Opposition to and Defence of them: all which, will doubtless be transmitted to you, in News Papers and single Pamphlets. However, I cant deny my Self this Pleasure of noticing one said to be wrote by your Friend G___l L___, which has afforded great Relief to the Minds of those who entertained, most fearfull Apprehensions of an open Rupture with the Parent State.[4]

The Officers of the Army, and their Friends, have carefully concealed the Diminution of their Forces both by Death and Desertion; but it is well known, that, so great a Number have died, out of the still Houses that were hired for Barracks, as to occasion their being removed to other Places: And by the

Numbers of Deserters, that have been seen and spoke with, all over N[ew] E[ngland] as well as to the southward, there is great Reason to believe, there will be scarce enough left to mount Guards when the season for Action arrives. This, if true, will surely *confound the Devices and frustrate the hostile Attempts of our Enemies.* The Circumstances, relative to the Removal of the Cannon, from the Fort at great Island in New Hampshire Government from New Port, and New London, you will receive a particular Account of in the News Papers; which in that Respect may be depended on.

Our Friend Mr G[oldthwai] t[5] tells me his Endeavours to obtain a recommendatory Letter from Lord P[erc]y were unsuccessful which perhaps by this Time you may no great Reason to regret, as it is generally thought, his Abilities or his Connections do not render his Influence very extensive.[6]

I should have told you before, that we were no sooner relieved from our Anxiety about your safe Arrival, and the Recovery of your Health, than our Concern commenced, or rather revived to know, you were safe Arrived in London, and what Reception you met with from the Court and City: Whether your Enemies are to be gratifyd by mob Persecutions, or your Friends, by the Esteem and Honor with which they hope to hear you are received and entertained not only by those Friends to whom you was recommended, but all those Friends to Liberty and the Rights of Mankind, who may honor you with their Acquaintance and Friendship.

You will readily believe me when I tell you we are all, whether Whigs or Tories, quite solicitous to hear, how the new Parliament opens: what the King's Sentiments are relative to american Affairs; how many new Members have obtained Seats in the House of Commons, because they are esteemed Enemies to Despotism, and Friends to Liberty; whether they are like to gain a Majority by being above Corruption? Or whether for Want of a sufficient Number of inflexible Patriots, the publick Affairs of the Nation are, as has been often foretold, running headlong to Ruin, and the Enemies of the British Constitution in its Purity, are likely to succeed, in their Endeavours for its Subversion?

In one of my former Letters I acquainted you with the premature Deaths of Mr. T. Gray who left a very handsome Estate, which he judiciously distributed amongst his near Relations.[7] I am now to inform you of the sudden Death of our Sister Marsh the 8th Instant who left her disconsolate Husband as sincere a Mourner, as, perhaps, ever lost a Wife.[8] May God! Of his infinite Mercy prepare us both for that Seperation from each other, which must sooner or later take Place; indeed, so violent has been the Return of the chronicle Disorders under which I labor, that for more than this fortnight past I almost dispared of Life but, I thank God, I am now much better. Your Wife, her Sisters, her Brother and his Wife with some of Mr. Mason's Family, were to dine with Us last Tuesday, had not Sister Marsh's Death prevented. Speaking of Mr. Mason's Family puts me in mind to tell you, of his Brothers Death in Newport about 3 Weeks since.[9]

You must excuse my rambling from one thing to another: Mr. W___ d brings Intelligence from Boston, that the Seamen on board the Fleet are grown mutinous. That one of them was hanged at the Yard Arm a few Days since. That his Body was sent by 4 men who thought Trustworthy in a Boat to be buried in one of the Islands but they all run off and left the Corpse and Boat when they landed. That one of the Navy Officers, meeting with a Land Officer at K[nox]'s Shop, told him that on board all the Ships, their Men were grown so uneasy and tumultuous, that it was with great Difficulty they could govern them. Upon which the Land Officer observed, "that the uneasiness among the Soldiers was full as great or greater than among the Seamen.[10] With how much Truth I can't say, but, it has been currently reported for this fortnight past, that the Arms of the 10th Regiment have been taken from them, and locked up every Night: and that the Marine's distributed in Barracks at the North End, have absolutely refused to do Duty as they are neither paid nor fed according to Contract. That the Discipline in both Departments is so Severe, and the Duty and Service so disagreable, the Impatience both of Seamen and Soldiers is every Day more and more visible and extensive, and it has been repeatedly hinted, that many of the Officers, as they become more acquainted with the Merits of the Cause they are engaged in, discover great Uneasiness.

If it was certainly known, that, an open Rupture was to take place in the Spring, there could not be more Diligence or greater Application, in studying the Science of War, than there is at present throughout N.E. And I believe through the Continent, which, surely must convince the M[inistr]y, that not only an immense Treasure, but Rivers of Blood must be expended, before the Spirit, of freeborn Americans can be made to submit, to parliamentary Legislation, and submissively bow their Necks to the Yoke of Bondage, their fellow Subjects in Power have prepared for them.

Pray make my affectionate friendly Regards acceptable to good Dr. F[ranklin] and Alderman Tanner and any other Friends who are kind enough to remember and ask after Me.

I can't express how near your Interest, your Health and your Happiness lyes to my Heart, nor how ardently I wish my longing Eyes may be blessed with the joyfull Sight of you, before they are closed in everlasting Darkness and the dear Relation is anihilated between you and

Your unalterably affectionate Parent
Josiah Quincy

PS. All present join in wishing you the Return of many happy new Years.

1. QP 51 (reel 29) MHS; "Memoir," 2:163-64, QP 46 (reel 6) MHS; *Memoir*, pp. 183-85.

2. He was referring to the prize money that he made as a result of the privateering exploits of the *Bethell* in the summer of 1748. Commanded by Isaac Freeman, the *Bethell* had traversed the Atlantic to Gibraltar and back, in search of targets. Freeman's success in securing prize money added considerably to Josiah Sr.'s fortune and that of his business partners, brother Edmund and brother-in-law Edward Jackson. The August 1748 letter that Freeman wrote to Quincy, detailing his activities, is reproduced in L. H. Butterfield's pamphlet *A Pride of Quincys* (Boston: Massachusetts Historical Society, 1969), n.p. The tale of how the *Bethell* captured its largest prize, a Spanish merchantman with a cargo of bullion, by a clever ruse is recounted briefly in the biography of Josiah Jr.'s son, written by Josiah the Mayor's son (Josiah Jr.'s grandson), Edmund Quincy, *The Life of Josiah Quincy of Massachusetts* (Boston: Ticknor and Fields , 1868), pp. 4-5.

3. Eliza Susan Quincy transcribed this paragraph for the "Memoir," but did not carry it into the *Memoir*.

4. He probably had in mind Charles Lee's *Strictures*, published anonymously in Philadelphia roughly a month before–see supra p. 270, n. 1.

5. Possibly Ezekiel Goldthwait.

6. Neither this paragraph nor the one above it appear in the "Memoir" or the *Memoir*.

7. This is the Thomas Gray that Josiah Sr. referred to in a letter to Josiah Jr. of 3 November 1774, a Boston merchant who was injured in a carriage accident and never recovered. See supra, p. 285.

8. A relative by marriage. Anne Marsh had become Josiah Sr.'s third wife in 1762; she died in 1805. Her brother Joseph, who had been in Josiah Sr.'s 1728 Harvard class (as a Hollis scholar—see supra p. 426 n. 608 for Thomas Hollis), served as the tutor for Josiah Jr., and earlier, John Adams, to prepare them for entrance to Harvard.

9. This paragraph and the one above it are not in either the "Memoir" or the *Memoir*.

10. This paragraph, but only to this point, is in the *Memoir;* it is not in the "Memoir" at all.

JQ TO ABIGAIL QUINCY

7 January 1775[1]

My very dear friend, Bristol Jany 7th 1775

The holydays have been improved by me in visiting Bath, Bristol and some manufacturing towns in the vicinity.

Did Americans realize their *commercial* powers, spirit and obstinacy would characterise their future measures. Had the Non-exportation agreement been appointed to commence on the first of March, Britain would e're this time been in popular convulsions. This is the sentiment even of Adversaries.

The manufacturing towns are now in motion, and petitions to Parliament to repeal the late acts on *commercial* principles will flow from all quarters. London is setting the example, and this city and other manufacturing towns are preparing to follow the example.

The commonality of this kingdom are grossly ignorant. The tools of the ministry (for their reward) are incessantly retailing the same stale falsehoods and the same weak reasonings every day. The consequences are easily conceived.

The people of this country must be made *to feel* the importance of their American bretheren. If the Colonies have one spark of virtue, in less than a twelve month, Britain must *feel* at every nerve. Believe me, the commonality of America are statesmen, philosophers and heroes compared with *the many* of G[reat] Britain. With *the former* you may reason: *the latter* you must drive. I have endeavoured to study the character of both countries; this sometimes is the result of my observations.

I have lately read divers Letters from several inland manufacturers to their mercantile correspondents; and I find that the Address to the People of their country hath wrought, and is still working wonders.[2]

Oh my dear friend! Reach hither thy hand and feel how my heart beats in the cause of my Country: their safety, their honor, their all is at stake. I see America placed in that great tide in the affairs of men, which taken at the flood leads on to fortune. Oh snatch the glorious opportunity! Or for "a warning voice" our lives are bound in vassalage and miseries.

The ministry I am well satisfied are quite undetermined, as to the course they must take with regard to America. They will put off the final resolution to the last moment. I know not, and any further than mere humanity dictates I care not, what part they take. If my own Countrymen deserve to be free, they will be free. If born free, they are contented to be slaves, e'en let them bear their burdens.

You must know, that I am a perfect Infidel in matters of mercantile virtue. It will not, therefore, be sufficient when we fund a commercial apostate to mouth "perdition catch the villain."[3] The Patience, the lenity, the humanity, of Americans towards public conspirators and public traitors hath been the source of infinite mischief.

From this circumstance our friends have become despondent, and our foes have taken courage.

I have a thousand things to say, which I would wish to "speak without a Tongue, and be heard without ears."[4] For this reason, therefore, if the three Acts relative to the Massachusetts bay are *not* repealed, I intend to be in Philadelphia in May next.

I am sure, if you knew all that I could tell you, it would strengthen your hand and inspire your hearts.

I have this day wrote very similar sentiments to my friend, Mr. Dickinson, at Philadelphia. You will perceive part of this letter copied, by my friend Williams, from mine to that great and good man. We are both now writing in the midst of a Coffee house, surrounded with the intolerable rackett of Dice boxes and the noise of party-cabal.

If, therefore, you make public any part of this letter, print that which relates to the cause of my transcribing part of my letter to Mr Dickinson, which will carry an apology to that gentleman, who may otherwise be displeased at seeing the same sentiment to different persons.

Last Tuesday and Wednesday I spent with Lord Shelburne at his magnificent seat at Bowood. His politeness would have prevailed with me to have stayed a few days longer, if my other engagements had permitted that indulgence.

Once since I arrived I spit a small quantity of blood, owing to some exertions of my lungs that brought on that old disorder. Since that time, I have had no symptoms of it; and, at this time, and indeed ever since I have been in Britain, I never enjoyed greater health and spirits. This climate undoubtedly agrees with me much better than my own: neither colds nor fevers have molested me since sojourning in this land of my fathers.

Capt Caldwell, who engages to deliver this with his own hand, calls upon me to finish.

Adieu! The blessings of my heart rest upon You.

JQ——y

You may show my Letters (in general) to our friend Samuel Adams

1. QP 51 (reel 29) MHS; "Memoir," 2:236–39 , QP 46 (reel 6) MHS; *Memoir,* pp. 247–49. Quincy mistakenly dated it 1774.

2. Printed in Ford, ed., *Journals of the Continental Congress,* 1:82–90.

3. Quincy may have taken a passage from *Othello* (Act III, Scene 3)—spoken by Othello as Desdemona leaves him and the suspicions planted by Iago begin to fester—and changed it for his purposes. The original reads: "Excellent wretch! Perdition catch my soul But I do love thee! And when I love thee not, Chaos is come again."

4. Quincy could have had in mind the riddle about the wind; he may also have been quoting from Edward Search, *The Light of Nature Pursued,* 7 vols. (London: T. Jones, 1768–1777), 1:3, speaking of the "Faculties of the Mind." He did not turn to it for his commonplace book nor is it listed in the 'Catalogue of Books." Abraham Tucker, the author, used Edward Search as a pseudonym.

JQ TO ABIGAIL QUINCY

11 January 1775[1]

My very dear friend London Jany 11th 1775

Last night I returned from Bath and Bristol, where I have been to spend a few of the holydays. From the last of which places, I wrote to my friend Mr. Dickinson and yourself: the Letter to you (together with several others on board the same ship, written sometime since) the Capt. (Caldwell who sails in Messers Mackay and Mitchell's employ) engaged on his arrival to deliver with his own hand.

Last evening I was regaled with yours of the 3 & 14 of November; James Lovells of the 10, 25, & 28th of October; Dr. Chaunceys of the 21st of October and the 3rd of November; and Oliver Wendells of the 15th of November. To all these, my remembering friends, present my acknowledgment and thanks. Inform them I shall write answers, if the time limited for the sail of this vessel (which is at present fixed for tomorrow morning) is extended.*

If the many letters, I have sent, come safe to your hands, my friends will see that I am neither less idle, nor less pregnant of my cause, than when I sojourned with them beyond Jordan. My avocations are so many and incessant, that I find but little time that I cannot employ more to the service of my country by attending to men and things here, than by writing my sentiments to those on the other side of the water. But that little time, whenever it occurs, is sacredly dedicated to that correspondence with my Bretheren in America, which is a substantial pleasure of my life. But let my friends in Boston and the Massachusetts be *reminded,* that my litterary connexions are extended through the Southern Colonies, and that, therefore, when they think themselves forgotten or neglected, my time has been so wholly employed with occurences here, or in transmitting advices to our Southern friends, that I have been denied any opportunity of paying that tribute of gratitude, respect and applause, that my Massachusetts friends may justly claim.

But as I have wrote to you very constantly and largely upon the subject of our great concerns I must entreat, that those *confidential* friends, to whom you may show my letters, would consider them as information sent the Brotherhood in general, and in correspondence (by way of return) favor me with their advice and council, for which, as I shall ever stand much in need, so I shall be accordingly gratefull.

The cause of the Colonies every day grows more *popular;* that of the ministry more desperate. The merchants are alarmed: the manufacturers are in motion; the artificers and handy craftsmen are in amaze, and the lower ranks of the Community are starving. Petitions are framing in all parts of the kingdom† in favor of *their own dear selves*; and if America reaps any advantage by this movement, be assured her tribute of gratitude is not due either to merchants or manufacturers. America might sink into bondage and long drag the load of misery and shame, before either of these orders (as a body of men) would feel one generous sentiment, or make one feeble effort—unless *immediate* and *obvious* interest prompted that exertion. I say *immediate* and *obvious,* for all know, that if the distance is beyond their own nostrils, or clouded by any thing deeper than a cob web shade, they will neither see, nor understand. I speak here of the governing majority; individuals are among them, who have knowledge, sentiment and spirit. But Heaven knows how little, how incredibly little, these noble qualities have influence here.

There can be no doubt, that the peacefull, spiritless and self-denying warfare, in which the Colonies are now engaged, would yield an ample victory: to be sure not the most glorious and splendid of any on record. But the times of splendor and the parade of glory may de dispensed with, if we can obtain the object of our wishes, by attacks which are truly *mock-heroic,* and weapons, which are most certainly *carnal.* My great doubt is, whether oeconomic virtue is a quality deeply engrafted in the human mind, and whether it contains a spirit sharp and active enough to cement and animate any large popular body for any length of time. However, if my Countrymen, after deliberation are convinced, that they can sacredly keep the pure faith of oeconomy, that they can follow the simplicity of their fathers, and what is more, can compell and keep to the ordinance of self-denial *their whole household,* I will venture to *assure them*, that they shall obtain a bloodless victory, and be crowned with the most ample success. I am so certain of the truth of what I now say, and that my words are indeed the words of soberness, that I would put my life and my all on the hazard of the trial. Let the non-importation agreements be observed for one year, and this whole kingdom will be in agonies and convulsions. Let the non-exportation be kept at the same time, and this nation must starve—or emigrate to America.

These are not the hasty opinions of a moment: they are sentiments founded upon enquiry and reflection. And I am convinced of no one truth more strongly, and I have no one judgment (in my own opinion) better founded, than what is above transmitted.‡

I am thus explicit, because you very well know, that I not only wish the safety, but the *glory* of my country. I have heard its *valour* questioned. I have seen its honour touched. Of that valor I have an elevated idea; of that honor I am jealous. As I wish, therefore, the peace, the wellfare and the bloodless deliverance of my native land, I hope to see my Countrymen prudent, frugal, saving oeconomists. But when I shall wish to see them *great* and *glorious,*

"I sure must view them in a nobler field."[2]

Permanent slavery or a full deliverance from their present burdens is the alternative now before America. No other country hath ever yet had any choice, but that of the sword for their emancipation from bondage. America, favored above the nations of antiquity, hath an alternative. If her Children can withstand the blandishments of luxury and the delusions of false pride, they may purchase liberty without it's price. But if attachments to commercial leaks and onions (an idolatry equally degrading and, in the present case, almost as impious as that of Egypt) have debauched the appetite and blinded all sense, they must soon make their election of *the load of slavery,* or *the sword of blood.*

The ministry are evidently plunged. Every thing bears the mark of distraction. Bute and Mansfield are not less your enemies, and Hutchinson is *still the same man.* Lord Dartmouth is _____ but America can at this day want no information as to his character. When hypocrisy throws away her mask, credulity must renounce her faith.

No measures are yet determined upon in the cabinet. Every thing will be done at the meeting of Parliament on the spur of the occasion.

The nation are 15 in 20, your friends and hearty well-wishers to your cause. The Lords and Commons are *what they are,* but another character is *in principle* your adversary, and will never be reconciled to your deliverance, till he sees (what, peradventure, he will not wait long for) a spirit going forth which compells rulers to their duty.

I shall take care to keep you constantly informed of events as they rise. Very important ones must occur in a short time.

The staunch friends of Our Country are here in high spirits. I should flatter your national vanity, if I told you all that is said and thought of Americans at this day. But the sentiments of this people are as fluctuating, and sometimes as boisterous, as the ocean.

I find I shall have no time to write to the friends I mentioned above. Send them, therefore, this Letter to peruse by way of apology.

My best wishes attend you. Present me to friends and relatives in the bonds of respect and love. In the same bonds continue to hold

Your Henry Ireton

PS. I would not have you make public, what is said of Lord Dartmouth, because great men have always some powers to hurt, and we generally find a proneness to revenge is co-equal with abilities to injure. I have wrote you already, if the acts are *not* repealed I shall be at Philadelphia in May next. I am in fine health and spirits, with many friends.[3]

Post PS. Tell Samuel Adams I can scarcely forgive his breach of faith and neglect of me. Tell Mr. Morton, I imagine he does not expect forgiveness. Remember the rule I gave you in my former letters: Print nothing without an absolute necessity and the consent of your father.

*Since writing the above I have received another letter from Dr Chauncey of the 4th of November, but have not as yet received the two pamphlets. Let him be the first to whom you transmit this letter. I have also receive a very *usefull* letter from my good friend Nathaniel Appleton. Let him be the next.

†That of London hath this day past in a very large meeting *unanimously*. The assembly was larger and more respectable than upon any like occasion. The contents of the petition will not be published, till delivered, which will be on the first day of the setting of Parliament. The draught was much extolled by my informant, who was a member of the meeting.

‡January 11th. Having this instant received a letter, from a gentleman of rank and character in this city, which confirms my own opinion, I herewith transmit it to corroborate my own sentiments. You will take care not to publish his name, so as to reach this side [of] the water.

1. QP 51 (reel 29) MHS; "Memoir," 2:240–47, QP 46 (reel 6) MHS; *Memoir*, pp. 250–54.

2. Although I have not been able to find this full statement anywhere but here, the phrase "a nobler field" turns up in a dozen or so sources known to Quincy, from a translation of Ovid to Shakespeare's *Troilus and Cressida* to poems by John Dryden and James Thomson.

3. The "Memoir" includes the two postscripts, but not the paragraphs after that, which Quincy had marked with insertion points in the text, then squeezed into the margins. The printed *Memoir* only has the material above "Henry Ireton."

JQ TO ABIGAIL QUINCY

12 January 1775[1]

My very dear friend, London Jany 12th 1775

Yesterday I finished a long letter to you, which will accompany the present. By a consideration of both, my friends will see how difficult the task would be to write *severally* to them all.

I have just come from spending three hours in private conversation with Governor Pownall, and without a moment's delay set down to transmit some parts of what passed between Us.

After having given him some general account of my intelligence from America, he said, "now, Sir, I will give you some news also. A King's ship has arrived from Boston with dispatches from General Gage. She sailed the 16th of December from that place. She brings certain accounts, that notwithstanding the non-importation agreement was to take place the first of December, yet since that day, by connivance, a considerable quantity of piemento and other articles forbidden by that agreement have been imported and stored in the city of New York." I replied, "I don't believe that what you have heard is true." "You may depend upon it, Sir; I am satisfied of it, perfectly, myself," was his answer.

See that this matter be enquired into. Don't entertain ill-grounded jealousies of each other, yet watch over one another for good.

"I will tell you more, Sir," added Governor Pownall: "the *Provincial* Congress have chosen their General Officers. Two of them are Colonel Prebble and Colonel Pomroy; I have forgot the third. They have also chosen a Committee to manage the office of Governor; and another that of the Supreme Court of Justice of the Province."[2]

I shall suspend a comment on this matter.

After a long conversation with him on the subjects which grew naturally out of our conversation I asked him (he is now a member of Parliament) what he thought the Ministry would do at the approaching sessions. He answered: "They will not repeal the Boston Port Bill because it executes itself. They will not repeal the acts altering your form of government, because these late advices, show that you have taken that matter out of their hands. They will not repeal the Quebec Bill, because it is the sense of all parties here that that is a matter with which no other Colony, but Quebec, hath any thing to do. If *they* don't complain, the other Colonies have no right to intermeddle."

I replied to Governor Pownall, I wished I could be satisfied that what he now said would be true. "It will ease my mind (add I) and would determine my conduct, to sail to America in four and twenty hours. I should then be in no doubt what the Colonies ought to do; and (with a little elevation of voice) I am sure I should not hesitate what part to take myself." "I tell you Mr xxxxxx, continued Governor Pownall, what I now say. I do not deliver as what I am informed of by the ministry, but as what I have not the least doubt of. It is my solid judgment founded upon facts on which I have reflected, and laid together, again and again."

My answer was: "I have lately been in the western part of the kingdom. I have conversed (ever since I have been there) with all ranks of people, who think or converse at all upon these subjects. I am a stranger in this country: I do not pretend to be thoroughly acquainted with their genius, temper or character; but this I will venture to say, that if the actions of this country are as correspondent with the sense, words and declarations of its inhabitants, as *the words* and *doings* of my American countrymen, I am sure, that this country will be convulsed. I am sure these will be very astonishing commotions, if those acts are not repealed, and that very speedily too after the Parliament have got well together. But as I said before I don't pretend to know this people as well as those who were bred and have always dwelt among them. Indeed I have been confirmed more and more every day, that *the Commonality* in this country are no more like *the Commonality* in America, than if they were two intire, distinct and unconnected people."

"Very true, Mr. xxxxxx," replied Mr Pownall; "your observation is certainly just. You have formed a right judgment; and you will see more reason to strengthen your opinion every day you live in this island."

You see I am faithfull to the good old cause. *I feel* that I shall continue so.

Governor Pownall presented me with two of his late productions to be sent to Dr Cooper, which I shall do, if I am able by this opportunity.[3]

I have wrote you that I shall be in Philadelphia in May next, if the acts are *not* repealed. I have made that determination, because I think I shall be able to do some good there. In conversation we can say and do more, than by whole folios of writing. But my being there at that time is so uncertain that I would not, *upon any account* have my friends omit sending their letters of intelligence to me here. Such letters are of amazing service. With them I can do more good, than you would think possible, if you had never experienced the effect.

Adieu. May the great Father of spirits inspire you! Act worthy of yourselves and you must be successfull and happy.

Henry Ireton

PS. I intend to send you Burke's Speech and Mrs Macaulay's Address (published this day) to the People of England &c.[4] They will be read in America with avidity and applause.

Excuse my not writing to my *two* fathers. I think, if they reflect a little, they will find no reason to blame me. Don't print the name of Governor Pownall, unless you find that putting his name at large will do considerable service to the Cause. He and I too must submit to inconveniences when our Country is in their Care. It is a necessity we must acquiesce in with contentment.

Post PS. Since writing the within, I have received the original Manuscript of a Letter from a Merchant here to his friend in Virginia. I now transmit it for your information and judgment. Mr. Samuel Adams will know the hand, if he sees it. Mr Sheriff Lee desires, that I would inform Mr S. Adams, that he inclosed a Letter to him under cover to Thomas Bromfield, by the New York Packett.

I am well informed, that Mr Hayley on receiving a large parcel of Letters from America without one order inclosed, sincerely said, "I find there is not even an inclination in Boston to smuggle now." Mr Sheriff Lee my informant.

A certain Mr. _____ lately arrived from Boston said "a few more troops would be sufficient to inforce all the measures of the Ministry." Mr. Bromfield my informant.

NB.[5] Be extremely carefull of Mr Bromfield's and my name.[6]

I have neither room, nor time nor for comment.

1. QP 51 (reel 29) MHS; "Memoir," 2:247–52, QP 46 (reel 6) MHS; *Memoir,* pp. 254–60.

2. Jedediah Preble and Seth Pomeroy; Artemas Ward was the third. This was part of the selection of various individuals to serve under the authority of the provincial convention, including a standing committee of safety—which Thomas Gage, not surprisingly, condemned, as illegal

and unconstitutional. See Lincoln, ed., *Journals of the Provincial Congress,* p. 35 for the appointments noted above, and p. 21 for Gage.

3. Pownall had revised and expanded his *Administration of the British Colonies* to a fifth edition in two volumes (see p. 318, n. 4, supra). Over the previous five years he had also had reproduced as pamphlets a couple of his speeches in the Commons and his reflections on the "wretched state" of the East India Company. Quincy's impressions of Pownall ought to be contrasted with those he left of Thomas Hutchinson, in what the former governor had hoped (unrealistically) would be a temporary London exile. In Peter Orlando Hutchinson, ed., *The Diary and Letters of Thomas Hutchinson,* 2 vols. (London: S. Low, Marston, Searle & Rivington, 1883–1886). Samuel Cooper, the minister of Boston's Brattle Street congregational church, had befriended Pownall when he was the Massachusetts governor and kept up a correspondence with him after he left. Cooper chose the patriot side in the imperial contest and welcomed independence when it came. See Charles W. Akers, *The Divine Politician* (Boston: Northeastern University Press, 1982).

4. Burke had delivered the first of his two most famous speeches on American affairs the previous April (the second would be on 22 March 1775, after Quincy had begun his fatal voyage) but it was not published until January 1775, as the *Speech of Edmund Burke, Esq., on American Taxation , April 19 1774* (London: J. Dodsley, 1775). Catharine Macaulay's *An Address to the People of England, Scotland, and Ireland, on the Present Important Crisis of Affairs* (London: Edward and Charles Dilly, 1775) had also just been published. Quincy had long admired Macaulay as a writer, quoting from both her 1770 *Observations* and her five-volume *History of England* in his political commonplace book. He had in fact just returned from his trip to Bath over the New Year's holiday, taken in part to meet her. For the commonplace book entries and Bath excursion see Coquillette and York, eds., *Portrait of a Patriot,* 1:102, 109–12, 120, 125, 138, 171, and 246, resp. Macaulay's *History* is in the "Catalogue of Books" in ibid., 5:898 (no. 230). There is no listing for the *Observations.*

5. NB—Nota Bene: to note well.

6. Eliza Susan Quincy transcribed most of this lengthy postscript in the "Memoir." Somewhat less ended up in the *Memoir.*

JQ TO ABIGAIL QUINCY

12 January 1775[1]

My very dear friend London Jany 12 1775 12 at night

I have been all this day toiling for our oppressed country. I have just closed my advices to the Southward. I should not now resume my pen, having wrote you very largely to Day and yesterday, had I not been just gratified with your and my good friend James Lovell's favors of October and December, yours dated 10 November and 9 December, his November 25 and 9th December.[2] Thank him most heartily for his zeal and industry in the cause of his country, and his affection and good wishes for me. Show him my Letters: tell him to consider them as addressed to him, and *command* him to persevere in his way of well-doing.

If you are satisfied, that what you wrote me relative to the speeches of Major Paddock[3] and Judge Sewall is really true in fact, please to convey word to Mr. Paddock and assume *in my name* that I have "*dared* to show my head in London," that I have *dared* to enter into the presence of Lords North and Mansfield, and what he may think more, on two days successively, to stand before the throne of a king, *literally* within reach of his royal sceptre and the sword of justice. Neither one, or the other dazzled or terrified me. Even the eloquence of a Sovereign did not so confound my judgment, but that before the royal charm was over, I was able to recollect, and remind a friend who stood near me, of the memorable saying of Henry Marten to Edward Hyde—"*I do not think One man wise enough to govern us all.*[4] Nay the splendor of royal robes, the pomp of State-attendants, or the glitter of a Diadem never once so fascinated my understanding or beguiled my heart, as that I did not realize the solemn and eternal truth delivered by the illustrious Milton—"*The trappings of a monarchy will set up a Commonwealth.*"[5]

You may tell Judge Sewall, that I am not yet "hanged", and whether, he or I shall first *dangle upon a gibbet* is a matter altogether problematical. But whether *he or I deserve it most,* I am willing to submit to a Jury of freeholders in his own vicinity. And if he will move for sentence upon their verdict, I will agree not to move in arrest of judgment.

Politicks you see so engross my time, that I have no time to think or write of those affections that are very deep in my heart. I know you will excuse the indulgence.

Write by every *possible* way so *little* memorandum of the state, of letters received. It will gratify me much to hear of the safe arrival of any of my Letters.

My duty and affection present to our Common Parents and relations. Tell them my health and spirits still continue high. As to my sentiments and opinions, my integrity and firmness, they must judge of those by my conduct.

Yours most affectionately

Josiah Quincy jun.

PS. Don't think I forget my Little Ones because I don't talk of them. They are subjects I had rather fondle in my arms, than employ my pen upon.

Post PS. Since writing the above last night, Governor Pownall hath this morning (January 13, 1775) called upon me, and I having Mr. Brand Hollis with me, he had only time to say, "you will hear terrible news from Boston town: The matter is decided before this time."

1. QP 51 (reel 29) MHS; "Memoir," 2:252–56, QP 46 (reel 6) MHS; *Memoir*, pp. 260–62.

2. Lovell's letters are here; Abigail's are not—their whereabouts, now unknown. None of the letters that Abigail wrote to Josiah in fact survive, or at least that I have been able to find.

3. Adino Paddock was a successful coach maker in Boston, an officer in the town's train of artillery. He sided with Gage when the General arrived as Governor, remained in Boston during the subsequent siege, evacuated with other Loyalists in March 1776, and took up residence on the Isle of Jersey.

4. Clarendon, *Life*, p. 41. Hyde claimed Marten made that statement very early on in the English civil war, an indication of republican tendencies that only became more pronounced and more militant with time. Marten's sympathies for the Levellers carried him to regicide and deep involvement in the attempt to create a commonwealth in the wake of Charles I's execution. Tempestuous, irascible, Marten did not get on well with Cromwell as lord protector and narrowly avoided execution himself when Charles II took the throne. Hyde, like Marten, had been a barrister who held a seat in the House of Commons as the nation split between crown and parliament. Unlike Marten, he chose monarchy, served as a diplomat on the Continent and had attached himself to Charles II when the future king was still a prince during the civil war. He was eventually rewarded with an earldom. Rising to become lord chancellor, his falling out with Charles II led to his exile in France, where he died. He had begun his history of the rebellion while it was still being waged and wrote his autobiography just a few years before his death in 1674. There is a good bit on Marten, Hyde and their differences in David Norbrook, *Writing the English Republic* (Cambridge, Eng.: Cambridge University Press, 1999). It seems likely that Quincy owned a copy of the 1759 edition of Clarendon's *Life* (see the citation in his allusion in his "Pro Lege" essay at supra, p. 16, n. 8), even though he did not turn to it for his political commonplace book, nor is it listed in the "Catalogue of Books"—evidence, again, that his intellectual world cannot be perfectly reconstructed.

5. An observation he also made in his London journal on 29 November 1774. See Coquillette and York, eds., *Portrait of a Patriot*,1:237. He was probably quoting (from memory) the introduction to the 1753 edition of Milton's *Works* that he used for the commonplace book—not Milton himself, but the editor, Thomas Birch.

JQ TO ABIGAIL QUINCY

14 January 1775[1]

My best friend, London Jany 14. 1775

I was this moment closing my advices to you, when I received from Mr. Blowers your Letters of October 15, November 3 and 8, my father's of November 3rd and Sister Nancy's.[2]

I am so fatigued with writing &c that *I can write no more.* The Person by whom I send this goes in ten minutes.

Thank my friends most heartily for their Letters. Don't let them think I neglect their favors. They must consider my letters to you as addressed to them all. I am so hurryed I have no other way.

Having sent out to Mrs. Bromfield (that most amiable lady) to transcribe some of my writings, I forward you her letter inclosing the Copies to her *equally* worthy husband, as a specimen of her accomplishments, and an evidence of my *own Labors* and some of my Shifts.

I have acknowledged to you the receipt of all the Letters I have received . I have told you all that I most wish you to know, excepting how much I am

Your affectionate and constant,

JQ——y

PS. My health was never better. I have as yet had no symptoms of a seasoning.

Post PS. Ingersoll hath had a severe touch of the gout in his stomach and is now ill. Jonathan Bliss is also confined to his room with a cold.[3]

1. QP 51 (reel 29) MHS; "Memoir," 2:256–57, QP 46 (reel 6) MHS; *Memoir,* pp. 262–63.

2. The letter from Josiah Sr. to Josiah Jr. survives and is printed supra, pp. 283–87. The others are apparently lost.

3. The first postscript is in the "Memoir" and *Memoir,* but not this second one.

JQ TO JOSIAH QUINCY SR.

22 January 1775[1]

Honored and Dear Sir, London Jany 22d 1775

I intend to say nothing more in this Letter than that I am in health and spirits, having never had an ill day since my arrival in this Island. *I am here doing my duty.*

Last Friday was a day of great happiness to me; I heard a Chatham and a Cambden speak for hours on the concerns of my country.[2]

This letter is intended to contain nothing, but what the spies at the Ministry may be willing to let pass. And having gratified their own curiosity, I wish they may be candid and generous enough to let my friends gratify theirs also.

Your affectionate and obliged
J Quincy Junr.

1. QP 51 (reel 29) MHS; another copy by a different hand in the Simon Gratz Autograph Collection, Case 8, Box 16, #250B HSP mss.; "Memoir," 2:27, QP 46 (reel 6) MHS; *Memoir,* p. 278.

2. Simmons and Thomas, eds., *Proceedings and Debates,* 5:268-87; and the note on Quincy's place in the record of this debate in Coquillette and York, eds., *Portrait of a Patriot,* 1:252–53, n. 95.

WILLIAM PHILLIPS TO JQ

25 January 1775[1]

Dear Sir Boston Jany 25th 1775

We have had the pleasure of hearing of your good State of health by your Letters dated Falmouth November 8th and are in expectation of receiving more from London soon. Wish they may give us favourable accounts of American Affairs, but of this fear much. Hitherto we have got much better than I expected, but what is to come know not, nor can I form any conjecture. A Storm seems to be gathering by the conduct of some of the Officers in the Army towards the Inhabitants. The particulars I cannot give you; enquiry is now making into facts before Justices Quincy, Hill and Pemberton. The greatest efforts are practiced to divide the People with little success for they appear as determined as ever. They have great dependance on your giving them the best of intelligence, and doubt not of your exertions in their cause which they view as just and will finally prevail.

I have receive the Principal of James Butler's Bond and £22.4 / Principal and Interest on Jonathon Bulkley's who is since dead. Jonathan Bass has discharged his and three others have paid their Interest.

I must refer you to Mrs. Quincy for the state of your family and only say they are very well.

Who am yours with much Affection
Wm Phillips

1. QP 51 (reel 29) MHS. Abigail Quincy's father, who was helping manage the family's finances. In a notice printed in the *Boston Gazette,* 10 October 1774, Quincy had informed the public that he had left for London and former clients should take their concerns to Perez Morton, who had taken over his office. "Those Persons who owe the said Quincy, on Bond or Note, are hereby notified to make their payments to WILLIAM PHILLIPS, Esq;" with whom Quincy had left power of attorney.

HUGH BAILLIE TO JQ

28 January 1775[1]

Sir, Jany 28. 1775

When I consider the present sittuation of our Publick affairs, I compare them with that of *Rome* and the Free States of Greece, just before they lost their liberty. It gives me very melancholy Ideas. *Philip* of *Macedon*, before he could conquer that brave free people of *Greece,* he introduced Luxury, Venality, and dissipation among them, and by corrupting their Leaders and Orators in their Assemblys by Money, he was enabled to conquer that brave people. And *Julius Caesar* by the same methods, laid the foundation for the destruction of the liberties of *Rome*, and the example of *Curio,* a Roman senator, who oposed him with great apearance of Patriotism, and was afterwards among the keenest of his friends, may shew us what we have to fear, from the inumerable Posts and Pensions, that now exist among us. To get the better of his Patriotism, it cost Caesar more than £400,000. And that brave people who whilst they continued free were unconquerable, were so dispirited in a few years after they lost their liberties, that the Senate itself in the Reign of Tiberius, the second Prince from Caesar, durst not make any resolve, without previously knowing the commands of the Prince, and in *Caligula's* time (his imediate successor) they were so far degenerated from brave Free men to Brutes, that they durst not oppose his making his Horse a Consul.

Our sittuation is such, that our only safety depends upon our Fleet. I was with that great Man the late Lord *Stair,* when Ambassador at *Paris,* and he was my relation, I often had the honour of conversing with him, at home, after his return from Paris.[2] And as his love to his country was sincere, when Mr. *Robert Walpole,* cajoled by Cardinal *Fleury,* to a neglect of the national trade, he wated upon the King and told him, that by neglecting trade his Minister was sacrificing him and the Nation to *France,* for said he, if by the loss of our Trade, our sailors are not double the number of those of *France,* we are undone, and the King of France can make us a Province to France, when he pleases, as our Fleet cant all be in one place, and the invasion from France may be from different Ports of France, and our Army compared to that of France is a nothing.

Now let us consider the sittuation of our trade at the present. Our chief trade lies with America. By our breaking with them, the number of our sailors will be decreased the one half of what they are, as I am told from Merchants, and instead of having the assistance of America, we shall be at War with them, and our Troops and Navy will be employed to destroy the very people by whose assistance and friendship we may be the greatest Nation in Europe. We can have from thence, all sorts of Naval stores, which costs us near two millions a year, to the northern powers of Europe. And from America we should have them in exchange for our manufactures, and in a few years when that large Continent is better peopled, we should be furnished with Wines, Raw Silk and Fruits &c from thence, which costs us at present, more than our naval stores, so that by a breach with America, we not only lose all these advantages and their Assistance against our enemies, but we likewise deprive Manufacturers at home of bread, and force the Americans to take what they wanted from Great Brittain, from France and Holland. And indeed had I been asleep for some years past, I should have thought that some late Acts of Parliament, had taken their rise at the court of Versailles, as I am afraid they must have consequences big with the destruction of the Brittish empire, and may probably end in our becoming a Province of France, when ever that ambitious nation, find our Fleet and Army, engaged to destroy our own strength, by attacking our own Collonys, and I believe nobody doubts of their taking hold of that opportunity, when ever it is in their power, and we may consider wether it is better for us to continue as we are, or to be treated by France as the Island of Corsica now is.

I was amazed some days ago, to hear of a speech in the house of Commons mentioning the Merchanets of Great Brittain, as not to be regarded though they should all concur in Pettitions and speaking of the landed interest, as what had no connection with Trade. The Gentleman who made this speech, I have heard spoken of as a man of sense, and yet there is no mathematical proposition clearer than this, by Trade this nation is become one of the most powerful in the World, and by losing its trade it would dwindle as to nothing, with regard to the rest of the powers of Europe, and the landed interest would fall to below a half of what it now pays, and the number of inhabitants would decrease a one half, and upon the number of inhabitants, the power and riches of any country depends.

I have never heard that the inhabitants of America desired any more from

Great Brittain, than to continue in possession of what they have possessed for 200 years past, and what their Charters entittled them to, which are granted by the Crown, and which the parlement have virtualy confirmed more than once, and I can't see how it can consist with the honour of the Mother Country, to break through these Charters and priviledges. The *Latin* inhabitants of Italy, were long the Allies of Rome, they thought themselves entitled to the priviledges of Roman Cittazens. The Romans refused them that priviledge, which occasioned a long and bloody War. Afterwards the Romans granted their desire, and never afterwards attempted to deprive them of these priviledges. The case of the Americans is much stronger in their favour. They are our bretheren, and were indued by the Charters and priviledges granted them, to attempt to settlement at the risk of their lives and fortunes in a Wilderness, and would it be fair and honourable, for their mother country to break through the Charters and priviledges they have granted them. And indeed had no priviledges been granted them, it would be the interest of Great Brittain, to give them all they ask; for no nation can be great under an Arbitrary and despotick Power. And a very great author observes Arbitrary power is political damnation, and particularly a trading nation, and therefore I hope there may be some real friends about his Majesty, who may convince him, that entering into a War with America must destroy the greatest Bulwark for his and the national safety, and that all attempts to introduce Arbitrary power and Popery, to any part of the brittish dominions, is contrary to the intentions of the act of settlement, in favour of the Royal Family.

I bore Arms under his Grace the Duke of Argyle, in 1745, against the Rebels in Scotland, at the head of a company of 52 volunteers, which besides of venturing my life and fortune, it cost me a considerable sum of money. I thought I fought against Popery and slavery, and should be sorry to live so long to see any encouragement given to these things I fought against, or to see any measures followed that may occasion jealousy in the minds of his Majestys subjects.

As I have no concern with any party, I am too Old to have any view of Ambition, and don't so much as expect repayment of the money I expended in the service of the Crown, and therefore have no view by this letter, but an honest wish to see the Eyes of my Countrymen opened, to perceive that the loss of *America,* may in all probability prove the destruction of Great Brittain, and therefore to induce them to prevent a War with America.

I am
Sir,
Your most Humble Servant,
Hugh Baillie
Doctor of Laws

P.S. I believe there never was a time, when there was a better correspondence between a great majority in parlement and the ministry than now, and it puts me in mind of what Cicero observes with regard to the sittuation of *Rome* in his time. Says he, you must either speak and vote with the *Triumverate Pompey, Caesar,* and *Crassus* or through[3] away your speeches and votes, by speaking or voting against them. We seem to be galoping into Arbitrary power and we won't find it easy to get another Prince of Orange to bring us out of danger.

1. QP 51 (reel 29) MHS; Howe, ed., "Quincy Letters," pp. 486–89. Baillie used few commas or periods, writing, seemingly in a grammatical stream of consciousness. I made a a few changes, similar to those made by Mark Antony DeWolfe Howe. Joseph Reed had written Quincy a letter of introduction (see Reed to JQ, 25 October 1774), supra, p. 279; Quincy met with Baillie on January 20th, after hearing debates in the House of Lords (see Coquillette and York, eds., *Portrait of a Patriot,* 1:261). Baillie had long been living in retirement in London, after a stormy career as a judge in Ireland. During this period he wrote a tract taking on both John Shebbeare and Samuel Johnson for their position on American affairs. For Baillie's background see Kevin Costello, "The Court of Admiralty of Ireland, 1745–1756," *American Journal of Legal History* 50 (2008-2010):23–48.

2. John Dalrymple, second Earl of Stair, who served as George I's minister plenipotentiary in Paris from 1715 to 1720. He had risen as a protégé of the Duke of Marlborough in the fighting on the Continent that led to the great victory at Blenheim in 1704.

3. That is, "throw."

THOMAS BRAND HOLLIS TO JQ

2 March 1775[1]

March 2 1775

Mr. Brand Hollis desires Mr. Quincy to accept of this small parcell of books the only ones he has by him at present to amuse him in his passage and as a mark of his esteem and regard. Wishes he may arrive in health and good spirits in his native soil and has no doubts but that the magnanimity and good sense of his countrymen will fix their Liberties on a solid basis and knowing the errors of England will avoid them and hopes they will show to the world a perfect form of Government where Liberty and Justice shall act in Union.

2 March 1775

1. QP 51 (reel 29) MHS; Howe, ed., "Quincy Letters," p. 489. Quincy noted in his London journal for March 3rd that he received "eight valuable books and eight pamphlets" from Hollis, and two more books and pamphlets from Theophilus Lindsey. See Coquillette and York, eds., *Portrait of a Patriot,* 1:267.

ALEXANDER MCDOUGALL TO JQ

2 March 1775[1]

Sir Newyork March 2 1775

The utility of Communicating to the Friends of Liberty every important transaction, relative to our important struggles is too obvious to those who have had any concern in Public affairs to require any elucidation. You have no doubt beheld with concern, before you left the Continent the vile artifices practised by the Tools of administration in this Colony, to induce a belief in the other Colonies, that this would not join the Common cause. Notwithstanding we sent Delegates to the Congress, and have since religiously observed the Association, yet those miscreants are indefatigable, in their old acts of circulating falshoods misrepresenting and magnifying every event, to excite Jealousies and distrust in our neighbours. This inveterate and inimical temper to America will doubtless prompt them to extend the same baneful correspondence to the Capital of the Empire, which if not contradicted, may at this important Crisis, have a fatal influence on the Councils of the Nation. Our mutual Friend Mr. Samuel Adams in a Friendly conference I had with him and your Delegates, apprehending the expediency of my commencing a Correspondence with you, gave me your address. This and a solicitude to contribute my mite to prevent that mischief I hope will apologize for this abrupt address. The Creatures of administration, will doubtless magnify to them the importance of our Assembly's not approving of the acts of the Congress, which may be improved by them as a matter of great Triumph. But the inclosed report of the committee of Grievances of the Assembly will demonstrate to the nation, that notwithstand[ing] all the artifices which have been used with the ignorant members of [the] House, and the wickedness of others, which prevented an enquiry into, and approbation of those acts, yet the Political Creed of the assembly accords with the Congress. Yesterday, the day appointed for the Committee of the whole House to go into the consideration of the report, they proceeded as far as Mr. Billops previous Question, and approved you will see in the notes in, and at the close of the report. And as there was but Two members absent who can attend this sessions, and as they will be on contrary sides, the report of the Committee of the House will certainly be approved by it. And what is not yet considered by the

Committee of the House will be more in favor of Liberty when perfected than against it.

The departure from this port of the ship James Captain Watson from Greenwich, which arrived here the 2nd [of] February without being suffered to enter or Land any of her Cargo, and the preparation of the ship Beulah Captain Mr. Busssell from London, to depart without being suffered to come into the Harbour are incontestible evidences of our determined resolution to maintain the Association. And our General Committee determined last night to convene the Citizens on Monday next, to select Deputies to represent them in a Provincial Congress to be called, immediately, in order to Chuse Delegates to represent the Colony in the Continental Congress to be held at Philadelphia in May next. Hence you see the assembly will adopt the Creed of the Congress, the People are carrying their active determinations into execution, and the advice of the Congress to send Delegates to another will be followed so that you will be able fully to meet and refute the misrepresentations of our Common Enemies. As I was obliged to write this, in the utmost haste, I must therefore intreat you to view it with an indulgent Eye.

I am, Sir, your Humble Servant.

1. Draft copy, with various excisions and insertions, in the Alexander McDougall Papers, New-York Historical Society, to be copied and sent to Quincy through Thomas Bromfield. Son of Scottish immigrants, McDougall, a onetime privateer, had risen to become a wealthy merchant in New York City and leader of the local Sons of Liberty by the end of the 1760s. His subsequent challenges to imperial authority led some to consider him New York's John Wilkes. He went as a delegate to the First Continental Congress, served in the New York provincial congress, and rose to major general in the Continental army during the war, earning George Washington's respect along the way.

THOMAS BROMFIELD TO JQ

9 March 1775[1]

Dear Sir London 9 March 1775

Mr. Buxted the Patriot delivered me both your Acceptable favors of the 6th Instant.

I rejoice to learn you are in good spirits, and from your Account doubt not the Voyage will be of service to you, at same time I am sorry for the Accident which has happened to your Cloaths &c. Misfortunes like that must be expected and it will be well if we meet with no greater to encounter.

Captain Tucker from Salem who you mention has been Arrived at Bristol a Month ago, and consequently brought no Letters new, but I yesterday received some for you from the Glasgow Pacquet. Captain Porterfield arrived at Glasgow, which are here enclosed. I have also for our House some from Brother Henry and Brother Phillips of 28 January, beside several others. They write that they continue firm, but expect to be involved in great trouble if coercive measures are pursued, but hitherto nothing material has happened. No Letters are come to hand for Captain Lyde nor has Mr. Haley received any respecting his Trip in any wise.

Robson was expected to sail about the Middle of February and we hear of no other Trip coming. If any thing very Material turns up while I have a prospect of the Letters reaching you, I will not fail to Advise, for as I can procure Franks it will be Attended with no expence to you.

You know that Mr. Hyslop has given me hopes he would put his West India concerns into our hand, and that he had wrote Deacon Greenough and Doctor Chauncey to that purport, shall therefore be much Obliged to you on your Arrival, if you would use your interest with Mr. Phillips to get Deacon Greenough and Doctor Chauncey, to grant a power to Abraham Dupuis and Co. without making us the substitute of Mr. Hyslop, who it is not impossible might alter his mind, and this matter pass into some other hand.

I have inquired about your Scions and find it is much too late in the present Season, but shall take care to find them in the fall. Mr Dilly had your Memoranda. He sends you a Pamphlet &c by this post. Mr. Lee desires his respects and says he has nothing new to communicate. Mrs. Bromfield and the rest of the Family desire to be remembered to you.

I am (in haste) Dear Sir,
Yours most sincerely,
Tho. Bromfield

1. QP 51 (reel 29) MHS; Howe, ed., "Quincy Letters," pp. 489–90.

CHARLES DILLY TO JQ

9 March 1775[1]

Dear Sir, Lond. Mar. 9th 1775

I am glad to hear by Mr. Bromfield this day that you are in good spirits and now lying in the Downs.

I found the wind was favourable on Saturday Evening to take you from Gravesend and therefore it was unnecessary to send the News Papers of the Day, but as I see by the Papers Captain Lyde's ship is yet in the Downs and probably may be detained there by contrary winds some Days longer, I embrace the opportunity of sending you a few of the last P[ublic] Advertisers and a Pamphlet published this Day; written by the Court Pensioner Dr. Samuel Johnson against the Votes of the American Congress;[2] I thought you would be glad to see it. It seems by the Essay in this Day's P[ublic]. Adv[ertiser] from the State Tinker that an officious friend put a Paragraph into the Public Adv[ertiser] on Tuesday signed *Plain Truth,* noticing your Illness, and of Embarking at Gravesend for Salem. This has afforded the State Tinker an opportunity of exercising his wit upon Dr. Franklin and yourself, which you will see. The P[ublic] Advertiser of Tuesday I could not get, but cut the Paragraph out of the Paper of that Day from the File at the Printers.[3]

Some Illnatured fellow in the London News in Yesterday's paper has put in a reflecting paragraph against you, but anonymous squibs are not worth your notice.[4]

I have neither heard or seen in any other news papers besides the Pub[lic] Advertiser that your name has been mentioned since you left London, except the Public Ledger of Tuesday [h]as a piece of News that you had left London on your return home to N[ew] England.

Mr. Bromfield gave me the direction to write under cover to you for Mr. Robert Ashington, North End of Deal, and to forward on board any packet which may be sent to him for you, and having procured Franks, they will all come free. And if I find the wind in the same corner tomorrow I shall probably send some more News Papers. If you are in tolerable health and able to write, I shall be happy to receive a few lines before you quit the English channel.

Brother Edward has been out the whole day, and will not be home till late in the Evening. He enjoys great good health, and the same unremitting flow of spirits. I wish he could keep a little in the bounds of moderation, but nothing but real illness will bring him to that.

Lord North carries every motion with a high hand. I understand he has this day made another to include two or three more Provinces from Fishing on the Banks of New Foundland.[5] The New Yorkers are to have peculiar marks of favuor shown to them by which distinguishing privileges the ministry are in expectation to have the people of that province on their side. I am Dear Sir, with the sincerest wishes for the re-establishment of your health—Your most obedient friend and humble Servant

Chas. Dilly

P.S. I think by the memorandum given to Mr. Bromfield to show to us—that you have lent Mr. Hollis your set of Burgh's Political Disquisitions, 3 Vols.—and when he sends them to our House, you desire they may be changed for Lord Chesterfield's Letters, or some other book of reputation about that value. If otherwise ment, please, Sir, to explain it.[6]

1. QP 51 (reel 29) MHS; Howe, ed., "Quincy Letters," pp. 490–91. The Dilly brothers, Edward and Charles, London printers, had produced the London edition of Quincy's *Observations*, less than a week before he arrived in London. Bachelors who lived above their London shop, they sold as well as published books and pamphlets. Edward was the more passionate politically of the two, a champion of John Wilkes and friend of Benjamin Franklin, but also on good terms with James Boswell and Samuel Johnson. Like Quincy, he died of consumption (in his late forties, unlike Quincy). Very little is now known of the brothers, despite their prominence in the book trade and their place in London social circles; hence the value of the two letters that Charles wrote to JQ, included here.

2. The literature on Dr. Johnson is large, his biographers, many. For his view of the American crisis as expressed in *Taxation No Tyranny* (London: T. Cadell, 1775), his one pamphlet-length piece on the subject, the best starting point is Donald Green's introduction in *Political Writings*, volume 10 in John H. Middendorf, et al., eds., *The Yale Edition of the Works of Samuel Johnson*, 23 vols. (New Haven, Conn.: Yale University Press, 1958–2010), 10:401–11, with the text of the pamphlet itself on pp. 411–55.

3. The note by "Plain Truth," with a retort by "A State Tinker," which included comments on Quincy, appeared in the *Public Advertiser* for 7 March and 9 March 1775, resp. "Americus" entered the newsprint fray on April 20th to defend the "State Tinker" by disparaging Quincy (and his "feigned illness"). "A State Tinker" had started it all with a jibe in the February 28th issue that accused "Dr. Quinancy" and the "notorious Electrical Doctor" of attempting to "kindle the Sparks of Sedition." Quincy's passing was noted sympathetically in the June 1st issue: "Josiah Quincy, Junior, Esq. of Boston, who came here last Winter to give a true State of the

Province of Massachusetts Bay to our obstinate and willingly misinformed Ministers, unfortunately died the Evening after he landed in his own Country. This Gentleman's Loss is peculiarly to be lamented at this Time, as his Abilities, Virtue, and Patriotism, would be an Ornament to any Age, and would surely have been of Essential Service at this alarming Crisis to the Liberties of England as well as America."

4. "A Friend to Government desires us to say that a certain swivel-eyed, scribbly Lawyer lately from Boston New-England who has taken great Pains in his impudent Attempts to traduce the spotless Character of the late amiable Governor of that Province (struck with a panic at hearing of the spirited Measures going forward against the Rebels) has very precipitately embarked for his own Country, justly apprehending he might fall under the Hands of the Crown Lawyers for publishing an impudent, treasonable Pamphlet." *Public Advertiser,* 8 March 1775.

5. North in the Commons, 9 March 1775, in Simmons and Thomas, eds., *Proceedings and Debates*, 5:518–19.

6. Quincy had used Chesterfield's two volume *Letters* in his political commonplace book–see Coquillette and York, eds., *Portrait of a Patriot,* 1:183–184. It is not listed in the "Catalogue of Books," which is perhaps why he was hoping to trade James Burgh's three volume *Political Disquisitions,* which the Dillys had just published, for a new or replacement set. He had met briefly with an ill Burgh as he was preparing to sail for home–see Coquillette and York, eds., *Portrait of a Patriot,* 1:264.

CHARLES DILLY TO JQ

10 March 1775[1]

Dear sir London 10th Mar. 1775

I hope the Three Packets under cover to Robert Ashington, north end of Deal, which I sent by the Post last night, he hath caused to be safely conveyed to you.

I hinted to you my dear Sir, the Day I last had the pleasure of being in your company, that a friendly hint, or caution from you would be taken in good part by my Brother Edward who has got into such extravagant wild notions in Politics, and stigmatizes the characters of great men merely postulatory; that to a stranger, he must, and does appear in a disagreeable point of view. I do think a few lines of admonition respecting his unpleasing conduct and ridiculous self importance, written in the style of Friendship may have the desired effect. I should not have presumed to ask you to do this piece of kindness to him, if I had not heard you coincided with some other gentlemen that he had not yet learned to *know himself.*

Though he may be inflexable in folly, yet I hope not so obdurate as to reject advice sincerely ment for his good. My Brother is really a good natured and well disposed man; but is dreadfully contaminated with false ideas in politics; and could he be diverted from the prattle of Government affairs, he would then return and be the useful man in business, as he has heretofore been. I must beg Sir, you do not take notice to Brother Edward what I have requested of you, because that would at once destroy what I wish to have produced—a reformation in him. Pray do not read or mention to a second person concerning my Brother, though I needed not to have cautioned you as your superior understanding will I know have no occasion for it. Mr. Bromfield's Clerk has just now been to me and says he shall send you the Ledger of Yesterday and to Day. I hope after this is received the wind will alter in your favour and waft you to Salem with utmost expedition in safety and in perfect health.

I remain Dear Sir,
Your obliged friend and Humble Servant,
Chas. Dilly

1. QP 51 (reel 29) MHS; Howe, ed., "Quincy Letters," p. 492.

JQ TO THOMAS BROMFIELD

18 March 1775[1]

Dear Bromfield, March 18th 1775

Going into Plymouth Harbour

Paper being scarce, I am obliged to take the remains of a Letter I was beginning to you 2 days since, when the boat put off and left the Ship.

I suppose you have received a Letter from me.

The sea runs high and I shall scarce write legibly.

In one of my Letters Mrs Q desires me to purchase for her Mamma and two Sisters Morrocco Pocket-books. They were pleased with one I gave Mrs Q which was made of bright Mazarine bluecoloured Morroccan Leather.

I want much to gratify Mrs Q and worthy relations. Please to purchase one for Mrs. P at a guinea. Those for the young Ladies lower priced: there must be a difference between Mamma and her daughters.

I also intended when in London to have purchased me one peice of handsome elegantly figured Chintz for a Summer Gown for myself and the use of the family. I should have chose one well filled with the figure, because I am a very careless fellow about my clothing.

I also wanted a peice of dark, strong stuff of the Chintz or Calico kind for to make Children's *Jams* with. I don't know whether you use the term with you. I should chuse the figure neat and yet well filled, so as never to show dirt.

Mr. W—ms will sail soon for New England and so will Captain Hill in the Boston or Bristol Packet. Either of these will put any small package in their Chests for me with pleasure. Hill I sailed with to Carolina, when he was mate of the Brigg he now commands; and it may be in some measure owing to my strong recommendation of him to Mr. Rowe, that he is in his present station.[2] He is a very worthy fellow.

If you think you can send these articles without making a puzzle and *noise* on the other side the water, please to purchase and send them.

I would have both pieces of these Stuff cut up so far as to make me a Summer Gown with a side of *each vert[icil]*. Mr. Jones has my measures, and if he ever makes such kind of garment, I would have him make up the gown. If not, get those who do; and only inform them, that it [is] for a person 5 foot 11 Inches high (and Arms in proportion) who loves his outward garments *full.*

These I think may be sent as articles, left behind, my trunk being unable to hold anything more than I brôt.[3]

A word as to my health. My Cough and rising are far from better, though in the day time I am troubled a very trifle with either. And though in the morning my tongue is a little furred, yet all day, it *appears* as clean as a person in health.

I wrote you I had been ill used and deceived. I discover every day more instances of it. If we reach into Plymouth tonight I shall have a thousand minds to go to Bristol.

I am perplexed much what I ought to do.

The sea runs so high and my head swims so much I must only wish you and yours (what my heart does every day as its duty and delight) the Best of Blessings.

JQuincy jun.

PS. If these articles can't be sent pretty soon, I would not have them sent at all.

1. QP 51 (reel 29) MHS; "Memoir, 2:284–85, QP 46 (reel 6) MHS; *Memoir*, p. 284. This appears to be the last letter that Josiah Jr. wrote before he died. His final message (on April 21st) was dictated to a sailor on the packet taking him home. He began it two days earlier (with that date scratched out), as the ship was preparing to sail down the Thames.

2. Boston merchant John Rowe, one of Quincy's friends. Quincy, but not Hill, is mentioned in Anne Rowe Cunningham, ed., *Letters and Diary of John Rowe* (Boston: W. B. Clark Company, 1903).

3. Everything between "write legibly" and "A word to my health" was left out of the "Memoir" and the *Memoir*.

CHARLES DILLY TO JQ

30 March 1775[1]

Dear Sir, Lond. March 30th 1775

I hope you had a pleasant voyage and are in perfect good health. The P[ublic] Adv[ertiser] of the 20th signed Americus takes notice of you for which reason I have procured it for you and the Essay cut out of the P. A. of yesterday is a continued piece of abuse of Dr. Franklin from the State Tinker.[2]

In haste I remain Dear Sir,

Yours sincerely,

C Dilly

1. QP 51 (reel 29) MHS; Howe, ed., "Quincy Letters," p. 492n.

2. For "Americus" see supra, p. 381, n. 3. Once again the "State Tinker" does not mention Franklin by name, referring to him sarcastically as "the *great* ELECTRICAL DOCTOR," a "skunk," a "polecat," preparing to return to his own country–and good riddance to an ingrate. *Public Advertiser,* 29 March 1775.

WILLIAM LEE TO JQ

3 April 1775[1]

Dear Sir London 3 April 1775

I wrote you a short line to Boston, inclosed to Mr. Phillips. I hope the sea air and exercise will restore you to a perfect state of health and that you will have a happy meeting of your Family. After you left us the Merchants with a good deal of dexterity were brought to the enclosed petition to the King, which is tolerably explicit.[2] You know how the Comittee in general were affected; your friend Bromfield stood close by the stuff to the last.

You have a Pamphlet written by my B[rother] in support of the Congress' petition to the King.[3] The Lords protest, an address to the Soldiers which was enclosed [to] you before.

Be pleased to communicate the contents to Samuel Adams Esq. and let him know that in the course of last summer I wrote him many letters which were inclosed to a Mr. Bromfield Glover in Boston, with several inclosures and that I should be glad to know if he has received any of them.

Late letters from Massachusetts give the friends of Liberty much pleasure, as they declare the firmness of the People and their determination to support their Liberties like men. For my own part I see the hand of Providence most evident in this business. Jerusalem was visited for its Sins but after a time it arose with redoubled splendor; so I hope will Boston, where the wickedness of some Merchants, the Hutchinsons, Olivers, Sewalls &c is great enough to draw down on that unhappy Town the vengeance of Heaven. Some of the Merchants there have wrote to several houses here for goods however they are not sent, but large quantities under the Patronage of the Ministers have been sent in the Francis, late John Wilkes, for *Boston* and Captain Deverson is at this moment loading with Merchandize for the same Port. He will be quite full, the value at least £50,000, which is paid for to the Tradesmen before the goods are shipped. Part of his Cargoe is 300 hhds[4] of refined Sugar, 3 or 400 chests of bohea Tea besides Bale goods Trunks &c. These Ships belong to Massachusetts, are both Transports in the Government Service and the goods are to be landed at Boston under the Military Protection. As all the other associating Colonies have religiously adhered to the Association of the last Continental Congress you will take care to prevent the above transaction from creating a division. The Enemies in New York will take every advantage and will be glad of every trivial circumstance to revile the friends of their Country and to contrive a division.

Besides the money, £1000 a man paid to several members in the New York Assembly previous to their meeting in January last, large sums have since been sent there and to some other Colonies to Bribe particular men. Dr. Smith in Philadelphia should be watched. You have Mr. Burkes motions in the H. of Commons the 22nd of March, which are the Rockingham parties creed with respect to America.[5] The Livery of London are to meet the 5th Instant in Common Hall to petition the Throne for redress of American grievances. The States of Holland have at the instigation of our Minister prohibited the exportation of Arms &c—but Spain is still open, so you know what you have to depend on. I trust you will find America united, but in my opinion if the 4 New England Provinces and Colonies were left alone they ought to persevere in support of their Liberty.

I am with Great Esteem
Dear Sir,
Your most Obedient. Servant
William Lee Esq.[6]

1. QP 51 (reel 30) MHS; Howe, ed., "Quincy Letters," pp. 493–94.

2. James E. Bradley discusses the petition to George III, along with failed attempts to sway Parliament by the same method, in *Popular Politics and the American Revolution* (Macon, Ga.: Mercer University Press, 1986), pp. 37–58.

3. [Arthur Lee], *A Speech, intended to have been delivered in the House of Commons, in support of the Petition from the General Congress at Philadelphia* (London: Edward and Charles Dilly, 1775). Not in line to inherit the family lands or fortune inVirginia, William Lee and his older brother Arthur had chosen to make their way in London society, William as a merchant, Arthur without really settling on a profession, despite his training in both medicine and law. Both were involved in the city's opposition politics and loosely associated with John Wilkes. William was elected a sheriff, then an alderman for London, but failed in his bid to win election to the Commons. Arthur wrote various pieces for the London press, most notably as the essayist "Junius Americanus." He attached himself to Benjmain Franklin when Franklin was the agent for the Massachusetts House of Representatives. He and William thereby became acquainted with Josiah Junior–thus various references to Arthur in Quincy's London journal (see Coquil-

lette and York, eds., *Portrait of a Patriot,* 1:221–69, passim). The brothers left London for the Continent, seeking their fortunes in a new venue, after the rebellion became a revolution. The best introduction to them can be found in Garraty and Carnes, eds., *DNB,* 13:356–58 and 406–7, in essays by Louis W. Potts.

4. Abbreviation for hogsheads, or large barrels, with specific weights varying according to the contents, which could run from tobacco to wine to rum.

5. *The Speech of Edmund Burke, Esq.* (London: J. Dodsley, 1775); and in Simmons and Thomas, eds., *Proceedings and Debates,* 5:598–631.

6. Lee's signature is crossed out.

ALEXANDER MCDOUGALL TO JQ

6 April 1775[1]

Dear Sir New York April 6th, 1775

Your favours of the 17th and 19th of December last, inclosed with Letters for the Friends of the common Cause in Boston, and Philadelphia, arrived here the 10th ultimo; but they were not handed to me, before the 25th, owing to their being in a Package belonging to a Gentleman who was absent when they arrived. Your directions respecting them were strictly observed and they were forwarded the 27th, by safe conveyances. And I shall take great pleasure, in transmiting your future communications to your Friends. I wrote you by the March Packet, under cover to Mr. Thomas Bromfield, in which I informed you of the progress then made, by our House of Assembly on American Grievances. The assurances I gave you, that what remained of the Report of the Committee of Grievances, not then considered by the Committee of the House, would rather be more in favour of Liberty, than the Report, has since been confirmed, the particulars of which, you have in the inclosed Printed proceedings of the House. After the state of Grievances were agreed to, and approved by the House, Several of the Members who are warm Friends to the Cause of Liberty, having attended the Assembly two Months, and their Families being very remote from the Capital, and urgent Business demanding their return, and considering the most important Transactions of the Sessions finished, went Home. This gave an opportunity to the wicked and designing Members of the House, contrary to all order, to depart from the Spirit of the list of Grievances, in the Petition to the King, memorial to the Lords, and remonstrance to the Commons. But the state of Grievances agreed to by the Fullest House, during the Session, must be considered as the Basis of all their proceedings, on the American Controversy. If any regard is to be paid to the sense of the Legal Representatives, that sense, is the state of Grievances agreed to in a full House; and therefore whatever difference, appears in the Petition &c, from the State of Grievances is a mere nullity. If the Ministry make any dependance on the Petition as declarative of the Sense of the Colony, they will find themselves egregiously mistaken. This City will publickly disavow, the vile Slavish Sentiments contained in the Petition &c the moment they make their appearance. So far as they are now known, they are condemned, and the patrons of them despised. And if the Provincial Convention, who are to meet upon the 20th instant to Elect Delegates for the Continental Congress, do not disavow the Petition &c (which I have reason to conclude they will,) they will certainly join with the Continental Congress in doing it. During the Ship Bulah's stay in our Bay, she was continually watched by a Sub Committee, and did not enter. But while she lay at the Hook, waiting for a fair Wind, the night before she departed threatned a Storm and as the Boat on Board of which the Sub Committee attended, was not so well provided with Ground Tackling as the Ship, the Boat was obliged to go into a Cove of Safety, at some distance from the Ship. Messers Robert and John Murray the owners, who had some goods on board, having previously meditated a plan to land them, availed themselves of this opportunity, and effected it in the Night. Of this they were Suspected, and our Sub Committee of Observation, and the Committee of Elizabeth Town, having got a Clue to a discovery, the Owners Confessed the Matter upon oath. Our Citizens were so enraged at them for the horrid Deed, that it was with great difficulty they were prevailed upon not to Banish them. The fearful apprehension of these Miscreants, and the terms on which they are suffered to abide here, are fully expressed in the printed papers, which you have herewith. This is the only violation of the Association, we have had since it took place. The punishment they now, and will endure, is sufficient to Deter any Man, however Base from another Breach. The Friends of the Association, and the great Cause are Daily increasing, so that you have no reason to fear a defection of this Colony. Time will not permit me, to be more particular. I shall continue to inclose you all printed papers, which I may Judge of importance to you, regardless of Postage, untill you direct me to the Contrary.

I am Dear Sir,
In great Haste but with great Respect
Your Humble Servant
Alexander Mcdougall

PS. As my political Character may tempt the Tools of Government, to open Letters to me, please to Cover your favors, to me, to Samuel Broome & Co, Merchants in New York.

1. QP 51 (reel 29) MHS; with a draft copy in the Alexander McDougall Papers, New-York Historical Society. Printed in the *Memoir*, pp. 255n–57n, and Force, ed., *American Archives*, 4th series, 2:283–84. Addressed "To Josiah Quincy Junior Esq. London, by the Duke of Cumberland Packet."

WILLIAM LEE TO JQ

12 April 1775[1]

Sir London 12 April 1775

Mr. L desires his respects and says that he has wrote you twice by via Philadelphia and once direct to Boston.

It is said that £25000 has been sent to General Gage for the purpose of Bribery, and that Major S ____ is now gone to Philadelphia with Money to Bribe the Congress.

Dr. P[rice]. desires his best respects to you and says he shall very soon send you what he promised. He tells me that of the Troops destined for America, Four Regiments are going for New York, and Two for Albany to intercept the communication between those two places; the remainder are for General Gage, upon the arrival of which he is to quit the Town and take the field, for they reckon the Americans are mere Cowards and will not fight. General G per his last Letters says he is more and more assured that they would quietly submit. This account he has from Colonel B __ 'Tis still his opinion that the quarrel can not be terminated without fighting, which the sooner it happens the better.

Mr. C a captial N.E. merchant told but a few days past a friend of mine that the Ministry's plan was a wise measure: If the principal Merchants trading to America are abettors of the Ministry, Men who as you justly observed ought to have America inscribed on their Carriages, Equipages, &c and gratitude on their Hearts! you need not be surprized that matters are carried with so high an hand. God grant they may meet with their just rewards; and I hope that those who have so barefacedly shipped for Boston at this time will not be overlooked by those who have it in their powers to resent it properly. From the several conversations I have had, I form my opinion that if the Americans should give up the points in dispute they will be despised not only by the Sons of Liberty every where, but by even the Ministerial hirelings, as numbers of them have acknowledged to me that they blame you not for endeavouring to prevent the imposition of unnecessary Taxes on you Three Millions and a half of free born Men cannot surely ever be brought to Submission by an handful of Mercenaries.

1. QP 51 (reel 30) MHS, written by a clerk practiced in calligraphy; Howe, ed., "Quincy Letters," pp. 494–95.

THOMAS BROMFIELD TO JQ
6 May 1775[1]

Dear Sir London 6 May 1775

I wrote you a little while past, since which I have reminded your Friends not to Omitt Acquainting you with every thing material regarding publick Affairs. Doctor L[ee] has often been with me to know if I had received any Letters for him; he has received but one since your departure and that by Accident. I saw through the Cover of a pacquet for Folger, addressed to you. I therefore ventured to Open said Cover and deliver that to him; the Other two contained therein were Letters for you, which I shall return with others for some safe Conveyance. The Doctor thinks you should have given me leave to open the Pacquets addressed to you, as he judges there must among some of them be more Letters for him, but I told him I did not dare to Open any Others, that which I did open, I could not refuse to do, because his Name was so conspicuous through the cover, and the hand writing seemed to be Doctor Chauncy's.

The Accounts received some time ago from N York, respecting the Majority in the Assembly in favor of Goverment highly elated the Ministerial People here, but on receiving the last Accounts from thence that a great Majority of Free Men and Free Holders had agreed to send Delegates to the Congress, they are much chagrined, though they still entertain great hopes of what the Fleet and Army will do when the Regiments Arrive, and that the great Number talked of by some of your people, which are ready to join them, will enable them to Obtain Obedience without much trouble. I do think the People in general here, have no notion that there will be any Bloodshed, otherwise they surely would not be so contented, as they yet seem. It is the Opinion of most of the Ministerial Merchants that there will be none; for they, as well as others, think the bare Appearance of the Forces, will sufficiently intimidate you. I have desired Messers. Dilly to forward you from time to time, such Newspapers, as may contain any thing regarding you or be of material information, which he has promised to do. I hope soon to hear of your safe Arrival. I have sent you per Captain Jenkins the Parliamentary Register.

Mrs. Bromfield joins me in proper respects to you and Mrs Quincy, our Dearest.

Yours sincerely,
Thos. Bromfield

1. QP 51 (reel 30) MHS; Howe, ed., "Quincy Letters," pp. 495–96.

HANNAH LINCOLN TO SAMUEL QUINCY

11 May 1775[1]

My dear Brother, Braintree May 11th 1775

I write this, in hopes to put it in to my father's letter, which he has just written. If it should reach you it may serve to convince you, that I have not forgotten that you are my *only* brother. He must judge what I feel, when I tell him, that I fear I shall never see him again. Our two departed brothers died upon the seas: you will perhaps say your body is sound, it may be so, but the sick in mind call for more than Esculapian aid.

If anything could surprise me *now,* the hearing of your going home would, but of late everything that is marvellous and strange is to be expected. I have not time to enlarge upon the complicated distresses of our Country, of families, or of individuals, but shall briefly say, that all our connexions have experienced such a series of melancholy events, as are not to be paralleled. We my brother, I hope can sympathize in sorrowing for the loss of a brother, whose character was as far as any man's of his age ever was, unimpeachable. In his labours for the salvation of his Country he was indefatigable. His death I hope will prove a warning to others, not to pursue too eagerly *any point.* nature kept upon the stretch will give way. He did not sufficiently consider the tenderness of his frame, and it may truly be said he fell a *Martyr* in the cause of Liberty.

In the Monody on our eldest brother I find the following lines. They may with equal propriety be applied to the younger

"That heart which late inflamed with patriot zeal
Braved the bold insults of its Country's foe,
No more it's pious frenzy can reveal
Nor e'er in Freedom's cause again shall glow."[2]

Let it not be told in America, and let it not be published in Great Britain, that a brother of such brothers fled from his Country the wife of his youth, the children of his affection, and from his aged sire, already bowed down with the loss of two sons, and by that of many more dear, though not as near connexions, to secure himself from the reproaches of his injured countrymen. To cover such a retreat obliged to enlist as a sycophant under an obnoxious Hutchinson, who is a tool under a cruel North. And by them to be veered about, and at last to be blown aside with a cool—"tomorrow Sir": "Refusal, canst thou wear a smoother form."[3] My blood chills at the thought of the meanness of a seeker, and flames with indignation at such treatment from those in power.

Arouse from your lethargy—let reason take the helm: disregard all greatness, but greatness of soul: then the little trappings that royalty can confer will lose their lustre, that false lustre which I fear inclines you to the prerogative side.

Spare me, and do not call what I have written impertinent, but ascribe it to the anxiety of a sister really distressed for thee. I behold you leaving your Country a land flowing with milk and honey: and in which as yet iniquity of all kinds is punished, and its Religion as yet free from idolatry: (how long it will continue so God only knows, we have reason to fear a depredation on our religious system next) for a Country where evil works are committed with impunity. Can you expect there to walk uprightly? Can you take fire into your bosom, and not be burned?

I take a long farewell and wish you success in every laudable undertaking.

Your affectionate sister
H[annah] Lincoln

1. QP 45 (reel 6) MHS, as transcribed by Eliza Susan Quincy for her "Memoir," 1:95–96, from an original not in the MHS collections. Also printed, with slight changes, in George Atkinson Ward, ed., *Journals and Letters of the Late Samuel Curwen* (New York: C. S. Francis and Co., 1842), pp. 562–64.

2. She quoted from *A Monody Inscribed to Benjamin Church jun. M.D. in Memory of Mr. Edmund Quincy, tert* (Boston, 1768), p. 4.

3. She quoted here from Edward Young's *The Complaint; Or, Night Thoughts on Life, Death, and Immortality* (1742), which would have been available to her in many editions.

ABIGAIL QUINCY TO JOSIAH QUINCY SR.

18 September 1775[1]

Honored and dear Sir Norwich Sept. 18th 1775

I received your favor of the 5th of August, and should have gratified myself by answering it, if an opportunity of sending directly to Braintree had offered but this is the first since I left you. Be assured Sir that as long as any affection remains in my breast to the memory of my dear partner, and which will remain tell I cease to breathe the vital air, so long every near relation or friend that he was fond of must be dear to me and there can be none nearer than a parent.

To pretend to inform you of what I have felt, and what I still feel, on the painful reflection on what I once enjoyed would be undertaking a task too great for my pen to execute. Alas! I find it very different from what I have often been told would be the case, that time would wear out the greatest sorrow. Mine I find is still increasing. When it will have reached the summit I know not. I dread the thought of going among my friends that were his friends and acquaintance—as though they were enemies—and feel a secret pleasure in thinking we are not likely to see Boston this winter. I feel sorry to renew your grief if it had subsided but my heart is too full to write to the father of my husband and not mention a word of him.

Forgive me, Sir, the pain I have given you and may the God and fountain of all good sanctify this afflictive providence to our everlasting happiness and may *we* be enabled to say from the heart as well as the lips "his holy will be done."[2]

Upon opening the trunks of my dear partner I found two greater curiosities than those which I now send you. These are some other books of history and politics which as they are very handsomely bound, I should not chuse to send so long a journey, for fear they should be hurt. I hope some time or other you will have an opportunity to peruse them. Everything in his chests returned safe except his watch which I suspect was stolen as one of the chests was broken open when Mr. Boice went on board. But in the same chest I found near one hundred £ sterling in cash, and it seems strange they should take a watch and leave the money. I have now sent you by Mr. Mason the journal and all the letters you have not seen before. You will be pleased to remember Sir, that I set a high value on them, both on my own account and my sons. If you incline to take a copy of the Journal it will be very agreeable to me, but the one that is in his own hand writing I must beg you would return before winter together with the letters. My father or brother will be down in a month or six weeks. If they should not you may have some other opportunity you can trust. The pamphlets you may keep as long as you please.

Josiah has been very ill with a fever, but through the goodness of God he is now so well as to ride out. I told him I was going to write to you and he of his own accord sent his duty.

Please to give mine to Mama, and my love to my sisters Mrs. Storer, Betsey and Nancy. My parents and sisters desire their sincere regards may be returned to every branch of your family.

Accept Sir, of the affectionate and dutiful regards of your
Abigail Quincy

1. QP 45 (reel 6), MHS; as pasted into the "Memoir," 1:68–70 by Eliza Susan Quincy.

2. She refers, of course, to the Lord's prayer, as offered by Jesus Christ at the Sermon on the Mount, and in Matthew 6:10 of the New Testament ("Thy kingdom come. Thy will be done, on earth as *it is* in heaven." KJV)

JOSIAH QUINCY SR. TO ABIGAIL QUINCY

25 September 1775[1]

My dear and amiable Daughter, September 25th 1775

I am very sorry I had not the Pleasure of seeing Mr. Mason, who would have been quite welcome to the best Accommodations with Us, till Mr. Adams Family will have received him.

Your kind and affectionate Letter of the 18th Instant, together, with the long wished for Journal and Letters, of my dear deceased Son, were safely delivered; and have since afforded me, and will continue to afford me, that melancholly Pleasure which results from an imaginary Conversation, with one who was dear to me as Life; and whose *Memory* will be precious, as long as it shall please God to continue to me the Exercise of that *Faculty.*

I can't remember whether I acquainted you, that, some time before he sailed for England, he gave me a large Packet, sealed and inscribed, not to be opened 'till after his Death: the Date of it is June 3d 1774, which he said would be an amusement to me, if I should survive him. I have some Time since opened it, and find it contains original Manuscripts, and proof Sheets from 1767 to 1774. If my Capacity was equal to my Inclination, his Pamphlet upon the Boston Port Bill, his Journals, and this Manuscript, would furnish me with sufficient materials for a considerable Volume, perhaps, as entertaining and instructive, and upon as interesting Subjects, as any of american Production. Pray let me know your Sentiments upon it; whether his Journal to and from Carolina or any other of his original MS. are in your Possession. Mr. Morton tells me that all his Books and Papers were carefully packed in Boxes and are locked up in his Office, but heard it was broke open.

I received, I hope, with due Gratitude to the Father of Mercies! the joyfull News of my dear grandSon's Recovery, from the Sickness wherewith he has been exercised. Oh! that his Life and health may be preserved and prolonged; his Powers, cultivated and improved, he grows up to be as eminently serviceable in his Day and Generation, as his dear dec:d Father was before him!

"'Tis Education forms the human Mind
Just as the Twig is bent, the Tree's inclin'd."[2]

As I am seperated, (perhaps forever) from this dear Object of my Love, embrace him for me, with the tender affections of a fond Parent, who devoutly, and earnestly prays for his temporal and eternal Happines!.

I have repeatedly perused, with Pleasure and Pain, the political Pamphlets you was so good as to send me: *Pleasure,* to find, there were still remaining among *Britons,* such warm Advocates for the civil and religious Rights of Mankind: *Pain,* to see the Learning and Ingenuity of such an elegant Writer, as the Author of the *Rambler,* prostituted and disgraced, in Defence of a stupid xxxx a venal P[arliament] and to an abandonly wicked A[dministratio]n. *Taxation* is certainly no *Tyranny* under given Circumstances. Neither is *Resistance,* under given Circumstances, *Rebellion.* But, in both Cases, who are to be the Judges? If the great Mr. Locke's opinion is decisive, certainly not the *Tyrant,* but the *People,* who suffer oppression; and whenever it becomes intolerable,[3] they have a Right to resist. If ever therefore *Resistance is lawfull,* it is so under our Circumstances; for, we are not all but destroyed; as far, as the Powers we oppose, are capable of effecting their bloody Purposes; and for no other Reason our unwillingness to have our Lives, Liberties, and Property at their *absolute* Disposal. For this, we are traduced, calumniated, and abused in this most opprobrious Language. For this, our Capital is seized, the Inhabitants Prisoners, and their Property spoiled. Many Houses have been burnt; some of the innocent Inhabitants of them murdered!

This Moment Doctor Cooper and his Lady are arrived to take a Lodging with us, in their Way to Middleborough, on a Visit to Mr Bowdoin, who it is feared will not continue long in this World. G[age]s Perfidy. The consequent cruel, and Barbarous Treatment of the Inhabitants of Boston, after he had them in his Power; together with the bodily Infirmities under which Mr. Bowdoin laboured, will probably soon prove too hard for him. His Death, will certainly prove a great publick Loss.

I have only Room to add, my affectionate Regard to your worthy Parents, and the rest of your amiable family; in which, my dear Mrs. Quincy, and all present, desire to join. Be assured, that whilst my Life is spared, of every Testimony of my Esteem and Love, to you and my dear grandson, that is in the Power of,

Your Affectionate &c: J Q____

P.S. Please to present my respectfull Compliments Deacon Mason and his good Family. I have received a Letter for his Son which I shall preserve 'till I see him or can send it by some safe Conveyance.

P.S. Lieut. Col. Pitkin, who is posted for the Defence of Squantum, informed me, the last Evening, that the Mate of a Vessel, that was seized and carried into

Boston, overheard an Officer say, to his Friend in Boston, that general Gage has positive Orders to attack the Rebels at all Hazards. But upon acquainting his Officers, they unanimously refused to go out, because, it would be certain Death to them, as we were so strongly entrenched; and had rather resign their Commissions than hazard their Lives at so great a Disadvantage. God grant it may be true!

Sept. 26th: Last night 30 Whaleboats and about 200 Men went to Governors Island, Burnt the House, and a boat that was building there, and carried off 3 horses and 12 Cows.[4]

1. QP 51 (reel 30) MHS.

2. He quoted from Alexander Pope, *An Epistle to the Right Honourable Lord Viscount Cobham* (London: Lawton Gulliver, 1733), p. 6—or perhaps from later Edinburgh or Dublin printings—changing "vulgar" to "human."

3. A portion of the letter at the top right edge, one inch wide by three inches long, is missing, so a few of the words that follow have been deduced.

4. Writing perpendicular to the regular text, Quincy Sr. squeezed his postscripts into the margins. For the context of the events Quincy reported, see Frothingham, *Siege of Boston,* pp. 207–45; and Allen French, *The First Year of the American Revolution* (Boston: Houghton Mifflin Company, 1934), pp. 466–546.

ABIGAIL QUINCY TO HANNAH LINCOLN

11 November 1775[1]

My dear Sister Norwich November 11th 1775

All I have to say in excuse for not writing to you before, is that no opportunity has offered of sending directly to Braintree since that by which I wrote to our Father, except when my parents went down. They did not determine to go till the night before, and as Dr. and Mrs. Gordon were then here, I was unwilling to lose their company.

I cannot describe to you my dear the emotions of heart I feel when writing to the sister of my departed friend. They are inexpressible! If you could see, if you could witness, how often I am obliged to lay aside my pen, to give way to my tears, you would pity me. I can write upon no other subject but this. Therefore you must not expect that my letters can give you any pleasure. They must give you much pain, as they must recall to your remembrance a Brother who possessed every qualification to make him dear to all his relations. And I should not think that they could soon forget him. As to me, how can I ever cease to dwell in the remembrance of one, who loved me with such a constant, such an undeserved affection, one who was so peculiarly formed for friendship and domestic happiness? I see no command from Reason or Revelation that we should forget our friends as soon as they cease from doing kind offices for us—cease did I say; no, I believe with the poet that

"Nor lands nor seas nor suns nor stars
Can soul from soul divide
They correspond from distant worlds
Though vision is denied."[2]

Indeed my dear sister, were it possible for me ever to forget the many aggravating circumstances which attended his death, intended by providence for my notice and improvement, I should be without feeling or understanding. May my greatest concern be that the designs of an infinitely just and holy God, in so severely afflicting me, may be fully answered by my improvement. You knw that I was always fond of retirement. It is now more desirable to me than ever.

"For him all thoughts of pleasure I forego
For whom my tears can never cease to flow."[3]

But I shall always be happy to hear from or see any of the friends or relations of my dear husband, and you must unless you injure me, believe that your happiness must give me pleasure. As to my health I am as well as usual. The country air is very favorable to me. My dear little boy is well. I asked him what he had to say to his Aunt? he says , "tell her I go to school and stay *all day,* and that I send them all many kisses."

Give my duty to Father and Mother, and love to my sisters. Give also the love and compliments of our family to yours, out of which you are to take a share. Write when you can. Love me for your dear brother's sake and accept of woe for his sake and your own. From

A. Q.

1. "Memoir," 2:300a–301a, QP 46 (reel 6) MHS; as transcribed by Eliza Susan Quincy.

2. Taken from Edward Young's poem "Resignation." Abigail altered the fourth line, which Young had written as: "Tho' Transports are denied."

3. From "On the Death of Mr. Thomas Rowe," by Elizabeth Singer Rowe, which appeared in *Philomella* (London: E. Curll, 1737), p. 184, but had also appeared earlier as "A POEM, by a Lady on the Death of her Husband" in the *London Magazine* 4 (May 1735):271, and under that same anonymous title even earlier in *Musapaedia, or Miscellany Poems* (London: B. Francklin, 1719), p. 67. The poem was also reprinted in later anthologies—meaning, Abigail had any number of sources to which she could have turned. Thomas Rowe died of consumption in 1715, which Abigail probably knew, and which could explain why his widow's poem offered her comfort. Abigail altered the lines as originally written to fit her circumstances, as Josiah Jr. often did when quoting others. The original reads: "For Thee, all thoughts of pleasure I forego, For Thee my Tears shall never cease to flow."

JQ SR. TO JOSIAH QUINCY (HIS GRANDSON)

16 March 1784[1]

My dearly beloved Grandson, Braintree March 16 1784

Your Uncle Phillips, was yesterday so good, as to wait on your dear Mamma, and made us happy in a friendly Visit, by whom, came safe to hand your welcome Letter, of the 10th ultimo, where in you have given me, not only a Testimony of your filial Affection, but a convincing Proof of your Proficiency in Learning. Be assured, your Pleasure in writing, could not exceed mine in reading, whilst I indulged the pleasing Hope, that by your Assiduity and Perseverance in the Paths of Science, you will one Day *equal,* at least, if not exceed your Predecessors in every respect; though some of them were remarkably distinguished for their superior Abilities. However, you will please to remember, and ought never to forget that, from early youth, through every Stage, and in every Department of Life, they owed their Emminence to their unwearied Dilligence and Application. But, besides Dilligence and Application to your Studies while young, it is indispensibly necessary to the forming a distinguished Character in public Life, that, Truth should be the invariable Object of your Pursuit, and your End the public Good. These are Maxims of Wisdom, which I have every Reason to think, your Great Grand father, as well as your dear deceased Father also, strictly adhered to; and by which the *Former* became emminent as a Judge and the *Latter* was highly esteemed in his Profession as a Lawyer; and had he lived, it is probable he would have been equally emminent as Statesman in public Life. For he was early taught, and strongly inculcated upon him, what I hope you will ever carefully remember; "if a Thing is *not right*, never to do it, and if it *not Truth* never to speak it, as also that,

"True conscious Honor is to feel no Sin:
He's armed without That's innocent within."[2]

These are Sentiments, which you may not be so able to comprehend at present, as when Experience and Observation have matured your Judgment; but, should they be preserved, 'till that happy Period arrives, and are duely attended to, the inestimable Importance of them, I hope, will fully appear, and have its genuine Effect.

It is more than probable, you will soon hear that, your aged parent is numbered among the dead[3]; but to the last Moment of my Life your temporal and eternal Happiness will be devoutly implored, and ardently wished for, by—

Your affectionate
Grandfather
Jos. Quincy

P.S. Present my respectful Compliments to the reverend Mr. French and Lady.[4]

1. QP 69 (reel 32) MHS. Young Josiah was at school at the Phillips Academy in Andover; his grandfather sent the letter to his mother, for her to forward to him.

2. From Alexander Pope's *First Epistle of the First Book of Horace Imitated,* lines 92–93. The elder Quincy could have been quoting from a number of London editions printed in the late 1730s or even from memory.

3. He died within days of writing this letter.

4. Jonathan French, a Harvard graduate and congregational minister who taught religion to students at the Academy. He was a native of Braintree.

SOURCES, IN HAND AND ONLINE

I NOTED the basic sources, secondary as well as primary, for the life of Josiah Quincy Junior, in a "Bibliographical Note" at the close in Volume 1 (on pp. 271–73). I neglected to include there the fine essay written by Clifford K. Shipton for John Langdon Sibley, et al., *Biographical Sketches of Graduates of Harvard University*, 18 vols. (Boston: Massachusetts Historical Society, 1873 —), 15:479–91. It is an omission as ironic as it is ungracious, considering that Shipton's sketch was one of the first places that I went to for background on Quincy, over twenty years ago. The reader will find various points in these volumes where I turned to that collection for information on the Harvard men who played such a decisive role in shaping Revolutionary Massachusetts.

I listed in that original note the microfilm reels in the Quincy, Wendell, Holmes, and Upham Family Papers pertaining to Josiah Junior. Since then one of Dan Coquillette's law students and research assistants, Kevin Cox, put together a more detailed listing of what is contained on those reels in an appendix for Volume 2 (pp. 429–37). Readers may also go directly to ABIGAIL, the online catalog for the Massachusetts Historical Society, to see the complete shelf list for all 67 reels, and their relation to the manuscript collection itself at P-347 in the MHS library. Not all of the individual items in that collection were filmed. Only by consulting the bound volumes in the reading room of the MHS library, with their combined alphabetical/chronological entries for individual letters, can readers have a precise sense of what is in the Quincy papers. Even then there is no substitute for searching the collection itself to be certain that something housed at the MHS library is not missed. There is nothing more frustrating in doing research than learning, too late, that something was hiding in plain sight.

Very early in my career I came to appreciate what the noted author Dee Brown called the importance of serendipitous discoveries in historical research. I made several during my work on Josiah Quincy Junior and they were greatly facilitated by what has only recently been made available through the Internet. I learned a hard lesson about using that resource effectively, when Dan

Coquillette wondered out loud in his office at Harvard Law School how to find the source for a particular Quincy quotation. As soon as I returned to my office at BYU I went to what I was sure was the source, could not find it there, checked a few more, then confessed my failure to Dan—all of this in the space of a few days. Dan told me not to worry, that one of his former students—Brian Sheppard, now a law professor in his own right—had googled the lines in question and had pinned down the source, all within a matter of minutes.

To be honest, most of the passages that Quincy quoted from other writers that had no clear source cited I too found on the Internet—if not by going to Google, then by consulting the online edition of Early American Imprints, often called series one of the Evans collection (for all known copies of books published before 1800 in what became the U.S.) and Eighteenth Century Collections Online (essentially all books published in the British Isles during the 18th century). Both collections are text searchable, putting at a user's fingertips information that would have required months, if not years, of digging in archives to find a generation ago. Quincy's *Observations* can be found in the Evans collection (Boston and Philadelphia printings) and ECCO (Boston and London printings). Quincy's essays for the *Boston Gazette* and *Boston Evening-Post* are text searchable in GenealogyBank.com. All of this has been done just in the years since I completed work on the first Quincy volume.

When I first started on this project I considered Martin Spevack's massive printed Shakespeare concordance a godsend, a rare gift that made the complicated simple. Spevack's compilation stands as a remarkable achievement for its time; compared with the ease of "googling" lines from Shakespeare, it now seems quaint indeed. But then I will ask a two-part question in closing that I first posed a few years ago, in completing another book for the Colonial Society of Massachusetts: With printed and even manuscript texts online that can be downloaded and sent as email attachments, will the serendipitous discovery become more common or less? And will research in general become more exacting and more precise, or sloppier because seemingly so simple? I wish I could say; perhaps we will know soon enough.

INDEX

Page numbers in *italics* indicate illustrations. Book titles are generally found under the name of the author, unless anonymous, in which case they are alphabetically listed by title. Information in [square brackets] indicates alternative spellings. The British nobility generally are listed under their titles rather than their surnames.

Portrait of a Patriot, Volume Six

HAS BEEN TYPESET IN CASLON TYPES

PRINTED AT KIRKWOOD PRINTING, WILMINGTON, MASSACHUSETTS

BOUND AT ACME BOOKBINDING, CHARLESTOWN, MASSACHUSETTS

DESIGN BY PAUL HOFFMANN

LANCASTER, NEW HAMPSHIRE